제13권

近代韓國外交文書

거문도 사건 Ⅱ

제13권

近代韓國外交文書

거문도 사건 Ⅱ

근대한국외교문서 편찬위원회 편

서울대학교출판문화원

본 편찬사업은 2010년도 정부재원(교육과학기술부 인문사회연구역량강화사업비)으로 한국연구재단의 지원을 받아 연구되었음. (NRF-2010-322-B00011)

This work was supported by the National Research Foundation Grant funded by the Korean Government. (NRF-2010-322-B00011)

간행사

1876년 조·일 수호조약, 1882년 구미 열강과의 수호조약 체결로 조선 문제는, 1882~1884에는 간접적으로, 그리고 1885년 영국의 거문도 점령부터는 직접적으로 세계정치와 연결되었다.

임오군란은 이리(伊犁) 문제와 연결되었다. 문제 해결을 위해 러시아와 여러 고비를 넘기고 조약 체결에 성공한 쩡지쩌(曾國藩)는 국경의 중요성을 강조하는 상소문을 올리고 1880년 7월 21일(음력 6월 15일) 황제의 재가를 받았다. 서양 공법에서 말하는 국경과 주권 개념에 입각해 러시아의 위험을 방지해야 한다는 것을 정확하게 인식하였다. 이런 정책은 만주와 몽골에도 적용되었다. 이는 중대한 의미를 갖는 것이었다. 예(禮)관념의 속방을 서양 공법의 속국으로 전환하는 정책이었다. 중국 주변 지역의 지각 변동이 일어나지 않을 수 없었다. 이런 정책이 한반도에 적용되자 소용돌이를 몰고 오게 되고 임오군란과 그 사후처리의 방향은 이미 예고되었다.

갑신정변은 중국과 프랑스의 월남 분쟁과 밀접히 연관되어 있다. 이 분쟁으로 한반도에 주둔하고 있던 중국 군대의 절반이 철수되면서 갑신정변이 야기될 수 있는 국제 여건이 마련되었다. 특히 갑신정변이 왜 12월 4일에 일어나지 않을 수 없었는가 하는 시기 문제는 월남 전쟁과 깊이 연결되어 있다.

1885년에 들어서면서 중앙아시아에서 영국과 러시아의 대립은 새로운 국면에 접어들었다. 3월 30일 러시아 군대가 아프가니스탄 북부의 펜제(Penjdeh)에서 영국 군대의 훈련을 받은 아프가니스탄 군대를 전멸시켰다. 펜제는 헤라트(Herat)로 가는 길목이고 헤라트는 인도로 가는 관문이었다. 영국 내각은 3월 24일에 이미 헤라트는 전쟁을 의미한다고 결의하였다.

그러면 어디에서 러시아와 전쟁을 결행해야 되는가? 다음 4개 지역 중 하나일 것이다. ① 발트해를 거쳐 러시아 본토를 공격하는 전략이다. 그러나 크림전쟁 때 영국 해군이 올란드(Åland) 섬을 점령한 이후 이 전략을 포기하였다. 러시아 본토의 방어 태세로 보아 그 공격이 용이하지 않다고 판단하였기 때문이다. ② 발칸반도 지역을 거쳐 러시아의 남서 지역인 몰다비아 · 왈라키아 두 공국으로부터 러시아를 공격하는 방안이다. 그러나 발칸반도에서 전쟁이 발발하는 것은 다민족 국가인 오스트리아 제국의 해체를 의미하는 것으로 현실적으로 불가능한 것이었다. ③ 다르다넬스-보스포루스 해협을 거쳐 러시아의 크림반도 또는 코카시아 지방을 공격하는 전략이다. 이 전략 가능성의 전제는 터키와 서유럽 열강이 영국을 지지하는 데에 있다. 크림전쟁 때는 가능하였으나 1885년의 유럽 정세는 판이하였다. ④ 동북아 지역이다. 블라디보스토크를 공격하는 전략이다. 영국의 인도 총독 킴벌리 경(Earl of Kimberley)이 재치 있게 표현한 바와 같이 "개의 목을 졸라 물고 있던 뼈다귀를 떨어트리게 만드는" 구상이었다. 블라디보스토크를 공격해 러시아로 하여금 헤라트로부터 철수시키는 전략이다. 공격의 전진기지가 필요하였다. 영국은 거문도를 지목하였다. "조선 사람들은 야만인이어서 점령하는 데에 아무런 의식(儀式, ceremony)도 필요 없었다." 점령은 일정한 절차가 필요한 유럽 공법의 한 제도이지만 야만의 지역은 이런 절차가 적용되는 것은 아니었다.

영국 해군성은 1885년 4월 14일 중국해 사령관에 거문도 점령을 명령하고 근 2년 후인 1887년 2월 27일 거문도에서 영국 국기를 내린다. 그러나 거문도 점령을 강행한 영국은 국제정치의 승자였다. 러시아로 하여금 근 10년간이나 한반도에 진출하지 못하도록 하였기 때문이다. 마치 크림전쟁(1853~1856)에 승리해 러시아의 지중해 진출을 20년 가까이 저지할 수 있었던 것과 같은 맥락이다.

한편 러시아는 한반도에서 후퇴하는 정책을 채택하지 않을 수 없었다. 1886~1887년 사이에 개최된 일련의 특별위원회에서 조선의 항구를 점령하는 것은 러시아 극동 방위력을 약화시키는 결과를 초래한다고 결정하였다. 1887년 1월 8일 기르스(N. K. Girs) 외상이 해군 본부장 쉐스타코프(I. A. Shestakov)에게 보낸 서한에서 조선에 러시아 영향력을 확장시키면 안 된다고 강조하고 있다. 동북아 지역에서 러시아의 정치적 관심은 오로지 중국과 일본이라고 단정하고 있다.

1888년 5월 8일 특별위원회에서는 아무르 총독 코르프(A. N. Korf)와 외무성 아시아 국장 지노비에프(I. A. Zinoviev)가 작성한 다음과 같은 내용의 보고서를 조선 정책의 기본 노선으로 채택하였다.

(1) 조선을 점유하는 것은 러시아에 아무런 이득도 가져오지 않을 뿐 아니라 매우 좋지 않은 결과를 분명히 가져올 것이다. 조선은 매우 빈곤한 국가로 러시아에 이익이

되는 무역 시장이 아니다. 또한, 조선의 긴 연안을 방어한다는 것도 러시아의 연해주 병력으로는 곤란하다. 조선을 점령한다면 중국, 영국, 그리고 일본과의 관계에서 매우 위험하다.

(2) 조선이 중국이나 일본의 지배를 받게 된다면 러시아에 위협이 되기 때문에 이런 사태가 야기되지 않도록 해야 한다. 갑신정변 이후 일본은 조선에 대한 무관심 정책으로 전환하였으나 최근 중국이 조선을 점령하는 것을 방지하기 위해 다시 고민하기 시작하였다. 러시아는 일본의 이런 정책을 지지해야 한다. 중국이 전통적인 사대 질서의 테두리 안에서 조선을 지도한다면 러시아는 찬성한다. 그러나 현재 중국의 조선 지배는 이런 전통적인 관계에 머물고 있지 않고 중국의 한 지방으로 예속시키려 하고 있다. 이런 사태가 발생하면 남 우수리의 상황은 매우 위험하게 될 것이다. 더욱이 열강들은 중국이 조선의 독립을 위협하는 것에 무관심하고 중국과의 우호 관계를 희망하고 있어서 문제의 심각성이 있다.

(3) 중국의 조선 내정 간섭은 러시아와 조선의 비밀 관계에서 대부분 비롯되었다는 사실을 묵과할 수 없다. 따라서 러시아가 조선 문제에 간여하여 중국과 분쟁을 일으키면 안 된다. 중국의 조선 정책이 조선을 점령하려는 것이라면 러시아는 중국과의 긴 서부 국경에서 군사적 위협을 가해야 한다. 조선 문제로 중국과 전쟁을 하는 것은 모든 면에서 바람직스럽지 않기 때문에 극단적인 조치는 중국 해역에서 군사적 시위를 하는 것, 또는 우리 국경에서 가장 가까운 조선 연안의 어떤 지역을 점령하는 것이다.

러시아의 이런 조선 경시 정책은 오래 지속되지 못하였다. 육군 위주의 군사전략을 채택하였고, 이 전략은 시베리아 철도 부설로 연결되었다. 1892년 2월 27일과 3월 5일 내각회의에서 드디어 철도 부설을 의결하고 조속히 공사에 착수토록 하였다. 동북아 지역은 다시 격동의 국제정치 현실에 직면하게 되었다.

2017년 10월

『近代韓國外交文書』 편찬위원장 김용구

편집방침

1. 본 문서집은 한반도의 역사적 현주소를 밝히는 데 중요하다고 판단한 좁은 의미와 넓은 의미의 국내외 외교문서를 망라해 수록하였다. 좁은 의미의 외교문서는 정부의 토의 문서와 훈령, 외무 담당자들의 교섭 과정 문서documents préaratoires와 왕복 문서, 본국 정부에 발송한 보고문, 그리고 국제조약을 가리킨다. 그리고 넓은 의미의 외교문서는 이 밖에 교섭 담당자들의 회고록이나 문집을 비롯한 개인 문서를 포함한다.

2. 본 문서집의 편집은 주요 열강의 외교문서집 편찬 방식에 따랐다. 주요 국가들은 외교문서를 보관하는 특별 기관을 보유하고 있어서 이 기관의 문서들 중 대외관계에 중요하다고 판단되는 문서들을 기사본말체로 편집하고 있다.

3. 중요하다고 판단하는 편집자들의 인식이 외교문서집 발간의 국제정치적 성격을 나타내 주고 있다. 대외관계 문서집의 효시인 19세기 각국의 칼라 북스Color Books, 미국의 *Foreign Relations of the United States*를 비롯하여 제1차 세계대전 이후 발간되기 시작한 독일의 *Grosse Politik der europäschen Kabinette 1871-1914*, 소련의 *Vneshnaya politika Rossii: XIX i nachala XX beka*, 그리고 *Dokumenty vneshnei politiki SSSR*, 영국의 *British Documents on the Origins of the War, 1898-1914*(G. P. Gooch & H. Temperley eds.), *Documents on British Foreign Policy, 1919-1939*(R. Butler & E. L. Woodward eds.), *British Documents on Foreign Affairs*(K. Bourne & D. C. Watt, eds.), 프랑스의 *Documents diplomatiques français 1871-1914*, 일본의 『日本外交文書』들이 모두 이런 방식을 취하고 있다.

4. 이들 외교문서집은 자국의 문서보관소의 문서들을 선별하여 편집하고 있다. 이들 선별된 문서들과 이를 채록한 원문서와의 관계를 검증하는 작업은 특수 분야를 연구하는 전문 연구자들이 담당하고 있다. 외교문서 편집과는 차원이 다른 연구 분야이다. 그러나 본 문서집은 한국의 문서집이기에 조선 문서의 경우 채록 문서와의 관계를 가능한 한 규명토록 노력하였다.

범례

1. 조선에서 사대질서의 '外交' 개념과 전혀 다른 diplomacy의 번역어로 '외교'란 낱말이 사용되기 시작한 것은 1880년 이후의 일이다. 따라서 1866년 병인양요와 1871년 신미양요의 대외문서를 '외교문서'라고 지칭하는 데에는 비역사적인 측면이 있다. 그러나 본 문서집은 1910년까지의 문서를 편집하는 사업으로 1880년 이전의 자료를 편의상 외교문서로 분류하였다.

2. 조선은 1895년에, 중국은 1912년에, 그리고 일본은 1872년에 양력을 채택하였으나 본 문서집에서는 그 이전의 음력을 모두 양력으로 환산해 적었다. 이들 날짜를 모두 양력으로 환산시킨 것은 특히 아편전쟁 이후 한반도 문제를 포함한 동아시아의 역사가 세계외교사의 흐름과 밀접하게 연관되기 때문이다. 다만 독자들이 동양 자료를 검색하는 데 도움을 주기 위해 중요한 날짜인 경우 음력을 병기하되 한자로 표기함으로써 양력 날짜와 구분하였다. 또한 1917년 소련혁명 이전의 제정 러시아력(曆)도 마찬가지로 양력으로 환산하여 수록하고, 러시아력은 괄호 안에 병기하였다. 19세기 제정 러시아력은 양력보다 12일이 앞서 있다.

3. 중국과 일본의 인명, 지명은 모두 원음으로 표기하였다. 러시아어의 영문 알파벳 전자(轉字)는 The Current Digest of Post-Soviet Press 방법에 의거하였다. 한글 표기는 한국 교육인적자원부 편수자료를 따랐다.

4. 본 문서집은 연구자들에게 검색상의 편의를 제공하기 위해 문건별로 문서의 내용에 관하여 간략한 정보를 표시하였다.

예

> **1** ①
> ②
> 군란 발발 및 경과 통보
> ③ ④ ⑤ ⑥
> 高宗 (1882. 7. 24/高宗十九年六月十日) ➡ 禮部 (1882. 8. 27/光緒八年七月十四日)

① 본 문서집이 부여한 고유의 문서번호이다.

② 본 편찬위원회에서 부여한 문서의 제목이다.

③ 문서의 발신인(기관)을 가리킨다. 문서의 수/발신인(기관)은 직함 등을 생략하고 인명만을 원어로 적는 것을 원칙으로 하였다. 인명을 특정하기 어려운 경우에는 문서에 나타나는 관직명만을 표기하였다.

④ 문서의 발신일을 가리킨다.

⑤ 문서의 수신인(기관)을 가리킨다.

⑥ 문서의 수신일을 가리킨다.

5. 문서의 수/발신일을 특정하기 어려운 교섭 담당자들의 회고록, 수기, 메모, 일기와 같은 사문서의 경우는 수/발신인 대신에 문서작성자의 이름을 표시하였으며, 회담의 경우는 해당 회담의 기록자 이름을 표시하고, 제목에 회담 참석자를 나타냈다.

예

> **35**
> 金允植 - 周馥 회담(1)
> 金允植 (1882. 8. 1/高宗十九年六月十八日)

6. 문건의 배열은 발신일을 기준으로 하였으나, 발신일을 확인할 수 없는 문건의 경우는 수신일에 의거하여 배열하였다. 어떤 문건의 발신일과 또 다른 문건의 수신일이 동일한 날짜에 겹치는 경우는 수신된 문서를 먼저 배열하였다. 문서에 발/수신일이 나타나지 않고 월(月)만 표시된 경우는 그 내용을 분석한 후, 문맥상 다른 외교문서와의 전후 관계를 고려하여 발송되었다고 추정되는 날짜에 의거하여 배열하였다. 내용으로 선후 관계를 추정하기 어려운 문서는 해당 월의 말미에 배열하였다.

7. 중요한 외교문서의 경우, 각 국가의 외교관들이 이를 자국 언어로 번역해서 본국에 보고하는 것이 일반적인 관례이다. 이와 같이 특정한 문서에 대해 여러 언어로 작성된 번역문이 존재할 경우, 본서에서는 이를【英譯文】,【漢譯文】,【日譯文】등으로 표시하고 해당 문서에 첨부하였다. 특정한 외교 교섭에 관해 참석자들이 서로 다른 언어로 기록한 문건 역시 번역문의 범주에 포함된다. 번역은 단순히 문자 기호 사이의 등가적 교환이 아니고 번역자의 특정한 정치적 의도나 작위가 개재되는 실천적 행위이다. 특히 외교문서와 같이 정치적 성격을 띠는 문서에 있어서는 번역 과정에서의 특정한 언어의 선택, 미묘한 어감의 차이, 오역의 발생 여부 등을 더욱 면밀하게 살펴볼 필요가 있다. 본서에서는 원문서와 번역문을 병행 수록함으로써 연구자들로 하여금 사건의 시말을 보다 다각적으로 파악하는 데 도움을 주고자 하였다.

8. 독립된 외교문서로 간주하기에는 형식적·내용적 측면에서 부족한 면이 있으나 특정한 외교문서의 작성 과정이나 사후처리 과정을 이해하는 데 도움이 되는 문서는【관련문서】라고 표시하고 해당 문서에 첨부하였다. 또한 회고록이나 수기, 대화기록, 광범위한 보고서 등 근대한국 외교사에서 중요한 사료적 가치를 가지는 자료들은 관계자료로 분류하여 각 권의 말미에 별도로 수록하였다.

9. 동일한 외교문서인 경우에도 이를 기록하고, 전달하고, 재수록하는 과정에서 일부 자형이 변경되거나 오탈자가 발생하는 경우가 있다. 이 경우 본 문서집에서는 각 국가의 공식 외교문서집에 수록된 문서를 기준으로 수록하였으며, 오탈자가 있다고 의심되는 경우에는 (*sic*)라고 표시하였다. 이들 오탈자 가운데 문맥으로 미루어 원자(原字)를 추정할 수 있는 경우에는【　】안에 표기하였다. 이와 함께 각국의 미간문서 중에는 문서 자체의 훼손이 심하여 글자나 단어를 판독하기 어려운 경우가 있다. 이 경우 로마자는 [___], 한자와 일본어는 □의 기호로 대체하였다.

차례

7-4. 철군 이후 러시아의 극동 군사정책 437

關係資料

6. 거문도 사건 관련 각국의 교섭

1
榎本武揚·李鴻章 회담

榎本武揚·李鴻章 (1885. 4. 20)

同年四月廿日

榎本公使李鴻章ノ官廳ニ於テ閑話ス左ノ如シ

榎本云 伊藤大使ハ予ニ伍大人ノ見送竝ニ太沽砲臺等ヲ中堂ニ代謝センコトヲ托セリ大使ハ貴我兩國和局ノ成リシヲ滿足シテ復命セラルヘシ

李云 大使ノ和衷ナルニ由リ今次ノ事件妥議ニ歸セリ亦貴使ノ幇助周到ナル大ニ與テ力アリ予ハ既ニ此旨ヲ總署王大臣等ヘ函致セリ只予ハ今次ノ査辦ニ對シ言官等ノ異說ナキヲ保シ難シ貴使能ク總署大臣等ヘ懇諭セラレンコトヲ望ム

我 假令言官等可否スル者アルトモ北京政府ハ違言アルヘキ筈ナシ是レ大使前日王大臣等ヘ切論シ置キ而シテ王大臣ヨリ伊藤大使ヘ宛タル照會文モ案ニ在レハナリ只本使ハ貴意ヲ諒シ總署ニ向テ貴皇帝ノ御批准ヲ促スヘシ

彼 批准ハ今ヨリ一ヶ月モ過レハ可相濟ト察スレトモ猶ホ貴使ヨリ時ヲ候テ總署ヘ催促セラルヽヲ可トス

我 前日伊藤大使ヨリモ話サレシ如ク中堂若シ我邦ヘ來ラレナハ兩國ノ交誼信懇篤ナルニ至ラン中堂ハ同時ニ我邦ノ百工製造場ヨリ鐵道礦山及ヒ船渠武庫等ヲ歷觀セラレナハ必ラス裨益アラン何トナレハ我邦近來西洋ニ傚テ創立セシ事業中ニ就テ國益ヲ興セシコトヽ失錯セシコトヽノ跡ヲ判然見分ケ得ヘケレハナリ且ツ中堂ノ雷名ハ我邦朝野ニ轟ケリ我カ朝廷ハ勿論人民モ必ス喜テ之ヲ接待センコト疑ナシ

彼悅テ云 予モ貴國ニ一遊センコトヲ望ム久シ惟現職ノ繁劇ナルヲ以テ其暇ヲ得ス此ヲ憾トス貴使若シ總署王大臣ニ說キ我皇帝ヨリ予ニ二個月ノ暇ヲ賜ハルニ至ラハ幸甚シ

我 中堂佛國ノ談判ヲ了シテ後來ル八九月頃東鴻セラレナハ更ニ妙ナリ大使以爲ク我皇帝ハ既ニ伊藤大使ヲ貴國ニ遣ハサレタレハ貴國皇帝モ亦一大臣ノ我邦ニ遣ハサレ以テ善隣ノ厚意ヲ表セラレテ可ナリ

彼 予ノ貴國行ハ隣交上ニ於テモ一己ノ利益上ニ於テモ倶ニ完キヲ知ルト雖奈何セン

我朝廷ニハ此理由ヲ解了スル者ナシ故ニ欽命ヲ以テ東派セラルヽカ如キハ殆ント夢想モ及ハサル所ナリ

我 中堂ハ奉命東派ノ名義ナキヲ苦シマルヽカ如シ本使玆ニ一說アリ設ヘハ貴皇帝ノ御佩セラルヘキ寶星ヲ我皇帝ニ奉スルノ使ニテモ可ナラスヤ我カ皇帝御佩ノ寶星ハ大抵皆ナ締盟各國帝王御佩ノ寶星ト交換セラレタリ然ルニ貴國ト我邦トハ近隣舊交ノ間柄ナカラ未互ニ此盛事ナキハ一ノ缺典ニアラスヤ本使以爲ク貴皇帝ニシテ其御佩ノ大寶星ヲ貴國皇帝ニ贈ラルヘシ

李 貴諭ハ道理アリト雖總署大臣等ハ徒ニ奇異ノ思ヲ爲スノミニシテ之ニ盡力スヘシトモ思ハレス

我 貴皇帝モ旣ニ各等ノ寶星ヲ欽定セラレシニアラスヤ

李 然レトモ矢張了解セサルヘシ貴國ハ舊慣ヲ打却シ百事西洋ニ傚ヒ而シテ之ヲ行フ日アルヲ以テ西洋各國ノ風習ヲ奇觀セラレサルヘシト雖中國ハ一切舊慣ニ因襲スルヲ以テ往々其所見ヲ殊ニスル所アリトテ是ヨリ日本富貴ノ子弟ハ私費ヲ以テ海外ニ留學スル者多シト聞ケトモ中國ニハ官費ヲ仰クニアラサレハ自ラ奮テ外遊ヲ事トスル者ナシ又日本ハ外遊成學ノ徒ヲ採用シテ高官ニ就カシムレトモ中國ハ然ラストテ一二ノ苦情話ノ後次件ニ轉ス

李 今次ノ事件伊藤大使ノ來淸ヲ以テ妥議ノ結局ニ至リシノミナラス幾分カ兩國ノ交誼ヲ親睦ナラシムルノ基ヲ開ケリ只惜ムラクハ琉球一案未局ヲ結ハス是レ猶關心ノ一事也伊藤大使ハ滯津中該案ニ談及セラレシコトナカリシヤ

我 否

李 貴使ハ該件取纒メノ良案ナキヤ

我 無シ句中堂若シ良案アラハ承リ置カン

李 該件ハ宍戸公使負擔セシトキ結局セハ都合好カリシニ今日トナリテハ予モ別ニ策ナシ

我 元來該件ハ宍戸公使ノ時雙方ノ辦法將ニ成ラントスルニ際シ貴政府ニ於テ突然其議ヲ變セラレシニ付我方ニテハ爾來該件取纒ノコトヲ斷念スルニ至リシナリ初メ本使カ貴國ニ駐紮ノ命ヲ奉セシトキ琉案談判ノ訓令ヲ帶ヒタラントノ說ヲ爲セシ者アリシト聞ケリ然レトモ本使ハ決シテ斯ル訓令ヲ受ケシコトナシ

李 乍併宍戸公使歸國後貴國ノ某大臣ハ該件ヲ憂慮セラレ竹添氏ニ內命シテ予ト談判セシメシコトアリ貴使ハ御承知ナキ哉

我 該件ニ付竹添氏ト中堂トノ對話書ナル者ハ曾テ一閱セシコトアリト雖是レ蓋シ竹

添氏一己ノ考ヲ以テ閑話セシナラン本使ハ竹添氏カ此種ノ内訓ヲ受ケシトノコトハ未曾テ聞カサレハナリ

李 當時竹添氏ハ予ニ向テ眞ニ内命ヲ受ケシト稱シ且ツ云ク若シ談判ノ基礎整ヒタラハ北京ニ赴キ田邊署大臣ヲシテ公然總署ト開談セシメント語レリ

我 夫ハ本使ノ解セサル所ナリ當時竹添氏ハ天津ノ領事ナリシカト思ヘリ如何

李 然リ

我 領事ハ外交官ニアラス我カ朝廷若シ眞ニ琉案ヲ處理セント思ハヽ北京駐紮田邊署大臣ニ命シテ總署ト開談セシムヘキニ主任者ヲ差措テ竹添領事ニ内訓ヲ與フヘキ謂レナケレハナリ恐クハ竹添氏ノ造意ニアラサルナキヲ得ンヤ

李 予モ亦當時其疑アリタレトモ竹添氏ハ直ニ内命ヲ受ケタリト自稱セリ故ニ予ハ同氏ノ對話書ヲ當時總署ニ送リテ田邊署大臣ト談判ノ資ニ供セリ

我 田邊署大臣ハ北京ニ駐紮セシコト三箇年餘ニ及ヘリ然レトモ其間總署ニ向テ球案ヲ再ヒ提出セシコトアリシヲ聞カス

李 予モ亦未其事アリシヲ聞カス今更思ヒ回セハ竹添氏ニ計ラレシナルモ未知ルヘカラス同氏ハ予舊相識ナレトモ兎角事ヲ好ムノ士タルニ似タリ乃チ昨年漢城ノ變ノ如キモ亦以テ其然ルヲ證スヘシトテ冷笑ス

李又 琉球ノ現況如何

我 廢藩以來彼地ニ裁判所ヲ置キ學校ヲ設ケ兵營ヲ分駐スル等渾テ內地ニ異ナルコトナシ

李 琉球ノ物産ハ貴國歲入ノ助ヲ爲スニ足ル者アリヤ

我 該島ノ物産ハ砂糖及ヒ絹布類ナレトモ其我ニ入ル所ハ出ス所ヲ償フニ足ラスト聞ケリ是レ實ニ然ルヘシ何トナレハ置縣以來我政府ハ該島從來ノ苛政ヲ改メテ諸税ヲ輕クシ又裁判官幷ニ巡査ヲ派遣シテ寃民ナカラシメ加之我內地ノ兵ヲ分駐シテ外寇ニ備フルカ如キ皆出入相償ハサルノ源タリ然レトモ是レ主權者ノ義務ニシテ不得已次第ナリ

李 琉球ハ九州ヨリモ臺灣ヲ距ル近キヤ

我 沖繩本島ハ大約九州ト臺灣ノ中間ニ位スト雖八重山宮古島ノ如キハ臺灣ヲ距ルコト本島ヲ距ルヨリモ近シ

李 宮古諸島ハ貧窶ノ島嶼タルヘシ

我 特ニ此島ノミナラス琉球本島トテモ亦然リ乍併貧島ナリトテ從前ノ如キニ任セ置

カハ萬一他國ニ占据セラルレハ內地ノ防禦ニ關スルコト鮮ナカラス是レ我カ政府費額ヲ厭ハス平時トテモ兵卒竝ニ巡査等ヲ分駐シ置ク所以ナリ本使コレヲ聞ク宮古八重山諸島ノ人口ハ共計三萬人許ニシテ我邦人ノ貴重スル一種ノ蔴布　ヂヨーフ　ナル者ヲ產シ且ツ島中石炭脈ノ現出スル所アリト恐クハ鷄籠ノ石炭脈ト相聯絡スル者ナルモ未知ルヘカラス

李 其石炭ハ貴國ニテ既ニ探掘ニ從事セラルヽヤ

我 否其脈ノ大小サヘモ未我礦學士ノ硏究ヲ經タルヲ聞カス

李 該島ヘモ貴國人住居セラルヤ

我 我商民ノ有無ハ知ラサレトモ官吏竝ニ還卒等ハ駐留セリ試ニ思惟セラレヨ該島ノ如キ我政府若シ保護ノ勞ヲ怠リ置カハ頃日英艦　ハミルトン　港ニ据リシカ如キ虞ナキヲ保スヘカラス又佛艦カ鷄籠ヲ攻ムル時ニモ宮古諸島ニ假據セサリシハ他ナシ我屬島タルヲ知レハナリ

李 其島ハ臺灣トノ距離大凡幾里許ナリヤ

我 悉シクハ記臆セサレトモ大約海里一百里强タリシト思ヘリ故ニ汽船ハ該島ヨリ十時乃至十二時間ニシテ能ク鷄籠港ニ達シ得ヘシ

李 然ルカ

是ヨリシテ李氏ハ朝鮮製ノ地圖ヲ出シ　ポルトハミルトン　ノ位置ヲ本使ニ質問ス本使ハ答フルニ該港ハ好碇泊所ニシテ淸水モアリ亦魚族ニモ富ミ人口ハ約一千五百人許ナル由ヲ以テス

李 英艦カ　ハミルトン　港ニ假據スルハ貴國ニ於テモ好ム所ニアラサルヘシ

我 固ヨリ然リ此擧第一朝鮮ノ爲ニ憂フヘキ而已ナラス我邦ニモ貴國ニモ又露國ニモ關係アリ甚タ不穩ノ擧動ト謂フヘシ只我邦ハ對馬島ニ良港アリテ能ク數十艘ノ軍艦ヲ泊シ得ヘキヲ以テ未認テ以テ直接ノ害アリト爲スニ足ラス之ニ反シテ貴國ノ爲ニハ敵船　ハミルトン　港ヲ以テ根據トシ石炭及ヒ糧食ヲ此ニ貯ヘ置キ以テ芝罘若クハ旅順口邊ニ出沒セハ頗ル不容易ノ事ニ屬スヘシ

李 然リ甚タ憂フヘキ事ナレトモ差當リ之ヲ遮ル能ハサルヲ奈何セン只英ノ占據ハ專ラ露ノ南侵ニ備フル爲ニシテ且ツ假據タレハ早晚引彿フヘキヲ賴ムノミ恐クハ貴國ニ於テモ詮方ナカルヘシ

我 乍殘念實致方ナキニ似タリ且ツ此擧ハ露ヲシテ其尤ニ傚ヒ朝鮮ノ　ラザレフ　港等ニ假據スルノ口實ヲ得セシムヘキノ虞ナキ能ハス假令直チニ　ラトレフ　港ニ據ラ

サルモ譬ハ松島ノ奪領セラレナハ是亦朝鮮竝ニ我邦ノ爲メ戒心ナキ能ハス

李 松島トハ何處ニアリテ何國ノ所屬ナルヤ

我 朝鮮ニテハ鬱陵島ト稱ス我カ西海岸ト朝鮮元山津ノ間ニアリ二百三四十年前迄ハ我邦民住居セシ由ナレトモ其後ハ專ラ朝鮮人民ノミ往來セリ此島良好港灣ナシト雖其東岸ハ船舶假泊スルヲ得ヘク島上良材多シ亦海岸處〻清水アリ吸ムヘシ魚類モ亦鮮カラス此島現ニ朝鮮ニ屬スレトモ常住民ナク朝鮮ノ官吏三年ニ一次巡回スルノミト聞ケリ

李 露艦濟州ニ據ルヘシトノ風說アリ如何

我 同島ハ船ヲ泊スヘキ所ナキヲ以テ露艦ノ占據スヘキ筈ナシ露若シ英ノ尤ニ傚ハント欲セハ巨濟島ナリ其他ニ占據スヘキノ島嶼一ニシテ足ラス是レ憂フヘキナリ

李 實ニ然リ願クハ將來貴國ト我ト同心合力シテ朝鮮ヲ他人ニ割據セラレサル樣致シ度者ナリ

我 本使モ亦御同見ナリ畢

2
거문도 점령의 전략적 가치 보고

Patenôtre (1885. 4. 21) ➡ Ferry

Ministre des Affaires Etrangères
Cabinet du Ministre
21 avril 1985

Note sur l'annexion par l'Angleterre de l'archipel Hamilton

Il vient de se produire dans l'Extrême-Orient un fait d'une réelle importance, dont l'opinion russe s'est émise à bon droit, serait qui n'a eu en France qu'un faible retentissement.

Le drapeau britannique flotte depuis quelques jours sur l'archipel des îles Hamilton, situé au sud de la péninsule de Corée. Voici comment cet événement a eu lieu.

Au milieu des complications survenues en Asie et en présence de l'éventualité d'un conflit armé qui aurait les mers de Chine pour théâtre principal, l'Angleterre s'est demandé si Hong-Kong pouvait être considéré comme protégeant suffisamment la commerce de ses nationaux dans ces parages et elle a conclu à la négative. Hong-Kong, en effet, est excellent pour garantir toute sécurité aux transactions maritimes sur les côtes méridionales [__] la Chine et l'on peut admettre sans trop d'invraisemblance que son influence s'étend jusque vers l'embouchure du Yang-sse-Kiang mais, passé l'estuaire de ce grand fleuve, Hong-Kong en [__] que station navale, n'exerçant plus aucune action efficace que faire dès lors, sinon chercher plus au nord, and le voisinage de la Corée, par exemple, une autre position assez avantageusement placée pour remplir cette fonction protectrice: on a cherché et on a trouvé.

L'attention du gouvernement britannique s'était d'abord protée sur l'île [__] qui, pareille à une sentinelle avancée, face à la pointe sud de la péninsule coréenne, aurait permis de surveiller à la fois l'entrée de la mer Jaune et du golfe de Pe-seni-li, d'une part, le détroit entre la Corée et le Japon, de l'autre, mais cette solution, simple en apparence, présentait un inconvénient capital[__] n'a pas de port; sa possession ne pourrait donc que créer des difficultés au Cabinet de Londres sans offrir en retour aucune utilité pour la marine anglaise, condamnée à l'emploi de mouillage plus que médiocres, battus par les vents et les courants.

L'Angleterre, qui avait caressé quelque temps ce projet y a donc renoncée résolument et elle a fait choix, pour y établir sa station navale des mers septentrionales de la Chine, d'un petit groupe d'îles, d'apparence chétive, l'archipel Hamilton, qui, situé par 34° de latitude nord, à 92 kilomètres seulement de la côte coréenne et à 240 de Shanghaï, renferme un port magnifique, le port Hamilton.

Ce bassin maritime, destiné à devenir avant pour le Hong-Kong du nord, est compris entre deux îles monstrueuses, en forme de croissant, et précédé d'une troisième île, de l'observatoire.

La sonde y accuse des profondeurs variant entre 14 et 22ème et les collines latérales le mettent complètement à l'abri des vents dangereux; on peut y mouiller partout et la forme du mouillage est très bonne.

Ce sont là, on en conviendra, des conditions exceptionnelles. En outre, les navires ne peuvent y pénétrer que par deux passes, le cheval du nord n'étant accessible qu'aux bâtiment d'un courant d'eau inférieur à 4° de part et d'autre de l'île de l'observatoire qu'il serait très aisé de fortifier. Les navires calant près de 6ème peuvent pratiquer la passe entre l'îlot et la grande Hamilton, ceux qui calent jusqu'à 11ème entrant librement par la passe qui sépare la Petite Hamilton de l'îlot nul doute que les Anglais ne s'empressent de mettre à profit ces remarquables conditions naturelles pour rendre bientôt Port Hamilton absolument inexpugnable.

Ainsi se trouve réalisé le dessein que l'ambassadeur anglais, sir Harry Parkes, avait connu l'ancienne date. Les derniers événements ont eu pour effet de décider l'Angleterre à brusquer l'exécution d'un plan depuis longtemps mûri, mais qu'elle hésitait encore à révéler, le Port Hamilton a été acheté au roi du Corée et l'on parle déjà d'y établir de grands dépôts de charbon.

Les Russes peuvent jeter les hauts cris, protester contre cette prise de possession soudaine, et prétendre ce en quoi ils ont raison que Port-Hamilton constitue une menace directe pour Wladivostok et leurs établissements de la côte sibérienne; les Anglais feront à Port-Hamilton ce qu'ils ont fait à Malte, en 1802: ils y sont, ils y resteront.

3

영·러 전쟁 발발 가능성에 대한 주독 청무관의 우려 보고

Patenôtre (1885. 4. 21) ➡ Ferry

Ministère des Affaires Etrangères
Cabinet du Ministre
21 avril 1885

Note sur une opinion émise à Berlin par le général Tchen-Ki-Long, de l'Ambassade de Chine

Il paraît résulter d'une conversation tenue par le général chinois Tchen-Ki-Long, attaché militaire à l'ambassade de Chine à Berlin, que cet officier croit fermement à la guerre entre l'Angleterre et la Russie et [__]que les hostilités s'ouvriront entre ces deux puissances au mois de juin prochain. M. Tchen-Ki-Long entretient en ce moment une correspondance des plus actives avec Londres où il est en relations avec plusieurs personnages anglais; les termes dont il s'est servi dans la conversation précitée donnant lieu de penser que la conclusion de la paix avec la France de rattacherait pour la Chine à une immixtion éventuelle dans la querelle anglo-russe la Chine serait entrée, ou sur le point d'entrer dans l'alliance anglaise, avec prouesse et sa part de faire une diversion en faveur des Anglais, en attaquant les Russes sur leurs frontières de la Sibérie et du Turkistan, dès l'ouverture des hostilités dans l'Asie Centrale.

Ce renseignement important qui prouvait du service secret des renseignements au ministère de la guerre, se complète par la nouvelle de l'attente où serait en ce moment Li-Fong-Pao, d'être envoyé d'un jour à l'autre à Paris, par un ordre de Tsong-Li-Yamên, pour y traiter de la paix avec le gouvernement français ou pur renouer des relations diplomatiques régulières avec le gouvernement de la République.

Le renseignement fourni n'est pas très explicite sur ce dernier point; il semble donner à entendre toutefois que Campbell aurait été un négociateur sans mandat.

4
청 정부에 전신 설치 승인 요청 지시

E. Granville (1885. 4. 27) ➡ N. R. O'Conor

No. 14.

Earl Granville to Mr. O'Conor.

Foreign Office, April 27, 1885.

(No. 85. Confidential. Ext. 16.)

Sir,

I HAVE to request that you will ask the Chinese Government to allow the Telegraph Construction Company to land a cable, and establish a cable house, at North Saddle Island, at the entrance of the Yangtze River.

This cable will be laid between that point and Port Hamilton for the use of Her Majesty's Government.

The substance of the above was sent to you this day by telegraph.

I am, &c.

(Signed) GRANVILLE.

5
거문도 점령에 대한 청 정부의 입장

曾紀澤 (1885. 4. 27) ➡ E. Granville (1885. 4. 27)

No. 13.

The marquis Tsêng to Earl Granville.—(Received April 27.)

Chinese Legation, April 27, 1885.

Confidential.

My Lord,

I BEG to acknowledge receipt of the letter which your Lordship did me the honour to address to me on the 16th instant, replying to the inquiry which, in conformity with instructions received from the Imperial Government, I made on the 8th of the same month, relative to the reported occupation by Her Britannic Majesty's Government of the islands forming Port Hamilton.

As these islands belong to the Kingdom of Corea, a country which is not only conterminous with China, but which is a vassal of the Chinese Empire, the reported occupation of them by a foreign Power naturally could not be viewed without concern at Peking.

This feeling, however, I am happy to be able to inform your Lordship, has in some measure been allayed by the assurance contained in the communication under reply, that the occupation would only be of a temporary nature, and that Her Majesty's Government, being desirous of not doing anything which would be injurious to the prestige of China, would be prepared to come to such an agreement with the Chinese Government as would not be hurtful to Chinese rights and interests in those parts.

The Imperial Government, after having taken due note of this assurance, and of the statement that, but for the exigency of circumstances, Her Majesty's Government would, before authorizing the occupation of the islands, have sought to come to an understanding with the Chinese Government on the subject, have instructed me to request your Lordship to inform me of the kind of agreement which Her Majesty's Government would propose in order to secure these objects.

I have, &c.
(Signed) TSÊNG.

6
거문도 점령에 대한 영국과 청의 협정문 초안

E. Granville (1885. 4. 28) ➡ 曾紀澤

No. 15.

Earl Granville to the marquis Tsêng.

Foreign Office, April 28, 1885.

M. le Ministre,

I HAVE the honour to acknowledge the receipt of your note of yesterday's date, and in accordance with your request to be informed of the nature of the Agreement which Her Majesty's Government would propose in regard to the occupation of Port Hamilton by Great Britain, I beg leave to forward a draft of Agreement on the subject, which I shall be prepared to sign with you.

I have, &c.
(Signed) GRANVILLE.

Inclosure

Draft Agreement between the British and Chinese Governments respecting the British Occupation of Port Hamilton.

EARL GRANVILLE, K. G., Her Majesty's Principal Secretary of State for Foreign Affairs, and the marquis Tsêng, Envoy Extraordinary and Minister Plenipotentiary from His Imperial Majesty the Emperor of China, having met this day at the Foreign Office, an exchange of views took place with regard to the possible occupation of Port Hamilton by Great Britain.

The Marquis Tsêng stated, in answer to Lord Granville's inquiry, that he was authorized by his Government to declare that, in the event of the British Government desiring, at any time, to occupy the islands lying off the south coast of Corea, known by the name of "Port Hamilton," His Imperial Majesty the Emperor of China would offer no objection to such occupation; and Earl Granville having taken due notice of this declaration, it was mutually agreed that from the day on which Her Britannic Majesty should deem it advisable to occupy those islands they should be acknowledged by His Imperial Majesty the Emperor of China as lawfully occupied and administered by England.

It is understood between the two High Contracting Parties that Her Britannic Majesty's Government shall, at the expiration of twelve months from the date of occupation, pay to the Corean Government the whole of the revenue that may have been received by them from the islands, and a similar sum at the expiration of every twelve months during the continuance of the occupation of the islands by Great Britain, deducting therefrom and paying to China any portion of that revenue which has hitherto been paid to China by Corea as tribute in regard to these islands.

It is also understood that the British occupation is not to prejudice either the rights or the privileges of the subjects of Corea inhabiting the islands.

7
영국의 거문도 점거에 관한 李鴻章과의 회담 보고

原敬 (1885. 4. 28) ➡ 榎本武揚

別紙寫之通昨夜外務卿之訓電ニ接シ候ニ付 文中不分明之廉も不尠候へ共 不取敢本日李氏ヲ訪問致シ追々同件之談話ニ移リ候所 彼之意見ニテハ目下ハ此まゝニ差置ク之外ニ策ナキモノヽ如ク相見得候 尤も彼ニハいよ々々英國ニ於テ永ク該島ヲ占有スルニ於テハ 朝鮮政府ニ問合セ 奪レタルカ但シハ通知之上借入たるかヲ糺シタル上ニテ 略奪ナレハ此まゝニ致かたく 貸與ナレハ朝鮮之土地ゆゑ如何トモ難致ナトヽ申候へ共 結局拙官より推察致候所ニテハ 目下無策ニテ先ツ暫ラクハ此まゝニ置クヘシト云フニ外ナラサル樣相見得候 尚ホ本日談判之詳細ハ追而可申上候へ共不取敢大要を申上候

歸途吳大澂ヲ訪問致候所 同人も前件ニ言及シ 朝鮮政府ニ勸告シテ該島貸與等之事アルモ決シテ條約等ヲ結フ勿レ 若シ條約等アリテハ他日ニ口實ヲ殘シ 縱ヒ英艦立去ルモ 露國ノ爲メニ再ヒ占據セラルベシ 依テ何分英國ガ勝手ニ一時占據シタル有樣ニ致シ[ママ]方可然ニ付 其旨書狀ニテ申送ルヘシト思居ヘ[ママ]リなと申候 尤も吳も李も英國ガ朝鮮ニ通知シタルカ否ヲ知ラスト申候ノミナラス 吳ハ朝鮮ハ恐クハ占據セラレタルコトヲ未タ知ラサル哉も難計ト申候

李氏ハ四日前旅順口より海定號(バイテン)ヲ朝鮮ニ派シテ日清談判之結局ヲ駐在之官吏ニ報知シ 且ツ兵隊ニも可成靜穩ニセヨト命シタリト申候 又此頃日清兵隊之中ニテ或る道筋ヲ日兵ノ通行スルヲ清兵止メタルヨリ事起リ喧嘩シ 清兵負傷シ 一時ハ大騷ナリシ旨報知アリト申候ニ付 拙官ハ 左もあるべし 日清兵彼地ニ在る間ハ其位之事ハ到底免かれまじト申候 彼も實ニ然リ 其事ハ伊藤大使も云ハレタリなと申候

[株消]
一 本日ハ大使御出發後始メテ之面會ニ御坐候故 彼之言語ニ注意致候處毫も先般已來之景況ニ異ラス候

一 又パトノー[ト欠]ル公使トハ未タ談判ヲ開[カ欠]ラセル趣 其故ハパトノートル之方ハ
未訓状到達セスト申候

右御含まて申上候 敬具

四月廿八日 領事原敬

特命全權公使榎本武揚殿

8
영국과의 협정문 서명에 관한 의견 요청

曾紀澤 (1885. 5. 1 / 光緒十一年三月十七日) ➡ 總署

附 曾侯致譯署

光緒十一年三月十七日子刻到

安島之事已屢次爭論 刻議約云 英據該島 中朝允不阻難 惟英據一年之後 察該島歲稅若干 每年以稅歸之高王 高麗入貢中國 安島應派費若干 應於稅中除出 送交中國作爲貢款 幷聲明英不得損該島居民權利 可照此訂約畫押否 乞示 東洋多方撓我上邦之權 澤意欲議此次約挽回之 刪

9
영국의 제안에 대한 李鴻章의 검토 지시

光緖帝 (1885. 5. 1 / 光緖十一年三月十七日)

관련문서 李鴻章의 의견 (1885. 5. 1)

丙辰 諭軍機大臣等 電寄曾紀澤 據電稱 安島之事 現議約云 英據該島 中朝允 不阻難 英據年後 察該島山戊不 稅若干 每年以稅歸朝鮮 派費若干 送交中國 作爲貢款 聲明英不得損該島居民權利 可否照此訂約畫押 東洋多方撓我上邦之權 欲藉此約挽回等語 屬國之地 豈可由我許其占據 且於中取利 尤非政體 倘爲他國藉口 流弊甚多 惟此事究應若何措置 方爲妥協 著李鴻章酌議速

奏 電寄

【관련문서】

寄譯署

光緖十一年三月十七日酉刻

洽電悉 英據安島洋名 哈米敦 華名巨磨島 當東海之沖 距朝鮮之釜山 日本之對與島較近 日使伊藤前曾商及 謂英久據於日本尤不利 但恐暫據備俄 可姑待之 玆曾紀澤允其古據 且令派費作貢款 誠如聖諭 非政體 多流弊 若謂借定約挽回上邦之權 日本雖不明認朝鮮爲我屬國 而朝屬名義自在 天下咸知 非東洋力所能撓 若允英據此島俄必將索占永興灣 日本亦必有詞 後患更大 似應暫置勿論 英果欲占據 須自與朝鮮議辦 朝雖弱小 諒不能無故允許 即允亦當疏報中朝 屆時仍可詰責 較爲名正言順 是否 伏候聖裁 請代奏 鴻

10
영국과의 협정 조인 불가 지시

總署 (1885. 5. 4 / 光緒十一年三月二十日) ➡ 曾紀澤

附 譯署致曾侯

光緒十一年三月二十日亥刻到

英約不可畫押 昨已電達 此事切勿輕許 致貽後悔 現聞俄使密謀 如許英據安島 俄亦欲據一島 且恐日本亦將效尤 是英之發難爲無名 徒貽害於朝鮮而利歸於他國 甚爲不值 希善爲說辭 勸令勿爲戎首 以利他人 看其如何答覆 電知 號

11
고종의 적절한 처리 지시
光緖帝 (1885. 5. 5 / 光緖十一年三月二十一日)

附 譯署來電

光緖十一年三月二十一日戌初到

本日奉旨 李鴻章電奏已悉 所陳派員往探各節 均依議行 昨已由總署電知曾紀澤毋庸畫押 幷令勸英勿爲戎首 以利他人矣 此意一幷密爲函致 令該國王斟酌妥辦 欽此 個

12
청 정부의 전신선 설치 승인 예정

N. R. O'Conor (1885. 5. 8) ➡ E. Granville (1885. 5. 9)

No. 17.

Mr. O'Conor to Earl Granville.—(Received May 9, 8 A. M.)

Peking, May 8, 1885, 7:15 P. M.

(No. 32.)
(Telegraphic.)
YOUR telegram No. 16.

Chinese Government will consent if I can assure them cable is landed temporarily in view of eventualities, will be removed afterwards.

13

러시아와 일본의 동향에 대한 청의 우려

N. R. O'Conor (1885. 5. 9) ➡ E. Granville (1885. 5. 9)

No. 18.

Mr. O'Conor to Earl Granville.—(Received May 9, 10:30 P. M.)

Peking, May 9, 1885, 2:55 P. M.

(No. 33. Confidential.)
(Telegraphic.)

CHINESE Government alarmed at temporary occupation of Port Hamilton as Russia and Japan have threatened to occupy other Corean islands. They ask if Her Majesty's Government will prevent such occupation. They also fear that Russia will take Port Hamilton when we leave it. They want, in fact, to save themselves vis-a-vis of Russia and Japan, and wish to consider occupation as meaning temporary employment of the island as a naval station; but I hardly think they will any how protest.

I am not sure about Corea, and have warned, confidentially, Her Majesty's Consul there.

Japanese Minister stirring Chinese against occupation.

Have informed Mr. Plunkett privately.

14
거문도 점령 기간에 대한 청 정부 견해

N. R. O'Conor (1885. 5. 9) ➡ E. Granville (1885. 7. 6)

No. 71.

Mr. O'Conor to Earl Granville.—(Received July 6.)

Peking, May 9, 1885.

(No. 218. Very Confidential.)

My Lord,

HAVING heard on the 2nd instant of the occupation of Port Hamilton by Her Majesty's naval forces, I called, accompanied by Mr. Hillier, Assistant Chinese Secretary, by appointment, on the Prince and Ministers of the Yamên yesterday afternoon.

I said that I had been instructed by your Lordship to inform the Chinese Government confidentially that Her Majesty's Government had decided, in view of present eventualities, to occupy temporarily the Island of Port Hamilton to the south of Corea. I had been aware for some time, I said, of this decision, but I had purposely refrained from alluding to it in my last interview, as I knew that his Highness was equally aware of it, and I judged from the silence which he had observed in the matter that he would prefer, for reasons of policy, to receive no official intimation of the action which Her Majesty's Government had thought it advisable to take.

His Highness replied that he was glad I had now alluded to this matter, as otherwise he would have been obliged to do so himself. It was a question upon which the Yamên felt that explanation could no longer be delayed. The Chinese Government did not for a moment question the bona fides of the British Government in this matter, and they had no doubt that the occupation was temporary, arid that the British Government would withdraw their forces when the circumstances which prompted the occupation no longer existed.

Nevertheless, the act was fraught with such grave danger to Chine and Corea, that it could not but be viewed with serious alarm. An example had been set which other and less friendly Governments would not be slow to follow. His Highness would even inform me confidentially that the Russian and Japanese Ministers had already called at the Yamên, and hinted at the probability of other islands being similarly occupied by other Powers, meaning, there could be no doubt, their own Governments. The danger with which China and Corea were menaced was very serious, as occupation by any other Power was not likely to be temporary. The Chinese Government felt bound, therefore, to put a plain question to Her Majesty's Government, which was this — to what extent were the British Government prepared to guarantee the immunity of Corean territory from annexation by foreign Powers?

In the occupation of Corean territory, without reference to the Corean Government or that of China, the suzerain Power, a serious invasion of sovereign rights had been made, and the Chinese Government would have felt it their duty to protest had their permission been previously asked. It seemed, therefore, to the Yamên, that under the circumstances the British Government would only be acting honourably, by coming forward and guaranteeing the integrity of Corean territory against all invaders. In the event of actual hostilities breaking out between Great Britain and Russia the former would, no doubt, prevent any such annexation as had been hinted at by the Russian Minister, but it was necessary to look to the future. It was to be feared that upon the withdrawal of the British forces the Russian Government might step in and say that political reasons dictated the occupation of the same island which the British Government had been allowed to occupy previously for a similar cause. Would Her Majesty's Government interfere in such a case?

Sir Harry Parkes, his Highness continued, had been very earnest in his insistance on the importance of securing the integrity of Corea, and the British Government had by their present action brought about the very thing which their Representative had been bo anxious to prevent. If Her Majesty's Government would undertake to hinder the seizure of any other portion of Corean or Chinese territory, the Chinese Government would not certainly, he intimated, offer any opposition to the occupation of Port Hamilton.

I replied that the Prince had opened a large question, and one of Imperial policy, upon which I had naturally no power to speak. It would, however, be my duty to report to your Lordship the remarks his Highness had thought fit to make.

I said that it seemed to me, however, that his Highness was attaching unnecessary importance to the occupation, for a temporary purpose, of a profitless island like Port Hamilton. Such occupation as had taken place was forced on us by the necessity of haying a secure coaling-station for our fleet, and was very different from a territorial annexation. It could not at present be viewed as a serious cause of complaint, either by Corea or by China. Moreover, the occupation of the island by the British forces in all probability had prevented the annexation of. the island by another Power, and in so far both the Chinese and Corean Governments should appreciate the service which the force of circumstances had thus rendered them; while the presence of the British fleet at Port Hamilton seemed to me the best guarantee, should the eventualities occur in view of which Her Majesty's Government had occupied Port Hamilton, against the annexation of other neighbouring islands by the Power to whom his Highness had alluded. The fact that no previous intimation had been made of the. intention to occupy the island had saved the Chinese Government from a good deal of difficulty vis-à-vis to other Powers. I had, however, been instructed by your Lordship to inform the Corean Government confidentially of this occupation, and I had, as a matter of fact, addressed a confidential note to the Corean Government in accordance with these instructions. His Highness asked if I would have any objection to let him have a copy of the note I had addressed to the Corean Government, and, as I saw little objection to doing so, I premised to comply with this request.

In the foregoing pages I have reported to your Lordship the substance of a conversation that lasted nearly an hour and-a-half, and I have tried to give as accurately as possible the pith of the remarks made by his Highness and the other Ministers of the Yamên. There was much, however, that passed between the Ministers themselves and in frequent interruptions that it is difficult to render verbatim.

The sum of the conversation was, however, pretty clearly to the effect that China did not herself object to the occupation of Port Hamilton by Her Majesty's forces, as she believed it would be a temporary one; but that both the Russian and Japanese Ministers had been very strongly urging her to protest, and had threatened, if she did not do so, to usurp the same liberty of action with regard to some other Corean island.

In order, therefore, not to injure her position vis-à-vis to other Powers, or to lay herself open to the reproach from other quarters of having in any way sanctioned the occupation of Port Hamilton, China thinks she is called upon to offer at least some form of objection to our occupation. That she had been moved by the threats of Russia and Japan to some such action was very apparent, but that she will now go the length of protesting I am inclined to doubt.

The tone itself of the Prince and Ministers was very friendly, and left no doubt on my mind that their chief preoccupation was how to answer Russia should she attempt a similar step. The assurance of a temporary occupation seemed to satisfy the Ministers of the Yamên, but would not, they appeared to think, satisfy other Powers, or prevent them from attempting something of the same sort; and his Highness said, in conclusion, that Japan they could manage, but Russia was more powerful, and it was necessary that their conduct towards us should not injure their position as against Russia. He would therefore like to be able to regard the "occupation" as consisting in making use of Port Hamilton as a temporary anchorage for British ships, and that if further questioned by the Representatives of other Powers he would explain the occupation in this way.

I did not further continue the conversation.

The following morning I sent your Lordship my telegram No. 33.

I have, &C.

(Signed) N. R. O'CONOR.

15

거문도 전신선 설치에 대한 청 정부와의 교섭 지침

E. Granville(1885. 5. 11) ➡ N. R. O'Conor

No. 20.

Earl Granville to Mr. O'Conor.

Foreign Office, May 11, 1885, 7 P. M.

(No. 19.)

(Telegraphic.)

YOUR telegram No. 32.

You may give assurances if absolutely necessary, but endeavour to avoid pledging us more than you can help as to its being temporary or removable.

Point out that such conditions are unusual, and that cable would be of great advantage to China, in affording her a means of communication with Corea; and that all the facilities would be given to "the Chinese Government which are usually accorded to countries granting landing privileges.

16
청 정부의 거문도 협정안 서명 거부

E. Granville (1885. 5. 11) ➡ N. R. O'Conor

No. 21.

Earl Granville to Mr. O'Conor.—(Received July 6.)

Foreign Office, May 11, 1885.

(No. 99. Confidential.)

Sir,

WITH reference to my despatch No. 93A of the 6th instant, relative to the question of the proposed arrangement respecting Port Hamilton, t have to acquaint you that Dr. Macartney was to-day informed that I had felt some surprise at the telegram from Peking, which he had communicated on the 6th instant. The Agreement, which the Chinese Government were now unable to authorize their Minister to had been proposed by me in consequence of the overtures which he made, by direction of the Marquis Tsêng, on the 8th and 9th ultimo, and which had led me to believe that the Chinese Government would not object to the occupation of Port Hamilton by Great Britain, and would be willing to come to an arrangement on the subject.

Dr. Macartney was further informed that if the communications which I had addressed to the Marquis Tsêng on the draft Agreement, forwarded to him on the 28th ultimo, were at any time to be made public, it might be necessary for Her Majesty's Government to publish the records of the communications made by Dr. Macartney on the 8th and 9th ultimo.

I am, &c.

(Signed) GRANVILLE.

17
영·러 전쟁 발발 가능성 저하 보고

J. Sienkiewicz (1885. 5. 15) ➡ Ch. de Freycinet

Direction Politique n. 93.

Tôkiô, le 15 Mai 1885

Monsieur le Ministre,

La solution de la question de l'Afghanistan et l'arrangement qui doit prochainement mettre fin à notre différend avec la Chine enlèvent aux tendances politiques que peuvent avoir les Cabinets de Tôkiô et de Pékin une partie de leur importance. Cependant, comme il existe désormais une question d'Extrême-Orient qui semble appelée à devenir l'objet de préoccupations de plus en plus sérieuses pour plusieurs Puissances européennes, il y a encore un certain intérêt à essayer de pénétrer l'idée qui a présidé à l'envoi d'une Ambassade Japonaise en Chine, et à se rendre compte des considérations qui ont pu amener le Gouvernement Chinois à modifier subitement l'attitude qu'il avait d'abord adoptée envers le Gouvernement du Mikado.

Des apparences plutôt belliqueuses, destinées à donner satisfaction au parti de la guerre, et le désir intense mais soigneusement dissimulé, d'éviter un conflit avec la Chine, tels ont été les traits caractéristiques de la politique japonaise depuis le jour où les troubles de Söoul ont créé une situation tendue entre les deux Empires. L'Ambassade du Comte Ito a été, si je puis m'exprimer ainsi, la mise en oeuvre de cette politique. Entouré de généraux et d'officiers, l'ambassadeur japonais semblait devoir tenir un langage très-ferme au gouvernement chinois. D'après les informations que je tiens de personnes qui ont été à même de bien voir et de bien juger, le Comte Ito aurait poussé la modération jusqu'à la timidité dans ses entretiens avec Li-Hung-Chang. Pour ne point s'exposer à un échec et peut-être aussi pour ne pas affaiblir les prétentions de la Chine sur l'Annam, il n'a point soulevé la question de l'indépendance de la Corée, et s'est presque exclusivement borné à faire ressortir les inconvénients graves que présentait la présence de troupes chinoises et japonaises à Sëoul. Li-Hung-Chang ayant objecté que le Gouvernement Chinois ne pouvait en aucune façon s'engager à ne pas envoyer de troupes en Corée dans le cas où des troubles agiteraient ce pays, M. Ito s'est contenté de réclamer en faveur du Japon le droit d'user de cette même faculté. On est donc convenu que chacune des deux puissances pourrait envoyer des troupes en Corée à condition d'en donner avis à l'autre. Le texte de la Convention n'ayant pas encore été publié, je ne puis que m'en rapporter aux indications verbales du Ministre des Affaires Etrangères. Cette combinaison qui ne remédie guère aux inconvénients de la situation actuelle, permet à la Chine d'embarasser le Japon dès qu'elle croira utile de le faire. Il lui suffira, en effet, d'envoyer des troupes en Corée sans en donner avis au Gouvernement japonais pour susciter un nouveau conflit.

Le Japon s'était avancé aussi loin que possible dans la voie de la conciliation et cependant le Comte Ito peut craindre au début des négociations d'être obligé de revenir à Tôkiô sans avoir rien fait. Heureusement pour lui l'aspect des choses se modifiait de nouveau dans l'Extrême-Orient. Un armistice venait d'être signé entre la France et la Chine et cet événement qui semblait devoir réduire l'Ambassade japonaise à l'absolue impuissance n'eut point les conséquences qu'on lui attribuait généralement. Et, d'ailleurs, une question nouvelle avait surgi dans l'Asie centrale. L'Angleterre et la Russie semblaient être sur le point d'en venir aux mains. Le Gouvernement chinois pouvait craindre que la Russie ne profitât des circonstances pour se donner enfin aux dépens de la Corée un port qui ne fût point fermé l'hiver. Et, comme tout porte à le croire, l'Angleterre exerça alors une vive pression sur le Gouvernement chinois pour l'engager à terminer au plus vite ses différends avec la France et le Japon afin d'être mieux en mesure de faire face aux dangers nouvaux qui menaçaient sa sécurité. Que la Chine ait agi d'après sa propre initiative ou qu'elle ait suivi les conseils de l'Angleterre, il n'en est pas moins probable que c'est à l'affaire de l'Afghanistan qui est due, en grande partie, la convention que le Comte Ito a conclue avec Li-Hung-Chang.

Cependant, l'Angleterre devançant la Russie prenait possession d'un territoire coréen dans des conditions qui ne laissent pas que de surprendre. Il semble qu'elle aurait dû demander à la Corée dont elle a reconnu l'indépendance, l'autorisation d'occuper les trois petites îles qui forment le Port Hamilton. Il résulte toutefois des affirmations positives du comte Ino-ouyé et de M. Dawydow que le Gouvernement Coréen n'aurait pas même été avisé de la mesure prise par le Gouvernement Anglais. Le Comte Ino-ouyé assure, il est vrai, que Li-Hung-Chang a protesté contre l'occupation de Port-Hamilton. Mais outre que cette protestation ne s'est produite que tardivement, il est possible qu'elle soit de pure forme, le Gouvernement Anglais n'ayant certainement pas manqué de prévenir le cabinet de Pékin que c'était dans l'unique but d'assurer l'intégrité de la Corée qu'il avait créé dans un de ses ports un dépôt de charbon.

Préoccupée du désir d'arrêter les progrès menaçants que la Russie fait en Asie, l'Angleterre semble même avoir en la velléité de s'attribuer l'hégémonie de l'Extrême-Orient; mais ce projet est trop vaste pour être réalisable et, d'ailleurs, le Comte Ino-ouyé ne m'a point caché que l'intention du Gouvernement Japonais était de ne point s'écarter d'une stricte neutralité dans le cas où la guerre éclaterait entre la Russie et l'Angleterre. Il est douteux, d'autre part, que la Chine consente jamais à se laisser entièrement guider par une puissance européenne.

Ces jours derniers la situation a de nouveau changé et le danger d'une guerre entre la Russie et l'Angleterre semble écarté pour le moment. Des incidents qui se sont produits depuis deux mois environ il ne restera que ce fait bizarre que le Japon et l'Angleterre qui ont été les premières puissances qui ont reconnu l'indépendance de la Corée, ont été également, les premières qui l'ont rendue douteuse.

Quoiqu'il en soit, il faut espérer que la bonne intelligence qui vient d'être rétablie entre l'Angleterre et la Russie, en rassurant la Chine, en faisant disparaître les périls qu'elle appréhendait du côté de la Corée n'aura pas pour effet de rendre plus pénibles les négociations qui se poursuivent à Tien-Tsin et ne nous empèchera pas de conserver les Pescadores.

Veuillez agréer,

Son Excellence
Monsieur de Freycinet,
Ministre des Affaires Etrangères
à Paris.

18
거문도 전신선 설치 관련 청 정부와의 교섭 경과

N. R. O'Conor (1885. 5. 15) ➡ E. Granville (1885. 7. 6)

No. 74.

Mr. O'Conor to Earl Granville.—*(Received July 6.)*

Peking, May 15, 1885.

(No. 227. Confidential.)

My Lord,

WITH reference to my despatch No. 217, Confidential, of the 9th instant, I beg to say that on the 12th instant I had the honour to receive your Lordship's telegram No. 19 of the 11th respecting the permission of the Chinese Government to land a cable at the North Saddle Island.

I called yesterday, accompanied by Messrs. Hillier and Everard, by appointment on the Prince and Ministers of the Yamên, and spoke to their Excellencies again on the subject of this cable. I said that it appeared to me your Lordship had not anticipated such difficulties as had been raised by the Yamên, or the imposition of such conditions as the Chinese Government wished to impose upon an undertaking which could not fail to be of benefit to the Chinese Government.

I pointed out to his Highness and their Excellencies that such conditions were unusual, and that the cable would be of great advantage to China as affording her a means of communication with Corea, and that it seemed to me that the Chinese Government should not lose the opportunity thus suggested of getting into direct telegraphic communication with Corea. Moreover, I was able to assure the Yamên that all the facilities would be given to the Chinese Government which were usually accorded to countries granting landing privileges.

His Highness replied that in the concession of permission to land a cable, even temporarily, at the North Saddle Island, they had run counter to the general rules laid down by the Chinese Government, and had given a very strong proof of the cordial relations which existed between the British and Chinese Governments. The permission had, in fact, been given in view of certain eventualities which they believed were no longer likely to occur, and they therefore presumed that the question of the cable at North Saddle would be put aside. Indeed, the great difficulty the Yamên experienced in consenting to this telegraphic connection was not so much in the cable as in Port Hamilton. The presence of the British fleet there was viewed with especial jealousy by Russia, and the Russian Minister had spoken to the Yamên on the subject, and had asked on what grounds they had allowed the British Government to lay a line of telegraph to the North Saddle Island. The Yamên were able to reply at the time that no such permission had been given, but this answer could naturally not be repeated when the fact was brought officially to their notice. His Highness and their Excellencies begged to assure me that it was from no unfriendly feeling towards Her Majesty's Government, or from any personal objections, that these objections were raised, but that they were prompted in order to save the Chinese Government from the suspicion of favouring one Government at the expense of another.

To this I remarked that the permission to land a cable at the North Saddle Island or elsewhere. in China was certainly within the power of the Chinese Government, and that I did not see that it could prove a cause of serious complaint on the part of any other country. The advantages to China were obvious, and became the more important from the anxiety the Yamên had manifested as to what might happen as regards certain other portions of Corean territory.

Besides, the fact of the British Government having a cable house at Port Hamilton seemed to me to be the best protection against the future annexation of Port Hamilton by any other country, which they stated as a cause of anxiety.

His Highness admitted' that the protection which a cable would afford against the annexation of Port Hamilton by another Power was no doubt to be considered, and that the fact of putting them in direct communication with Corea was also an important consideration. His Highness said that, nevertheless, he saw many objections to a line being laid direct from the North Saddle Island to Port Hamilton, and that the Yamên would much prefer if it were laid in the first instance to

Nagasaki, and thence to Corea, as it would relieve the Chinese Government from the charge of seeming to abet our occupation of Port Hamilton.

I was unable to answer an inquiry of the Prince as to what special reason made it desirable to establish a cable-end at the North Saddle rather than elsewhere, but I was sure it had been selected for some good reason in no way hurtful to China, and that I trusted the Yam en would accede to the request which I had preferred.

His Highness pointed out in the course of further discussion that a very strong objection lay in the fact that the permission would add one more to the previous landing places of cables, and thus be an infringement of the rules which the Chinese Government had laid down for their guidance, and intimated that now that our relations with Russia were reported as on a better footing, he hoped the request would be withdrawn altogether. He had much difficulty in continuing his consent to land the cable at all. He proposed to refer the matter again to the Viceroy Li Hung-chang, but I strongly combated this proposal, or, indeed, any delay in the matter, which had now been before their Excellencies for nearly a fortnight.

Finally, the Prince and Ministers agreed to their former conditions, namely, that the cable might be landed temporarily at the North Saddle Island to connect directly with Port Hamilton, on the understanding that it would be removed when its necessity, caused by the possibility of eventualities, ceased to exist. When this happened they would give permission to establish the cable-end permanently at Woosung, and allow it to be moved again to the North Saddle Should circumstances necessitate it.

If the cable should prove to be useful to the chinese Government as a means of communication with Corea, it will strongly favour our request for its permanent establishment on the North Saddle. Moreover, although China dislikes our occupation of Port Hamilton, she dislikes still more the idea of that island being taken possession of, as she fears may happen, by Russia, and thus we may be able to obtain her consent both to our occupation and to the natural resultant of a cable at the North Saddle. I am not inclined, therefore, to attach very much importance to the refusal, at the present moment, of a permanent cable, which I think is likely to follow the temporary landing of the cable-end.

Owing to the anxiety manifested by the Prince and Ministers as to the interpretation likely to be put on their action in this matter by the Russian Government, it was understood between us that my note asking permission to land the cable at North Saddle Island should be worded in the following sense: — "That, in view of the comparatively large maritime traffic which now exists between Hong Kong and different places in the China Seas, Her Majesty's Government propose to lay a cable-end at the North Saddle Island, and that as soon as the British maritime traffic is reduced the cable laid temporarily will be removed. I am, accordingly, requested to obtain the permission of the Chinese Government, &c" This arrangement offers the best; terms I was able to obtain at the present moment.

I propose, before addressing the Chinese Government in writing, awaiting your Lordship's reply to my telegram No. 37 of this morning, in which I gave the substance of this despatch.

I should add, however, that the Prince and Ministers assured me that as soon as they received my note orders would at once be given to allow the cable-end to be landed at the North Saddle Island.

I have, &c.

(Signed) N. R. O'CONOR.

19

청의 입장을 각국에 통보 제안

日本代理公使 ➡ 李鴻章 (1885. 5. 15 / 光緖十一年四月二日)

附 日本代理公使覆函

光緖十一年四月初二日

敬行密覆者 接誦貴密函內稱 以英國水師官將哈米囮暫行居守 貴公使及各與國公使下示明敎 以保自有之權等語 本公使竊念此事關係貴邦國權 似屬重大矣 乃閱英大臣密函 但言應防不測 試思英國之所可防者 假爲與貴國修好訂約之國 則攸關不更大乎夫同盟各國內若不幸有失和之國 其一欲據貴國地方 以防不虞 貴國許之 利於一國而害一國 恐反局外相待胥處之道 然而貴大臣旣答英大臣 以非徒貴國之不敢許 卽各國有請 斷無可准之理 誠至當之言也 今英國有此擧 各與國未知貴國之意之所在 將疑英國之擧或出於貴國之肯語也 爲今之計 似宜將所告英國之意告各與國 俾知英國占該島爲貴國之所未曾准 則各國自釋疑而公論有所歸 第此事本公使未奉有本國政府之訓令 除略抒私見奉覆外惟祈貴大臣妥當處辦 是所深望也 專此 順頌日祉 近藤眞鋤頓 陽歷五月十三日

20
거문도 전신선 설치 관련 추가 지침

E. Granville (1885. 5. 16) ➡ N. R. O'nor

No. 26.

Earl Granville to Mr. O'Conor.

Foreign Office, May 16, 1885.

(No. 107. Ext. 22.)

Sir,

I HAVE received your telegram No. 37 of yesterday's date in regard to the connection of Port Hamilton with Saddle Island by cable.

I have to request you to inform the Chinese Government that in view of increased maritime traffic in the China seas, great importance is attached by Her Majesty's Government to the connection in question, and to urge them to give their consent to it on that ground.

The Arrangement may be looked upon as a temporary measure, but considering the heavy expense entailed in laying down the cable, its removal will be a matter for consideration at a future time.

I have this day communicated to you the substance of the foregoing by telegraph.

I am, &c.

(Signed) GRANVILLE.

21
청 정부와 거문도 전신선 설치 합의

N. R. O'Conor (1885. 5. 18) ➡ E. Granville (1885. 5. 19)

No. 27.

Mr. O'Conor to Earl Granville.—(Received May 19, 1:45 P. M.)

Peking, May 18, 1885, 9:20 P. M.

(No. 38.)

(Telegraphic.)

YOUR telegram No. 22.

As Chinese Government have consented to cable being landed temporarily, to press matter further at present will certainly risk withdrawal from previous understanding.

Direct communication between Saddle Island and Corea will make them less likely to insist on removal; at any rate, the danger is remote.

22
청 정부와 거문도 전신선 설치 협상 내용

N. R. O'Conor(1885. 5. 18) ➡ E. Granville (1885. 7. 13)

No. 93.

Mr. O'Conor to Earl Granville.—(Received July 13.)

Peking, May 18, 1885.

(No. 230. Confidential.)

My Lord,

I HAVE the honour to acknowledge the receipt of your Lordship's telegram No. 22 of the 16th, in answer to my telegram No. 37 of the 15th instant, respecting the landing of a cable at the North Saddle. Island from Port Hamilton, and the conditions upon which the Chinese Government may be willing to give their consent to this arrangement.

In the interview which I had with the Prince and Ministers on the 14th instant, there was little doubt that his Highness and their Excellencies were inclined to withdraw altogether the consent they had previously given even to the temporary establishment of the cable-end at the North Saddle, and it was not without some difficulty that I succeeded in obtaining their adherence to the previous understanding. I did myself the honour to inform your Lordship of the substance of the remarks of the Prince and Ministers in my despatch No. 227, Confidential, of the 15th instant.

On this, as on the occasion of a previous interview, I did all I could to induce the Yamên to consent to more satisfactory terms, but without success. The understanding come to as to the wording of the note which the Prince and Ministers requested me to address to them was as liberal as it was possible to obtain, and will not bind Her Majesty's Government more than is absolutely necessary in order to obtain the Concession at all.

I feel sure that if I open the question again at this moment I have every chance of meeting with a direct refusal, on the grounds that since the request was first preferred circumstances are much altered, and the Chinese Government cannot risk giving a Concession which would be viewed with much ill-will by more than one foreign Power. As one of the Ministers remarked, when I appeared dissatisfied with the limited conditions offered, the Chinese Government had given a signal mark of their friendly feeling towards Her Majesty's Government in according, in one day, pretty much what had taken three years to obtain in the case of the establishment of a telegraphic line at Woosung.

As the matter at present stands, Her Majesty's Government is at liberty to land the cable-end at once at the North Saddle Island on giving an assurance that when the maritime traffic is reduced the cable will be removed. That the Chinese Government are likely ultimately to insist on its removal is even doubtful; while the fact of heavy expense having been incurred in laying it down will be a very strong argument against their doing so.

Much, no doubt, depends on the turn our occupation of Port Hamilton may take in their eyes. If Her Majesty's Government comes to an understanding with the Governments of China and Corea respecting the island, and connects the North Saddle directly with Corea, it is very likely that the cable will remain indefinitely. In any case, I feel that in urging the Chinese Government further in the matter, at this moment, I should not further the aim your Lordship has in view; and I trust that the impression gathered in my last interviews with the Ministers of the Yamên will seem to your Lordship sufficient justification for delaying, without further instructions, to make renewed representations to the Chinese Government in the matter.

I have sent your Lordship the substance of this despatch in my telegram No. 38 of this day's date.

I have, &c.

(Signed) N. R. O'CONOR.

23
거문도 전신선 설치 관련 總理衙門에 보낸 공문

N. R. O'Conor (1885. 5. 20) ➡ E. Granville (1885. 7. 13)

No. 94.

Mr. O'Conor to Earl Granville.—(Received July 13.)

Peking, May 20, 1885.

(No. 233. Confidential.)

My Lord,

WITH reference to my despatch No. 230 of the 18th instant, I have the honour to transmit herewith to your Lordship a copy of a note which, in compliance with the request of the Chinese Government, I have addressed to the Prince and Ministers of the Yamên with reference to the permission to land a cable-end on the North Saddle Island.

In order to meet the wishes of the Ministers, I have stated that the permission is requested in view of the large maritime traffic between Hong Kong and various places in the China Seas, and I have omitted any direct mention of Port Hamilton, it being privately understood that the cable is to be laid from that island to the North Saddle.

I have referred to the consent already given to this request, and I have stated the conditions laid down by the Ministers, and upon which they agreed to the cable being landed.

In an interview which I shall have the honour of having with the Prince and Ministers to-morrow I propose to hand in this note, and I hope his Highness and their Excellencies will not take objection to the wording by which I have reserved the question of the removal of the cable as a matter for future agreement between the two Governments.

I have, &c.
(Signed) N. R. O'CONOR.

Inclosure in No. 94.

Mr. O'Conor to the Prince and Ministers of the Tsung-li Yamên.

Peking, May 19, 1885.

IN accordance with instructions he has received from Her Majesty's Principal Secretary of State for Foreign Affairs, Her Britannic Majesty's Chargé d' Affaires has the honour to inform his Highness and their Excellencies the Ministers of the Tsung-li Yamên that Her Majesty's Government, in view of the large maritime traffic between Hong Kong and various places in the China Seas, propose to lay a marine cable in order to facilitate telegraphic communication, and they invite the consent of the Chinese Government to the landing of the cable-end and the establishment of a cable-house upon North Saddle Island.

At the interview which Her Britannic Majesty's Chargé d'Affaires had the honour to hold with his Highness and their Excellencies on the 14th instant they were good enough to signify their consent to this arrangement, adding, however, that the landing of the cable-end on North Saddle Island must be regarded as a temporary arrangement, and that as soon as the maritime traffic was reduced the removal of the cable-end elsewhere would have to be considered in agreement with the Chinese Government.

Her Britannic Majesty's Chargé d'Affaires has reported the above conditions to Her Majesty's Government, and in accordance with the desire of His Highness and their Excellencies he now records them in the form of an official note, to which he requests the honour of a reply, and begs that, in conformity with the promise of the Prince and Ministers of the Yam en, the necessary instructions may be sent to the local authorities to allow of the landing of the cable-end.

Her Britannic Majesty's Chargé d'Affaires avails, &c.

(Signed) N. R. O'CONOR.

24
거문도 전신선 설치 위한 선박 파견

E. Granville (1885. 5. 20) ➡ N. R. O'Conor

No. 30.

Earl Granville to Mr. O'Conor.

Foreign Office, May 20, 1885.

(No. 110. Ext. 23.)

Sir,

WITH reference to your telegram No. 38 of the 18th instant, in regard to the proposed telegraphic connection of Port Hamilton with Saddle Island, I have to state to you that it was not clearly understood, from your telegram No. 37 of the 15th instant, that the Chinese Government had given their consent to the cable being landed temporarily at Saddle Island. As, however, it appears from your last Report that the desired sanction has been granted, it will be unnecessary for you to press the Chinese Government further in the matter.

A ship with the cable on board will arrive at Saddle Island on the 28th instant, and I have to request you to use your own discretion as to informing the Chinese Government of this fact.

The substance of the above was sent to you this day by telegraph.

I am, &c.

(Signed) GRANVILLE.

25
영국의 거문도 점령과 조선의 협조 요청

G. C. Foulk (1885. 5. 20) ➡ Bingham

Enclosure No. 1 with Mr. Binghams No. 2061
Mr. Foulk to Mr. Bingham

Legation of the United States
Seoul, Korea
May 20th 1885.

Sir,

The diplomatic representative for England at Peking has addressed a despatch to the Minister for Foreign Affairs of Korea to inform him that England had sent a naval force to Port Hamilton, an island of Korea, on the south coast of that country, as a precaution, and to remain there as such temporarily. The despatch concludes forth sentiments for a desire to continue friendly relations with Korea. The Korean Government has replied on the 19th instant, to the English Representative of Peking in terms meant to convey its largest to desire to avoid any complication in a possible conflict between England and Russia, and emphatically refuses to sanction the use of any part of its territory for either Russia or England, or any other power, for war purposes. It will probably express the same to Russia at an early date.

The Korean Government realizing its utter weakness, expresses great anxiety over the reply from England to its despatch, and it is fearful of the maintenance of Port Hamilton by force. It has addressed all the foreign representatives in Seoul on the subject, asking for advice and assistance to be directed towards preserving its autonomy of its territory.

Believing that the Government of the United States, would regard with great regret any action of a foreign power tending to dismember Korea, or diminish her chances for forming an independent nation, it has seemed to me right, that its representatives could properly use their influence to avert such an action, There is no Russian representatives in Korea, nor are there any means for speedy communication with the Russian authorities elsewhere.

Under the circumstances, I venture to address you this communication, requesting your consideration of the case, and such action as may appear to you to be effective and proper.

I am, Sir, very respectfully
(Signed) George G Foulk
Chargé d'affaires, ad interim
The Honorable
Envoy Extraordinary and
Minister Plenipotentiary
For the United States,
Tokei, Japan

26

거문도 사건의 추이 보고

原敬 (1885. 5. 27) ➡ 井上馨

二十六號

巨文島一件ニ關シ李鴻章朝鮮王ヨリ書翰ヲ落手セシ大要ハ 電報幷機密信ヲ以テ申述置候所 去廿三日御發電ヲ以テモルレンドルフ長崎ニ赴キ英國水師提督ト談判致候ハ 拙官ヨリ差立候電報ト齟齬スル旨ヲ御申越相成候ニ付 熟ト電文拜讀致候所李鴻章ハ廿一日之面會ニ於テ 十八日ニ長崎ニ入港セシモルレンドルフ之一件ヲ談話不致候も甚タ不可解義ト存候 依テ不取敢翌廿四日李氏ヲ訪問致シ 其邊相尋ね候所 朝鮮王ヨリ之書翰ニ就キテハ 前日申候所ト同樣ニ御坐候へ共 過日李氏ハ英韓之問答ハ公然ニハ非サルカ如シト推察之樣ニ申所 此度ハ全ク公然ニアラスト斷言致候上ニ被申候ニハ モルレンドルフヲ經テ一應申入レ 其ニ對シテ返答セシまてニ付 更ニ朝鮮より官吏ヲ派シテ巨文島之實況ヲ取調べ 且ツ同島ニ碇泊スル英國水師提督ニも占據ノ說明ヲ求ムルコトノ必要ヲ感シタルニ付 明言ハセサレトモ 李氏之命令ナルカ如キ口氣有候 朝鮮官吏某とモルレントルフガ淸國軍艦ニ乘リテ該島ニ赴キタルニ六隻ノ英艦碇泊セシモ 提督ハ長崎ニ居ルトノ趣ニテ不在なりしゆゑ 其まゝ長崎ニ赴キタルなり 別ニ他意アルニハ非ラスト申候ニ付 然ラハ向後之所ハ矢張リ一時ノコトナラハ不問ニ置キ 永遠ノ占據ハ許サストノ御決心ナルヤト尋候所 彼レ手ヲ振リ 一時ナラハ不問ニ置クヘシ 朝鮮も淸國も同樣之趣なりト繰返陳述致候 其意ハ滋事ヲ招クコトヲ恐ルヽニ在ルカ如ク相見得候 然ラハ英國ノ處置ハ永遠ノ見込カ將タ一時ノコトカ モルレンドルフ之報告ヲ待タルヽヤト申候所 然リ 報知アルヲ待ツノ外ナシト申候 尤も李氏之口氣ハ別ニ策ナキニハ非サルカ如ク相見得候へ共 拙官より之疑問ハ全ク拙官一己之意見ニ出テ 我政府之意見ハ如斯ト明言スルコトヲ得サルニ付彼ハ充分ニ其見込ヲ吐露致サヌ樣推測致候 依テ語ヲ改メ 右御談話之趣ハ我外務卿ニ報告シテ宜シキヤト相尋候所 彼云 宜シ 乍去此事ハ頗ル機密ヲ貴フ事ニ付 實ハ我徐公使ニモ未タ何等之報告モ送ラス 貴官ヨリ問ハルレバコソ內話スル位之事ニ付 全ク外務卿ニノミ報告セラレ 他へハ決シテ口外セラレルヽ勿レト申候 又露英

之模様相尋候所　未タ平和ニ歸セサル趣報知ヲ得たりト申候ニ付　右不取敢其翌廿五日電信ニテ報告致候

右之外李氏ハ頻リニ我政府之意見如何ヲ尋候ニ付 先般內訓之趣ニ從ヒ 拙官一己之見込トシテ述へ候上 此事ニ關シテハ貴國ハ我國ヨリハ速カニ且ツ詳カナル報告ヲ得ラルヘキ筈ニ付 貴國ハ我國ヨリハ先キニ本件ニ關スル處分策ヲ立テラルヘキ筈也 我政府ニテハイヨ〻〻斯ク處分スルト決定シタル上ハ 閣下ニ告クルコトヲ否マサルヘシト信スレトモ 貴國モ其策ヲ決セラレタル上ハ 我國ニ秘密ヲ以テ告ケラルヽコトヲ惜マルヽ勿レト申候所　李氏ハ　其ハ勿論辭セヌコトナリ　然ルニ貴國モ軍艦等ヲ出シテ該島ノ様子ヲ探ラレタルヤト申候ニ付 未タ右様ノコトヲ聞カス 尤も仁川ニ往復スル我軍艦ハ實見セシ事ありト聞ケリ 何分他國之領地ニ勝手ニ軍艦ヲ送リテ實況ヲ取調フルコトハ出來ヌ譯ニ付 其邊ノ事ハ遺憾ナカラ能ハサルコトモアラント申候所 彼又云 然リ 貴國より突然軍艦等ヲ送ラルヽ譯ニハ參るまじ 淸國トテモ突然軍艦ヲ送ル譯ニハ參らヌニ付 朝鮮官吏ヲ載セテ送リタルナリ 予ノ此取計ハ不可ナカルヘシト申候ニ付　拙官ハ其ハ妙策ナリト稱贊致候　察スルニ 李ハ日本ハ此件ヲ淸國ニノミ打任カスルト云フ如キ疑心ハ邪推ナカラ强テナシトハ難申口氣ニ付　拙官よりハ 我國ハ淸國ノ朝鮮ニ施ス如クスルコトハ出來ヌ譯なりトノ主旨ヲ間接ニ述へ置候

一　淸佛談判之模様ニ付テハ　昨日李鴻章ハ其衙門ニ於テ佛公使領事等之一行ト午食致候所　世間ニテハ最早調印相濟タル哉之風說も有之候ニ付　不取敢今朝羅豐祿へ聞配候所　昨日ハ調印ニハ非サレトモ　北京ト巴里之間ニ於テ大概取極リタルニ付　當地ニ於テ調印スル事ハ未定ナレトモ　最早遠キコトニハ非サルト申候ニ付　不取敢本日電信ニテ及具報候

右御含まて申述候 敬具

明治十八年五月廿七日　　　　領事原敬

外務卿伯爵井上馨殿

27

거문도 조차 협상을 위해 청 정부와 사전 협의 필요성 설명

N. R. O'Conor (1885. 5. 30) ➡ W. G. Aston

Inclosure 1 in No. 123.

Mr. O'Conor to Consul-General Aston.

Peking, May 30, 1885.

Sir,

ON the chance of a steamer leaving Shanghae or Chefoo for Corea in a few days, I again write to you on the subject of Port Hamilton.

I have just been informed by Lord Granville that Her Majesty's Government are ready to pay Corea a sum not exceeding 5,000*l*. a-year as rent for Port Hamilton while used as a coaling-station. This sum, you will remark, is the outside limit which it is proposed to pay.

For reasons already known to you, I think an ultimate arrangement is more likely if China or Corea originates the proposal, and if, at the start, we secure the support and influence of the Chinese Government.

With this object in view I shall see the Ministers of the Yamên on the 1st June.

There will, however, be no objection to your sounding the Corean Government, and if you see your way to an arrangement in the sense desired, pressing the matter to a conclusion. It is possible that a much lower rent, considering the island has heretofore been an entirely profitless possession to Corea, may meet the demands of the Corean Government.

I am myself inclined to think that the Corean Government will do nothing without consulting China, or, at any rate, the Viceroy Li Hung-chang, and therefore it is desirable that I should be informed as speedily as possible of the result of your interview with the President of the Corean an Foreign. Office.

I am in hopes that the interference of China will put a check to any exorbitant demands advocated by M. von Möllendorff, and induce the Corean Government to agree to a satisfactory settlement of this question.

In view of the importance of not losing time in this matter, I have ventured to ask Vice-Admiral Sir W. Dowell whether he can spare a gun-boat to carry my despatches from Chefoo to Chemulpo, taking back on the return voyage any communications you may address to me.

I have, &c.

(Signed) N. R. O'CONOR.

28
청 정부를 통한 협상 타결 건의

The Secretary to the Admiralty (1885. 6. 1) ➡ Currie

No. 42.

The Secretary to the Admiralty to Mr. Currie.—(Received June 2.)

Admiralty, June 1, 1885.

(Confidential.)

Sir,

I HAVE laid before my Lords Commissioners of the Admiralty your letter of the 29th May, transmitting a telegram from Her Majesty's Minister at Peking reporting the protest of the Corean Government against the occupation of Port Hamilton by this country.

My Lords desire me to request that you will state to Earl Granville that they concur with the suggestion of Consul-General Aston contained in the above telegram that a pecuniary arrangement should be made with the Corean Government with respect to the occupation of Port Hamilton.

My Lords presume that the arrangement will be effected through the Chinese Government, with whom Her Majesty's Government are already in communication.

I am, &c.

(Signed) R. D. AWDRY, *pro Sec.*

29
영국의 거문도 점령에 대한 청 정부의 지지

N. R. O'Conor(1885. 6. 2) ➡ W. G. Aston

Inclosure 3 in No. 123.

Mr. O'Conor to Consul-General Aston.

Peking, June 2, 1885.

Sir,

I HAVE been assured, confidentially, by the Ministers of the Yamên that the Chinese Government is unable to interfere directly with Corea in favour of our occupation of Port Hamilton, but that she will not take any steps in opposition to the interests of Her Majesty's Government, and that if appealed to by Corea she will repeat the assurances she has received as to the temporary character of this occupation. At the same time, their Excellencies distinctly stated that China was not herself opposed to our occupation, though the fear of giving offence to Russia and Japan, and the probability that these Powers would take advantage of China's approval of our action to seize other portions of Corean territory, forced her to be very prudent in the line of policy she followed in this matter.

In answer to certain communications which I made unofficially to the Viceroy Li Hung-chang, his Excellency has assured me that he has already written to the King of Corea, advising His Majesty to say nothing more on the subject at present, and promising to undertake that Corea shall not offer any further objection if he (the Viceroy) is quite sure that the occupation is temporary. I have told his Excellency of the assurances which I have been instructed to make on the part of Her Majesty's Government to both China and Corea, and I have expressed the hope that he will accordingly communicate with the King in the sense intimated. The Viceroy has, moreover, expressed his willingness to come to an arrangement in respect to this question, but I have reason to believe that the bases of this agreement would' involve pledges in respect to the integrity of Corea which would not meet, I feel sure, with the approval of Her Majesty's Government.

It is just possible that it would be well for you to try and see the King in person in relation to this question, point out to His Majesty that our action is not directed by any unfriendly feeling towards Corea, and state that as a proof of this Her Majesty's Government would be willing to come to an agreement in respect to the occupation of Port Hamilton. I will do what is possible towards supporting you through the Viceroy Li Hung-chang, and inducing his Excellency to write to the King in the sense you are instructed to use to His Majesty.

I have, &c.

(Signed) N. R. O'CONOR.

30
李鴻章이 조선 정부의 반대 차단 약속

N. R. O'Conor (1885. 6. 2) ➡ E. Granville (1885. 7. 27)

No. 120.

Mr. O'Conor to Earl Granville.—(Received July 27.)

Peking, June 2, 1885.

(No. 255. Confidential. Ext. 44.)

My Lord,

I HAD the honour to telegraph to your Lordship yesterday afternoon that the Corean Government had requested an answer to the official protest which the President of the Corean Foreign Office addressed to me for transmission to Her Majesty's Government respecting the British occupation of Port Hamilton, the substance of which I did myself the honour to communicate to your Lordship in my telegram No. 43 of the 25th ultimo. I also ventured to say that further delay in acknowledging the receipt of the communication of the Corean Government would be likely to give umbrage, and would probably encourage that Government to carry out their threat to protest to the foreign Powers and foreign Representatives at Söul against the action of Her Majesty's Government. I stated that I considered a mere formal answer repeating previous assurances would be sufficient in view of the fact that the Viceroy Li Hung-chang had promised to undertake, on being assured that the occupation was temporary, that the King of Corea should not offer any farther objection to our occupation of Port Hamilton.

I have, &c.

(Signed) N. R. O'CONOR.

31
러시아의 반응에 대한 청 정부의 우려
N. R. O'Conor (1885. 6. 2) ➡ E. Granville (1885. 7. 27)

No. 122.

Mr. O'Conor to Earl Granville.—(Received July 27.)

Peking, June 2, 1885.

(No. 259. Confidential.)

My Lord,

I CALLED by appointment on the Prince and Ministers of the Yamên on the 1st instant, and after some casual remarks on the negotiations between Great Britain and Russia, the conversation turned to the question of the occupation of Port Hamilton.

I began by saying that I had been much disappointed to learn, on reliable authority, that Admiral Ting had countenanced the action of the Corean Government as far as to actually call in at Corea in order to convey two Corean officials to Nagasaki, in order to protest to the British Admiral against the occupation of Port Hamilton. I said that I had reason to believe, from the friendly assurances of the Prince and Ministers, that the Chinese Government would certainly refrain from any course of action likely to be disagreeable to Her Majesty's Government, and that I had not certainly expected to hear they had gone so far in an opposite direction as was implied by the conduct of Admiral Ting. I had also learnt that one of the Corean officials, whom the Chinese Admiral had conveyed to Nagasaki, was a German in the service of the Corean Foreign Office, and who, if late reports were true respecting his intrigues with an Aide-de-camp of the Russian Governor-General of Eastern Siberia, was not an official more favourable to the interests of China than to those of Great Britain.

The Prince and Ministers replied that the part taken by Admiral Ting was not at all intended as a mark of opposition to the action of Her Majesty's Government. The Coreans had asked the Admiral to take their officials on board, and to give them a passage to Port Hamilton and Nagasaki, and it would have been very difficult to have refused. But, as far as the Chinese Government were concerned, they had certainly not taken any unfriendly, much less hostile, part against England. The Yamên would not conceal from me that they could not conscientiously approve the action of Great Britain in seizing upon a part of Corean territory without leave or licence, but this opinion they kept to themselves, and they had given me repeated proofs of their good-will. They would again repeat that they had personally no objection to the occupation by Her Majesty's forces of Port Hamilton, and his Highness would even assure me that he thought the occupation was, at the present juncture, in the interests of China as well as of England. But between this and taking any active part to support us the way was long; it would offend several foreign Powers; it would leave them without an answer were Russia to adopt the same course; and (a consideration that must not be lost sight of) the relations of China to Corea were so peculiar that they could not risk the refusal of the Corean Government to listen to their advice. With China advice to Corea was tantamount to a command, and it was impossible for her to exercise her legitimate authority in a matter of this kind.

If, however, Corea asked their advice, they would repeat to them the assurances which they had received from Her Majesty's Government as to the temporary nature of the occupation, but they would not go farther.

I said that Corea, from reports I had had from Söul, had asked the advice of the foreign Representatives, and in the course she had followed she had been guided not only by the influence of M. von Möllendorff, but of some foreign Consuls. If Corea acted on the advice of foreigners, I did not see why China, who had heretofore shown so much good-will towards us, should not interfere on the other side, the more that she recognized that our interests and those of China were similar.

A further interchange of remarks ensued in the sense above reported to your Lordship, and finally the Ministers said they would be thoroughly frank with me, and give another proof of good-will by showing how impossible it was for them to do more at the present moment than promise not to interfere in the question, and not to take any step inimical to British interests. Their Excellencies then informed me, confidentially, that your Lordship had already spoken some time since to the Marquis Tsêng on this subject, and had asked him to solicit the influence of the Chinese Government in the interests of the British Government. The Marquis Tsêng had telegraphed the request of your Lordship, and the question had been laid before the Empress, who had issued a Decree to the effect that it would be inexpedient for China to interfere. In the face of the Imperial command, it was naturally now impossible for the Yamên to take any action.

It will not escape your Lordship's notice that the Yamên have gone back somewhat from the position of almost direct support which on previous occasions they seemed inclined to accord. It may, as stated, be owing in part to the fact of the Empress having pronounced an opinion, but I am inclined to think that it is equally due to the fear of other foreign Powers regarding their support of oar action as an excuse for seizing other parts of Corean territory.

In view of the pressure brought to bear by Russia, and also by Japan, on the Yamên, I thought it well to make known privately to the Viceroy. Li Hung-chang the substance of the remarks which I had made to the Ministers of the Yamên when speaking of the British occupation of Port Hamilton. The Viceroy is charged more immediately with all matters relating to Corea, and I know that if his influence were obtained it would do much to neutralize any action in an opposite direction.

I had the satisfaction of learning on the 29th ultimo that the Viceroy had written to the King of Corea, advising His Majesty to say nothing more on the subject of the occupation, and had added that if he could be positive that this occupation were really temporary, he would undertake that Corea would not offer any objection, but that he did not wish to make any assurances to the King unless he was sure of his ground.

I informed his Excellency, through Mr. Brenan, that I had already assured the Yamên and the Corean Government that the occupation was temporary, and that I therefore trusted these assurances would be satisfactory to his Excellency, and that he would accordingly advise the King of Corea in the sense he had intimated. There is good reason to believe that the Viceroy's influence with the Corean Government is very powerful, and that neither the King nor the Corean Government will feel inclined to disregard it.

I have, &c.

(Signed) N. R. O'CONOR.

32
영국의 거문도 점령에 대한 일본의 반응

Bingham (1885. 6. 4) ➡ T. F. Bayard

No. 2061.

United States Legation,
Tokei, Japan, June 4, 1885.

Mr. Bingham,
To Ho. Thomas F. Bayard,
Secretary of State, Washington, D. C.

Subject.

The seizure of Port Hamilton by a British naval force. Communication from Dir. Foulk Chargé d' affaires and interim at Seoul, Corea.

Sir,

Herewith I have the honor to enclose for your information, a copy of a note, dated the 20th addressed to me by Mr. Faulk, United States Chargé d' affaires at Seoul, wherein he acquaints me of the forcible occupation of Port Hamilton, a Corean Island, by the British naval forces, and that the British Minister at Peking after the fact, notified the Corean government of the action taken by Her Britannic Majesty's Naval officers in the premises, stating that the seizure of the island by the British forces was "as a pre-caution" and that "the force would remain there (as a precaution) temporarily."

Mr. Foulk, you will note further states that on the 19th the Corean Government replied to the British Minister at Peking to the effect that it desires to avoid complication in any possible conflict between England and Russia and refuses to sanction the use of any port of its territory by either Russia or England or any other power.

It is also stated by Mr. Foulk that the Corean Government has addressed all the Foreign Representatives in Seoul asking for advice and assistance to secure that Government's rightful autonomy over its own territory. In an interview with His Excellency, Count (*sic*), last evening in relation to this action of England, he informed me that His Japanese Majesty's Government considers the seizure of this island as an unfriendly act towards Japan as also towards Corea and that some representations have been made in the matter by this government to Her Britannic Majesty's Minister at this court.

Now that Great Britain challenges Russia for her passing upon the alleged but disputed territory of (*sic*) as to which territory so occupied by Russia the (*sic*) is reported to be in doubt, whether it is any part of the territory of Afghanistan, it seems strange that Great Britain should by force seize and occupy Corean territory as to the rightful and exclusive control of which by the Corean Government there is no room to doubt.

That this forcible seizure of Port Hamilton by the British naval force has been made with the approval of the British Government is not doubted here.

The value of Port Hamilton as a naval station was fully reported by Commodore (*sic*) U. S. N. to Admiral Bell, about the year 1870-71 which report I presume will be found in our Navy Department.

I have the honor to be,
Sir,
Your obedient servant,
(Signature)

33
러시아, 영국 사신에 대한 응대 관련 훈령

井上馨 (1885. 6. 5) ➡ 高平小五郎

今般露國公使館書記官 スパイア 氏俄カニ朝鮮國京城ヘ派出セラレタルニ付テハ極メテ其地着ノ上ハ爲スベキ方略モ多少アルベシト信ゼラル サレバ貴下ハ同書記官ノ擧動ニ常ニ注意セラレ ナルベク其筋ノ便路ニ就キ其ノ朝鮮政府ニ對シ所言等探問セラルベク 聞ク所ニ據レバ過般露國ヨリ朝鮮政府ト結約ノ委員タリシ ゼー・レデング 氏ハ 今般露國ノ代理公使ニ任ゼラレ 其地ニ駐在スルコトトナリタル由過般露 英ノ關係生起セシ以來 兩國ニ於テ朝鮮國ニ專ラ注目シ 兩國ノ爭ヒニ乘ジテ其利便ノ位置ヲ得ントノ模樣見ユ 就テハ英ノ アストン 氏モ既ニ來着シ 又露代理公使着京ノ上ハ 相互ニ計畫スル處アルベキハ勿論 双方ヨリ我贊助ヲ求ムルノ場合無シトモ限ラザレバ 兩國使臣ヨリ何等申出ヅルトモ 未ダ特ニ訓令無キ旨申述ベ双方ニ對シテハ全ク不偏ノ位地ニ立チ 貴下ノ見込ミヲ提出セラレズ 程能ク應接セラレタシ 而シテ其平素談話ノ模樣並ニ擧動等ハ不絶報告アランコトヲ乞フ

明治二(*sic*)十八年六月五日

伯爵 井 上 馨

高 平 小 五 郎 殿

34
거문도 사건에 대한 李鴻章의 입장
原敬 (1885. 6. 5) ➡ 井上馨

二十八號

[上欄書入]

〈清佛談判一件〉

清佛談判ハ前信ニテ及具報候通 去月廿六日兩全權之會合已後ハ不相替佛領事幷李氏之幕友等往復ヲ重ね居リ候ヘ共 未タ調印ニハ至ラス候 昨日李鴻章ニ相尋ね候所十之九まてハ既ニ決定セシも 何分字句之間幷譯文之當否等ニて 些少之事ニも四五日乃至七八日ヲ費シ 其上巴里ト北京之間ニ直接ニ取極ムル事多キニ付 今日まて調印ニ至ラサレトモ 最早不遠調印之見込なりと申候

[上欄書入]

〈巨文島一件〉

一 巨文島一件ニ關シ李氏ハ近頃朝鮮ヨリ書翰ヲ落手致候趣 其書翰ニはモルレンドルフハ既ニ朝鮮ニ歸着之由 又長崎ニ於テ英國水師提督ト談判セシニ 一時碇泊之趣ニ付歸韓セリ 此等之事情ハ近藤代理公使へも告ケ 同代理公使よりも回答有之たりとて其往復文寫ヲモ添來レリ云々と李氏之直話ニ付 拙官より 乍去英國水師提督ハ長崎ニ於テ獨斷ニテ回答スルコトヲ拒ミ 政府之訓令ヲ待タサル可ラスト回答セシ由ニ傳聞セシカ 果シテモルレンドルフは其邊ヲ詳悉之上ニ歸韓セシニヤト相尋候所 李氏云 成程英國政府之訓令ヲ待ツヘシト云ヘタル由ナルガ 英國水師提督は全ク一時之事なりト辯明シ 且ツ事情左もあるべき形況ニ付 其訓令之到達ヲ待タス歸韓せし趣なりト 又云 朝鮮ハドコまても永ク占領ヲ許サヌ積なりト 依テ再ヒ拙官より 既ニ一時之事ト明瞭したる上ハ 貴國ハ先ツ不問ニ置カルヽ御見込ナルヤト推問致候所 然リ 先ツ不問ニ置テ差支なかるべしとの覺悟なりト明言致候

[上欄書入]

〈吳大澂東界派遣〉

先頃より吳大澂北洋事宜會辦ヲ罷免セラレタル風說有之 又右之罷免ハ朝鮮事件取

調不行届之爲メなる由なと 其他種々之風說有之候所 何分信用難致樣被考　且ツ吳大澂ニハ過日も面會致候へ共 更ニ其景況無之候ニ付如何ト存居候所 此頃別紙李氏より其筋へ之內達書入手致候 此達書ニ據レハ吉林東界卽チ露國トノ境界勘定ノ爲メ派遣ヲ命セラレ候ニ付 罷免之風說ハ全ク其達之誤聞ニ出たる事ト判然致候 依テ右達寫御參考まて別紙ニ相添候 尤も右派遣之命ハ尋常之境界標ヲ立ツルまて之事ニハ有之間敷 客年六月中機密第四十三號ヲ以テ及具報候通 吳大澂之談話も有之候ニ付　事情探聞中ニ候へ共　未タ詳報接手[不欠カ]致候 又此達文ニ據レハ不遠起程可致樣相見得候へ共 今日まて請訓ノ爲メ北京ニ赴キタル事も無之候ニ付 多分何カ都合有之事ト存候

右御含まて及具報候 敬具

明治十八年六月五日　　領事原敬

外務卿伯爵井上馨殿

35
Plunkett · 井上馨 회담

F. Plunkett (1885. 6. 5) ➡ E. Granville (1885. 7. 10)

No. 81.

Mr. Plunkett to Earl Granville. — *(Received July 10.)*

Tôkiô, June 5, 1885.

(No. 158. Very Confidential.)
My Lord,

IN my despatch No. 150, Confidential, of the 25th ultimo- I mentioned that, although I had heard by telegraph from Vice-Admiral Sir William Dowell on the 12th ultimo that the British flag had been hoisted at Port Hamilton, I had not thought it necessary to inform Count Inouyé of a circumstance of which I knew him to be as well aware as myself.

In the course, however, of a visit which his Excellency paid me some days ago, I brought the conversation round to the subject, and said I presumed he knew that, in consequence of a Russian steamer having lately appeared at the entrance of Port Hamilton, the Senior Naval Officer had, at once, hoisted the British flag on all the islands forming the harbour.

Count Inouyé said he knew the flag had been hoisted, and it was, he supposed, still flying.

In order to continue the conversation I mentioned some of my personal experiences when I visited Port Hamilton in 1875, and I thus drew his Excellency on to an informal discussion of the matter of our present occupation.

Count Inouyé was very guarded in his language. He carefully avoided anything approaching to a protest against our proceedings, although he expressed his belief that the temporary occupation would necessarily grow into a permanent one, and he allowed me to understand that, if it were not for the excuse unfortunately given to Russia to take something else, there would be little objection in Japan to what England had done.

I reminded his Excellency that the principal reason we had acted as we had was to forestall Russia, and to prevent her taking a place of such strategic importance as Port Hamilton would be more especially to Russia.

His Excellency admitted that this argument had a certain value, but said there are still many other points about Corea, and in these waters generally, which would suit Russia's purpose just as well as Port Hamilton. Therefore, he said, whatever you do, I hope you will not try to make an official arrangement with Corea about Port Hamilton at present. Corea cannot lease or sell Port Hamilton to England and then refuse to sell or lease something else to Russia. Whereas, if England remains simply where she is, neither Corea nor China will try to turn her out, nor perhaps, on the whole, are they as sorry to see her there as fear of Russia makes them pretend to be.

The reason why I forced this conversation on Count Inouyé, and how I thus came to elicit the above important remark, was that Her Majesty's Chargé d'Affaires at Peking had again lately telegraphed to warn me that Japan was working against England at Peking.

Not only can I obtain no evidence here, of such action on the part of Japan, but all the information I can gather, both from official and private sources, goes to prove that the opposition originates in China; whether with Li Hung-chang or the Tsung-li Yamên, who seem for the moment to be working actively against each other, I am unable yet to discover.

Certainly, neither in the conversation herein summarized, nor in a subsequent one with me, has Count Inouyé in any way raised an official objection to the presence of Great Britain at Port Hamilton, and I have no reason to think that the instructions of the Japanese Minister at Peking authorize him in any way to work against England at the present moment.

I beg to forward herewith copy of a despatch which I addressed on the 30th ultimo to Mr. O'Conor in regard to the present attitude of Japan in the Port Hamilton affair.

I have, &c.

(Signed) F. R. PLUNKETT.

36
O'Conor · 李鴻章 회담

N. R. O'Conor (1885. 6. 6) ➡ E. Granville (1885. 8. 1)

No. 132.

Mr. O'Conor to Earl Granville. —*(Received August 1.)*

Peking, June 6, 1885.

(No. 268.)

My Lord,

ON receipt of your Lordship's telegram No. 32 of yesterday's date, ordering me to act on your Lordship's previous instruction stating that Her Majesty's Government were ready to pay Corea a sum not exceeding 5,000*l.* a-year rent for Port Hamilton while used as' a coaling-station by Her Majesty's fleet, I telegraphed to this effect to Mr. Aston, Her Majesty's Consul-General at Söul, and also addressed to him the despatch of which I have the honour to inclose a copy.

I have received fresh assurances from the Viceroy Li Hung-chang (who, as your Lordship is aware, has much influence in Corean affairs) that China is not at all opposed to our occupation of Port Hamilton, and that she will certainly not offer any opposition to our remaining there, and will advise Corea not to raise, on her side, further objection.

The Viceroy, however, sees many difficulties in the way of a formal agreement sanctioning our occupation, whether by renting the island or buying it, though he leaves it, pretty clearly to be seen that both China and Corea will shut their eyes to anything we do there, provided we do not require them to publicly proclaim their consent.

His Excellency has suggested an agreement with the local authorities to rent and occupy the island, and as the support of the Viceroy in this matter is all-important, seeing that Corea will be sure to follow his advice, I have ventured to telegraph to Admiral Sir William Dowell to inquire whether he thinks any such arrangement is feasible.

I trust your Lordship will approve of my having done so without reference to you beforehand; but I thought that, until I knew whether it was at all practicable, I need not trouble your Lordship in the matter. I have not much confidence in the success of an arrangement of this kind; but if it should prove feasible, there would not be much difficulty in obtaining the approval and sanction of the Corean Government; it would be, in any case, a step in the desired direction. The expense would not be great, and the Corean Government might be willing, for 2,000*l*. a-year, to sanction the arrangement in such a manner as would appear satisfactory to Her Majesty's Government.

I am anxiously awaiting Mr. Aston's first despatches to learn exactly how matters stand at Söul. I Shall not be surprised to hear that the Corean Government may be tempted to comply with our proposal if, instead of a yearly rent, they can count on receiving a round sum of some 20,000*l*. or 30,000*l*., for I understand they are in very great pecuniary straits, and that the King is especially in want of money.

As matters now look, no further serious objection is likely to be raised by Corea to the occupation of Port Hamilton by Her Majesty's fleet, but, at the same time, it may be very difficult to obtain a formal recognition of our occupation.

I have the honour to inclose to your Lordship a copy of the telegram above mentioned, which I ventured to address to Sir William Dowell, who is now at Port Hamilton.

I have, &c.
(Signed) N. R O'CONOR.

Inclosure 1 in No. 132.

Mr. O'Conor to Consul-General Aston.

Peking, June 6, 1885.

Sir,

ON receipt of instructions from Her Majesty's Principal Secretary of State for Foreign Affairs to delay, until further instructed, the offer to rent Port Hamilton from the Corean Government, I sent you my telegram of the 31st ultimo, which was recorded in my despatch of that day's date.

On receiving instructions this morning that Her Majesty's Government were again ready to pay to Corea a sum not exceeding 5,000*l.* a-year rent for Port Hamilton while the island is used as a coaling-station for Her Majesty's fleet, I telegraphed to you immediately to say that you were at liberty to act on my despatch of the 30th ultimo, in which I repeated to you the original instructions of Her Majesty's Government.

I learn that according to the opinion of Li Hung-chang a direct proposal on the part of Her Majesty's Government either to buy or lease Port Hamilton will probably frighten the Corean Government" and induce them, for fear of Russian aggression, even to offer farther objection to our temporary occupation. However, as I have already pointed out to you other possible objections against a formal proposal to rent Port Hamilton, I have no doubt that, being on the spot, you will be the best Judge as to the course to pursue in order to let the Corean Government understand that Her Majesty's Government is willing to rent the island, and to pay a sum yearly not exceeding 5,000*l.*, as long as it is used as a coaling-station.

The consent of Her Majesty's Government to an agreement of this sort shows in a way which I trust will appear to the Corean Government sufficiently explicit, that we do not at all dispute the question of Corean sovereignty, and that Her Majesty's Government merely propose to pay an annual rent for Port Hamilton and the cession to England of Corea's rights of sovereignty over that island as long as it may be used by us as a coaling-station.

The Chinese Government has frequently assured me, and I have received similar assurances from the Viceroy Li Hung-chang who, as you are aware is especially intimate with Corean affairs, that they have no objection whatever to our occupation, but they indicate pretty clearly that they cannot give it their consent in any formal manner. I am much inclined to think that Corea will look upon the question in much the same light, and that if we do not ask her for a formal consent she will offer no further objection.

I have thought it just possible that some arrangement might be come to with the British Admiral and the local authorities on the island with a view to renting to which the Corean Government would not hesitate to give their approval. An arrangement of this kind would, at any rate, be a step in the desired direction, which might be later on developed into an agreement such as is desired by Her Majesty's Government; and I have accordingly ventured to ask Vice-Admiral Sir W. Dowell, who is now at Port Hamilton, for his opinion. I have also inquired of his Excellency whether he can spare a gun-boat to carry your despatches to Chefoo early in next week.

I am, &c.
(Signed) N. R. O'CONOR.

Inclosure 2 in No. 132.
Mr. O'Conor to Vice-Admiral Sir W. Dowell.

Peking, June 6, 1885.

(Confidential.)
(Telegraphic.)

HER Majesty's Government adhere to proposal to rent island. Corea too frightened, I fear, to consent easily to formal agreement. Would it be possible arrange to rent in first instance from local authorities? Corean Government would no doubt approve. I hear privately Russia trying to get Port Lazareff. Can your Excellency spare gun-boat to carry Aston's despatches to Chefoo and take back mine? Important not to lose time.

37

입안 8개 조에 관해 李鴻章과의 협상 지시

井上馨 (1885. 6. 10) ➡ 榎本武揚 (1885. 6. 27)

英國其軍艦ヲ以テ朝鮮所屬巨文島占據ノ儀ニ付別紙甲號ノ通リ英國公使ブランケット氏ヨリ申來候ニ付乙號ノ通リ回答致置候右占據ニ付朝鮮政府ニ於テ執タル處置ハ別紙丙號近藤代理公使ノ機密信數通及丁號モルレンドルフ氏竝ニ嚴世永ガ長崎ニ於テ英國水師提督ダワエル氏ト往復セシ書簡ニテ御承知可相成候而シテ右ノ書類ニ依テ見ルニ英政府ハ右占據ニ付テハ豫シメ朝鮮政府ノ承諾ヲ得タル者ニ非ズシテ卽ニ之ヲ遂ゲタル後四月二十四日附ノ書翰ヲ以テ通知シタルニ止マリ最モ不道ノ處置ニ有之候得ドモ右ハ英韓兩政府間ノ事項ニシテ我ノ敢テ嘴ヲ容ルヽ義ニハ無之唯我政府ニ於テ本件ヲ傍觀シ不問ニ置ク事ヲ得ザルノ理由ハ卽チ地形竝ニ政略上ノ關繫ニシテ抑モ右ノ占據ヲ單ニ看過シ後來生ズベキ其結果如何ヲ推考セザルニ於テハ差シタル重大ノ事件ニモ無之樣見ヘ候得共熟ラ將來ノ成行ヲ考フル時ハ英政府方今ノ所爲ハ英露葛藤ノ際止ヲ得ザルニ出タルモ尚ホ持久ノ存意有之時ハ將來容易ナラザル關繫ヲ惹起シ獨リ朝鮮ニ付テノミナラズ大ニ東亞細亞全洲ノ利害ニ關繫ヲ生ズベキハ火ヲ見ルヨリモ易シ其譯ハ英國若シ果シテ永ク該島ヲ占有シ退去セザル時ハ露國モ亦其先轍ニ効ヒ元山釜山又ハ濟州島ニ占據スルヲ得ルノ讓與ヲ朝鮮政府ヘ開談セント欲スル意向モ有之而シテ朝鮮政府ニ於テ特許シタルモノヲ他國ニ向テ臺(ママ)ム事ハ大ニ苦ム所ノモノナルノミナラズ露朝條約中最恵條款ニ依リ必ズ他國ヘモ亦均シク許スノ外ニ策ナカベルク果シテ此場合ニ立至リ候時ハ卽チ亞細亞洲中一ノ新ラシキ困難ノ種子ヲ播クモノニシテ東亞コレヨリ多事ナラント相信候卽チ露國ヲシテ朝鮮地方ヘ着手ヲ始ムル最好機會ヲ與フルト云モ亦過言ナラズ其結果タル遂ニ追々朝鮮國ヲ分割シテ他國ニ贈與スル如クニ相成其際各國ノ競爭ハ必ズ甚敷我國ノ近海ハ爭亂紛議ノ中央トナリ東亞細亞ノ平和ハ殆ンド保持スル能ハザルニ立至ルベク候而シテ其原因ハ卽チ之ヲ英國政府現行ノ所爲ニ誘起シタルニ歸シ可申候是卽チ我政府ノ巨文島占據ニ付最モ苦慮スル所ニ有之候且又英國公使ヨリノ來旨ニ據レバ右ノ占據ハ一時ノモノナリトノ事ナレトモ其一時ト稱スル所ノモノハ其意義最モ曖昧ニシテ

卽チ尋常ノ意味ニテモ九十九ケ年迄ハテンポラリーヲキユペーション卽チ一時ノ占據ト稱スルヲ得ベク然ラバ斯ク曖昧ノ語ヲ以テ其制限ヲ爲シ以テ其不當ノ處置ヲ覆ハントスルハ素ヨリ不可許義ト存候又前陳ノ如ク英國ガ巨文島ヲ占據スルニ於テ先ニ朝鮮政府ノ承諾ヲ得ズ占據シテ而後タヾ之ヲ該政府ニ通知シタルニ止マル義ハ英韓兩國間ノ事件ニシテ素ヨリ我政府ノ嘴ヲ容ルヽ所ニアラザレドモ我邦ニ於テモソレガ爲メ受クベキ重要ノ影響アルモノナレバ此點ニ於テ黙視スルニ忍ビザル事ト存候前述ノ利害ハ獨リ我邦ノミナラズ清國モ均シク被ムルモノナレバ清國ニ於テモ亦同樣ノ注意ヲ以テ同樣ノ論議可有之筈ト存候乍併清國ト朝鮮トハ獨立屬國ノ關係ニ關シテ各國ノ最モ注意スル所ナレバ英政府ヲシテ清國ガ猥リニ朝鮮ノ事件ニ干渉スルヤノ疑ヲ惹起スニ至ラバ二個ノ問題ヲ合一シテ其解除ヲ一層困難ナラシムルノ恐モ不尠候ニ付巨文島一件ニ付清政府ガ英國ニ向テ異議ヲ唱フルニ當テ清國ノ爲メニ計ルニ務メテ朝鮮政府ニ干渉スルノ疑ヲ避ケ單ニ自國利害ノ一點ヨリ論議候方得策ナラント存候

巨文島占據一件ニ付拙者ノ考案大凡前陳ノ通ニ有之候間其主意李中堂ニ詳細御陳述相成彼ヲシテ英政府ニ向テ抗議致候樣御盡力有之度候尤モ我國ニ於テハ目下條約重修ノ件モ有之今日英政府ノ甘心ヲ失スルハ不得策ニ付本件ニ付テモ先導者ノ地位ニ立テ異議相唱ヘ難キ義ニ付可成清國ヲシテ直接ニ其衝ニ立タシメ候樣致度候間其御含ニテ御盡力有之度候尚本件付テ李中堂モ既ニ曾公使ヘ十分强ク異議相唱候樣訓令シタル趣徐公使ヨリ聞及候ニ付河瀨公使ヘハ曾公使ニ面會シ十分ニ彼ヲ誘促シ且ツ好機ニ乘シ英國政府ヘモ公然トナク我政府苦慮ノ趣ヲ陳述シ退去ノ義盡力可致樣及訓令候

近藤代理公使機密信第七十二號及七十三號露國トノ關係及魚允中責罰ノ件ノ如キハ實ニ驚歎ノ至リニテ朝鮮國王ノ暗弱内官等ノ驕愚恰モ自ラ其國ヲ虎穴ニ投スル有樣ニシテ今ニシテ或ル方法ヲ以テ國王内廷ニ在テ政ヲ執ルノ弊習ヲ押制シ内官ノ權力ヲ殺消スルニアラズンバ朝鮮ノ不利危害ハ扨置キ我國及清國ニ於テモ其餘禍ヲ蒙ル事明瞭ニ有之候依テ本月五日徐公使ト數時間ノ長話ヲ爲シ別紙筆記書ノ通リ韓廷監察ノ方法致陳叙候處徐公使モ至極同感ニテ速カニ李中堂ニ通信スベキ旨被答候就テハ貴官ニ於テ速カニ下津李中堂ニ面晤筆記中ニ記載スル拙者ノ主意ヲ詳述シ彼ノ賛成ヲ得監察ノ方策速ニ實施相成候樣御盡力可有之候右徐公使ト對話ノ模樣ハ筆記ニテ御承知可相成候其要ヲ擧候ヘバ左ノ方法ニシテ之ヲ設ケ置候ハヾ將來ノ危害ヲ防

グニ足ルベク存候ニ付李中堂ト極密御對話相成度候

第一 朝鮮ニ對スル政策ハ總テ最秘密ノ手續ニテ常ニ李鴻章ト本官ト協議ノ上李氏之ヲ施行スベシ

第二 朝鮮國王ヲシテ現今ノ如ク內廷ニ於テ自ラ政務ヲ執ラシメズ且內官ノ執權ヲ剥キ其政務ニ關スルノ途ヲ絶ツベシ

第三 擧國第一等ノ人物ヲ撰ンデ之ニ政務ヲ委任シ之ヲ進退スルニハ國王必ラズ李鴻章ノ承諾ヲ得ベシ

右第一等ノ人物トハ金宏集金允植魚允中ノ如キ其人ナルベシ

第四 右ノ人物ニ委任スル政務トハ外交軍事會計ノ三務ヲ以テ主要トス

第五 可成速ニモルレンドルフ氏ヲ退ケ至當ノ米國人ヲ以テ之ニ代ラシムベシ

第六 陳樹常ハ篤學ノ人物ナレドモ才力足ラズ他ノ有力者ヲシテ之ニ代ラシムベシ

第七 右陳氏ノ跡役ヲ李鴻章ヨリ任命シ米國人ヲ朝鮮ニ推薦シタル上ハ將來ノ政策ニ付十分ノ訓令ヲ與ヘ其者ヲ日本ニ送リ本官ニ面會セシムベシ

第八 陳氏ノ跡役ハ京城ニ在留ノ日本代理公使ト深ク交誼ヲ結ビ諸事協議シテ事ヲ執ルベシ

且又右ハ全ク亞細亞全洲ニ虎狼ノ侵襲ヲ防クヲ以テ其静謐安寧ヲ保全スルノ一點ヨリ出テ朝鮮政府ノ治略ニ干涉スルノ主意ニハ無之候條其趣李中堂ニ於テ明カニ諒知セラルヽ樣添テ御陳述有之度候

機密第十二號及十三號朝鮮ヲ日淸合同保護ノ下ニ置ク云々ニ付テハ御意見ノ趣一應御尤ニ候得共我國ト淸國トノ朝鮮ニ對スル政略ハ全ク相反シ我ハ之ヲ獨立ト認メ彼ハ尚屬國視スルノ場合ニ付若シ之ヲ公然共同保護スル時ハ他各國ニ於テハ誤テ或ハ淸國ノ屬國主義ヲ贊成スルナリトノ感覺ヲ起スニ於テハ大ニ我ニ取リ不利ナラントス存候ニ付我政府ノ政略一變シタル上ハ知ラズ今日ノ場合ニ於テハ到底難被行事ト存候乍併朝鮮國王及ビ政府ノ暗愚ナル露國ニ密使ヲ派遣ノ如キ處置有之候テハ到底何カノ方法ヲ設ケザレバ其禍我邦家ニモ波及候義ニ付卽チ今回徐公使へ叙述シタル如キ計畫ヲ立テ以テ內密常ニ李氏ト協議シ其コレヲ實施スルハ李氏其任ニ當ラシメント存候次第ニ有之候

十三號琉球ノ件ニ付テハ御申越ノ通リ先年トハ時勢モ相變シ條約改正ノ期限モ條約ノ順次ニ依テ既ニ到來シ又互相均霑ノ事モ却テ我ニ不利ナル次第加之爾來政治上琉球諸島ニ施行シタル事項モ鮮ナカラズ且最近歐洲諸邦ニ於テハ切リニ植民政略ヲ東

洋竝ニ阿弗利加ニ擴張スル際ナレバ一孤島タリトモ決シテ等閑ニ放棄スベキ時ニ無之候間既ニ我政府ニ於テ過日汽船一艘ヲ暫時琉球へ遣シ宮古八重山間ヲ往復セシメ置候其節工師ヲ派遣シ該地ノ石炭鑛モ調査セシメ候事ニテ右分與ノ義ハ好マザル義ニ有之候義貴官ニ於テモ御同案ニ付テハ李氏自然日本へ渡航候トモ右琉球案ヲ以テ使事ノ主眼トスル內意アリテ來航候時ハ我ハ事ヲ左右ニ寄セテ之ヲ否ムモ終ニ同人ニ於テハ不愉快ヲ其精神ニ感ゼシムルハ必然ニ付若シ眞ニ渡航相企テ居候ハヾ暗々裡ニ使事ノ目的ヲ酒杯ノ上ニ於テ御探リ被成右琉球案ヲ提出スル時ハ日淸ノ間ニ再ビ一ノ問題ヲ起スト同樣ナルノ理由ヲ貴官ノ意見トシテ御辯諭置相成候事最必要ニ有之候

尙韓廷監察ノ義ニ付テハ過日原領事へ別紙ノ通リ致通電候ヘドモ今般貴官下津相成候ニ付テハ右李中堂ト協議ノ義ハ貴官へ引繼候樣原領事へ及指令候間此段御承知相成度候

38
영국의 거문도 전선 설치 및 러시아의 흑포도 점거 사실 통보

李鴻章 (1885. 6. 11 / 光緒十一年四月二十九日) ➡ 總署

寄譯署

光緒十一年四月二十九日午刻

徐承祖二十八來電 據長崎理事電稱 聞英於巨文島設電綫通英京 又 電線傳俄艦據墨浦島 與巨文相近云 鴻

39
주청 영국 공사가 조선에 거문도 점령을 통지한 사실 확인

J. Sienkiewicz (1885. 6. 12) ➡ Ch. de Freycinet

Direction Politique n. 96.

Tôkiô, le 12 Juin 1885

Monsieur le Ministre,

J'ai l'honneur d'adresser, ci-joint, à Votre Excellence la traduction française de la convention conclue à Tien-tsin, le 18 avril, entre la Chine et le Japon et dont précédemment déjà je lui avait fait connaître les pincipales clauses.

Cet arrangement parait avoir donné, bien que pour des motifs différents, une égale satisfaction aux deux parties. Les Chinois le considèrent, non sans raison, comme un grand succès diplomatique qu'ils auraient remporté, alors que les Japonais y voient surtout un gage de paix et de tranquillité. Ce qui démontre, d'ailleurs, combien étaient factices ces tendances belliqueuses que certaines feuilles de Paris ont prêtées aux Japonais, c'est l'indifférence que j'ai constatée ici en ce qui touche la nature même des clauses de la convention du 18 avril. Quelques personnes font discrètement remarquer que pour obtenir de si modestes et si douteux avantages, il n'était point besoin d'envoyer en Chine une Ambassade extraordinaire. Mais généralement on n'y regarde point de si près; on désirait éviter la guerre, M. Ito a su satisfaire ce désir et l'on n'en demande point davantage pour décerner à M. Ito le titre d'habile diplomate.

Un télégramme de M. Patenôtre en date du 9 de ce mois, m'a appris, d'autre part, que la paix venait d'être signée entre la France et la Chine. Cette nouvelle m'est parvenue au moment où muni d'informations précises, j'allais adresser des remontrances au Gouvernement japonais au sujet des fournitures d'armes qu'il se disposait à faire au Gouvernement chinois par l'entremise d'un Agent d'une maison de commerce allemande de Shang-haï qui se trouve au Japon depuis le 5 mai dernier. Aussi ai-je cru devoir m'abstenir de soulever une question irritante du moment qu'elle ne pouvait plus donner un résultat pratique, me réservant de donner à entendre, à l'occasion du Gouvernement japonais que ses agissements ne m'étaient point restés inconnus. J'ai lieu de croire, toutefois, qu'il s'agissait surtout pour les Japonais de se débarrasser d'une manière avantageuses d'un armement ancien dont ils ne voulaient plus se servir.

La troisième des grandes questions qui agitent l'Extrême-Orient attend encore une solution définitive (On pense généralement ici que la chute du Ministère Gladstone et l'arrivée au pouvoir de Lord Salisbury rendront inévitable la guerre entre la Russie et l'Angleterre. C'est, ce me semble, exagérer beaucoup l'importance de ce changement de Ministère. Il n'en est pas moins constant que l'Angleterre, pour mieux protéger la Corée contre les envahissements de la Russie, a commencé par lui enlever Port-Hamilton et elle semble si peu disposée à renoncer à cette station qu'elle s'occupe à la relier par un fil télégraphique à sa colonie de Hong-Kong.

Le Comte Ino-ouyé qui a varié quelque peu dans sa manière d'apprécier cet acte tout arbitraire de l'Angleterre m'a déclaré aujourd'hui qu'il craignait que la Russie invoquant la clause de la nation la plus favorisée, ne réclamât à son tour de la Corée une compensation territoriale quelconque. Il résulte, d'autre part, des diverses informations que j'ai pu recueillir sur la manière dont s'est faite l'occupation du Port-Hamilton, que le Chargé d'Affaires d'Angleterre à Péking en avait donné avis par une simple note, en date du 19 mai, au Gouvernement Coréen, qui se serait empressé de protester contre ce procédé sommaire. Il paraîtrait même que le Gouvernement chinois, mieux éclairé sur la question, aurait agi de même.

Il est bien difficile de prévoir ce que fera la Russie. M. Dawydow prétend que les Anglais, ayant pris ce qu'ils convoitaient depuis longtemps, se trouveraient bien plus à l'aise si les Russes suivaient leur exemple; mais ce n'est là qu'une opinion qui lui est personnelle. Dans tous les cas, pour mieux suivre les incidents qui peuvent se produire en Corée, le Cabinet de Pétersbourg a décidé que M. de Speyer secrétaire de la Légation russe à Tôkiô, se rendait à Seöul en qualité de Chargé d'Affaires.)

Je profite de cette occasion pour informer Votre Excellence que je viens de faire une rapide excursion dans le nord du Japon. Je me suis rendu par mer à Sendaï vers la fin du mois dernier et de là je me suis dirigé par terre jusqu'à Morioka. Partout j'ai rencontré le meilleur accueil. Les fêtes que m'ont données les autorités ayant certainement été prescrites par le Gouvernement du Mikado, n'ont en que la caractère d'une courtoisie officielle. J'ai attaché plus d'importance aux illuminations et aux autres manifestations de ce genre qui ont été improvisées par les notables de plusieurs villes que j'ai traversées. J'ai même eu la satisfaction de voir flotter les couleurs françaises soit sur ma demeure, soit sur les divers bateaux qui ont été mis à ma disposition. L'explication de cet accueil exceptionnel qui m'a été fait est, d'ailleurs, des plus simples: à peine débarqué dans la baie de Sendaï, j'avais longé les côtes pour étudier l'endroit le plus favorable à la création du port par où pourraient s'écouler les produits du Nord du Japon. Or, cette question étant l'objet des constantes préoccupations des populations, on a pensé que je pourrais contribuer à sa solution. J'avais emmené avec moi le capitaine Bougouïn, qui m'a été d'un très-utile concours par la connaissance qu'il a des moeurs et des usages des Japonais.

J'aurai, d'ailleurs, l'honneur d'adresser prochainement à Votre Excellence sous le timbre de la Direction des Consulats et Affaires Commerciales un rapport spécial où je consignerai les remarques de diverse nature que j'ai été à même de faire pendant ce voyage de deux semaines dans un pays bien rarement visité par les Européens.

Veuillez agréer, Monsieur le Ministre, les assurances de ma très-haute considération.

Sienkiewicz.

Son Excellence
Monsieur de Freycinet
Ministre du Affaires Etrangères
à Paris

Convention de Tientsin entre le Japon et la Chine.

Notification N.3 du DaijoKan

Les questions pendantes entre le Japon et la Chine à propos des troubles, survenus à Séoul au mois de décembre dernier, ont été discutées avec le Gouvernement Chinois. Ces questions ont été résolues par la Convention et la lettre ci-annexées.

(L. S.) Prince Sanjo, premier Ministre d'Etat,

Comte Inouyé, Ministre des Affaires Etrangères,

Tôkiô le 27 Mai 1885

Convention

Le Comte Ito, ambassadeur extraordinaire du Grand Empire du Japon, Ministre d'Etat et de la Maison Impériale et Grand Cordon de l'ordre du Soleil Levant, et le Comte Li Hung Tchang, plénipotentiaire extraordinaire du Grand Empire de la Chine, Grand Gardien de l'héritier présomptif, Grand Secrétaire d'Etat, Ministre du Commerce de la Mer du Nord, Ministre de la Guerre, Vice-Roi du Chili et Shinuki (*sic*) du premier rang.

Après avoir délibéré officiellement et conformément à leurs instructions respectives et en vue de resserrer les relations amicales qui existent entre les deux pays, ont arrêté ce qui suit:

Afin d'éviter un conflit entre les deux Puissances, la Chine retirera les troupes qu'elle entretient en Corée; le Japon retirera celles qu'il y maintient pour la protection de sa Légation. Le retrait de ces troupes devra être effectué dans un délai de quatre mois à dater de la signature de la présente convention. Les troupes chinoises s'embarqueront à Masam-po et les troupes Japonaises à Ninsen.

Les Puissances contractantes s'engagent à conseiller mutuellement au roi de Corée de procéder à l'organisation de l'armée Coréenne, afin qu'elle puisse, le cas échéant, assurer l'indépendance de ce pays. Pour procéder à cette organisation, le gouvernement Coréen pourra engager un ou plusieurs instructions militaires, choisis parmi les officiers des armées étrangères, à l'exclusion, toutefois, d'officiers Japonais ou Chinois.

Dans le cas où des circonstances d'une gravité exceptionnelle obligeraient les deux Gouvernements de la Chine et du Japon, ou l'un d'entr'eux à envoyer des troupes en Corée, ils se donnerait l'un à l'autre avis préalable et par écrit de leur intention. Dès que les causes qui auront motivé, cet envoi de troupes auront cessé, les troupes seront immédiatement retirées et n'y seront pas maintenues plus longtemps.

le 18 Avril de la 18e Année de Méiji 1885

(L. S.) Comte Ito Hiroboumi, Ambassadeur extraordinaire, Sanghi et Ministre de la Maison de l'Empereur, etc, etc.

le 4e jour de 3e Mois de la 11e Année de Kotcho (Calendrier Chinois)

(L. S.) Li hungtchang, Plénipotentiaire du Grand Empire de la Chine, etc, etc.

Lettre de Lihungtchang, plénipotentiaire du Grand Empire de la Chine, etc, etc, au Comte Ito Hiroboumi, Ambassadeur extraordinaire du Japon, etc, etc, etc.

C'est avec un profond regret que nous avons appris que les troupes chinoises et japonaises se sont battues au palais royal de Séoul, lors des troubles survenus au mois de Décembre dernier (10e mois du calendrier Chinois). Ces actes se sont produits en dehors de la volonté des deux Gouvernements, Attachant le plus grand prix aux relations amicales qui existent heureusement entre les deux pays depuis les temps anciens. Je déclare que les troupes chinoises, tout en ayant été contraintes par les circonstances de faire usage de leurs armes, ont manqué toutefois de modération dans l'action. Je les réprimanderai officiellement à ce sujet.

En ce qui regarde les dépositions de la femme de Honda Shousnoské et des autres sujets japonais que vous m'avez communiquées, et d'après lesquelles des soldats chinois auraient pénétré dans les maisons des résidents Japonais de Séoul, et se seraient rendus coupables de crimes contre la propriété et la vie de plusieurs sujets Japonais. Je n'ai en main aucune preuve de ces incriminations, émanant des autorités chinoises. Mais j'enverrai à Séoul une mission chargée de faire une enquête minutieuse sur ces faits. Si j'acquiers la preuve que des soldats appartenant aux détachements chinois se sont trouvés ce jour-là dans les rues, causant du désordre et se livrant à des voies de fait contre la vie et la propriété des sujets Japonais. Je ne manquerai pas de les punir sévèrement suivant le code pénal militaire de la Chine.

Tel est l'objet de ma lettre.

Le 4e Jour du 3e Mois de la 11e Année de Kotcho

(L. S.) Li Hung Tchang, Plénipotentiaire extraordinaire.

40
영국의 거문도 점령에 관한 대응책 훈령

井上馨(1885. 6. 13) ➡ 河瀨眞孝

(前略) 在京英國公使 プランケット (Plunkett) ヨリノ來翰ニ依ルモ英國政府ハ右占據ニ付而ハ豫メ朝鮮政府ノ承諾ヲ得タル者ニアラスシテ旣ニ之ヲ遂タル後四月二十四日附ノ書翰ヲ以テ通知シタルニ止マリ最不道ノ處置ニ有之候得共右ハ英韓兩政府間ノ事項ニシテ我ノ敢テ嘴ヲ容ルル義ニハ無候唯我政府ニ於而本件ヲ傍觀シ不問ニ置ク事ヲ得サルノ理由ハ卽チ地形竝政略上ノ關係ニシテ抑モ右ノ占據ヲ單ニ看過シ後來生スヘキ其結果如何ヲ推考セサルニ於テハ差タル重大ノ事件ニモ無之樣相見候ヘ共熟々將來ノ成行ヲ考フルトキハ英政府方今ノ所爲ハ英露葛藤ノ際止ヲ得サルニ出テタルモ尙持久ノ存道之有ルトキハ將來容易ナラサル關係ヲ惹起シ獨リ朝鮮ニ付テ而已ナラス大ニ東亞細亞全洲ノ利害ニ關係ヲ生スヘキハ火ヲ見ルヨリモ易シ其譯ハ英國若シ果シテ永ク該嶋ヲ占有シ退去セサルトキハ露國モ亦其先轍ニ習ヒ元山釜山又ハ濟州島等ニ占據スルヲ得ルノ讓與ヲ朝鮮政府ヘ開談セント欲スル意向モ有之而シテ朝鮮政府ニ於テモ一國ニ特ニ許シタルモノヲ他國ニ向テ否ム事ハ大ニ苦ム處ノモノナルノミナラス魯韓條約中最惠條款ニ依リ必ラス他國ヘモ亦均シク許スノ外無之ルヘク果シテ此ノ場合ニ立至候トキハ卽亞細亞洲中一ノ新シキ困難ノ種子ヲ播クモノニシテ東亞是ヨリ多事ナラント相信候卽チ魯國ヲシテ朝鮮地方ヘ着手ヲ始ムルノ最好機會ヲ與フルト云フモ又過言ナラス其ノ結果タル遂ニ追々朝鮮國ヲ分割シテ他國ニ贈與スル如クニ相成其際各國ノ競爭ハ必ラス甚敷我邦ノ近海ハ爭亂紛議ノ中央トナリ東亞細亞ノ平和ハ殆ント保持スル能ハサルニ立至ルヘク候而シテ其原因ハ卽チ之ヲ英國政府現行ノ所爲ノ誘起シタルニ歸シ可申候是卽我政府ノ巨文嶋占據ニ付最苦慮スル處ニ有之候且又英國公使ヨリノ來旨ニ據レハ右ノ占據ハ一時ノモノナリトノ事ナレトモ其一時ト稱スル處ノモノハ其意義最曖昧ニシテ卽チ尋常ノ意味ニテモ九十九年迄ハ テンポラリー・ヲキユペーション 卽チ一時ノ占據ト稱スルヲ得ヘク然ラハ斯ク曖昧ノ語ヲ以テ制限ヲ爲シ之ヲ以テ其不當ノ處置ヲ覆ハントスルハ素ヨリ不可許義ト存候又前陳ノ如ク英國カ巨文嶋ヲ占據スルニ於テ先ニ朝鮮政府

ノ承諾ヲ得ス占據シテ而後只之ヲ該政府ニ通知シタルニ止マル義ハ英韓兩國間ノ事件ニシテ素ヨリ我政府ノ嘴ヲ容ルル處ニアラサレトモ我邦ニ於テモ夫レカ爲受クヘキ重要ノ影響アルモノナレハ此點ニ於テモ黙視スルニ忍ヒサルコトト存候前述ノ利害ハ獨リ我邦ノミナラス淸國モ均シク被ルモノナレハ淸國ニ於テモ亦同様ノ注意ヲ以テ同様ノ論議可有之筈ト存候乍併淸國ト朝鮮トハ獨立屬國ノ開係ニ關シテ各國ノ最モ注意スル處ナレハ英政府ヲシテ淸國カ猥リニ朝鮮ノ事件ニ干涉スルヤノ疑ヲ惹起スルニ至ラハ二個ノ問題ヲ合一シテ其解除ヲ一層困難ナラシムルノ虞不尠候ニ付巨文嶋一件ニ付淸政府カ英國ニ向テ異議ヲ唱フルニ當ツテ淸國ノ爲ニ計ルニ努メテ朝鮮政府ニ干涉スルノ疑ヲ避ケ單ニ自國利害ノ一點ヨリ論議有之候方得策ナラント存候

巨文嶋占據一件ニ付拙者ノ考察大凡前陳ノ通リニ有之候且又本件ニ付而ハ李鴻章モ大ニ心配シ曾紀澤公使ニ訓令シ英政府ニ向テ强ク異論ヲ唱ヘシムル趣淸公使ヨリ聞及候(ニ付卽別紙電報相發候義ニ有之候)就而ハ尙曾公使ヘ御面會前陳之趣十分御說明相成彼ヲシテ十分ニ英政府ヘ　プロテスト　致候樣御盡力有之度且又英政府ニ向テ好機ヲ見計談話ノ序ニ貴官ヨリモ前陳ノ旨趣御申入相成將來之利害得失御辨說相成度候要之我國ニ於而ハ目下條約重修ノ件モ有之今日英政府ノ甘心ヲ失スルハ不得策ト言ヘキニ付本件ニ付而モ我レ先導者ノ地位ニ立チ公然異議ヲ唱候樣ナル感覺ヲ英政府ニ起サシメサル樣御注意有之可成淸國ヲシテ直接ニ異論者ト成ラシメ度候間其含ニテ夫々御盡力相成度候

右申進候

41
거문도 전신선의 일시적 설치를 재확인

總署 (1885. 6. 15) ➡ N. R. O'Conor

Inclosure in No. 155.

The Prince and Ministers of the Tsung-li Yamên to Mr. O'Conor.

Peking, June 15, 1885.

(Translation.)

THE Prince and Ministers of the Yamên beg to acknowledge the receipt, on the 13th instant, of Mr. O'Conor's letter, in which he states, with reference to the exception taken by the Prince and Ministers to his version of the North Saddle cable question, that he cannot admit that. he is mistaken in his recollection of what passed.

The Prince and Ministers are really unable to set this matter aside without comment, for the refusal to permit the landing of a cable end is a prerogative secured by the sovereign rights of China.

It was distinctly stated, both on the 14th May and the 1st June, that the laying of a cable to North Saddle Island was a matter of temporary accommodation, and. that the cable would hereafter have to be removed.

As regards what was said about removal to Woosung, the remark had sole reference to amalgamation with the cable of the British Eastern Extension Company. The conversation that passed on this subject was heard by everybody, and was perfectly explicit, but in spite of this fact, Mr. O'Conor, in his earlier letter, added the words, "and land the cable," to the words, "remove to Woosung."

The Prince and Minsters positively did not make use of these words, and if Mr. O'Conor's memory has not served him incorrectly, then the Chinese Secretary must have misinterpreted their remarks.

In a word, the cable end can only be placed temporarily on North Saddle

Island; its position there must not be regarded as permanent; and should it hereafter be removed to Woosung, all that can be done is to amalgamate it with the Eastern Extension Company's cable the end cannot be brought on shore.

In the letter under acknowledgment the question is described as academical, and one which it is unnecessary to pursue further, and reference is also made to the friendly response to the wishes of Her Majesty's Government. In Mr. O'Conor's opinion, this matter is one the discussion of which it is unnecessary to go deeply into; but the Prince and Ministers are actuated by the prospect of having to make their words good in the future, and are therefore obliged to state distinctly the intention they had when they gave their promise with respect to this matter, that this may be placed on evidence.

They avail themselves, &c.

42
영국과의 협약 체결을 통한 중국의 권리 보전 제안

曾紀澤 ➡ 總署 (1885. 6. 15 / 光緖十一年五月三日)

관련문서 曾紀澤이 영국 외무성에 보낸 조회

五月初三日 出使大臣曾紀澤文稱 竊照英國佔據朝鮮濟洲東北之安島 本爵大臣前詢英國外部侍郎克蕾諺稱 水師官尙無確信 繼准尙書伯爵葛蘭斐爾密咨 始將暫據韓墨爾登海島之事說出 比將密咨譯漢於本月初十日 咨呈察核在案 先是初八日 承准貴衙門姑庚電示密約保權利 似屬空談 如何辦法 希探明電覆等因 本爵大臣思該島晩爲英俄兩國爭據之地 在我不能禁止該二國均不佔據 俄人若據該島 則與混□江口及海參崴等處呼吸相通 其不便於中國 較之英人據之爲尤甚也 英國已據該島 必不肯因我之爭論遽復退還 現准外部聲明 不欲有損中國聲望 甚願與中國相商立約等語 如能講訂一約 保全中國上邦之權利 則尙不至大傷中國體面 刻下遵電先行探明如何意見 乃與議約 已具一牘 於十三日照會英外部 講其見覆大略 除俟接准覆文若何 再行電聞外合將照會先行譯漢 咨呈貴衙門 謹請査核

【관련문서】

照錄粘單

照錄給英外部照會

爲照會事 照得本爵大臣前奉本國朝廷之命 於本月初八日 操詢英國佔踞韓墨爾登海島之說 頃接貴爵部堂本月十六日覆文 具悉一一 査此處各島皆屬高麗 高麗不僅爲中國之近鄰 而且爲中國之屬國 若被別國佔踞此等之島 中國國家宜能漠然置之不問 然本爵大臣猶幸

貴爵部堂覆文所稱 英國佔踞該島乃是暫行之事 又承示以英廷不欲作事 有損中國望幷願預備與中國立約 俾於該島等處無礙中國之權利 又承英廷剖釋 若非迫於事勢所

不得不行 則必願先與中國國家相商 然後再踞該島云云 中國國家是以特飭本爵大臣懇請貴爵部堂將英廷欲與中國國家立約式樣 及如何保護中國權利之處 示知大畧 曷騰盼感 相應照會貴爵部堂 請煩查照施行 須至照會者

43
Plunkett에게 청 정부의 반대 가능성 통보

N. R. O'Conor (1885. 6. 17) ➡ E. Granville (1885. 8. 11)

No. 145.

Mr. O'Conor to Earl Granville.—(Received August 11.)

Peking, June 17, 1885.

(No. 297.)

My Lord,

I HAVE the honour to inclose to your Lordship herewith a copy of a despatch which I have addressed to Mr. Plunkett in respect to the opinion which he seems to entertain that the Chinese Government has been active in remonstrating against the occupation of Port Hamilton by Her Majesty's Government. I have not [___] to keep Mr. Plunkett fully informed of the language held by the Prince and Ministers of the Yamên in this question, conveying assurances that the Chinese Government were not personally opposed to the British occupation.

I have, &c.

(Signed) N. R. O'CONOR.

Inclosure in No. 145.

Mr O'Conor to Mr. Plunkett.

Peking, June 17, 1885.

Sir,

I HAVE the honour to acknowledge the receipt of the despatches No. 143,

150, and 151 to Earl Granville, and of your despatch to Sir W. Dowell of the 31st May, copies of which you were good enough to forward to me in your despatch, marked Confidential, of the 31st May.

In your despatch No. 151 of the 25th ultimo to Earl Granville, marked Very Confidential, detailing the reasons which, in your opinion, make it desirable that Her Majesty's Government should now hold Port Hamilton, and in which, so far as I can venture an opinion in the matter, which seems to me essentially founded on naval and military considerations, I would generally concur, you allude to the representations made by China and Corea, at the suggestion of Russia, and against the British occupation' of Port Hamilton. So far as the Chinese Government is concerned, and so far as any weight can be attached to their assurances, I may be allowed to point out that neither in conversation with me, nor in any written communication, nor in what has been said to one at least of my colleagues here, is there any reason to believe that up to the present moment the Chinese Government are personally opposed to our occupation, or inclined to make representations with a view to this occupation ceasing. What may happen in the future it is difficult to predict, especially in a country like China, but I feel pretty sure that unless they yield to the pressure of foreign Governments, they will not of their own accord offer any opposition to the action of Her Majesty's Government in this matter.

I hope you will allow me to allude to one other point in the despatch which you were so good as to send me.

In your despatch to Sir W. Dowell of the 31st May, marked Very Confidential, you say that "there seems to be at present considerable friction between the Central Government at Peking and Li Hung-chang in connection with the French negotiations, and which of these two Chinese influences it is which is now so active against England I have not yet been able to discover."

In reply to this observation, which concerns, so to speak, the internal political feeling of China, I must say that neither during my experience in Peking, nor during the longer and far more valuable experience of the late Sir Harry Parkes, has anything tended to show that there was any considerable friction between the powerful Viceroy and the still more powerful Ministers of the Yamên, either in the matter of the French negotiations or other questions. The Viceroy bears a reputations for outspokenness, and even a somewhat reckless style of language, but there is invariable much system in what he says, and he would be the first to disclaim responsibility when his views were not shared in by the Chinese Government, by whom he is strongly supported in his present position, and to whom he admits the necessity of obedience.

That the Viceroy has not been active against England may, I think, be assumed from the fact of his having written to the King of Corea to offer no further objection to our occupation, and of his having sent this letter through Her Majesty's Consul.

I have, &c.
(Signed) N. R. O'CONOR.

44
Plunkett · 井上馨 회담

F. Plunkett (1885. 6. 23) ➡ E. Granville (1885. 8. 7)

No. 138.

Mr. Plunkett to Earl Granville.—*(Received August 7.)*

Tôkiô, June 23, 1885.

(No. 173. Very Confidential.)

My Lord,

COUNT INOUYÉ called on me this afternoon to show me confidentially a telegram which he had lately received from the Japanese Chargé d' Affairs in Söul, stating that M.de Speyer (whose departure from Tôkiô was reported in my despatch No. 156 of the 4th instant) calls himself Russian Provisional Agent; that he proposes to remain at Söul until the arrival of M. Waeber, the new Russian Consul-General; that M. Speyer has assumed a harsh tone, no doubt designedly, and that he had declared to several persons, including the Japanese Chargé d'Affaires himself, that he had instructions to take steps for the annexation of ten times as much Corean territory as had been occupied by Great Britain, unless the latter withdraws from Port Hamilton.

Count Inouyé, having read me the telegram above summarized, inquired whether I had received any information in regard to M. Speyer's attitude since his arrival in Söul.

I told his Excellency that the latest news I had from Corea had been brought to me by M. Carles, who had left Chemulpo just before M. Speyer's arrival; I could, therefore not throw any further light on the matter.

Count Inouyé observed that this telegram confirmed the fear he had always entertained, that the seizure of Port Hamilton by Great Britain would be made use of by Russia as a plausible excuse for making a similar demand on her own account in regard to some other portion of Corean territory. His Excellency went onto say that he would be greatly relieved if he could learn from me that our occupation of Port Hamilton was likely soon to come to an end. Did I suppose that the advent of a new Ministry in England would make any change in this respect?

I told his Excellency that, although I knew from the public telegrams that there had been a Ministerial crisis in London, and that the Marquis of Salisbury had been intrusted by Her Majesty with the task of forming a new Cabinet, I had no official information yet of the constitution of the new Ministry, and I suggested that it was somewhat indiscreet to ask me for any expression of opinion at such a moment.

I reminded his Excellency that the object of Great Britain going to Port Hamilton was to forestall Russia and to keep her out; that we should probably remain there as long as we considered desirable for such a purpose; and that really it was so much in the interest of the Japanese that Russia should not get hold of such an important strategic position, that Japan ought to be glad to see a friendly and unaggressive Power like Great Britain there; that I could well understand how fear of Russia might make Japan anxious not to appear in any way to encourage us, but that, under the peculiar circumstances of the case, the less Japan moved in the matter the better. That I had reason to fear that, both at Peking and Söul, the Japanese Representatives had perhaps not been as discreet as would have been judicious, and that I should greatly regret if any ill-advised language of some of her Agents abroad were to encourage an idea (which I personally believed to be false) that Japan was working in any way against the interests of Great Britain.

Count Inouyé disclaimed any desire to make difficulties, and had no wish to ask any question which I might consider inopportune; but the danger of the advance in Corea of Russia was one which interested Great Britain as much as it did Japan, and it was to warn me of the increasing probability of that danger that he had now spoken to me.

I said I entirely appreciated the friendly spirit which dictated his remarks, and suggested that the best course would be for him to send the telegram which he had shown me to Mr. Kawase, that Mr. Kawase should communicate it confidentially to the Foreign Office, and leave it to the authorities there to make or not any remarks upon it.

Count Inouyé said he would do so.

I have, &c.

(Signed) F. R. PLUNKETT.

45

거문도의 개항 제안

徐承祖 ➡ 總署 (1885. 6. 26 / 光緖十一年五月十四日)

五月十四日 出使大臣徐承祖函稱 本月十九日曾肅第十一號函 度已上邀賜詧 前日接徐叔鴻農部來電 囑先定買紅銅二百萬觔 昨經電達貴衙門 想必承轉回間中堂矣 玆特寄上請採辦銅觔一榾 乞代呈各堂憲閱後轉遞是叩 昨接李相來電 知法事已定約畵押化干戈爲玉帛 薄海賴以乂安 聞之不勝欣慰 惟願我國從此將水陸各軍實力從新 並速建造火車 開挖各礦 以生財源諸事 力圖富强 以弭將來之患 實爲深盼 前英俄搆釁英借朝鮮巨文島屯煤 現聞英人竟有久踞之心 如是恐日後英人或與我有違言 實有不利於我國 似宜早與理論 惟目前因此小島又未便與英廷過於力爭 鄙見與之極力理論如不能行 或請函致高王 囑其宣告各國卽以此島添爲通商口岸 一有各國牽制將來英人自不能獨踞作屯糧備兵之地矣 再前日與幷上馨晤談 論及高事 似有關擊 玆將問答另錄附上 叩請轉呈堂憲鑒閱酌奪 卽賜論覆 以便轉覆幷上 再我國文人到東 外務卿回不肯給予護照遊歷內地 經承祖屢與理說 告以岡千仞去年曾往我內地遊歷 我政府未嘗阻止 彼云容函詢榎本 再行回覆 究竟去年罔千仞到京 是否貴衙門給予遊歷憑照尙祈詳示 以使再向外務理論 中東旣係修好 此等小事似亦宜彼此平允也 諸乞代賜回明 是所幸禱 專此 敬請台安 統惟垂詧

敬再啓者 正在封南間 接奉大咨並批摺三件 均謹收領 容再恭錄咨呈鈞案 此次寄上請採買銅觔一摺 應另備安摺 前承允爲代辦 卽乞飭善一並恭遞 是所叩禱 專肅 再請台安

照錄問答

46

거문도 점령에 대한 李鴻章의 견해

N. R. O'Conor (1885. 6. 27) ➡ E. Granville (1885. 6. 27)

No. 56.

Mr. O'Conor to Earl Granville.—*(Received June 27, 11 P. M.)*

Peking, June 27, 1885, 7:30 P. M.

(Telegraphic.)

TELEGRAM from Mr. Aston, received 22nd, says:—

"President of the Foreign, Office does not see way to making arrangement regarding Port Hamilton. Fears public opinion and pressure from other Powers, and requests removal of ships."

Telegram received to-day says:—

"Corean Government repudiate agreement made by M. von Möllendorff to employ Russian officers to instruct Corean troops. If agreement not kept, Russian Secretary threatens seizure [of] Quelpaert[Quelpart].

"M. von Möllendorff dismissed."

(Sent to Mr. Plunkett.)

China moving troops Corean frontier contiguous to Russian territory.

Viceroy Tien-tsin proposes, through Consul, following arrangement:—

"That England should hold Port Hamilton provided that she undertakes never to use it against China."

Proposal, though unofficial, deserves consideration, as Viceroy directs Corean affairs.

47
李鴻章 견해 수용을 위한 總理衙門과의 교섭 진행

The Marquis of Salisbury (1885. 6. 28) ➡ N. R. O'Conor

No. 58.

The Marquis of Salisbury to Mr. O'Conor.

Foreign Office, June 28, 1885.

(No. 153. Ext. 36.)

Sir,

I HAVE received your telegram No. 51 of yesterday's date, relative to the views of the Corean Government with regard to the occupation of Port Hamilton by this country, and the attitude of the Russian Representative in Corea on the subject.

With regard to the last paragraph of your telegram, in which you state that the Viceroy of Tien-tsin proposes, through Her Majesty's Consul at that place, that England should hold Port Hamilton provided that she undertakes never to use it against China. I have to instruct you to encourage the Viceroy's proposal which you should endeavour, if possible, to have made to you by the Chinese Government at Peking.

The substance of the above was sent to you this day by telegraph.

I have, &c.

(Signed) SALISBURY.

48
청 總理衙門의 거문도 전신선 관련 입장

N. R. O'Conor (1885. 6. 29) ➡ The Marquis of Salisbury (1885. 8. 24)

No. 156.

Mr. O'Conor to the Marquis of Salisbury.—(Received August 24.)

Peking, June 29, 1885.

(No. 325. Confidential.)

My Lord,

WITH reference to my despatch No. 321 of the 27th instant, I have the honour to inform your Lordship that I consider it advisable to encourage as far as was possible the various suggestions of the Viceroy Li Hung-chang in respect to an arrangement regarding Port Hamilton on the chance of his coming round eventually to support the views of Her Majesty's Government with that of Corea.

Your Lordship is aware that Corean affairs are entrusted nearly entirely to the direction of the Viceroy, and that in the difference between China and Japan in respect to Corea the negotiations were confided almost exclusively into his hands.

For some time past his Excellency has been pretty free in his expressions, at first inclined to condemn much more severely than the Yamên the policy of Her Majesty's Government in occupying Port Hamilton, and then sending me messages that although China could not certainly acquiesce openly in our occupation, she would not oppose Great Britain. Later on his Excellency undertook that Corea should offer no further objection to our occupation provided we did not require her formally to agree to it, and he was even good enough, at my request, to write to the King of Corea not to oppose Her Majesty's Government or offer further objection. At the same time he refused to support any arrangement either to rent or buy the island, but was evidently gratified by my deferring to his suggestion in so far as to inquire if some arrangement could not be made with the local authorities which might later on receive the sanction of the Corean Government.

A few days ago I again sounded his Excellency through Her Majesty's Consul at Tien-tsin and found that he was now ready to go much farther in the line desired by Her Majesty's Government than previously. He did not refuse to use his good offices with the Corean Government in order to induce them to rent Port Hamilton to Her Majesty's Government, but made a proviso that the island should never be used as a base for operations against China.

I ventured to telegraph his proposal, and your Lordship was good enough to instruct me in your telegram No. 36 of the 28th instant to encourage it, and I trust that the result will be that his Excellency will be ready at all events to support the proposal with the Corean Government if he does not actually consent to let the offer come through him.

I hope before the mail leaves on the 1st proximo to be able to furnish your Lordship with further details in this matter.

I have, &c.

(Signed) N. R. O'CONOR.

49
李鴻章의 제안을 Aston에게 통지

N. R. O'Conor (1885. 6. 30) ➡ The Marquis of Salisbury (1885. 8. 24)

No. 159.

Mr. O'Conor to the Marquis of Salisbury. — *(Received August 24.)*

Peking, June 30, 1885.

(No. 328.)

My Lord,

I HAVE the honour to inclose herewith to your Lordship copies of two despatches which I have addressed to Mr. Aston, Her Majesty's Consul-General in Corea, in respect to the question of renting Port Hamilton from the Corean Government.

I have ventured, in order to save time, to forward to Mr. Aston a rough draft of an Agreement to be come to with the Corean Government, and I have done so without waiting for your Lordship's instructions, as it may be ten days before there is another opportunity of communicating direct with Corea, whereas, should your Lordship's answer to my telegraphic inquiry be opposed to these instructions, I can inform Mr. Aston by telegraph, before it is possible for him to have submitted the Agreement to the Corean Government. I trust that, under the circumstances, and in view of the importance of trying to arrange this question while the impression caused by M. von' Möllendorff's intrigues is favourable to Her Majesty's Government, I shall meet with your Lordship's approval.

I have, &c.

(Signed) N. R. O'CONOR.

50
러시아를 고려한 청의 입장

N. R. O'Conor (1885. 7. 1) ➡ The Marquis of Salisbury (1885. 8. 24)

No. 160.

Mr. O'Conor to the Marquis of Salisbury.—(Received August 24.)

Peking, July 1, 1885.

(No. 331.)

My Lord,

I CALLED by appointment, accompanied by Messrs. Hillier and Bullock, yesterday afternoon upon the Ministers of the Yamên.

I took the opportunity of informing their Excellencies of the news I had received from Corea Respecting an agreement between M. von Möllendorff, Under-Secretary of the Corean Foreign Office, and the Russian Legation at Tôkiô, and the consequent dismissal of that official from the Corean service. I observed at the same time that as this Agreement dated from a period certainly prior to any question of the occupation of Port Hamilton by Great Britain, it put at rest the complaint so often of late repeated by the Yamên that Russian activity in Corea had been instigated by the action of Her Majesty's Government.

The Ministers seemed to admit the force of this remark, but observed that the fact remained that the British Government was all the same in occupation of a part of Corean territory, and that this occupation, while advantageous to Great Britain, brought trouble and difficulty upon China.

It was even at this moment under consideration whether it would not be necessary to address a formal note to the British Government in respect to Port Hamilton, in order to have something to say when the Russian Minister again reproached them for their partiality towards England. This note, their Excellencies added, would he a mere formal document, drawn up "for the eye," but it would in no way diminish the good understanding between the two Governments. In fact, behind it there might be a secret understanding which would correspond to the views of both Governments.

I deprecated, I said, any exchange of formal notes such as was suggested, and the more so as the notes would contain statements which they admitted would have no importance and no meaning, except as a blind to the Russian Minister, and I was inclined to doubt whether the latter result would be attained. Thereupon the Ministers let it be understood that no final decision had yet been taken in the matter, and that consideration would be given to what I had said.

If the Ministers, I said, really attached the importance they wished me to believe to a strong and increasing friendship with Great Britain there was now a good opportunity for laying the first stone by acceding to an agreement in respect to Port Hamilton, and inducing Corea, at the same time, to come to an arrangement with Her Majesty's Government, and I would be ready at any moment to come to an understanding such as I knew would be in strict accordance with the wishes of my Government.

The Ministers replied at some length to the effect that there were great difficulties in the way of the Chinese Government, as well from the consequent entanglements with especially one foreign Power, as from the division of parties in Corea. It was very difficult for China to advise Corea; in the sense desired, without its being taken hold of by the opposition party in Söul. It seemed possible, however, that some arrangement could be come to between the Chinese and British Governments, by which China could acquiesce in the British occupation of Port Hamilton, and even come to an understanding that might go considerably farther; but it was particularly important that the consent of Corea and China to our occupation should not prove the cause of a further loss of territory to Corea. Would Her Majesty's Government be willing to guarantee the integrity of Corea if she recognized our possession of Port Hamilton?

I said that this was a very big question which I had no authority to speak about, but I had no hesitation in stating that pledges of this nature would certainly not be lightly given by Her Majesty's Government. For the present it was my duty to confine myself to the particular case of Port Hamilton, free from any pledges beyond such as might properly be demanded by either Corea or China, as, for instance, that the occupation should not be used against either country. I would not, therefore, follow their Excellencies on to ground involving considerations of general and Imperial policy. It was, however, by small and friendly acts in the beginning that more lasting friendships and alliances were built up, and such an opportunity seemed now present to the Chinese Government.

The conversation was prolonged owing to the presence of three Ministers all anxious to speak, but the gist of what was said may be briefly summarized, and was to the effect that an arrangement by which Her Majesty's Government should be authorized to occupy Port Hamilton would certainly meet with the approval of the Chinese Government, if Her Majesty's Government would join in a guarantee of Corea's future integrity, but that without this guarantee it would not be easy to get China formally to acquiesce in our occupation.

There is no doubt that overtures of a more direct and positive nature for a closer understanding between Her Majesty's Government and that of China were made in the course of the conversation than anything that had previously fallen from the Ministers of the Yamên. It was clearly indicated that the Chinese Government would be ready to enter into a secret understanding with that of Great Britain, and that it was hoped that the remarks of the Yamên might be deemed deserving of the consideration of Her Majesty's Government.

It was not, however, very clear whether these overtures were limited to the question of a guarantee of the integrity of Corea, or to the question of a private alliance between the two countries in case of certain eventualities. The remarks were probably thrown out as feelers of considerable political importance, which were meant to show that the Chinese Government is watching the course of the negotiations between Russia and England with keen interest, and that they are waiting on the upshot of these negotiations before taking any more-definite line. I was to-day strengthened in the impression, already reported in an earlier despatch, that should hostilities unhappily break out between Great Britain and Russia, it would not be difficult to bring China into a strong and practical alliance with Her Majesty's Government. The fact that Chinese troops have been moved to the Russian frontier in Corea, and that, as I am in credibly informed, the Chinese Government have already made inquiries from a British firm as to the possibility of a loan of 10,000,000*l.* for naval and military purposes, shows pretty clearly that they do not put out of mind the contingency of hostilities breaking out between them and Russia, either in respect to the Manchurian and Kashgarian frontiers, or to the policy of Russia in Corea.

I have, &c.
(Signed) N. R. O'CONOR.

51

조선 정부에 영국의 거문도 조차 제안 통보 지시

李鴻章 (1885. 7. 1 / 光緒十一年五月十九日) ➡ 劉含芳

寄旅順劉道

光緒十一年五月十九日巳刻

望密致陳道樹棠 云英據巨文島必不肯退 欲朝鮮暫租 歲給租銀二萬兩 其他地課 民人由朝管理 仍立密約 永不害朝 求我轉商 希密致朝政府 如可通融 即與駐朝英領事議辦 否則亦勿聲張 鴻

52
조선 정부에 러시아 요구 거절 권고 지시

李鴻章 (1885. 7. 2 / 光緒十一年五月二十日) ➡ 劉含芳

寄旅順劉道

光緒十一年五月二十日巳刻

密致陳道云 英接電 朝已革穆麟德 甚合公論 朝 俄若眞有密約 朝未派全權 又未批准 按公法可作廢紙 革穆更有詞 勿怖 俄若索島地 堅勿許 望密告政府轉告朝王秘之無泄 鴻 此電發後船即開

53
榎本武揚·李鴻章 회담

(1885. 7. 2 ~ 7. 3)

七月二日李鴻章ト總督衙門ニ會晤シテ對話スル如左

此 我邦ハ朝鮮ノ內治外交共ニ干涉スルヲ好マズ然レドモ朝鮮ノ近況內外ノ處置共ニ其當ヲ失シ特ニ自國ノ不爲ナルノミナラズ其害貴我兩國ニ波及スベキヲ以テ外務卿ハ徐公使ニ向テ其所見ヲ陳セラレシハ中堂既ニ御知ナルベシ外務卿ハ更ニ本使ニ令シテ下津ノ上親シク中堂ト同件ヲ面議スベキヲ以テセリ

彼 貴外務卿ヨリ徐公使ヘノ御話竝ニ徐氏ニ示サレシ一切ノ書類ハ漢譯ノ上徐氏ヨリ予ニ送越セリ但シ該書類中露韓事件ニ付在韓近藤署公使ヨリノ報告ハ予ノ得タル報告トハヤヽ異ナル所アリ

此 何ノ異ナル所アリヤ

彼 予ハ前件ヲ我ガ在韓陳樹常ニ命ジテ探偵セシメシニ陳氏ガ何某ヨリ得タリトノ報ニ據レバ過般漢城ノ變後中日兩國必ラズ開仗ニ至ルベシトテ韓國上下相擧テ恐怖シ以爲ク中國ハ現ニ佛國ト事アリ其勢大ニ兵ヲ韓ニ出シテ日兵ト戰フ能ハザルベシ然ルトキハ韓國孤立トナリ其存亡不可測ルヲ以テ金鏞元´ 權´ 申´ 金ノ四人韓王ニ說ヒテ曰ク今日ノ計露國ト相結ブニ如カズト於是四氏ハ密ニ韓王ノ命ヲ受ケ(但シ政府ノ憑據モ全權モ帶ビズ)上途シ咸鏡道ニ至テ將サニ露境ニ入ラントスルトキ咸鏡道ノ道台ハ四氏ノ露行ノ憑據ヲ帶ビザルヲ以テ護照ヲ與フルヲ許サズ四氏ハ不得已逗留四五日ノ後武器買入ヲ以テ名トシ遂ニ海參葳(浦鹽斯德港)ニ至リ露官ニ面シテ先ツ陸路通商ノ事ヲ約シ而後何カ計リシ由ナレドモ其事柄ハ何タルヲ知ルニ由ナシ恐クハ露韓同盟ノ密約タラン當時露官ハ彼得堡ニ電報ノ命ヲ待チシニ同府ヨリ明年四月ヲ以テ露ヨリ漢城ヘ使者ヲ派スベキニ由リ其時ヲ以テ商議スル所アラント下知セシ趣ナリ

此 其使者ハウエーバー氏ナルベシ

彼 然ルベシ頃日貴國駐劄露公使ノ書記官即チ昨年井上外務卿朝鮮行ノ節漢城ニ到リシ者再ヒ漢城ニ來リ居レリト聞ク

此 本使モ亦其事ヲ聞ケリ我ガ在韓近藤氏去月十九日漢城發ノ密信ニ據バ彼ノ露國書記官スペーヤナル者現ニ漢城ニ在リ自ラウエーバー氏來韓迄ノ代理ト稱シ擧動疎暴ニシテ大ヲ好ミ揚言シテ云ク英艦モシ巨文島ヲ去ラバ露國ハ巨文島ヨリ十倍ノ韓地ヲ占據スベシト渠ハ近藤氏ニ向テモ忌憚ナク此言ヲ吐キシ由

彼微笑シテ云 予モ亦同様ノ報ニ接セリ其他予ガ聞ク所ニハ該書記官ハ韓王ニ語テ曰ク朝鮮ノ兵ハ日本竝ニ中國ノ教練ヲ受ケ來リシガ今日中兩國ノ兵互相撤回スルニ由リ以後ハ露人來テ教練スベシ是レモルレンドルフ氏ノ依頼ニ因ルト於是韓王及ビ在廷ノ諸臣ハ斯ル事ヲ依頼セシ覺ナシト答ヘモルレンドルフ氏ヲ革職セリト

此 モルレンドルフ氏ノ革職ハ確實ナリヤ

彼 確實ナリ但シモルレンドルフ氏ノ革職セラレシハ抑モ亦他ニ緣故アリ其故ハ今次露韓密約一件ニ付當地ニ在ル英領事及ビ他ノ英人等予ニ説クニモルレンドルフ氏ハ露國ノ友ニシテ韓王ニ向テ露ト同盟ノ約ヲ訂セン事ヲ勸告セリト又貴國人民モ同説ヲ持セル趣徐公使ヨリノ報アリ是故ニ予ハ前日一使ヲ韓ニ派シ韓王ニ向テ其實否ヲ糺セリ　此時李氏稍得色アリ

此 其使ハ密約ノ事果シテモルレンドルフ氏ノ勸告ニ基クヲ復命セシヤ

彼 此使ハ船便ナキヲ以テ未ダ歸リ來ラズ

此 露韓密約ノ事タル本使ハ初ジメ信ゼザリシガ近頃聞ク所ニ據レバ實説ナルガ如シ如何

彼 予ハ凡ソ二ケ月前ニ其風説ヲ聞キ直ニ韓王ニ問糺セシニ王ハ別ニ密約ヲ結ビシ事ナク只露國ト陸地通商ノ事ヲ謀リシノミトシテ答ヘタリ

此 本使ハ本國ヨリ接セシニハアラザレドモ頃日或ル所ヨリ得タル報ニ據レバ所謂露韓ノ密約ナル者ハ六ケ條ヨリ成立テリト只未ダ其何タルヲ知ラズ中堂ハ多分御承知ナラン

彼 予モ亦六ケ條アル由ニ聞ケリ

此 密約ノ大旨ハ御承知ナキヤ

彼 承知ナリ然レドモ此密約タルヤ韓王ハ無シト稱シ加ルニ訂約セシ使臣ハ微賤ノ者ニテ全權ノ憑據モナク又固ヨリ國王ノ批准モナキユヘ初メヨリ成立セサル者ニ均シ其意ヲ以テ御聽取リアリタシ卽チ

第一條　金玉均海參蔵ニ渡來セバ露官捕ヘテ之ヲ朝鮮ニ引渡スベシ

第二條　朝鮮ヨリ日本ニ拂フベキ十三萬圓ハ露國日本ニ勸メ要求セザル事ヲ務ムベシ

第三條　何レノ國ヲ問ハズ朝鮮ノ土地ヲ侵略スルトキハ露國來テ之ヲ保護スベシ

李氏語ヲ添テ云朝鮮政府ハ既ニ貴國ニ償金ヲ完清セシヤ我云幾分カハ拂ヒタルベケレド貧乏國ユヱ未ダ完淸セシヲ聞カズ李微笑シテ云須ラク金額ヲ催促シテ拂ハシムルヲ良トス否ラザレバ露ハ己ノ盡力ニ由リテ日本ヨリ催促セザルナリト韓ニ對シテ誇ルベシ又云第三條モ實ハ貴國ヲ指テ云ヒシ者ナリ

第四條　露國ハ欽差大臣ヲ漢城ニ駐箚セシムベシ

第五條　朝鮮ハ三面海ニ瀕スルヲ以テ露國ノ軍艦之ヲ防守スベシ

第六條　陸路通商ノ事

以上ノ密約ナル者ハ固ヨリ正當ノ全權ヲ帶タル使節ノ結ビタル者ニアラズ況ヤ韓王ノ批准ナキ者ニ付露國ヨリ之ヲ實施セント迫ルモ韓王ハ之ヲ破棄セザルベカラズト予ヨリ韓王ニ申通セリ然レドモ俄ハ威力ヲ挾ミ必ラズ之ヲ實施セント言張テ韓王ノ抗論ヲ承諾セザルトキハ中國ヨリ露ニ向テプロテスト(辯駁)スル見込ナリ露ハ果シテ右ノ計ニ出ツベキヤ貴意如何

此　本使ハ露ノ必ラズ出言セザルヲ保シ難シ何トナレハ縱令其使臣ハ正當ノ權力ヲ帶ビタル者ニアラザルモ全ク韓王ノ使价ニシテ而シテ王ノ旨ヲ奉ジテ訂約セシコト事實タラハ露ハ之ヲ以テ口實トスルモ測ルベカラズ然リト雖ドモ斯ル所業ハ要挾ニ屬シ萬國普通ノ正理ニ悖ル者ナレハヨモヤ斯ル不條理ヲ言張ルベシトモ思ハレズ

彼　朝鮮ヲ露國保護ノ下ニ置クカ如キハ(卽チ前文密約中ノ第三條)實ニ特ク朝鮮ノ禍タルノミナラズ中國ト貴國ノ利益ニ關スル所甚ダ大ナリ只貴國ハ朝鮮ヲ獨立國ト認メタルヲ以テプロテスト(辯駁)スルモ露ハ借スニ耳ヲ以テセザルベシ反之中國ハ朝鮮ノ宗國タル天下ノ共ニ知ル所タレハ露國モ中國ノ駁辯ヲ無ニスル能ハザルベシ抑モ朝鮮ハ英米獨等ノ國ト條約ヲ結ビシ時必ラズ其成文ヲ中國ノ朝廷ニ奏聞シ來レリ然ルニ今次露韓ノ密約ノ如キハ正當ノ使者ノ手ニ成リシ者ニアラザルト韓王ノ批准ナキノミナラズ韓王此約ノ成レルヲ奏聞セシ事ナケレハ中國之ヲ以テ無効ノ條約ト看做スモ不當トスル者ナカルベシ貴意如何

此 貴論甚ダ理アリ只貴政府駁辯ノ論礎ニ宗國權ヲ提出スルトキハ議論枝生テ却テ面倒ナルベシ何トナレバ露ハ必ラズ言ハン 朝鮮ハ獨立國タレバコソ我皇帝モ對待ノ資格ヲ以テ之ト約ヲ結ビタルナリ其結約ノ成文ヲ淸廷ニ送ルガ如キハ我國ノ關スル所ニアラズ淸ニ送ルモ英ニ送ルモ朝鮮政府ノ勝手ニシテ我ト朝鮮ト對待ノ資格ニ對シ毫モ權力ヲ有スル者ニ非ズト 故ニ本使以爲ク貴國ノ論礎ハ 朝鮮ノ支那ニ於ケル樞要ノ地ニ接近スルヲ以テ其痒痛直ニ貴國ノ利害ニ關スルニ付默許スルヲ得ズ トノ意ヲ主張スルヲ良トス

彼默止良久 其點ヨリ論ヲ立レハ貴國モ亦露國ニ向テ駁辯シ得ベシ不知貴國ハ露ニ向テ駁辯セラルヽ否

此 夫ハ我政府ノ意中ニ存スル者ニ付果シテ駁辯スルヤ否本使ハ豫言スルヲ得ズ只本使一己ノ見ヲ以テスレバ駁辯スルヲ得ルノ理アリトス只朝鮮ノ貴國ニ於ケル關繫ト我國ニ於ケル者トハ世人ノ知ル如ク輕重ノ差アレバ貴國ハ首唱者タラザルベカラズト思惟ス

彼 默止

此 巨文島一件ハ如何

彼 予ハ英領事ニ向テ英艦巨文島退去ノ事ヲ請求セシニ英領事曰ク露英事件妥議ニ歸セバ退去スルナラントト予曰ク露モ亦英ノ所爲ニ傚テ朝鮮ノ或ル場所ヲ占據セバ如何英領事曰ク是レ英國ノ關スル所ニアラズト

此 中堂ハ露英ノ紛議平定セバ英艦ハ巨文島ヲ退去スベシト考ヘラルヽヤ

彼 今次ノ露英事件妥議ニ歸セバ又他ノ紛議起ルベク而シテ英ハ之ニ籍テ以テ辭柄ト爲シ到底退去スベシト思ハレズ

此 本使モ亦同見ナリ現ニ英ハ巨文島ヨリサヅルアイランド迄海底電線ヲ連絡セリ(此時津海關道台周馥傍ニ在リ獨語シテ曰ク英ハ巨文島ヨリ上海迄既ニ電線ヲ布ケリ)是レ一時占據ノ徵ニアラザルニ似タリ

彼 顰眉 予モ亦同見ナリ該件ニ付露公使ハ貴使ニ向テ何カ語リシ事アリヤ

此 中堂ニ限リ密語セン露公使ボヽフ氏ハ英艦巨文島ヲ占據セシ報ヲ得シトキ本使ニ語ルニ英政府ハ淸廷ノ許可ヲ得タルナラントノ疑念アリタリ本使ハ答フルニ淸政府斯ル事ヲ英ニ許可スベキ理ナキヲ以テセリ露公使ハ然ラバ全ク英政府自儘ノ所業タルベシトテ只管其不條理ヲ鳴ラシ居タレドモ別ニ露國モ亦英ノ所爲ニ傚フガ如キ口氣ハナカリシ只露國公使館附ノ人々ハ英ノ所業ハ直ニ露ノ利益ニ

關スルヲ以テ露モ亦朝鮮ノ一地ニ據リ以テ其衝ヲ折ラザルベカラズ杯語リシ者アリタリ前日本大使天津ヲ去ル時中堂ニ向テ英艦ノ所爲ハ露ヲシテ尤ニ傚ハシムルノ戸ヲ開キタリト稱セシハ中堂記臆セラルベシ是レ實ニ一難題ナリ

彼 洵ニ然リ其秋ニ至テハ如何處置スベキヤ貴見如何

此 此問題ハ實ニ緊要ニ屬スルヲ以テ我外務卿ハ中堂ノ意見ヲ聞キ以テ相共ニ圖ル所アラント欲スルナリ

彼 先ツ貴使一個ノ意見ヲ承タシ

此 實力アラバ難ヲ排スルニ難カラズト雖ドモ實力ナキ以上ハ外交上ノ手續ヲ踏ムノ外本使ハ他見ナシ其手續ナル者ハ種々アルベケレド先ツ差詰メ直接ノ關繫アル朝鮮ノ國王ヨリシテ英露兩政府ニ駁辯書ヲ送ラザルベカラズ兩政府モシ退去ノ意ナキトキハ更ニ訂盟各與國ニ書ヲ致シテ憐ヲ請フノ外ナカルベシ只其効能ハ覺束ナシ

彼 朝鮮政府ハ既ニ駐箚各領事ニ書ヲ致シテ其手續ニ從事シタリ

此 本使モ既ニ其事アルヲ知レリ只朝鮮統理衙門ヨリ各領事ニ致セシ書翰ハ措語頗ル妥ヲ欲キ外交上ノ體裁ヲ爲サズ且ツ右ハ只巨文島ノ事ノミニ止レリ露國モシ英ノ所爲ニ傚フニ至テハ其事件更ニ重大トナリテ自ラ各國ニ感觸ヲ與フル事モ深カルベシ此時ニ方テ韓土ヨリ正當ノ請求ヲ先ツ英露二國ニ提出シ併テ他ノ各與國ニ盡力ヲ乞ハヾ幾分ノ効アルモ知ルベカラズ

彼 予ガ所見ニハ米政府ノ政略ハ只貿易ノ一點ニ止ルヲ以テ右等ノ件ニ盡力スベシトモ思レズ獨逸ト英國ト交渉ニ於ケル勉テ厚誼ヲ傷ケザルヲ主トスルヲ以テビスマーク氏ハ英ニ向テ異議ヲ唱ヘザルベシ露英二國ハ當局者タルヲ以テ論ヲ俟タズ殘ルハ貴國ト中國アルノミ

此 此問題ハ暫ラク次會ニ讓リテ本使專任ノ事務ニ及バントス偖テ朝鮮內政ノ近況ニ至テモ大ニ掛念ナキ能ハズ近報ニ據レバ韓王ノ暗愚ニ乘ジ內監密勿ニ與聞シテ權威甚ダ熾ナル由既ニ韓廷屈指ノ人物ト聞ヘタル魚允中ハ忠直ヲ以テ內監ノ讒ニ逢ヒ罪ナキニ官職ヲ褫ハラレテ庶人ト爲リ金宏集ハ要路ニ留ルヲ得ズ今只金允植ナル者僅ニ一人アルノミ然レドモ伊ハ他ノ二人ニ比スレバ氣力稍弱キ由ニ聞ケリ今朝鮮國步艱難ノ際內監政權ヲ執リテ威福ヲ擅ニスルニ任セ置カバ內亂乍チ起リ外患次デ生ゼン其影響ハ即チ貴國ト我國ノ利益ニ關繫アル淺カラザルベシ故ニ何トカ法ヲ設ケ撿束セザルベカラズ是レ朝鮮ノ內政ニ干渉スル趣意ニ

アラズ只管貴我二國ノ利益ヲ保護スル爲ナリ

彼 予モ其事ヲ思ハザルニハアラザレドモ從來中國ハ朝鮮ノ內政ヲ不問ニ附シ置タリ今中國ヨリ賢才ヲ擧ゲ小人ヲ遠クヘシト申遣ハシタレバトテ韓王ノ柔弱ニシテ且ツ闇愚ナル乍チ左右ニ籠絡セラレテ陽ニ我言ヲ容レ陰ニ之ヲ實施セザルベシ

此 實施スルヤ否ハ貴國ノ理事官京城ニ在ルヲ以テ之ヲ檢査スルヲ得ベシ

彼 理事官一人ニテ能ク監督スルヲ得ザルベシ

此 是レ其人ノ能否如何ニ在ルノミ

此時旣ニ十二時ヲ過ギタルヲ以テ我云ク本使ノ陳述セント欲スル事ハ本日能ク盡シ得ベキニアラサルヲ以テ次會ニ讓ラントス李云明日午後四時貴領事館へ答禮トシテ罷出ベシ我云フ願クバ粗飯ヲ呈セン李云予主タレバ先ヅ招カザルベカラズ願クハ支那料理ヲ供セン原領事ヲモ御伴アラバ幸甚我云諾將サニ退席セントスルニ臨ミ

此 朝鮮人閔泳翊現ニ當地ニ逗留スル由定メテ御面會アリタルベシ

彼 然リ

此 渠ハ何等ノ用ヲ帶テ渡來セシヤ

彼 渠ハ漫遊ノ爲メ來リシ由ナリ前日面晤ノ節渠曰ク往キニ京城ヲ發セシ後中日兩兵互相撤回ノ事ヲ聞キ一書ヲ國王ニ奏シテ中國ノ兵撤回セバ內亂再ビ起ルベシトテ極テ其不可ヲ陳セリト予ハ撤兵ノ約已ニ成ルヲ以テ變換スルヲ得ズト答ヘタリ

此 閔泳翊ハ三十五日前ニ兩三名ノ官吏ト共ニ牛莊ニ着シタル趣ナレバ渠ハ本國ヲ發スル前業已ニ兩國撤兵ノ約成リシヲ知居タルナラン

彼 渠ハ閑散ノ身ニテ且ツ他道ニ在リシ由ユヘ蓋シ遲ク聞込ミシナラン

此 渠ハ現ニ何道トカノ御史ナリト聞居リシガ漫遊ヲ事トスルヲ見レバ辭職セシニヤ兎ニ角渠ハ撤兵一件ノ外別ニ中堂ニ向テ話セシ事ナキヤ

彼 予ハ渠ニ向テ露韓密約ノ有無如何ヲ糺セシニ渠ハ全ク知ラザル旨ヲ答ヘタリ

此 風說ニ據レバ渠ハ大院君ノ放還ヲ見合セ呉ヨト中堂ニ向テ懇請スル爲メ來淸セリト何カ似寄ノ事アリヤ

彼 渠ハ大院君歸國スルモ國事ニ關セザル樣諭シ呉ヨト予ニ申出タリ渠ハ好人物ト豫聞セシガ眞ニ然ル者ノ如シ

此 近日陳奏使トシテ閔種默ナル者大院君ヲ迎ヒニ來ルト聞ケリ眞ナルカ

彼 予モ亦左様ニ聞ケリ

此 大院君歸韓セバ韓ニ紛擾再起スベシト思ハザルヤ

彼 反對黨ハ不快ヲ抱クベシ然レドモモシ朝鮮ニアラバ露國ニ密使ヲ派スルガ如キ事ハセザルベシ朝鮮ノ紛擾ヲ再起セシムル者ハ現ニ貴國ニ潜伏スル金玉均ノ徒ナリ渠等ハ人心ヲ攪亂セン爲メ斯ル書ヲ隱ニ朝鮮ニ流布セリトテ其書ヲ出シ示ス

此 一讀了テ微笑

彼 朝鮮ノ内亂ハ貴我共ニ其餘波ヲ蒙ルヲ以テ其禍源ヲ斷タサルベカラズ貴國ハ何故ニ渠等ヲ朝鮮ニ引渡サヾルヤ

此 我ト韓トノ間ニハ罪犯引渡ノ約條ナキノミナラズ國事犯ハ文明各國互ニ引渡サヾル者ナリ是レ特ニ憐愍ノ情ノミニ止ラズ卽チ獨立國ノ權利ナリ

彼 朝鮮ニ引渡スヲ欲セザレバ中國ニ引渡サレタシ中國ハ決シテ渠ヲ刑セズ只幽閉シ置クノミ

此 朝鮮人ヲ貴國ニ引渡スベキ謂レナシ

彼 然ラバ貴國ニ於テ渠ヲ幽閉シ亂階タラシメザル樣御處置アリタシ

此 貴國ニ於テハ大官ノ獨意ヲ以テ人ヲ幽閉スルヲ得ベキモ我國ニ於テハ皇帝陛下ト雖トモ無罪者ヲ幽閉スルヲ得ズ

彼 渠ハ貴國ノ治安ヲ妨グ者ニアラズヤ

此 間接ニハ其理ナキニアラザレトモ直接ニハ罪名ヲ下スヲ得ズ況ヤ之ヲ捕テ幽閉スルヲ得ベケソヤ

但シ李鴻章モ亦罪犯引渡ニ關スル法理ヲ解セザル事全ク總署大臣等ニ同ジ通譯伍廷芳ハ法學者タルヲ以テ頗ル通譯ニ苦メル色アリ

我政府ハ金玉均等ノ遁來テ我邦土ニ居ルヲ許スト雖モ決シテ渠等ヲ保護スルニアラズ朴泳孝外一名ハ前日米國ニ赴キシ由金玉均ハ現ニ京攝間ニ落魄シテ衣食ニモ不自由ノ由中堂渠ノ恢復ヲ圖ルヲ憂ヘラルヽハ過慮ニ似タリ

彼 朝鮮ノ民ハ上下擧テ暗愚ナルニヨリ金玉均ノ流言ヲ信ジテ動揺スルハ明カナリ故ニ井上毅氏ハ過日我徐公使ニ大院君モシ歸國スルモ金玉均ヲ用ヒサル樣ニ注意セヨト語ラレタリ是他ナシ後患ヲ慮ルニ坐セリ貴使ハ井上氏ノ注意ヲ傳聞セラレズヤ

此 否縱令金玉均他日事ヲ擧グベキノ恐レアルモ是レ特ニ推測ニ止マレリ推測ヲ以テ渠ヲ幽閉スルヲ得ズ只中堂左迄ニ苦慮セラルヽナラバ本使ハ其旨ヲ我外務卿ニ

函知シ渠ヲシテ流言ヲ本國ニ致シテ人心ヲ攪亂スル等ノ事無之様相當ノ手段ヲ施サレ度ト請フベシ

彼 何分御依賴申候

此時殆ンド午後一時ニ近キヲ以テ談ヲ畢ル

翌三日午後四時ヨリ公使ハ李氏ト總督衙門ニテノ對話如左

彼 貴政府ハデトリング氏ヘ勲章ヲ賜ヒタル由眞ナリヤ

此 新聞紙ニテ其事ヲ讀ミタレドモ本邦ヨリ何トモ申越タル事ナシ何ノ廉ヲ以テ勲章ヲ賜ヒタリト聞カレシヤ

彼 伊藤大使談判ノ節盡力セシ功ニ因ルト聞ケリ(微笑)貴使モ同功ヲ以テ伯爵ニ叙セラレシニアラズヤ

此微笑 新聞記者ヨリ伯爵ニ叙セラレシ事アリデトリング氏ノ叙勲モ恐クハ同種類ナラン

彼 笑否デトリング氏ノ叙勲ハ新聞紙ニ載セタルノミナラズ横濱西字新聞記者ブリンクリー氏ナル者ヨリデトリング氏ニ送リシ私信中ニ其事ヲ載セ而シテ其勲章ハ高等ナル由二等トカニ聞ケリ

此 二等勲章ハ通例陸海軍ノ中將等若クハ高貴ノ文官ニ賜ハル者ニテ本使モ往年勲二等ニ叙セラレタリデトリング氏ニ二等勲章ヲ賜ハルベシトハ思ハレズ

彼 然ラバ三等ナラン三等モ頗ル貴キモノナルベシ

此 然リ

彼 ロベリト・ハート氏ハ未ダ英公使ノ職務ヲ執ラザルヤ

此 否ハート氏ハ未ダ公然英公使ニ任ゼラレタルヲ聞カズ久シク其風説ハアレドモ北京駐箚ノ同僚等ハ容易ニ信ゼザリシ然レドモ頃日ハ彌實説ナリト唱ル者多シ

彼 實説ニ相違ナシ

此 曾公使ヨリ確報アリシヤ

彼 即ニ拜命セリトノ事ハ報知ナシ

此 ハート氏ノ拜命ハ貴政府ヨリ英政府ニ請求セシニ基ケリト聞ク果シテ然リヤ

彼 否々

但シ總署大臣等モ清政府ヨリ請求セシニアラズト明言セリ眞ニ然ルベシ

此 ハート氏ノ跡役ハ其弟ゼームス・ハート氏ナリトノ説ハ眞カ

彼 其説極メテ多シ蓋シ眞ナラン

但シ該件ニ付テハ羅豊祿氏來館ノ節本使ハ(內訓ヲ體シテ)デトリング氏ヲ以デハート氏ノ後ヲ受ケシムルノ是ナルベキヲ諷セシニ羅氏曰ク李中堂モ同見ニテデトリング氏ヲ庇護セリ何トナレバゼームス・ハート氏總稅務司トナルトモ其實權ハ兄ロベルト・ハート氏ニアルベキヲ以テ我政府ノ不利タレバナリ然レドモロベルト・ハート氏ハ北京ノ王大臣等ニ知人多キト年來ノ功勞トニ由リ到底其跡役ハ其弟ノ手ニ落ツベシ羅氏又曰ク實ハハートニモセヨデトリングニモセヨ其本國ノ利益ニ對シテハ虛心ナル能ハザルハ必然ナリ稅務司ヲ擧テ西人ノ手ニ委シ置クハ我ガ政府ノ爲ニ之ヲ惜ムト

此 金玉均等ノ書翰ヲ返却シテ此書ヲ熟讀セシニ文章ノ拙劣ナルト立意ノ把握ナキト宛名ノナキ等ハ本使ヲシテ多分贋作タルベシトノ疑ヲ起サシメリ李中堂今一應閱讀セラレナバ蓋シ同感アラン

彼 熟讀良久朝鮮人ノ漢文ユヱ純粹ナル能ハズ

此 金玉均ハ頗ル詩文ヲ能クスル事本使ノ知ル所ナリ斯ル惡文ヲ爲ス者ニアラズ且ツ此書尾ニ二月四日ト記セリ其頃ハ韓廷ニ金玉均等ノ朋友アルベキ筈ナシ然ルニ致朝鮮廷臣ノ字アリ設令廷臣中ニ知己アリトスルモ此等ノ密書ヲ金玉均等ヨリ接收セリトノ事流布セバ其廷臣ハ必ラズ嚴罰ニ處セラルベシ況ヤ卽覧付丙ノ字アリ接手セシ者ハ祕シ置クベキ筈ナリ

彼 金玉均ノ作ニアラザレバ朴泳孝等ノ手ニ成リシナラン渠等漢城ノ人心ヲ動揺セント謀ル書類ハ此一編ニ限ラズ願クハ貴國渠ヲシテ不軌ヲ圖ル能ハザルノ手段ヲ施サレン事ヲ

此 昨日モ陳述セシ通外務卿ニ函知スベシ

彼 只管懇請スル所ナリ

此 昨日中堂ノ語ラレシ露韓密約中ニハ露人ヲ雇テ兵ヲ教練スルノ條ナシ然ルニ本使ガ刻下接手セシ二個ノ電報ニ據レバ其事アリ

彼 予ガ朝鮮ヨリ接手セシ電報中ニハ無之コト昨日陳セシ如シ只當所ニテ他人ノ得タル電報中ニハ其事アリト聞ケリ貴使ノ刻下接收セラレシ電報ハ外務卿ヨリノ報カ

此 一ハ外務卿ヨリ來リ(卽チ本月一日午後三時東京發ニシテ同三日午後三時ニ接到セシ者ヲ云フ)一ハ他所ヨリ來リシ報ナリ(卽チ本月三日上海發同午後三時二十分接到セシ者ヲ云フ)

彼 拜聽スルヲ得ベキヤ

此 二報共ニ密示セン其他所ヨリ得タル報ニ據レバ密約第一條ハ圖們江ヲ開ク事第二露國ノ士官ヲ雇テ韓兵ヲ練習スル事第三浦鹽斯徳ニ朝鮮ノ理事官ヲ置ク事第五或ル地方ニ郵便ノ道路ヲ開キ以テ露韓二國ノ便ヲ計ル事以上ノ通報者其實否ヲ知ラズト自ラ稱シ來レリ

彼 第二條ヲ除クノ外ハ皆陸路貿易ノ事ニ係レリ

此 外務卿ヨリノ報ニ據バ現ニ漢城ニ在ル露國書記官スベーヤナル者朝鮮政府ニ迫テ曰ク韓廷モシモルレンドルフノ約セシ露人ヲ雇テ韓兵ヲ練習スルノ條款ヲ履行セザル時ハ露ハ濟州島ヲ占據スベシト

彼微笑 其報ハ予モ英人ヨリ聞ケリ恐ラクハ一源ヨリ出タル報ナラン濟州島ハ碇泊所ナキ趣ナレバ露國必ラズ占據セザルベシ予ハ其報ヲ信ゼズ

此 濟州島ハ占據スルモ無益ニ付占據セザルベシ此事本使モ同見ナリ蓋シ韓廷ヲ恐怖セシムル爲メノ虛喝ナラン只所謂密約中ニ露國武官雇入ノ一事有無如何

彼 予ガ聞ク所ニ據バ露人雇入レ事ハ往キニモルレンドルフ氏貴國東京ニ赴キシ時露國ノ書記官ニ其ノ事ヲ約セリト聞ケリ

此時李氏此約ノ無効ナル理ヲ昨日同様ニ反復辯論セリ

此 本使ノ見モ亦然リ本使ハ是ヨリシテ今次下津ノ訓令ヲ受ケシ事ノ話ヲ續ク可シ只其事タル既ニ我外務卿ヨリ徐公使ニ面談セラレシヲ以テ中堂ハ我外務卿ノ論旨ヲ疾ク了解セラレシナラン問フ徐公使ノ報告ハ長文ナリヤ如何

但シ閣下六月五日徐公使ト對話筆記ハ頗ル長文ナルヲ以テ徐氏果シテ閣下ノ論セラレシ要點ヲ悉ク領承シテ李氏ニ送附セシヤ否ヲ慥ムル爲メ此問ヲ設ケシナリ

彼 徐氏ノ報告ハ簡短ナリ願クハ改テ貴使ヨリ承タシ

此 (六月六日外務卿ガ徐公使トノ對話筆記ヲ出シテ)是レ卽チ我外務卿ノ徐公使ニ語ラレシ筆記ナリ本使英語ヲ以テ之ヲ譯讀セン意味不分明ノ廉ハ直チニ質問セラレヨ

彼 諾

是ニ於テ本使徐々ニ之ヲ譯讀ス李氏頻リニ耳ヲ傾テ之ヲ聽ク彼ノ通譯ハ羅豊禄ナリ本使ノ十分ニ譯讀スル能ハザル所ハ呉書記生ヲシテ支那語ヲ以テ之ヲ助クシム原文中ノ 今貴國ノ邊疆露ト接壤スル者正ニ其幾萬里アルヲ知ラズ只黑龍江ノ下流ニ沿フ者ノミニシテ已ニ七百有餘里云々ヨリ外人ノ講スル公法ハ恃ムベカラズ彼ハ利ヲ見テ義ヲ忘レ競テ人ノ物ヲ取ル云々(但シ此段ハ原語過激ニ付稍

斟酌シテ譯讀セリ)ニ至テハ李氏眉ヲ揚ゲ氣ヲ吐テ眞ニ快論ナリト賛賞セリ偖大略讀了リテ後

徐公使ノ報告ト詳粗如何

彼 徐氏ノ報告ハ未ダ此一事ヲ得ル能ハズ渠ノ報告ハ啻ニ粗ナルノミナラズ或ハ自家ノ意ヲ交ヘタル如キ所モアリ渠ハ外務ニ熟練セザルヲ以テ貴外務卿ノ論旨ヲ悉ク了解スル能ハザルベシ困リタル人物ナリ

此 若クハ本使ノ讀過セシ趣意ト徐公使ノ報告ト齟齬セル所アルカ

彼 否大意ハ同ジト雖ドモ貴使ノ讀レシ如ク剴切ナラズ徐氏ハ好外交官ニアラズ(李氏失意ノ色アリ)

此 報告ノ簡短ナルヲ以テ徐公使ヲ咎ムル事ナカレ入組タル論旨ヲ漏レナク報告スルハ筆者側ニ在ルニアラザレバ頗ル六ケ敷事ナリ只大要ヲ失ハザレバ可ナリ本使ヲ以テ之ヲ見レバ徐氏ハ粗ボ英語ヲモ解シ人ト爲リモ活潑ニシテ前公使黎氏ヨリ勝レリ本邦ノ氣受ケモ前公使ニ比スレバ善シト聞ケリ

彼淵黙不答良久 只今讀過セラレシ貴外務卿ノ論旨ハ漢文ニ譯シテ恵送セラレン事ヲ乞フ

此 漢文ニ譯スルハ容易ナラズ且ツ譯送スベキ者ニアラズ

彼 貴外務卿ノ懇篤ナル論旨ヲ貴使ノ譯送スルヲ拒マルヽハ何ノ故カ貴使モシ漢譯ヲ難ンゼラルレバ羅豊禄ヲシテ漢譯セシメン

此 祕スベキ書類ナレバ本使ハ始ヨリ之ヲ讀マズ只此種ノ書付ハ目前ニテ讀過スルヲ以テ外交上ノ慣習トス中堂ハ本使ノ讀過セシヲ以テ卽ニ我外務卿ノ論旨ヲ悉皆了解セラレシニハアラズヤ然ルニ何故必ラズ漢譯ヲ得ント欲セラルヽヤ

彼 他意アルニアラズ忘却ニ備ル爲メノミ

此 備忘ノ爲メナレバ忘レザル中ニ書留メ置カルベシ本使ハ譯送スルヲ得ズ

(是ニ於テ李氏復タ再ビ强ヒズ)

偖今讀過セシ外務卿ノ論ノ如ク外國ノ要挟如彼ナルニ朝鮮ノ内政如此キヲ以テ貴我共同利益ノ爲メ坐視傍觀スルヲ得ズ故ニ我ガ外務卿ハ既ニ徐公使ニ面論セラレシ上ニモ猶ホ今次本使ニ下津シテ中堂ト面議スベキノ命ヲ以テセリ卽チ其條款ハ左ノ八ケ條タリ

是ヨリ本使ハ逐條英語ニ譯讀ス李氏淵黙シテ之ヲ聴キ畢リ

彼 御尤ノ立案ナリ只當方ヨリ勸告スル大臣ノ如キモ朝鮮國王必ラズ登用スルヤ否ヲ

慥ムル能ハザル事ヲ奈何セン去トテ當方ヨリ强ヒテ登用セシムルヲ得ズ只勸告ニ止ルノミ

此 如是要件ヲ只勸告ニ止ルノミト云ハルヽハ本使ノ解セザル所ナリ何ンゾ强テ之ニ從ハシメザル

彼 朝鮮ハ我ガ藩服ニシテ國王ハ予ト同等ノ地位タレドモ我政府ハ從來彼國ノ內政ニ干涉セザル政略ニ付必ラズ我言ニ服從セシムルヲ得ズ況ヤ前日伊藤大使トノ約ニ基キ我ガ駐韓ノ兵ハ程ナク悉皆撤回セザルヲ得ザルニ付國王ノ所爲ヲ監督スルニ甚ダ不便ナルヲ覺フ

此 貴國ハ朝鮮ノ內政ニ干涉セズト云フヲ得ルカ又貴國ハ自家ノ勸告ヲ韓廷ノ收捨ニ聽セ置クト云フヲ得ルカ此二者ハ本使ノ信ゼザル所ナリ

彼微笑不答 貴外務卿ノ立案ハ羅豊禄ヲ貴館ニ遣ハシメ漢譯セシメント欲ス如何

此 諾

是ヨリ晩餐ノ饗ニ與ル道台周馥等モ亦坐ニ在リ食事中雜話ノミニテ別ニ記スベキ程ノ事ナシ

當日ノ對話筆記末ニ李鴻章ノ所謂ル貴外務卿ノ立案トハ前顯榎本公使ヘノ訓令章內ニ一應記載アレドモ爾後聊カ修正ノ廉アリシニ由リ李氏ノ言ノ通リ羅豊禄ガ在天津我領事館ニ來リテ漢譯セシモノヽ文句ヲ其儘ニ直譯シテ參考ニ供スル如左

朝鮮外務ノ辦法ハ日本中國ノ利權ト大イニ關繫アリ如シ其ノ自力ヲ爲スニ任セバ必ラズ外交ノ枝節ガ橫生シテ中日ノ利權ハ重ネテ其累ヲ受ルニ至ラン井上伯爵因テ辦法ヲ擬スル如左

一李中堂ハ井上伯爵ト密ニ朝鮮外務主意ノ辦法ヲ議ス既ニ定マルノ後ニ李中堂ヨリ朝鮮ニ飭令シテ照辦シ務メテ其ヲシテ辦到セシム

二朝鮮國王ハ內監ト國政ヲ商議スルヲ得ズ應サニ內監ガ國政ニ與聞スルノ權ヲ將テ除去スベシ一切ノ國事ハ均シク內監ノ干預スルヲ准サズ國王ハ當サニ其ノ例ニ照シテ委任スルノ大臣ト商議スベシ

三朝鮮ノ大臣中ニハ必ラズ其ノ最モ忠藎タル者ヲ擇ビ託スルニ國政ヲ以テス國王如シ重臣ヲ擢用スル有ラバ如何ヲ論スルナク必ラズ先ツ李中堂ト相ヒ商リ中堂ハ再タビ井上伯爵ト斟酌ス金宏集金允植魚允中ノ諸人ハ皆ナ託スルニ國事ヲ以テスベキ者ナリ

四國事ノ最要ナルモノ外部兵部戶部ノ事務ノ如キハ均シク應サニ以上ニ擧ル所ノ

忠藎ナル重臣ニ委託シテ辦理セシムベシ

五應サニ米國ノ才アル者一人ヲ擇ビ朝鮮政府ヲシテ委用シ以テモルレンドルフ氏ニ代ラシムベシ

六中國ヨリ漢城ニ駐箚スルノ坐シテ國政ヲ探ル大員ハ急ニ宜シク才幹ノ較ヤ現在ニ駐箚スルノ員ヨリ長ズル者ヲ遴派スベシ

七中國委派ノ坐シテ國政ヲ探ル大員ハモルレンドルフ氏ニ替代スル米國人ヲ朝鮮ニ薦與シ必ラズ中堂ヨリ詳細ナル訓條ヲ奉有シ日後ニ辦事ノ主意ヲ暁ラシム其ノ朝鮮ニ赴ムク時ハ其ヲシテ順途ニ日本ヲ過キ往テ井上伯爵ヲ見セシムベシ

八中國ノ坐シテ國政ヲ探ルノ大員ハ必ラズ日本ノ代理公使ト情誼ヲ敦篤ニシ要事アルニ遇ヘバ互ニ相ヒ商酌シテ辦理スベシ

三日ノ對話ニ引續キ尚一回ノ對話ニテ李氏ハ我外務卿ノ對韓政略ヲ大イニ賛成シ甚ダ満足ノ段ヲ口演セシニ由リ榎本公使ハ七日附ヲ以テ電報ヲマタ八日附ヲ以テ書信ヲ外務卿ニ差立テヽ報告以後將サニ北京ニ歸任セントシテ其翌九日李氏ヲ總督衙門ニ訪ヒ本官歸京後ニ朝鮮ノ交渉事務一切ニ關スル者ハ新任ノ領事波多野氏ヘ掛合呉候様依頼シ尚又念ノ爲メ對韓ノ八ケ條ハ悉皆同意ナル事前夜面述ノ通リニ相違有之間敷ト相糺シタルニ李氏云ク八ケ條ノ大要ハ異議ナシト雖モ同意難致條款モ有之譬ヘバ第三ケ條中ノ末文ニ大臣ノ忠藎ナル者ヲ擇ブニ井上伯爵ト斟酌スベシト有之是ハ東京天津懸隔ノ地ナルヲ以テ實際上施行難致ノミナラズ予ヨリ韓王ヘ勸告スル良臣ヲ必ラズ採用スベシト强制スルヲ得ズ是レ我邦是迄屬國ノ内政ニ干渉セザル習慣ニ反スレバナリト其言甚ダ漠然ニシテ而カモ一兩日前ニ同意ヲ表セシ口舌未ダ乾カザルニ斯ル不都合ノ申分ハ甚以テ其意ヲ得ズトテ榎本公使云ク東京天津土地相隔ルヲ以テ我外務卿ト商議スルヲ得ズトハ餘リ受取難キ論理ナリ寧ロ直言シテ不同意ノ本意ヲ吐露セラレヨトノ問詰ニ對シ李氏曰ク譬ヘバ予ガ忠藎ノ人ナルベシト認テ韓王勸告スル重臣ヲ貴外務卿ニ於テ不同意ノ節ハ其人ヲ勸告スルヲ得ザルベシ右同様ニテ井上君ノ忠藎ト認メラルヽ人モ予ニ於テ必ラズ同見ナリト妄定スル能ハズ是レ此末文ノ實際上ニ施行難致所以ナリ加之我ノ韓王ニ於ル宗國ノ權アルヲ以テ賢才ヲ擧ケ小人ヲ遠ケヨト勸告スルヲ得ベシト雖モ貴國ハ韓ヲ獨立對等國ト認メラルヽヲ以テ固ヨリ其内政ニ干渉セラルベキ謂レナシ然ルニ予ハ韓王ニ賢才ヲ勸ムル毎ニ必ラズ貴國外務卿ト商議ヲ經タル後ニアラザレバ其言行ハレ難キ時ハ恰モ予ハ井上君ノ指揮ヲ奉ズル地位ニ陥入ルニ似タリトノ言ニ對シ公使云ク夫ハ以ノ外ノ誤解ナリ

過日モ緩々ト我外務卿ノ底意ヲ縷述シテ中堂モ既ニ同意セラレシニアラズヤ抑モ朝鮮國内治外交ノ近況ハ言フニ忍ブベカラザル者アリ是レ畢竟政府其人ヲ得ザルニ坐セリ而シテ其影響ハ直ニ貴國ト我國トノ利益ニ關スルヲ以テ其勢默視傍觀スルヲ得ザル場合ニ立至レリ故ニ我外務卿ハ中堂ト相謀リ其弊ヲ矯メテ以テ朝鮮ノ危難ヲ救ント欲シ而シテ且ツ中堂ヨリ韓王ニ勸告スル事ト爲セシハ貴國ト朝鮮ト從來特殊ノ關繋ナルヲ以テセシナリ然ルヲ中堂ニハ此條ヲ以テ暗ニ貴國ノ權利ニ撞觸スル所アルガ如ク看做サルヽハ畢竟我政府ノ厚意ヲ了解セラレズシテ猜疑ノ念アルニ坐セリト迄ニ反覆辯論シタルニ李氏ハ依然前説ヲ固執シ何分ニモ三ケ條ノ末文ハ實施難致ト申張タルニ付公使ハ公使ノ獨見ヲ以テ此條ガ不同意ニ於テハ八ケ條ノ精神ハ烏有ニ均シ實ニ惜ムベキ事ナガラ是非ナク中堂ノ異見ヲ直ニ外務卿ヘ電知スルノ外ナシト明言シテ其夜ハ別ヲ告ケ歸館明治十八年在清公使館機密第二十二號信其翌々十一日附ヲ以テ李氏ハ我立案ノ第三條ニ不同意ノ次第ヲ外務卿ニ電報セシトコロ外務卿ハ七月十五日附機密第三十一號信末ニ貴官下津今日迄ノ談判ヲ取消シ北京ヘ歸還可致旨返電セリトアリタル通リナリシモ尚ホ他ニ要事アリシガ爲メ公使ノ天津出立ハ十九日迄延引其翌二十日出發北京ニ歸任

54

Plunkett·井上馨 회담

F. Plunkett (1885. 7. 3) ➡ The Marquis of Salisbury (1885. 8. 7)

No. 139.

Mr. Plunkett to the Marquis of Salisbury.—(Received August 7.)

Tôkiô, July 3, 1885.

(No. 176. Very Confidential.)

My Lord,

THE two last conversations I have had with Count Inouyé show me that he continues to fear the early annexation by Russia of some portion or other of Corean territory, and that he is most anxious to prevent what he considers would be a catastrophe for Japan and also for China.

The imminence of the common danger from Russia has, as I have already reported in previous despatches, drawn Japan and China closer together. Since the mission of Count Ito to Tien-tsin the Japanese statesmen and Li Hung-chang have come into closer intercourse than formerly, and, as far as I can gather here, the relations between them seem now of a friendly and intimate character.

I received on the 28th ultimo from Her Majesty's Chargé d'Affaires at Peking a telegram, stating that M. von Möllendorff had been dismissed from the Corean service, and Count Inouyé has also received a somewhat similar telegram from the Japanese Consul at Tien-tsin.

This news has given his Excellency profound satisfaction, for he considers M. von Möllendorff to be a bitter enemy to Japan, and to have been gained over entirely to the Russian cause.

His Excellency told me that he had already been in communication with Li Hung-chang in regard to the choice of a successor to M. von Möllendorff, and had suggested the selection of an American as being the least likely to offend the various international susceptibilities which have to be considered in connection with Corea.

Count Inouyé having pressed me for my opinion, 1 said that it was for Her Majesty's Representative at Peking to decide what was best for British interests in Corea; I did not deny, however, that the United States might be a good source whence to draw M. von Möllendorff's successor.

Both to me and to others Count Inouyé has mentioned his fear that the example set by Great Britain in Port Hamilton may be followed by Russia, Germany, or some other Power in regard to one or other of the outlying islands of Japan, as, for instance, the Tshushima, Goto, Bonin, or Meacosima groups, and his Excellency has stated that any attempt by any Power on any of them will be resisted by arms. Steps have been lately taken to place police and soldiers in these places, so as to prove that they form part of the Japanese Empire, and thus to deprive foreign Powers of the excuse of these islands not being defended by the nation to which they belong.

Count Inouyé has stated to me on more than one occasion that no monetary compensation from Russia or any other Power would induce Japan to surrender any of her outlying islands; on the contrary, he has told me in confidence that she is determined to fight if any attempt should be made upon them, no matter by whom this attempt should be made.

I have, &c.

(Signed) F. R. PLUNKETT.

55
거문도 점령에 대한 일본의 반대

N. R. O'Conor (1885. 7. 5) ➡ The Marquis of Salisbury (1885. 9. 7)

No. 172.

Mr. O'Conor to the Marquis of Salisbury.—(Received September 7.)

Peking, July 5, 1885.

(No. 339. Confidential.)

My Lord,

IN previous despatches I have ventured to state that I had good reason to believe that the Japanese Minister in Peking, Admiral Enomotto, was very active in his opposition to the occupation of Port Hamilton by Her Majesty's fleet, and that from the personal character of this Minister it did not seem likely that he would take so strong a line without instructions from his Government. I have lately again learned that the Viceroy Li Hung-chang has repeated his statement that the Japanese Government have been urgent in their request for China to join with them in protesting against the British occupation, and that he says that Admiral Enomotto, who is now in Tien-tsin, is still much disturbed at our occupation.

The Japanese Minister had, the Viceroy further stated, suggested to him that Corea should be advised to apply to the Powers who had Treaties with her to summon an International Conference on the subject.

The Viceroy, in reply, had represented the inutility of such a step. Of the Powers having Treaties with Corea, Russia, from the nature of the case, could not be heard. The United States would not interfere. Germany had been so active in appropriating territory of late that she would find it difficult to raise her voice, and Japan's remonstrances would be of little avail. Thereupon Admiral Enomotto admitted that he was convinced.

I have sent a copy of this despatch to Her Majesty's Minister at Tôkiô.

I have, &c.

(Signed) N. R. O'CONOR.

56
거문도 점령 관련 영국 정부와의 협의

曾紀澤 ➡ 總署 (1885. 7. 7 / 光緖十一年五月二十五日)

五月二十五日 出使大臣曾紀澤文稱 竊照英國佔據朝鮮濟洲東北之安島一事 二月二十三日 承准貴衙門夾養電示 英據濟洲究是何意 能否詰問布酌等因 當卽遵電前往外部面詢侍郞克雷 該侍郞諉稱 水師官現無確信 迨本爵大臣再三詰問 於三月初二日接准該外部伯爵尙書葛蘭斐爾 西歷四月十六日密咨 始將佔據韓墨爾登海口之事確實告知 並於文尾聲明 英廷作事 不欲有損中國聲望 甚願與中國相商立約 以保中國之權利等語 比於二月二十九三月初二等日 兩次電陳在案 査韓墨爾登海口 以中口守之地口對其部位 似是安島 本爵大臣無由確知彼處情形 刻下與英國外部談論 卽以韓墨爾登立言 合將英外部密咨一件 譯漢咨呈貴衙門 謹請督核

照錄抄單

英外部來文 密咨謹致大淸欽差大臣 本月初八日 承詢英國佔据韓墨爾登海口是否確實 當貴爵大臣探詢此事之時 英廷尙不能將此事之確音告知貴爵大臣 惟其時英廷思現在之時勢 必須諭令水師提督看景而行 暫据此島 若照平常情形 英廷本欲先時此事告知中國 緣見別國有佔据此島之意 英廷不得不急於下手 英廷並不欲行有損中國聲望之事 是以甚願與中國相商立約 不致於該段等處或有損於中國之權利也 爲此照覆貴爵大臣 請項查照

57
거문도 점령 관련 청 정부와의 협의

N. R. O'Conor (1885. 7. 8) ➡ The Marquis of Salisbury (1885. 9. 7)

No. 175.

Mr. O'Conor to the Marquis of Salisbury.—(Received September 7.)

Peking, July 8, 1885.

(No. 349. Confidential.)

My Lord,

I HAVE the honour to acknowledge the receipt of your Lordship's telegram No. 38 of yesterday's date, in answer to my telegram No. 52 of the 2nd instant.

In my despatch No. 331 of the 1st instant, I reported to your Lordship, after an interview with the Prince and Ministers of the Yamên, that the Chinese Government had very strong objections to entering into any formal agreement with a view to recognize the occupation of Port Hamilton, unless Her Majesty's Government consented to join with China in a guarantee of the integrity of Corea, and I beg to say that it was to this point that I referred in my telegram when alluding to the objectionable pledges respecting Corea's integrity.

It seemed to me that pledges of this onerous and responsible kind would not be agreeable to Her Majesty's Government, and I continue to direct my efforts to trying to induce the Chinese Government to agree to an arrangement free from such obligations. For this purpose I made use of the information conveyed in Lord Granville's despatch No. 85 A respecting the proposed draft Treaty between the Marquis Tsêng and his Lordship, and represented that after what had passed on this occasion the Chinese Government could not well refuse without seeming unfriendly to come to an arrangement in respect to Port Hamilton. The tone of the Ministers was decidedly apologetic, but they repeated that any such action would place them in a very difficult position vis-a-vis to Russia, and that under present circumstances they were obliged to look after their own interests before any other.

They would be very willing to oblige Her Majesty's Government, but in view of the fact that if they gave their consent to our occupation, Russia would immediately claim some other portion of Corean territory, it behoved them to be very cautious in what they did. We were in occupation of Port Hamilton and it was all right. But they could not appear to sanction openly what they had assured me privately they did not object to.

In my above-mentioned despatch of the 1st instant, I have alluded at some length to the concluding paragraph of my telegram No. 52, so that I need not trouble your Lordship with further remarks for the present.

I have, &c.

(Signed) N. R. O'CONOR.

58
거문도 개항에 대한 부정적 입장 전달

李鴻章 (1885. 7. 8 / 光緒十一年五月二十六日) ➡ 總署

覆總署 論朝鮮國政

光緒十一年五月二十六日

密覆者 昨奉五月十八日直字八百八十四號公函 以徐孫麒函述日本外務井上馨密議朝鮮近事 欲請中國爲之主持 罷斥奸黨 引用正人 詢及如何維持補救 答覆井上等因 仰見保衛屬藩 綢繆未雨 欽佩莫名 先是四月杪 日本駐津領事原敬來告 接井上電 云有朝鮮要事已告知徐公使轉達 并令駐京使榎本接信後來津會商 嗣得孫麒四月二十九日來書 附寄節略三件 與致鈞署語意相同 五月二十日榎本到津 往復籌商 譯出井上與徐使談論節略 與孫麒所錄情節小異 內有英據巨文島 俄允保護朝鮮各事 榎本謂措語傷時 不便鈔送 但將井上另擬朝鮮辦法八條面遞存覽 謹照鈔原文呈核 二十四日榎本復詢如何主意 鴻章告以此事 關係重大 井上持論甚正 第中國於屬邦用人行政向不與聞 日本系朝鮮與國 亦不應攙預朝鮮外交內政 若欲中國變通舊制代爲主持一切 借保中 日藩籬 用意非不甚善 兩國無不同心 必須密商總署 酌寄可否 請旨辦理云云 榎本謂先將此語電告井上 俟其電覆 或令在津候信 或回京靜候鴻章答復等語 竊查井上八條 如朝鮮國王不得與內監商議國政 擇大臣忠藎者如金宏集 金允植 魚允中等皆可托以國事 中國駐朝大員遇有要事與日本駐使互商酌辦各節 尚中肯綮 惟諸要政均請由鴻章遥制 旣懼無此權力 若朝王不能遵辦 亦斷難使其事事辦到 況朝鮮外務如與井上密議 相距皆遠 何從面籌辦法 至用人旣由中國商定 又與井上斟酌 未免越界攬權 事多窒礙 顧其立意 似欲護持朝鮮勿被俄人呑幷 洵與中 日兩國大局有裨 鴻章暫未峻拒 俾之別生趨向 究應如何酌量答覆之處 敬祈察商詳密 賜示爲幸 榎本若久駐津候信 或婉勸其先行回京 孫麒處似可暫置不覆 以待謀定後動也 至駐朝道員陳樹棠謹厚有餘 才智不足 自是確論 前派陳道專爲照料通商起見 幷未令其與聞國政 朝爲屬藩 若派大員 朝王旣嫌相逼 體制亦難妥洽 且各國公使均駐漢城 久之更滋口舌 應俟現議酌定後 徐籌更替 鈞意有無通達外務 政體可靠者 幷求示悉 昨朝王內戚閔泳翊來津面謁 謂朝京事勢不成體段 請由中朝擇本邦藎臣有民望者 俾付之以政府之事

與井上所論差同 可否請旨略予變通 密飭朝王 以後與各外國議約必先請示 其擢用外務及兵 戶各置大臣 須先申報核准 然後施行 庶借皇威震慴 得以隨時操縱 使就范圍幷希卓裁 至英踞朝之巨文島 孤懸海中 無商可通 誠如尊論 卽使許作通商口岸 各國未必願往 英已布置水雷 炮台 亦無他國能往 榎本謂伊外務照復英使 不准久踞 英置弗答 固無如何 朝鮮密約俄人保護一節 陳樹棠前報已咨冰案 鴻章批令設法挽回 昨又由便船密電陳道云 英接電 朝已革穆麟德 甚合公論 朝 俄若眞有密約 朝旣未派全權 又未批准 按公法可作廢紙 革穆更有詞 勿怖 俄若索島地 堅勿許 望密告政府轉達朝王云云 盖英領事及榎本均接朝電 謂俄派參贊赴朝 要求遣弁敎練朝兵 朝王弗許俄使謂與穆麟德有成約 朝王因革穆 俄使仍索一大島等語 俄勢日逼 鴻章不得不陰助之 以我敵謀而堅朝志 質之高明 當亦謂然 第俄爲東方患 較法尤甚 竊謂奉之邊門鴨綠江 吉之琿春 必豫籌勁旅移駐 以觀動靜而備不虞 朝 俄陸路僅圖們江數十里可通未必不懼我軍之橫截而拊其背 幸早留意 毋致後時 專肅密覆 祗叩中堂 王爺 大人鈞祺 李鴻章謹啓 直字四百四十號 附抄折

59
조선에 대한 청의 종주권 활용 방안

The Marquis of Salisbury (1885. 7. 10) ➡ N. R. O'Conor

No. 85.

The Marquis of Salisbury to Mr. O'Conor.

Foreign Office, July 10, 1885.

(No. 170. Ext. 39.)

Sir,

INFORMATION has reached Her Majesty's Government that the German Consul in Corea has reported to his Government, by telegraph, that the Government of Corea are engaged in the preparation of a protest to the Powers against the occupation of Port Hamilton by this country.

I have to instruct you to spare no effort both at Peking and through the Acting Consul-General at Söul to prevent the protest in question from being sent, it might be suggested to the Tsung-li Yamên that a protest such as this, made without the concurrcnce of China, ignores her suzerainty; and that it would, moreover, be an unfriendly act on the part of the Chinese Government, after the communications which took place between Earl Granville and the Chinese Minister here, if the Chinese Government did not exert their authority to put a stop to a proceeding which would be embarrassing to this country. Her Majesty's Government arc prepared to make a full acknowledgment of the suzerainty of China over Corea and its dependencies, and to come to an arrangement, through the Tsung-li Yamên, for an annual payment to Corea so long as the British occupation of Port Hamilton may last.

I have this day sent you the substance of the foregoing by telegraph.

I have, &c.

(Signed) SALISBURY.

60
영국의 거문도 점령 관련 조선의 동향 보고

Patenôtre (1885. 7. 10) ➡ Ferry

No. 3.

Mr. Patenôtre
Ministre de France à Pékin

10 juillet 1885.

Dans la dépêche dont vous trouverez ci-joint copie, notre ministre au Japon me transmet les indications qu'il a recueillies tranchant la prise de possession, par le marin britannique, des trois îles formant le territoire de Port Hamilton, au Sud de la Corée.

[__] fait remarquer que l'Angleterre ayant été l'une des premières Puissances qui ont reconnu l'indépendance de la Corée, il semblerait qu'elle eût aviser la Cour de Séoul de cette occupation. Le gouvernement coréen paraît n'avoir reçu, à ce propos, aucune communication du Cabinet de Londres. Les difficultés qui se voicnt levées à plusieurs reprises entre la Chine et le Japon au sujet de la Corée auront certainement mis en éveil le Cabinet de Pékin sur l'intervention de l'Angleterre qui, à certain moment, a été démentie par des informations de forcer de [__].

Aussi transmets-je avec intérêt des [__]moments que vous aurez été [__] en mesure de me transmettre de votre geste au sujet de [__] le Port Hamilton, en me rendant compte de l'impression qu'il aura produite [__]de vous.

Recevez att.
Le ministre

61
井上馨 · Plunkett 회담(1)

F. Plunkett (1885. 7. 14) ➡ The Marquis of Salisbury (1885. 7. 14)

No. 99.

Mr. Plunkett to the Marquis of Salisbury.—(Received July 14, 10·30 A. M.)

Tôkiô, July 14, 1885, 10·17 A. M.

(No. 23. Confidential.)
(Telegraphic.)
REFERENCE to your telegram No. 10.

Foreign Minister asserts that he never authorized action against England, either in China or Corea. He invokes frequent information given to me about Russians in proof of good-will towards England. He only seeks to prevent our occupation serving as a precedent elsewhere. Enomotto (*sic*) went to Tien-tsin to urge Viceroy to prevent Russian military teachers, and to ask him to exercise henceforth stricter control over Corea. King of Corea's protest appears to have collapsed. Foreign Minister had already telegraphed to Japanese Chargé d'Affaires to return Corean note. He read me a telegram stating that Russian Secretary had failed and probably returns here soon. He said Japan very much afraid of Russia, and fears she may seize Tsushima if any excuse offers.

62
井上馨 · Plunkett 회담(2)

F. Plunkett (1885. 7. 14) ➡ The Marquis of Salisbury (1885. 8. 25)

No. 162.

Mr. Plunkett to the Marquis of Salisbury.—(Received August 25.)

Tôkiô, July 14, 1885.

(No. 182, Very Confidential.)

My Lord,

I HAD the honour to receive on the afternoon of the 11th instant your Lordship's telegram No. 10, informing me that the German Consul in Corea had telegraphed to his Government that Corea was preparing a protest to the Powers against our occupation of Port Hamilton.

Your Lordship further added that Her Majesty's Government was desirous of stopping this protest, which they suspected was the result of a Japanese intrigue.

I also received the following day a telegram from Her Majesty's Chargé d'Affaires at Peking, warning me that Admiral Enomotto was in Tien-tsin, and was, under instructions from his Government, urging the Viceroy to join action against the British occupation of Port Hamilton, and that the representations made by the Japanese were increasing the difficulty of an arrangement.

I was not able to see Count Inouyé until yesterday morning, when I had with him a long and earnest conversation, the result of which, in order to prevent any mistake, I condensed into the short Memorandum, herewith inclosed, and which his Excellency, after careful perusal, at a second interview in the afternoon entirely confirmed.

I have accordingly just informed your Lordship, by telegraph, that Count Inouyé assures me that he never authorized action against England either in China or Corea, and invokes the frequent occasions on which he has given me private information about Russian movements in proof of his good-will towards England. His Excellency's only object is to prevent as far as possible our temporary occupation of Port Hamilton serving as a pretext elsewhere. He had sent Admiral Enomotto to Tien-tsin to urge the Viceroy to exercise in future a more strict and direct control over the King of Corea, and to take steps immediately to prevent him from accepting Russian officers as military instructors to the Corean forces.

I also informed your Lordship, by telegraph, that the Corean protest to which your Lordship's telegram alluded appeared to have collapsed, and that Count Inouyé had already instructed the Japanese Chargé d'Affaires at Söul to return the note of the 27th June, in which the Corean Government had asked for the good offices of the foreign Powers.

I also informed your Lordship that Count Inouyé had read me a telegram from Söul stating that the mission of M. de Speyer had failed, and that he would probably return to Tôkiô shortly.

I further informed your Lordship that Count Inouyé had stated that Japan continued to be much afraid of Russia, and had reason to fear that, if an excuse presented itself, Russia would try to seize the Island of Tsushima.

In case your Lordship should not have already received a copy of the document from Mr. Aston, I inclose herewith a translation made by Mr. Hall of the Corean note above referred to, and which, according to a telegram from the Japanese Chargé d'Affaires, had already been returned by the American Minister; but the German Consul had so far declined to return it.

I have the honour to inclose herewith copy of the telegram which I have just sent to Her Majesty's Chargé d'Affaires in Peking on this subject, and I trust that the instructions which have been sent to Admiral Enomotto by the Japanese Foreign Minister will cause him in future to be more prudent and discreet than I fear has sometimes been the case.

Nothing could be more emphatic and categorical than the denials which Count Inouyé gave to my insinuations that fear of Russia might have made Japan work against us. He admitted, to the fullest extent, how terribly afraid Japan is of Russia, and how uncertain she feels of any support elsewhere if she were to offend Russia, but he gave me his word of honour that he had never authorized any action, either in China or in Corea, against us, nor had he suggested the Corean protest which, before I had spoken to him, he had already instructed the Japanese Chargé d'Affaires to return.

I impressed on Count Inouyé that it was not sufficient for him to entertain towards England a platonic good-will. I did not ask him to join England, I had no authority to encourage him to run risks from Russia; but I had a right to insist that he should prevent his Agents in China and Corea from using language which seemed to have been interpreted not only by English, but also by foreign Agents, as exciting China and Corea against our occupation. I said that the quieter Japan remained the better for her interests. The last telegrams from Europe seemed to show that England and Russia might come to an understanding. Japan must take care not to find herself in the position of having offended both her big neighbours, and thus be left in the lurch by both.

His Excellency said that his position was a most trying one. He could not please either of us, and yet what he wanted was to be entirely neutral. Here was the British Minister coming to-day to accuse him of working against England. Three days ago the Russian Minister had called on him to cease favouring England, which, he said, Japan was unfairly doing by allowing the British naval authorities at Port Hamilton to draw stores, labourers, &c., from Nagasaki. He, Count Inouyé said he had argued in vain with the Russian Minister that Japan had no right, in time of peace, to prevent such trade. The Russian Minister would not admit the excuse, and went away asserting that Japan was favouring our occupation.

I told Count Inouyé that I quite sympathized with the difficulty of his position, and was quite sure your Lordship would do so likewise, but that I must again ask him to warn his Agents to be more prudent in their language. I said the valuable nature of the information he had frequently given me privately about Russian movements convinced me of his personal good-will towards England, and I therefore asked him to give me further proof of it by preventing a revival of the protest of Corea against our temporary occupation of Port Hamilton. His Excellency said the position for him was one of the most extreme delicacy, but he would do what he could to meet my wishes, and, at all events, he would not countenance any action by Japanese Agents against us.

I thanked his Excellency very warmly for this assurance, which, I said, I felt sure your Lordship would much appreciate.

I have, &c.
(Signed) F. R. PLUNKETT.

Inclosure 1 in No. 162.

Memorandum shown to Count Inouyé and approved by him.

(Confidential.)

FOREIGN Minister asserts that Enomotto was not authorized to press Viceroy to join action against English occupation. He was sent to Tien-tsin to urge Viceroy to prevent Russian instructors, and to ask him to exercise henceforth stricter control over Corean King.

Foreign Minister denies authorizing action against England either in China or Corea. He only seeks to prevent our occupation serving as precedent elsewhere. He invokes frequent information given about Russians as proof of his good-will towards England.

I have urged on Foreign Minister prudence and avoidance of interference which may easily be misconstrued; he has telegraphed to Enomotto in this sense. Proposed Corean protest seems to have come to nothing; he has already instructed Japanese Chargé d'Affaires to return Corean letter asking for good offices. Foreign Minister has shown me telegram stating that Russian Secretary has failed, and probably returns here soon.

Tôkiô, July 13, 1885.

Inclosure 2 in No. 162.

Corean Note.

June 27, 1885.

(Translation.)

KIM, Corean Minister for Foreign Intercourse and Commerce, makes a communication: —

With reference to the occupation by the British naval forces, on the 31st of the 3rd month, of the Island of Kiyobun (Port Hamilton), my Government dispatched Gen, Councillor of State, and Mo (Möllendorff) Vice-President of this Department, with instructions to proceed to that island, and take observations of the state of affairs there. They did so, and actually found the British ships of war at anchor there, and flags flying on' the islands, whereat they were greatly astonished. Thence they proceeded to Nagasaki, where they saw the British Admiral, and they inquired of him the grounds of such a proceeding, and formulated their queries in writing. In the reply which the Admiral sent to them it is stated: —

"I have communicated by telegraph with my Government, and am awaiting their reply, which, on receipt, I shall lose no time in imparting to you."

The two above-named emissaries have returned for some time, yet the answer is not received. In the first week of the present month, however, the British Consul-General, Aston, came to this Office and had an interview, when he stated that a communication from his Government had been received by the British Minister at Peking, who had transmitted it to him (Aston), and was to the effect that the occupation of Kiyobun Island was for a while only, and was not intended to be permanent, the object being merely to locate on the coast some sheds for the storage of coal, but that, beyond that, there was no other design whatsoever.

On examination, I find that the VIIIth Article of the Treaty with England provides that depots for stores, ammunition, &c., for the use of the British navy may be erected at the open ports, and be kept under the supervision of a British official. Coal is, no doubt, included under the designation of naval stores, but it is not to be stored elsewhere than at the open ports. In the event of hostilities between foreign States, this country will maintain neutrality, and cannot lend to them its terrors. Even a temporary occupation, therefore, finds no justification in international law, and positively cannot be given effect to.

I have thus minutely set forth the circumstances in the hope that your Excellency (the Chargé d'Affaires) will give them your careful attention, and communicate them to your Government for its mature consideration, and that they will view them in the light of the claims of good neighhourhood and of long-standing friendship, and that they will quietly intermediate in the matter.

The above is the purport of the communication which] respectfully make.

To Jakahira,

Japanese Chargé d'Affaires.

Inclosure 3 in No. 162.

Mr. Plunkett to Mr. O'Conor.

Tôkiô, July 14, 1885.

(Confidential.)

(Telegraphic.)

FOREIGN Minister denies that Japanese Minister was authorized to press Viceroy to join action against English occupation. He went to Tien-tsin to urge Viceroy to stop Russian military teachers, and also to exercise in future more direct control over Corean King. Foreign Minister telegraphed yesterday to Japanese Minister to abstain from interference against occupation.

Japanese Chargé d'Affaires in Corea had been already instructed to return Corean letter of 27th, asking for good offices of the Powers. Japan hears that Russian Secretary has failed, and probably returns here. Japan much afraid of Russia.

63
거문도 점령 및 러시아에 대한 청의 입장

N. R. O'Conor (1885. 7. 15) ➡ The Marquis of Salisbury (1885. 9. 7)

No. 178.

Mr. O'Conor to the Marquis of Salisbury.—(Received September 7.)

Peking, July 15, 1885.

(No. 352. Confidential.)

My Lord,

I HAVE the honour to acknowledge and to return my best thanks to your Lordship for your telegrams Nos. 39 and 40 of the 10th and 13th instant.

In reply to your Lordship's telegram No. 39, I lost no time in informing your Lordship that the note addressed by the President of the Corean Foreign Office to the foreign Representatives at Söul, asking for their good offices in respect to the British occupation of Port Hamilton, in accordance with Article I of the British Treaty, had been withdrawn at the instance of Her Majesty's Consul-General.

Since Mr. Aston's return to Söul I have frequently urged upon him the necessity of doing all he could to prevent any fresh protest on the part of the Corean Government, and I have no doubt that he did everything that was possible under the circumstances. I am not as yet in possession of his full report of the interview he had with the President of the Corean Foreign Office, but from the sudden and unexpected manner in which the note was sent out, it would appear as if it was sprung upon him suddenly, so as to enable the Corean Government to say to Russia that they had not allowed the occupation of Port Hamilton to pass without appeal to the foreign Powers.

As your Lordship is aware from previous despatches, I have exerted what efforts I could to influence the Corean Government, and to prevent any further action in the way of protest or written remonstrance. I had been assured of the support of the Viceroy, Li Hung-chang, and had obtained a promise from the Chinese Government that they would not advise Corea to take any action in opposition to England, and that, if appealed to, they would repeat the assurances which they had themselves received from Her Majesty's Government.

There is no doubt, however, that fear of Russia is the one great objection on the part of both China and Corea in agreeing to any formal recognition of our occupation, and that the publication of a secret agreement between Russia and M. von Möllendorff has for the moment made any arrangement with Corea almost impossible, though it would offer a plausible reason for not abandoning Port Hamilton, should Her Majesty's Government wish to retain possession. China as well as Corea believes Russia as a "limitrophe" Power is a serious menace to Corean integrity, and only waits a fair pretext to seize upon a part of her territory. Corea is helpless, and only has force by appealing to right and to the Suzerain Power. But China feels that it is a serious matter for her, and though she values the friendship of England, and would do more to oblige us than any other Power, she asks, What will England do to protect Corea from the consequences of acquiescence in our occupation. What material guarantee will we give that Corean territory shall not be seized by Russia. "We are alone, and Russia is powerful. The brunt of the trouble that would follow would fall upon us. Therefore, if we are to do as you want, you must be prepared to lake some of the burden off our shoulders or bear it equally. In that case we shall be only too happy to consent to your occupation of Port Hamilton, but, short of this, you offer us really nothing, for which we can endanger our own position and run the risk of a quarrel with Russia on our hands, while England arranges the Afghanistan question at her pleasure."

In the interviews I have had with the Ministers of the Yamên in this matter 1 have at various times urged upon them the considerations set forth in your Lordship's telegrams, and had no difficulty in extracting the admission that they preferred our occupation to that of Russia, and that they had no personal objection to our being at Port Hamilton, and would certainly not offer any serious remonstrances, as they knew that it did not betoken any unfriendly feeling to China. Your Lordship's late instructions have enabled me to let them see that Her Majesty's Government would be willing to undertake to respect the integrity of Corea, would agree not to use Port Hamilton as a base of operations against either China or Corea, and would recognize the suzerainty of China over Corea; but all this is not enough to counterbalance in their eyes the risk of being involved in difficulty with Russia.

Yesterday I saw the Ministers again, and told them that I had heard Corea had proposed addressing a note to the foreign Representatives appealing to the good offices of their Governments, and that such a proceeding would certainly be viewed by Her Majesty's Government as very unfriendly, and I represented that, after what had passed between Lord Granville and the Marquis Tsêng, the Chinese Government ought surely to interfere to prevent it, and I begged of the Government to use their influence with Corea to stop the note being again sent forward.

The Ministers said that the Chinese Government was, frankly speaking, in a very difficult position. They had strained their friendly feelings towards Her Majesty's Government so far as not to raise objections to an act which, committed by any other Power, would have called forth earnest remonstrance if not even more positive opposition. They had been questioned by Russia as to what action they had taken against our occupation, but, in deference to my request, they had refused to send in any note asking for explanations, and had thus left themselves without an answer to Russia. To interfere now directly with Corea, and endeavour to induce her not to remonstrate against our action, would leave them open to a charge of direct partiality and involve them in difficulties and embarrassments with that country which they were not anxious to bring about at present. They deprecated any further efforts just now to come to an arrangement about our occupation. We were there, and the best plan would be to allude to it as little as possible. If the Chinese Government were eventually forced to do so, it would be a mere formal note. They did not see, at the stage to which things had come, and in view of the report of a Treaty by which Russian officers were to be forced upon Corea, how they could urge her to consent formally to our occupation, and they thought that it would be more advisable not to press it upon her. I failed to extract a promise that they would prevent Corea acting as she thought fit, and though they let me see that they would not urge her to take any action hostile to us, they were, at the same time, opposed to further pressure for a formal and definite arrangement.

If Her Majesty's Government decide on holding Port Hamilton, a more favourable opportunity for an arrangement will not be long wanting, and I have no doubt that the pecuniary difficulties of the Corean Government will induce her, ere long, to accept terms, particularly if a yearly rent is commuted into a bulk sum.

I do not propose to broach the question of the possible evacuation of the island by Her Majesty's Government for the present. For the moment the Chinese Government has made up its mind that we are there and mean to remain, and that it is not in their interest to offer any opposition. It will besides be a card in reserve in case there appears no other way of stopping an appeal from Corea to foreign Powers such as would be embarrassing to Her Majesty's Government, and would force me to avail myself of your Lordship's suggestion to prevent it.

I send your Lordship, by telegraph, the substance of this despatch, as it embodies the present state of the question and the opinions of the Chinese Government, as gathered during an interview of some length yesterday afternoon.

I have, &c.

(Signed) N. R. O'CONOR.

64
李鴻章·榎本武揚 협의 경과

N. R. O'Conor (1885. 7. 15) ➡ The Marquis of Salisbury (1885. 9. 7)

No. 177.

Mr. O'Conor to the Marquis of Salisbury.—*(Received September 7.)*

Peking, July 15, 1885.

(No. 351. Confidential.)

My Lord,

IN continuation of my despatch No. 339 of the 5th instant, with reference to the active opposition displayed by Admiral Enomotto, the Japanese Minister in Peking, to the occupation of Port Hamilton by the British fleet, I now have the honour to inclose copy of a despatch from Mr. Brenan, Her Majesty's Consul, at Tien-tsin, reporting the substance of some remarks made to him by the Viceroy Li Hung-chang, in the course of an interview which Mr. Brenan had with his Excellency on the 10th instant.

The Viceroy stated that Admiral Enomotto had informed him that he had come to Tien-tsin under instructions from his Government to consult his Excellency as to the possibility of joint action on the part of China and Japan in the event of Russian encroachments in Corea, or the refusal of the British Government to evacuate Port Hamilton.

The Viceroy informed Admiral Enomotto, in reply, that while encroachment on the part of Russia would be forcibly resisted by China, it was not the intention of the Chinese Government to allow the British occupation of Port Hamilton to be the occasion of quarrel with the British Government. His Excellency added that if Corea refused to give her consent to the British occupation, the action of China would be limited to friendly representations on the subject to Her Majesty's

Government.

As Admiral Enomotto's action in Tien-tsin was calculated to do mischief, I thought it advisable to warn Mr. Plankett, in a telegram, of which I have the honour to inclose a copy, of the Japanese Ministers representations to the Grand Secretary Li, and I am happy to be able to report the receipt this day of a telegraphic reply from Mr. Plunkett, in which he informs me that Admiral Enomotto had no authority from his Government to make any proposals on the subject of Port Hamilton, and that he has been instructed to interfere no further in the mutter.

I have, &c.
(Signed) N. R. O'CONOR.

65
거문도 점령 및 러시아에 대한 청의 입장

N. R. O'Conor (1885. 7. 16) ➡ The Marquis of Salisbury (1885. 9. 21)

관련문서 전신보고내용

No. 182.

Mr. O'Conor to the Marquis of Salisbury.—(Received September 21.)

Peking, July 16, 1885.

(No. 354. Ext. 54.)

My Lord,

I HAD the honour to inform your Lordship by telegraph this day that the Chinese Government said that they could not formally recognize the British occupation of Port Hamilton unless Her Majesty's Government would be ready to join in a guarantee to protect Corea from any act of aggression on the part of Russia that might possibly follow. Under present circumstances, the interests of China were against any agreement of this kind, and equally opposed to advising Corea in favour of it, as it would be likely to give a pretext to Russia. At the same time, the Chinese Government renewed their friendly assurances towards Her Majesty's Government, and informed me confidentially that they entertained no objections to the occupation of Port Hamilton; and that, if obliged eventually to ask for any explanation, it would merely be in order to save themselves from any embarrassments with the Russian Government.

I added that the note of the Corean Government invoked the good offices of the Representatives of the Treaty Powers in accordance with Article I of the British Treaty, but that it had been withdrawn for the present, and would not be sent out again until the Corean Government wrote to me officially, and time had been allowed to receive my reply, and that I hoped it might be quashed altogether.

I observed, in conclusion, that it seemed to me that by hinting to the Chinese Government that Port Hamilton might be evacuated in favour of China under certain conditions, the withdrawal of the Corean note would almost certainly be secured, and that the proposal would be viewed as a very friendly act by the Chinese Government.

I have, &c.
(Signed) N. R. O'CONOR.

【관련문서】

No. 103.

Mr. O'Conor to the Marquis of Salisbury.—(Received July 16, 9:30 P. M.)

Peking, July 16, 1885, 6:25 P. M.

(No. 54. Telegraphic.)

UNLESS Her Majesty's Government will join in guarantee to protect Corea from possible Russian aggression, Chinese Government cannot formally recognize occupation Chinese interests forbid under present circumstances entering agreement or advising Corea as likely pretext to Russia. They renew friendly assurances; confidentially state no objection to occupation. If forced eventually to ask for explanations, it would be merely to save embarrassments with Russia. Corean note invoked Article I of British Treaty; delayed until they write officially and receive my reply; hope to quash it altogether. Your Lordship's contingent instruction evacuate in favour of China would certainly effect this and viewed friendly act.

66
조선 정부에 대한 청 정부의 압력 기대

N. R. O'Conor (1885. 7. 17) ➡ The Marquis of Salisbury (1885. 9. 21)

No. 184.

Mr. O'Conor to the Marquis of Salisbury.—*(Received September 21.)*

Peking, July 17, 1885.

(No. 356.)

My Lord,

I LEARN from Mr. Aston that he has forwarded direct to your Lordship a copy of his despatch No. 81 of the 10th instant, inclosing a copy of a letter which the President of the Corean Foreign Office has addressed to me, respecting the occupation of Port Hamilton, and for the answer to which he has agreed to delay the note he had lately addressed to the Representatives of the Treaty Powers at Söul, as mentioned in my despatch No. 346 of the 8th instant.

In answering the note of the Corean Government, I shall have to be guided in great measure by the extent to which the Chinese Government may be ready to go in order to prevent further action on the part of Corea. If they undertake, on condition of our not pressing the Corean Government at present for a formal recognition of our occupation, to prevent its revival, I propose merely acknowledging its receipt, and stating that, in accordance with the custom in communications of this sort, I have not ventured to give a reply without putting my Government in possession of the exact terms of the note of the Corean Government, and pointing out that, though considerable delay must necessarily intervene, still it will be more satisfactory for the Corean Government to receive an answer from London, and that in the meantime I trust they will not renew the question of a note to foreign Powers, as, by so doing, they would only make more difficult the satisfactory arrangement of the present question.

If, on the other hand, the Chinese Government decline to interfere, and to prevent such action as Corea thinks necessary in the matter, 1 shall make out as good a as I can for our occupation and endeavour to prove to Corea that there is nothing in it of which she need be afraid, and press for time to be allowed for the official reply of Her Majesty's Government.

In a subsequent despatch, I shall have the honour of forwarding to your Lordship a copy of the answer to the Corean Government.

I am encouraged, however, in hoping that I can to some valuable extent rely on the support and influence of the Chinese Government, as I learn from Tien-tsin this morning that, after my interview of the 14th instant with the Ministers, the Viceroy, Li Hung-chang, received orders from the Yamên to try to prevent the King of Corea from raising any farther objection to our occupation, and was told to allay his anxiety in respect to it.

At Söul, Mr. Aston will spare no effort to prevent the Corean Government again addressing a note to the Representatives of the Treaty Powers. His task is considerably increased by the fact that, though M. von Möllendorff has been officially dismissed from his post of Under-Secretary, he still continues to influence the decisions of that office, and to dispatch notes to the foreign Representatives. The Viceroy, whose protégé he was, seems determined on his dismissal, even though he fears he will afterwards give trouble by taking sides with Russia.

I have only just received Mr. Aston's despatches, and the mail is about to start for Shanghae.

I have, &c.

(Signed) N. R. O'CONOR.

67
李鴻章에 대한 Colquhoun의 거문도 점령 반대 권고

N. R. O'Conor (1885. 7. 18) ➡ The Marquis of Salisbury (1885. 9. 21)

No. 185.

Mr. O'Conor to the Marquis of Salisbury.—*(Received September 21.)*

Peking, July 18, 1885.

(No. 357. Confidential.)

My Lord,

I HAVE the honour to acknowledge the receipt of Earl Granville's despatch No. 115 of the 23rd May last, inclosing a copy of a despatch from the Colonial Office containing copies of telegrams which, at the request of Mr. Colquhoun (the "Times" correspondent at the time in these parts), had been sent by the Acting Administrator of the Straits Settlements to the Viceroy of India.

With much reluctance, I feel bound not to let these telegrams pass without some observations, as at a very critical moment they were addressed to so high and influential a person as the Viceroy of India, and conveyed what I cannot but consider a greatly exaggerated, if not erroneous, impression of the policy of China at that period.

I have good reason to believe that the proposals emanated from the Viceroy Li Hung-chang, who, as your Lordship is well aware, is an official of very great rank and influence in China, but at the same time one who holds a position which, as far as the Central Government is concerned, except in special instances, allows him to speak without any great feeling of responsibility, and under the idea that what he says does not in any way bind his Government. He is reputed, and, as far as I can judge, with very good reason, to be wild and extravagant at times in his proposals and ideas, often no doubt with a set purpose, and in order to draw out his interlocutor, but quite as often because he feels that he can either deny or smooth down any statements he may make in the course of conversation. As a matter of fact, at the very time Mr. Colquhoun reports China as making positive and specific overtures for an alliance with Her Majesty's Government, the attitude of the Central Government was extremely cautious, and the most that could be said was that there were symptoms that, if war broke out between Great Britain and Russia, the Chinese Government might seriously consider the advantages of an alliance with England against Russia.

I trust your Lordship will not think I am going out of my way to pass remarks on a matter which is long passed, and to which Lord Dufferin was the last person to attach the political importance which was desired.

But, curiously enough, under date of the 10th May, I received from an entirely reliable source the following information: "Mr. Colquhoun advised the Viceroy Li to protest against the occupation of Port Hamilton, and told him that Japan should protest too. These countries should not allow themselves to be made a cat's-paw of by England. England was always ready to accept substantial assistance, but when other countries were in trouble, all she had to give in return was sympathy and fine phrases."

I have, &c.

(Signed) N. R. O'CONOR.

68
거문도 점령 철회를 위한 독·러 협력 도모

M. de Giers (1885. 7. 18) ➡ M. de Staal

관련문서 (1) 거문도 사건이 러·독의 공통 위협이라는 견해(1885. 7. 3)
(2) 영국의 거문도 점령을 철회를 위한 독·러 협력 제안(1885. 7. 3)
(3) 독·러 협력 불가 및 비스마르크에게 대책 마련 촉구(1885. 7. 12)

127. GIERS A STAAL. L'occupation de Port-Hamilton par l'Angleterre (avec Annexes). Tentative russe d'une entente avec l'Allemagne à ce sujet. Saint-Petersbourg, le 18 juillet 1885.

Monsieur l'Ambassadeur,

J'ai l'honneur de transmette ci-après à Votre Excellence les copies d'une dépêche et d'une lettre très confidentielles que j'ai cru devoir adresser à notre Ambassadeur à Berlin, au sujet de l'occupation de Port-Hamilton par les Anglais, ainsi que de la lettre que je viens de recevoir de M. le comte Schouvalow. Les informations contenues dans ces pièces sont destinées pour votre information personnelle. — Giers.

【관련문서 1】

ANNEXE 1

Copie d'une dépêche réservée de M. de Giers au comte Schouvalow, en date de Saint-Pétersbourg, le 3 juillet 1885. N°169. L'ambassadeur d'Allemagne a été chargé de m'entretenir confidentiellement d'une démarche que le Gouvernement coréen vient de faire auprès des représentants étrangers à Séoul au sujet de l'occupation de Port-Hamilton par les Anglais.

Considérant cette occupation comme une atteinte à ses droits, le Gouvernement en question a cru pouvoir réclamer l'assistance des Puissances, en se basant sur l'article I des traités conclus entre celles-ci et la Corée, qui porte que, dans le cas où des discussions s'élèveraient entre la Corée et l'une des parties contractantes, celles-ci seront tenues, sur la demande de la première, de lui prêter leur concours afin de contribuer à une solution pacifique du malentendu.

Le général de Schweinitz m'a dit qu'avant de 'arrêter à un parti quelconque, le Cabinet de Berlin tiendrait à savoir si le Gouvernement impérial serait disposé à s'associer à des démarches que les Puissances pourraient se trouver dans le cas de faire auprès de la Grande-Bretagne à la suite du recours du Gouvernement coréen.

J'ai répondu à l'Ambassadeur d'Allemagne que nous n'avions aucune connaissance de la démarche faite par la Corée et que, d'ailleurs, notre position vis-à-vis de ce pays n'était, pour le moment, pas analogue à celle d'autres Puissances qui, telles que l'Allemagne, la France, les Etats-Unis d'Amérique et l'Angleterre, avaient déjà des représentants à Séoul. Les ratifications du traité que nous avions conclu l'année passée avec le Gouvernement coréen n'ont pas encore été échangées, et M. Weber, désigné pour représenter la Russie à Séoul, se trouvait encore en route. Néanmoins, en notre qualité de Puissance limitrophe, nous ne pouvions rester indifférents en présence d'une prise de possession d'une partie du territoire coréen. Nous nous réservions de profiter de la première occasion favorable pour provoquer de la part de la Grande-Bretagne des explications positives sur ses projets, et nous ne saurions, par conséquent, que favoriser des démarches d'autres Gouvernements tendant à sauvegarder l'intégrité de la Corée.

Je n'ai pas caché au général de Schweinitz que j'avais déjà interpellé l'Ambassadeur britannique sur le motif de l'occupation de Port-Hamilton par une escadre anglaise, et que sir E. Thornton m'avait répondu qu'il n'avait reçu aucune communication à ce sujet de Londres, mais qu'il supposait que cette occupation n'était que provisoire et qu'elle n'avait été résolue qu'à la suite de complications surgies sur la frontière afghane et la crainte d'une rupture éventuelle entre l'Angleterre et la Russie. Je n'ai pas manqué de prendre acte de cette réponse.

En communiquant ces détails à Votre Excellence, je viens vous prier, Monsieur le Comte, de vouloir bien vous expliquer à ce sujet avec le Cabinet de Berlin et de bous faire connaître la décision qui aura été arrêtée par lui. Vous êtes en même temps autorisé à lui déclarer que, dans le cas où l'Ambassadeur d'Allemagne à Londres serait chargé d'adresser au Cabinet britannique des représentations au sujet de Port-Hamilton, nous n'hésiterions pas à profiter de la même occasion pour insister, de notre côté, auprès des Ministres de la Reine sur la nécessité de mettre fin à l'occupation d'une partie du territoire coréen, que rien ne saurait justifier. Si même les ratifications du traité que nous avons conclu avec la Corée, et qui renferme également l'article I ci-dessus reproduit, n'étaient pas échangées jusqu'alors, nous ne manquerons pourtant pas de nous prévaloir auprès du Cabinet de Londres du droit qui nous appartient de veiller à la sécurité de nos possessions sur le littoral de l'océan Pacifique et à celle de nos communications.

La position de l'Allemagne n'est point analogue à la nôtre, mais cette Puissance a pourtant de vastes intérêts commerciaux à sauvegarder dans ces parages, et il nous semblerait que l'établissement d'une station nouvelle anglaise dans le détroit qui relie la mer du Japon à la mer Jaune pourrait, à un moment donné, devenir une menace pour ces intérêts aussi. — Giers.

【관련문서 2】

ANNEXE II

Copie d'une lettre très secrète de M. de Giers au comte Schouvalow, en date de Saint-Pétersbourg, le 3 juillet 1885. — N°10.

Pour faire suite à ma dépêche du jour au sujet de la démarche faite par le Gouvernement coréen à la suite de l'occupation par les Anglais, je crois de mon devoir d'initier Votre Excellence à la nature de nos rapports avec la Corée.

Les instructions secrètes dont a été muni M. Weber, nommé en qualité de Chargé d'affaires et de Consul général à Séoul, et dont je crois nécessaire de vous transmettre ci-après une copie, suffiront pour vous mettre au courant des vues du Cabinet impérial. Cette pièce est destinée exclusivement pour votre information personnelle.

Le départ de M. Weber pour son poste ayant subi quelque retard, nous avons jugé nécessaire d'inviter M. Speyer, secrétaire de notre légation au Japon, à se rendre provisoirement à Séoul. Cet employé fut chargé: 1° de demander au Gouvernement coréen une prolongation du délai fixé pour l'échange des ratifications du traité conclu l'année passée, pour le cas où M. Weber ne serait pas rendu à temps à son poste; 2° de contrecarrer les démarches du représentant britannique tendant à obtenir du Gouvernement coréen la cession définitive de Port-Hamilton; 3° et de veiller à ce que le Gouvernement coréen n'acceptât pour l'instruction de ses troupes que des officiers russes.

M. Moellendorff, premier conseiller aux Ministères coréens des Affaires étrangères et de la Guerre, ayant donné à notre Ministre à Tôkiô l'assurance positive que le Roi de la Corée était fermement résolu à nous confier l'instruction de ses troupes, M. Speyer fut autorisé à promettre à Sa Majesté l'envoi de nos instructeurs.

Un télégramme de M. Davydov vient de nous mettre au courant de la tournure inattendue qu'a prise la mission de Speyer à la suite d'un revirement subit qui semble s'être opéré à Séoul et dont la position personnelle de Moellendorff s'est gravement ressentie.

Informé que le Gouvernement coréen était sur le point d'engager des instructeurs américains, M. Speyer ne se laissa pas décourager par cette circonstance, et il fit dire au Roi que l'envoi d'instructeurs russes avait déjà été résolu par le Cabinet impérial; que, pour sa part, il ne pouvait pas admettre une rétractation des assurances données par M. Moellendorff, et qu'il n'était venu que pour discuter les conditions du séjour des susdits instructeurs en Corée. Le Roi consentit d'abord à souscrire à l'arrangement proposé par notre agent, mais il ne tarda pas à se rétracter de nouveau, à la suite de quoi M. Speyer se vit placé dans la nécessité de quitter Séoul. Ignorant pour le moment les motifs qui ont poussé M. Speyer à s'écarter des instructions dont il avait été muni, nous ne pouvons nous empêcher, en attendant, d'appréhender les conséquences de son départ. Cette circonstance nous paraît surtout préjudiciable au point de vue des résultats auxquels pourraient aboutir les efforts des agents anglais tendant à persuader le Gouvernement coréen d'abandonner Port-Hamilton à la Grande-Bretagne moyennant une indemnité pécuniaire. C'est un arrangement semblable qu'il s'agissait surtout de conjurer, et c'est dans des démarches simultanées des Puissances intéressées à Londres que nous voyons le moyen le plus sûr d'empêcher une éventualité qui pourrait servir de précédent fâcheux à d'autres Puissances jalouses d'étendre leurs communications avec les pays riverains de l'océan Pacifique.

Une entente à ce sujet entre le Gouvernement impérial et le Cabinet de Berlin ne saurait, selon notre avis, rester sans effet sur les résolutions de la Grande-Bretagne. — Giers.

【관련문서 3】

ANNEXE III

Copie d'une lettre secrète du comte Schouvalow au Secrétaire d'Etat de Giers, en date de Berlin, le 12/24 juillet 1885.

Me conformant aux ordres contenu dans la dépêche de Votre Excellence en date du 3 juillet, je me suis rendu chez le comte de Hatzfeldt pour m'expliquer avec lui sur la démarche que le Gouvernement coréen venait de faire auprès des représentants étrangers à Séoul, par rapport à l'occupation de Port-Hamilton par les Anglais.

Je communiquai au Ministre des Affaires étrangères les détails de la conversation de Votre Excellence avec le général Schweinitz et je lui demandai en même temps de bien vouloir me faire connaître la décision prise à ce sujet par le Cabinet de Berlin. J'ai ajouté que, dans le cas que (*sic*) l'Ambassadeur d'Allemagne à Londres serait chargé d'adresser au Gouvernement britannique des représentations au sujet de Port-Hamilton, nous n'hésiterions pas à nous joindre à cette démarche, pour protester contre cet état de choses. Les ratifications du traité conclu entre nous et la Corée n'ayant pas encore été échangées, nous nous fonderions, dans cette démarche, uniquement sur notre droit de Puissance limitrophe, qui ne nous permettrait pas de rester indifférents, eu égard à cette prise de possession d'une partie du territoire coréen.

Le comte de Hatzfeldt me répondit que la démarche faite par le Gouvernement coréen, il y a de cela quelque temps, lui était parfaitement connue. Dès que le Roi de Corée avait réclamé l'assistance des Puissances, sur la base de l'article I du traité conclu entre celles-ci et son Gouvernement, le Cabinet de Berlin s'était empressé d'en faire part à Votre Excellence pour connaître le point de vue du Gouvernement impérial à ce sujet. Depuis, la situation avait complètement changé. Le Gouvernement coréen avait révoqué sa demande d'intervention après des Puissances et, comme cette demande n'avait été formulée que sur la base des traités existants, il n'en avait plus été question.

Les détails que Votre Excellence a bien voulu me donner par sa lettre très secrète, en date du même 3 juillet, expliquent cette volte-face. Je ne doute pas un instant que les derniers événements qui se sont produits à Séoul sont la cause de ce revirement subit, aussi bien dans les intentions du Gouvernement coréen que dans celles des Puissances qui naguère auraient pu se trouver dans le cas de protester contre les empiétements de l'Angleterre.

Ignorant les motifs qui ont poussé M. Speyer à une procédure aussi précipitée et, comme Votre Excellence veut bien l'observer, peu conforme aux instructions qui lui avaient été données, je ne puis que regretter les conséquences qui en découlent et qui produisent le revirement actuel.

Toutefois, je ne voulais pas terminer ma conversation avec le comte de Hatzfeldt en me contentant d'une simple fin de non-recevoir. C'est au Cabinet de Berlin qu'appartenait l'initiative de nos pourparlers à ce sujet; or, pour ne pas me priver du moyen de reprendre la conversation selon les circonstances, je me suis permis d'adresser au comte une question personnelle, celle de savoir si l'Allemagne, en vue des intérêts commerciaux à sauvegarder dans ces parages, ne serait point disposé à intervenir tout de même pour empêcher une éventualité qui ne saurait point ne pas toucher les Puissances intéressées.

Le comte de Hatzfeldt me déclara ne rien pouvoir me dire à ce sujet, mais il s'engagea à transmettre aussitôt le sujet de ma conversation au Chancelier, et il me promit de me mettre le plus tôt possible au courant du point de vue du prince de Bismarck.

Avec ou sans intention, le comte Hatzfeldt ne prononça pas un mot, ni au sujet du départ de M. Speyer, ni sur les derniers événements en Corée. En conséquence, je me suis abstenu de toute parole sortant du cadre tracé par Votre Excellence. Je me suis borné à la question concernant l'intervention du Cabinet de Berlin à Londres, malgré la révocation faite par le Gouvernement coréen. — Schouvalow.

69
조선의 교섭 상황 및 러시아 군함의 동태 보고

李鴻章 ➡ 總署 (1885. 7. 19 / 光緒十一年六月八日)

六月初八日 北洋大臣李鴻章文稱 本年六月初五日 據駐紮朝鮮辦理商務陳道樹棠五月初十日稟稱 竊職道前將丁提督赴巨文島 並日本長崎會英提督等情形 備由具稟 於光緒十一年五月初五日 奉憲台批開 四月十二日來稟並摺均悉 仍將續後情形隨時探詢明確稟報 奉此 同日又奉密諭開 據徐孫麒星使來電 英人於巨文島設電 直達英京 俄艦已據高麗墨浦島 與巨文相近等語 墨浦島究在何處 距巨文若干 是否有艦駐泊 等因奉此 職道伏查 英人於巨文島設電一節 查係通至江浙交界之豬山 洋人稱馬鞍山云 接釜山分辦委員陳令爲焜來稟稱 有日本兵艦抵埠 據說在巨文島見有英國兵船七八艘 停泊島內 其四面入口之處均批置水雷 外加鐵索 每島最高處設有兵丁瞭望之所 並確朝鮮多人填築馬頭 濟州一帶時有俄兵船停泊等云 又查墨浦島卽木浦 距巨文島三百八十里 該處人煙稠密 爲民漁船灣泊之所 亦有市面買賣 俄船停泊濟州一帶 與木浦相近 往購食物容或有之 寔未聞其佔據也 昨英領事阿須頓接見外部金允植稱 接有北京代理英使來書言 巨文島爲暫住計耳 並不設砲台建房屋 只要權藏煤炭 如朝鮮肯允則更有爲朝鮮便宜好意等云 金允植答以巨文一事擧國皆爲不可 該處非通商口岸 不宜屯煤炭 致啓人疑 應請稟明貴政府 速將該島兵艦撤退 以敦友誼 至有何便宜好意不宜偏厚於一國 當俟公平再議等云 職道查釜山分辦委員陳令來稟係四月二十日所發 英領事與金允植所談係在本月初七日 特未知其所接北京代理英使之信係何日所發耳 近日傳聞已有和議 則巨文島兵船不久當須退去 隨後有聞 自當續報 等情到本大臣 據此 相應密咨 欽命總各國事務衙門 煩請查核

70
李鴻章에 대한 榎本武揚의 거문도 철수 요구 제안

N. R. O'Conor (1885. 7. 20) ➡ F. Plunkett

No. 186.

Mr. O'Conor to Mr. Plunkett.

Peking, July 20, 1885.

(Confidential.)

Sir,

I HAVE already had the honour to acknowledge the receipt of the telegram you were good enough to send me on the 14th instant, saying that the Japanese Minister for Foreign Affairs denied that Admiral Enomotto was authorized by his Government to press upon the Viceroy Li Hung-chang to join action in opposition to our occupation of Port Hamilton, and that he had been instructed to abstain from any such interference in this question.

It seems to me advisable to inform you, confidentially, that the Viceroy has since then stated to Her Majesty's Consul at Tien-tsin that Admiral Enomotto had read out his instructions to him. These were to the effect "that England's occupation of Port Hamilton was a source of danger to China and Japan. Admiral Enomotto was therefore to endeavour, in consultation with the Viceroy, to bring about our evacuation of the place."

The Viceroy had pointed out to Admiral Enomotto that merely formal protest would mean nothing, and that before more weighty language was used Japan must consider the next step should her remonstrances be unheeded Was Japan prepared to resort to force? To this Admiral Enomotto had replied that the consideration of this question might be deferred until remonstrance was found to be useless.

The Viceroy had said to Admiral Enomotto that it was almost certain that

England had decided to retain possession of Port Hamilton, and asked him whether Japan would be reassured by a promise that Port Hamilton would never be used against Japan. To this Admiral Enomotto had replied that such a promise would be as easily broken as the wine-glass he then held in his hand.

The Viceroy seems to be under the impression that Japan, disliking our proximity to her coasts, wished China to undertake the disagreeable duty of causing us to withdraw, a idle which, bis Excellency said, China would certainly not play.

I have, &c.

(Signed) N. R. O'CONOR.

71
거문도 점령에 대한 청의 즉각적인 항의

G. S. de Bezaure (1885. 7. 24) ➡ Ch. de Freycinet

Direction des Affaires Commerciales et Consulaires
N°1

Tientsin le 24 juillet 1885
Consulat de France à Tientsin

Monsieur le Ministre,

J'ai cherché depuis quelques jours à recueillir sur les affaires de Corée tous les renseignements de nature à intéresser Votre Excellence, et je n'ai pas manqué d'interroger sur cette question, qui passionne vivement l'opinion publique à l'heure actuelle, toutes les personnes avec lesquelles je me suis trouvé en rapport depuis mon arrivée à Tientsin. Il ressort pour moi la conviction qu'aucun débat ne s'est encore ouvert au sujet de la Corée entre la Chine et la Russie. C'est avec le Japon seul, que les Chinois sont en discussion, pour le moment. Ainsi que vous le savez, Monsieur le Ministre, les Japonais demandent que l'indépendance de la Corée soit reconnue par son puissant suzerain; mais les désirs du Japon ont peu d'autorité à Pékin et la Chine, au reste, parait formellement décidée à maintenir les droits qu'elle prétend avoir sur son vassal.

Quant au prétendu différend russo-chinois, je crois qu'il faut le ramener aux préparations suivantes: M. Mollendorf aurait eu l'intention de créer en Corée un corps militaire destiné à maintenir l'ordre dans le pays, et aurait voulu confier à des officiers russes le commandement et l'instruction des soldats. Les Chinois eurent connaissance de ce projet et s'empressent de protester contre la dernière partie du programme, c'est-à-dire contre l'engagement d'officiers russes. Ils se proposent, à ce qu'on dit, de mettre à exécution l'idée de M. Mollendorf, avec cette seule modification, qu'il ferait appel au service d'officiers américains. Il est fort possible que M. Mollendorf ait voulu préparer l'intervention de la Russie en Corée et qu'un projet de traité ait même été élaboré par ce personnage: il semble faux, cependant, que le gouvernement coréen en soit venu avec la Russie à un accord stipulant des conditions contraires à son état de vassalité vis-à-vis de la Chine, et qu'un conflit ait ainsi éclaté, dès maintenant, contre la Cour de Pétersbourg et celle de Pékin.

Il n'en est pas moins vrai que les préparatifs en vue d'une résistance à opposer à une tentative des Russes contre la Corée, parmi les mieux armés et les mieux disciplinées, sont dirigées vers la frontières coréenne et massées des les environs de Port Lazareff. Des personnes bien informées me disent qu'il y a environ trente mille Chinois sur ce point. Je tiens d'une source sûre que les Russes n'ont dans ces parages qu'une quinzaine de mille hommes et que l'envoi de renforts exigerait beaucoup de temps et de grands sacrifices.

Je crois que la Chine fera tout son possible pour éviter d'être obligée d'entrer en guerre, soit avec la Russie, soit avec toute autre nation. Mais je suis convaincu, en même temps, que dût-elle prendre les armes, elle s'opposera à l'intervention directe de qui que ce soit dans les affaires de Corée, et qu'elle soutiendra, jusqu'à la limite de ses forces, son droit de suzeraineté et l'intégrité territoriale de son vassal. La politique chinoise parait être, sur ce point; celle de l'expectative : ainsi que je le disais plus haut, des mesures vont être prises pour que l'ordre ne soit plus troublé en Corée. D'un autre côté, on s'occupera d'assurer la sécurité du commerce étranger dans les ports de ce pays. Le gouvernement chinois compte ainsi enlever tout prétexte aux étrangers d'intervenir sur le sol coréen. J'apprends, en autre, que de nouvelles protestations vont être faites contre l'occupation de Port Hamilton par les Anglais.

Veuillez agréer l'hommage du respect avec lequel j'ai l'honneur d'être, Monsieur le Ministre,

de Votre Excellence, le très humble et très obéissant serviteur,

[__]de Bezaure.

72
거문도 전신선 연결 완료 보고

The Secretary to the Admiralty (1885. 7. 27) ➡ J. Pauncefote (1885. 7. 30)

No. 38.

The Secretary to the Admiralty to Sir J. Pauncefote.—(Received July 30.)

Admiralty, July 27, 1885.

Sir,

MY Lords Commissioners of the Admiralty desire me to forward herewith, for the perusal of the Secretary of State for Foreign Affairs, an extract of a letter, dated the 3rd June, from the Commander-in-chief on the China Station, reporting that the telegraph cable connecting Port Hamilton with the main cable of the Eastern Extension Telegraph Company has been laid.

I am, &c.

(Signed) EVAN MACGREGOR.

Inclosure

Vice-Admiral Sir W. Dowell to the Secretary to the Admiralty.

"Audacious," at Nagasaki, June 3, 1885.

(Extract.)

IN confirmation of my telegrams of the 30th ultimo and of yesterday's date, I beg leave to report that the telegraph cable connecting Port Hamilton with the main cable of the Eastern Extension Telegraph Company has been successfully laid, and is now in working order.

2. The two telegraphists stationed here to work the instruments are for the present living on board the "Merlin," which vessel is anchored close off the position chosen for landing the cable. The wooden building sent from Hong Kong as a residence and office for these gentlemen has been erected by he carpenters of the squadron, and is now nearly complete. In the meantime, the telegraphic operations are carried on in a temporary shed.

3. The cable has been landed on North Saddle Island, where the Company have erected a station. Her Majesty's Chargé d' Affaires at Peking informs me, by telegraph, that the Chinese Government have consented to this arrangement.

73
거문도와 홍콩 간의 해저 전신선 부설을 덴마크 전신회사가 담당했음을 보고

A. P. Davydov (1885. 7. 30) ➡ N. K. Girs

AVPRI, F. Glavnyi arkhiv U-Az, 1885 g, D.45, L.312-4.

Токио, 18/30 Июля 1885 года.

Его Высокопревосходительству Н. К. Гирсу.

Милостивый Государь, Николай Карлович.

Телеграммой от1/13 минувшего Июня я имел честь донести Вашему Высокопревосходительству, что между Портом Гамильтон и Гонконгом установлено телеграфное сообщение, и высказал при этом предположение, что это сделано с согласия Китайского Правительства и при участии Датской Телеграфной Компании.

Г. Стен, помощник Директора Японским Телеграфом, с которым я говорил об этом, сообщил мне на днях конфиденциально полученное им частное письмо от Г. Гелланда (Helland), агента Great Northern Telegraph Company в Шанхае. Копию с этого письма имею честь при сем приложить. Из оного оказывается, что устройство этой телеграфной линии держалось в тайне, и что Датская компания заявила протест в Лондоне, как только ей об этом стало известно. Г. Гелланд также выражает предположение,что кабель был положен уже после состоявшегося по сему предмету соглашения между Великобританским и Китайским Правительствами.

В конце письма говорится о приводимом уже в исполнение намерении

Китайцев провести телеграф из Сеула к Китайской границе и таким образом соединить Кореи с Китайской сетью телеграфов. Эти сведения уже дошли до меня и с другой стороны, Китайц по-видимому действуют по наущению Англичан, желающих как можно теснее связать вассала с его сюзереном.

С глубоким почтением и таковою же преданностью имею честь быть

Вашего Высокопревосходительства

покорнейший слуга

А. Давыдов

74
유사시 거제도 점거 건의

榎本武揚 (1885. 7. 31) ➡ 井上馨

酷暑之節不被爲相替御鞅掌之義ト遙察仕候然者拙官義本月廿三日ヲ以て任所歸着仕候處妻兒臥蓐いたし居今日迄も晝夜之看病等に逐ハれ乍不本意之至天津談話擧記第二編以下を完整して貴閱ニ供する暇無之何卒御諒察被下度候乍去幸ニ妻兒之病証も昨今回復之徵相顯れ候間次便ニは幾編歟差進候運ニ可相成希望致居候

一　去ル廿九日貴機密卌一號より卌三號迄接手披閱仕候三十二號ハ殊ニ緊要之件御記載有之朝鮮ニ對する御政略ハ彌不干涉主義ニ被立戻候御決意之旨并ニ英公使プランケット氏ト御內話之旨一概致領承候抑此頃日淸廷が朝鮮ニ對する政略ハ英に協合して露を扞制するに如かずとの一點ニ相決候ニ相違無之右ニ付巨文島一件之如きハ乍不本意も姑ラク且ツ之を坐視ニ附シ置隱ニ其甘心を失ん事を恐居候(タトヘ一應ハ異議ケ間敷事を唱へしにもせよ)依之見解を下シ候ヘハ異日英露葛藤之日ニ際シ淸廷ハ中立を唱ふるも露より朝鮮え手を出シ候ハヽ(譬ハ防英名義にて)淸政府は遂ニ英ト合力するに立至可申下心有之候(是トテモ鍔際ニ至らされハ保証シガタシトハ云ヘ)是れ畢竟日本トノミ合力するも未た英也露也を防禦するに足るの見込無之御坐すべし況や日本之政略ハ危急之秋ニ至りて眞ニ實力ヲ以て共同利益を保護すべき哉否を洞觀する能ハざるに於てをやト拙官以爲らく是れ至極尤之儀也是れ猶朝鮮が昨年之變亂に淸國之實力能く日本兵を韓より驅逐する能ハざるべきを慮りて姑らく露に保護を依賴セシト殆ンド同工異曲とも可申歟傍に我政府之朝鮮政略たるjoint protectionハ之を避ケられ候以上ハタトヘ平常無事之日ニ於て幾分歟輔助手段を執らるゝも一旦緩急之秋ニ方り我國家之利益を擧て朝鮮ニ犧牲すべき程の要を見さるニ付其節ハ我中立を確守して傍觀するの外可無之トも可申歟乍去拙官之鄙見ニハ朝鮮之獨立を訂盟各國より確認して互ニ不相侵之約ヲ立る云々ハ到底「アカデミカル」理論にして實施するを得さるべきニ付我ハ平日ニ在テハ不干涉主義を執りながらも一旦有事之日ニハ朝鮮西東海岸中我ニ取て最要害たるべき土地譬ハ巨濟島之如きを占據して露英會社之株券シエールホールダルを買ふ方却て可然奉存候就ては朝鮮事件ニ付餘

り淸政府ト相謀るを止め獨立自重之御政略こそ願敷候貴機密三十二號中御記載之旨ハ粗此御趣意たらバ誠ニ以て御同見ニ候但シ同號中ニ李氏ハ今次拙官との內話を密ニ「ハート」氏ニ通知せしならんとの御疑念有之候へ共是は斷然其事なかるべしト被察候第一「ハート」氏ハ未た公然公使之資格なく又事務も執らず其上李氏ト從來不折合ニ候加之李ハ隨分時々其說を左右する事不少候へ共マサカニ拙官ト密話せし國事ヲ「ハート」に內通する程の小人ニハ可無之候(是モ退引ナラヌ大關係アルコトナレバイザ知ラズ今次之談話ハ夫程ノコトニアラザレバ也)同氏ハ今次八ケ條中の一二ケ條ニ異議ありと雖共大体ハ御同意也ト吳々も申居候ニ付矢張自家之都合を慮り幾分歟我國ト共同利益を保護せんとの內願ハ有之候(總署ハ漠然ニ相違ナシ)故に閣ト向後渠ト韓事ヲ餘り商議セラレズ却テ渠より商議を乞ふに至らしむる方得策たるべく候

右ハ兼てより申述度存居隨懷隨記御判談被下度猶內信ヲ以て御高諭ヲ仰き度候

七月三十一日　　　　武陽

井上盟臺閣下

75
李鴻章과의 협의 경과 보고에 대한 답신

井上馨(1885. 8. 15) ➡ 榎本武揚

外務卿ハ八月十五日附ヲ以テ本件ニ關シ第三十二號ノ機密信如左

貴官天津ニ於テ朝鮮ニ對スル政略ニ付李中堂ト御協議ノ次第ハ追々電報ニテ致承知候處去十二日附貴官御電報ノ趣ニ依レバ李氏ニ於テハ全體ノ利害ニ暗ク瑣々タル體裁曲節ニ拘泥シ本官カ主眼トスル亞細亞全洲ノ平和ヲ保持セント欲スル誠意ヲ了解セサルモノヽ如シ今日迄多少ノ匠意モ爲メニ徒爲ニ屬シ候ハ實ニ遺憾ト存候得共浩歎ニ附スルノ外無之元來本官カ此政略ヲ彼ヲシテ實施セシメント欲スルハ只管我方ニ於テ其責任ヲ取ル事ヲ忌避スルニ非ズ專ラ亞細亞全局ノ利害得失ヲ考量セシヨリ右ノ畫策ニ出候事ニ有之候其故ハ日清兩國ガ朝鮮ニ對スル政略ハ從來異同アリ卽チ清國ニ於テハ其屬邦ト視做シ我邦ニ於テハ早ク既ニ獨立ト視做スガ如ク從テ兩國ガ同國ニ對スル關繫ニ於テモ多少ノ差異アルハ自カラ免ル可カラザルモノニ有之然ルニ兩國各自ニ其所思ヲ施サント欲スルトキハ所謂其本ヲ揣ラズシテ其末ヲ斉フセント欲スルガ如シ到底其目的ヲ達スル能ハザルノミナラズ日清間ノ意嚮ニ支離逕庭スル所アルハ最モ賭易キノ理勢ナリトス故ニ我方ニ於テハ是等ノ困難ヲ避ケ專ラ清國ヲシテ着手セシメ　內實其意嚮ヲ同クスル爲メニ協議ヲ盡シ　目下朝鮮國ニ關シ將サニ萌生セントスル所ノ困難ヲ消却セントスルノ精神ヨリ出テ候事ニテ此辦法ヲ措テハ他ニ良策ヲ見出サズ且我方ニ於テ此精神ノ外ニ他意ナキハ明瞭ニ有之候處彼ノ如キ管見ヲ持シ疑念ヲ抱キ候テハ縱令ヒ協同事ヲ謀ルモ到底其良結果ヲ不可期ト存候ニ付此上ハ我ニ於テモ朝鮮ニ對スル政略ヲ一變シ之ヲ放任シテ自然ノ成行ヲ傍觀スルノ外致方無之就テハ過日申進八ケ條ノ發案モ其三條及ビ七條ヲ同意セズシテ他ノ條款ノミヲ實施セシムル事トスルトキハ兩國協同ノ實益ナキノミナラズ却テ清國ノ主權ヲ擴張スル事ヲ我ニ於テ認メタルトノ形迹ヲ存シ後來不都合ト存候故三條七條ニシテ同意セザルニ於テハ全體ノ發議ヲ撤回スルハ要用ト存候故電信ニテ其趣申進候議ニ有之候巨文島一件ニ付テハ本月十三日英公使プランケツト氏特ニ本官ニ內晤ヲ乞ヒ外務卿サリスバリー侯ノ訓令ナリトテ本件ニ付テハ日本政府ノ痛ク抗論ヲ主

張シ清韓兩國ノ間ニ在リテ異論スル事ヲ誘導スルニ非ズヤトノ推問有之且今般貴官下津李中堂ト面議セラレシ事ヲモ引用シ英政府ハ果シテ此事ノ眞實ナル事ヲ臆測スルトノ事ニ付拙者之ニ答フルニ該島占據ノ處置ニ對シテハ我邦ノミニ關スル意見ハ既ニ已ニ先般該件ヲ通知セラレタル際陳述セシ通リニシテ貴國ノ此行爲ニ就テハ邦々ニ於テ之ヲ甘諾ス可ラザル事ハ既ニ已ニ了解セラルベシ而シテ我邦ガ該件ニ關シ清韓兩國ヲシテ異議ヲ起サシムル事ヲ誘導セシヤ否ヤノ點ニ於テハ固ヨリ公然タル訓令ヲ公使ニ付與シタルニ非ズ或ハ榎本公使ノ如キモ曩ニ我政府ガ貴政府ノ通知巨文島占據ノ事ニ係ル　ニ對シ答ヘタルノ意ヲ以テ幾分カ清國政府ニ其意見ヲ吐露シタル事アルモ不可測ト雖モ日清兩國其關繫ヲ異ニスレバ固ヨリ我政府ハ公然タル訓令ヲ我公使ニ付與セシ事無之又朝鮮政府ガ在京城ノ我代理公使ニ書翰ヲ送リ巨文島占據ノ事ニ關シ意見ヲ聞キ且中裁ヲ請求セシモ曾テ之ニ對シ異論ヲ主張スベシトノ訓令ヲ政府ヨリ付與シタル事無之且今ヲ距ル事凡ソ二三ケ月前英公使拙者面談ノ際英公使ノ意嚮ヲ揣摩スルニ我政府ハ萬一英露事アルノ日ニ當テハ日清英ニ合縱シテ攻守ノ內約ヲ結バント欲スルノ端倪ヲ露ハシ候事モ有之候故我邦ニ於テ他日英露ノ葛藤ヲ戰爭ニ訴フル場合ニ於テハ只此困難ヲ避クルノ一法ハ嚴ニ中立ノ位置ヲ守ルノ外無之候今一層ヲ進メテ之ヲ言フトキハ孰レノ友國タリトモ我邦土ニ對シ侵略スル事アルカ若クハ脇迫スルノ擧動アルニ於テハ不得已右不理ノ行爲ニ抗敵セザルヲ得ザル場合モ可有之トノ旨趣ヲ述ベ置タル事アリ竝ニ露國賛參官スペーヤ氏ガ朝鮮國ニ到リ朝鮮政府ト談判セシ事ニ關スル近藤ヨリノ電信ヲ示セシ事アリシヲ再應引證シ此等過去ノ事實ニ依リ我政府ハ誘導ノ行爲ニ出デザルトノデナイヤル　否答ヲ陳ベ彼ノ猜疑ヲ釋キ置候此辯解ニ依リ英公使ニ於テモ大イニ我意向ノ大略ヲ曉リ直チニ外務卿サリスバリー侯ニ電報ニ及候右本官ノ辯明中ニハ貴官ヘ先般來御內訓ニ及候事實ト殆ンド支吾スル所アルヲ免レズト雖モ今日我邦ノ位置ニ於テハ英露孰レニ對シテモ其歡心ヲ失フ可カラザルノ事情有之加之清國今日ノ有樣ニテハ貴官御見込ノ如ク殆ンド憑伏ス可カラズ殊ニ今回英公使ノ口氣竝ニサリスバリー侯訓令ノ模樣ニ依リ揣摩スルトキハ清政府ハ露國ガ朝鮮ニ手ヲ着クルヨリモ寧ロ英國ヲシテ扞制ノ任ニ當ラシムル方可然トノ淺薄ノ政略ヲ執リ該件ニ關シテハ貴官ガ李氏ト御談判ニ相成候事ヲ李氏ヨリ在清英公使ハート氏ニ相洩シ候ニ相違ナシト被察候就テハ今後我政策ニ付總理衙門及ビ李氏ト御談判相成候事ハ御助才無之候得共一層注意ヲ要シ候事緊要ト思考致候此段申進候也

76
거문도 탐문 결과 보고
(1885. 8. 16)

十八年八月十六日

別紙電報之趣外務卿へ御通知可相成哉左按取調仰高裁候也

按 普第二一六四號ノ二

朝鮮國巨文島景況別紙之通リ海門艦長ヨリ報告有之候ニ付此段及御通知候也

十八年八月十七日(附箋 外務省へ通知取計濟)

海軍卿

外務卿アテ

普第二一六四號ノ三

朝鮮國巨文島景況御届

朝鮮國巨文島ニ於テ英國人擧動別紙ノ通リ該地派遣海門艦長ヨリ報告有之候ニ付此段御届仕候也

十八年八月十七日

海軍卿發名

太政大臣着名アテ

普第二一六四號　來電譯

海門艦ハミリトン島エ回艦「アカメムノン」號艦長ニ面談スハミリトン島港內國旗ヤ水雷器其他取除キタル機見請タリ英國魯國ノ談判モ平定セシヤト問合セ同艦長云フ然リ然シ魯國未タ結局ニ至ラス現今廟議決定スルワケニハ至ル間敷トノ事ナリ海

門艦釜山浦トリ電信報告

十八年八月十六日午前七時五十分

横須賀

中艦隊司令官

川村海軍卿アテ

77
거문도 점령 사건으로 인한 오스트리아-헝가리제국과 한국 간의 조약 체결 보류

A. P. Davydov (1885. 8. 17) ➡ N. K. Girs

AVPRI, F. Glavnyi arkhiv U-Az, 1885 g, D.45, L.319-20.

Токио, 5/17 Августа 1885 года.

Его Высокопревосходительству Н.К. Гирсу.

Милостивый Государь, Николай Карлович.

Австро-Венгерский Посланник Граф Залуский, получив телеграмму из Вены накануне отплытия своего в Корею для заключения трактата, отложил свой отъезд на неопределённое время.

Как Министру Иностранных Дел, так и коллегам своим, Граф Залуский объявил, что Цислейтанское Министерство не успело еще прийти по этому вопросу к соглашению с Транслейтанским и что поэтому заключение трактата должно быть на некоторое время отложено.

Это объяснение до такой степени противоречит всему тому, что говорил до этого Австрийский Посланник, что очевидно поездку свою он отменил по другим причинам, но по каким именно – здесь никому не известно.

Японцы предполагают, что занятие Порта Гамильтона Англичанами составляет ныне предмет переговоров между Европейскими Державами и что Австро-Венгерское Правительство предпочитает держаться в стороне от осложнений, в которых оно совершенно не заинтересовано.

С глубоким почтением и таковою же преданностью имею честь быть

Вашего Высокопревосходительства

покорнейший слуга

А. Давыдов.

78
영·러 분쟁 미결 시 각국의 움직임에 대한 풍설

李鴻章 ➡ 總署 (1885. 8. 22 / 光緒十一年七月十三日)

七月十三日 北洋大臣李鴻章文稱 據委辦朝鮮商務陳道樹棠稟稱 竊職道前以英據巨文島事 疊稟憲聽 計均達到 玆探得英兵船照舊停泊 毫無動靜 昨日接見英總領事阿須頓 言及英俄結怨 恐難解釋 不免以干戈從事 倘果能修好 自當撤兵回去 斷無久佔他人島嶼之理 據其所言 然則英俄不和 巨文島無退讓之日 當時金允植行文各國 暫緩調停 係受英總領事之愚 近日各公使皆有中國密約英人聯兵拒俄之說 而英總領事從中刁猾 唔相附和 遂致各公使文椆探問 職道雖告之以並無其事 然終不知此說之何由而起 日前日斯巳尼亞公使游歷到朝 亦有北說 職道云 此係謠傳所致 若我中國果然結英制俄 究有何益 公使曰 益則未能言也 不過英俄若在阿富汗開仗 中國以新疆之兵逼近俄境 則俄不能不多爲之備 而俄兵爲之牽制 大英之有益也 職道云 照則中國仍無所益子 公使曰 此不過有事之際 圖其肯售軍火 借國債 派員幫戰而已 言畢復微笑曰 善法之戰 曾亦聞之否 臨行復謂職道曰 頃問一席談皆私語也 非爲公事耳 可勿存意云云 德使亦有此說 丘云 中結英不若結俄 盖俄與中隣 地方相連之故云 以上皆職道與各公使接談而得 承諭有聞必報 不得不據以瀆陳 諒憲台自有權衡 當不責以悠悠之言有惑淸聽也 惟祈察鑒 等情到本大臣 據此 除排各公使謂中國密約英人云云確係誤傳 寔無此說 如再有人談及 該道應力辯其無 勿任以說沿說外 相應密咨貴衙門 請煩查照

79
거문도 경비병에 대한 보고

(1885. 8. 24)

巨文島ノ戍兵(本年八月十三日チヤイナ オウアーランド トレード レポート)英國政府ハ今回巨文島海岸衛戍トシテ水兵百名ヲ該島ニ派遣セリ又該島家屋建築用材ハ昨今香港及長崎ノ兩所ニ於テ調製中ナリト云フ

80
波多野承五郎·吳大澂 회담

波多野承五郎(1885. 8. 25) ➡ 井上馨(1885. 9. 12)

機密第五拾貳號　　　　　　　　　　九月十二日接收

過日吳太(*sic*)澂ニ面會ノ時露國ハ永興港(ポルトラザレツフ)ヲ占據シ其海軍碇泊所トナサントストノ儀專ラ世上ニ風說致候而シテ若シ實ニ其事アラバ貴我兩國ノ利害ニ關係スル所頗ル少ナラサルガ如シ豫メ之ヲ防クノ策ハ如何可有之哉トノ趣拙官ヨリ問試候處吳太澂ハ

露ヲシテ永興港ヲ占據セントスルノ意ヲ斷タシメント欲セハ先ツ豫メ永興ヲ以テ各國共同ノ船所(原語)トナシ各國ヲシテ之ガ安全ヲ保護スルノ任ニ當ラシムヘシ若シ斯クノ如クセハ露ト雖トモ手ヲ永興ニ下スコト能ハサルヘシ

ト申候ニ付拙官ハ頗ル之ヲ稱贊シ

此議甚タ妙ナリ貴國若シ此議ヲ朝鮮政府ニ照會シ而シテ之ヲ各國ニ發議セハ露ヲ除クノ外殆ント皆ナ之ニ同意ヲ表スヘシ特ニ米獨英ノ如キハ之ヲ實行スルコトニ付大ニ盡力スル者ナルヘシ

ト相答候處彼レマタ話次ヲ繼キ

是レ余カ一箇人ノ私見ノミ斯ノ如キノ議ハ我總理衙門ニ呈出スルモ之ヲ理解シ得ル人ハナカルヘシ該衙門ノ人ハ皆ナ內國ノ事ニノミ着目スルヲ知リテ廣ク眼ヲ放チテ海外ノ情ヲ察視スルヲ知ラス又唯タ家ヲ富スコトヲ思フテ國事ノ重ンスヘキヲ思ハス貴國伊藤大人ノ如キハ歐米ノ事情ニ通シ頗ル聰明ノ人ナレハ余カ此說ニハ必ス同意ヲ表セラルヽナルヘシ

ト申候ニ付拙官ハ蓋シ然ラント相答候然ルニ吳太澂ハ更ニ話次ヲ繼キ

貴領事若シ伊藤大人ニ書ヲ贈ルノ序モアラハ吳太澂此說ヲ有スト同大人ニ告ケラレヨ

ト得意ニ物語候ニ付拙官ハ承諾ノ旨相答置候

右吳太澂ノ共同船所說ハ同人一個ノ私見ナリトスレハ左マデ價値モ有之間敷候得共彼ノ在朝鮮獨逸領事主張スル所ノ朝鮮中立說ニモ幾分歟符合スル所モ有之殊ニ同人

ヨリ伊藤參議ニ傳語スル懇請シタル事情モ有之候ニ付右吳太澂說話ノ趣同參議ヘ御轉說相成且ツ拙官ヨリ吳ニ對シ何等ノ返答可致哉御訓示被下候樣致度願上候

此日拙官ハ

上海ノ新聞紙ニ記スル所ニヨルニ露ハ淸國ノ境界ニ三萬ノ兵ヲ集ムルヲ得ヘシ而シテ之ヲ集ムルノ日ハ淸國ト日本トハ手足ヲ縮メテ命ヲ聽クヘキノミ云々トアリタレトモ余カ聞ク所ニヨルニ露ハ三萬ハ偖テ置キ一萬ノ兵ヲモ集ムルヲ得サルヘシト聞ケリ果シテ然ルカ

ト相尋候處吳太澂ハ

然リ然リ露ハ其境界ニ於テ此所ニ百人彼所ニ二百人ノ兵ヲ置クノミ固ヨリ多數ノ兵ヲ備ヘタルニアラス若シ之ヲ集ルモ想フニ三千ニハ足ラサルヘシ好シ又露ヲシテ三萬ノ兵ヲ集ムルヲ得セシムルモ我ヨリ二萬ノ兵ヲ出シ貴國ヨリ壹萬ノ兵ヲ出サルレハ之レニ當テ何ノ恐ルヽ所アルヘキゾ余ハ其時淸兵ヲ率ヒテ境界ニ向ハント欲ス

ト誇言致候ニ付拙官ハ

然リヽヽ此時ニハ余モ亦タ日本軍ニ從ハント欲ス

ト戲ニ相答置候

又朝鮮ニ大員ヲ派出スルノ議ニ關シ吳太澂ハ

朝鮮ニ人ヲ派スルニハ先ツ外交ニ長シ兼テ內政ニ巧ニ且ツ朝鮮ノ民情ニ通スル者ヲ用ヒサル可ラス然レトモ我國殆ント此等ノ人ナシ或ハ之レアルモ皆ナ內國ノ要機ニ富ルヲ以テ出テヽ朝鮮ニ行クヲ得ス畢竟其人ヲ得サルニ苦ムナリ

トノ趣申候ニ付拙官ハ

貴國ニ於テ其人ヲ得サルニ苦ムトハ余カ信セサル所ナリ

ト申候處彼レ

余ヲシテ自ラ此任ニ當ラシメハ如何

ト自得ノ言相發候依テ拙官ハ

大人ニシテ自ラ此任ニ當ラハ甚タ可ナラン然レトモ此事未タ大人ノ力ヲ勞スルニハ足ラサルヘシ

トノ趣相答候

右之通此日ハ吳氏得意ノ談話有之候後ニ前顯共同船所說ヲ呈出致候儀ニ付亦是レ太澂一個ノ得意談トノミ御見做可然歟ト推察致候凡ソ得意ノ談話又ハ開進ノ意見等開說致候節ニ總理衙門ノ譯ノ分ラサルヲ慨歎シ或ハ罵詈致候儀ハ李鴻章始メ淸官(但

シ當天津)ノ習慣ニ有之候樣ニ被察候ニ付前顯吳カ說話中總理衙門云々ト云ヘルハ例ノ習慣ニ有之候儀ト是亦推察致候

右具報ニ及候也

明治十八年八月廿五日　天津

領事　波多野承五郎 (印)

外務卿伯爵　井　上　馨 殿

81

波多野承五郎·李鴻章 회담

波多野承五郎(1885. 9. 7) ➡ 井上馨(1885. 9. 21)

機密第五十六號　　　　　　　　　九月二十一日接受

丁汝昌ハ過般以來暫ク太沽ニ滯在罷在候處頃日再ヒ當地ニ歸着致候同人儀ハ去廿四日付機密第五拾壹號ヲ以テ略ホ具申候通リ大院君歸國ノ節同行致候積リニ有之由李鴻章明言致候

金明圭來津ノ用向ハ電線ノ事ノミニハアラサルヘシトノ趣去廿四日付機密第五十一號ヲ以テ具申ニ及置尚ホ一昨日李鴻章ニ面會ノ節右相尋候處李ノ云フ所ニヨルニ

金明圭ハ露國ノ關係ニ付キ余ニ諮詢スル爲メ來津セリ余ハ何等ノ儀ヲ露國ヨリ申出候モ朝鮮政府ニ於テ斷然之ヲ拒絶スヘシ若シ何故ニ之ヲ拒絶スル歟ト問ハバ李鴻章之ヲ准サズト云フヘシト金明圭ニ傳語シ且ツ此趣旨ヲ以テ國王ニ書ヲ贈レリ

右談話ハ曩ニ機密第五十二號ヲ以テ具申ニ及候吳太(*sic*)澂共同船所說ニ付李ノ思想ヲ問試候機會ト存候ニ付右相尋見候處李ハ之レニ付キ何等直接ノ回答ヲ爲サス却テ其坐背ナル例ノ比斯馬克(ビスマーク)公ノ銅像ヲ指シ

此ノ比斯馬克ハ聰明ノ人ナリ彼レ露ガ東洋ニ於ケル擧動ヲ評シ朝鮮若シ正經ノ道ヲ守ラハ露ト雖トモ之ヲ如何トモスルコト能ハサルヘシ而シテ露國兇暴ニシテ正經ノ道ヲ守ル所ノ朝鮮ヲ犯ス如キハ我レ實ニ之ヲ承知ス可ラスト謂ヘリト獨國ノ新聞紙ニ見ヘタリ余ハ中國ノ比斯馬克ナリ恰モ比斯馬克ト同一ノ思想ヲ有ス朝鮮正經ノ道ヲ守リテ尚ホ露之ヲ犯サハ余ニ於テモ之ヲ承知セサルヘシ凡ソ萬國ノ交際ニハ交際ノ法則アル者ナリ正經ヲ守ルノ國ヲ他國ヨリ之ヲ犯サハ萬國既ニ此事ヲ許ス可ラス英國ハ露英ノ葛藤ニヨリテ一時巨文嶋ヲ占據スト雖トモ此葛藤ノ落着スルノ日ハ速ニ該嶋ヲ退去スヘシ英人ハ皆ナ此說ヲナセリ

永興港ヲ以テ共同船所トナスコトハ先ツ朝鮮政府ノ意ヲ問ヒ其承諾ヲ經サル可ラス

ト申候然ルニ英ハ巨文嶋ヲ退去スヘシトノ儀ハ餘リ可笑ク聞ヘ候ニ付拙官ハ英國領事ヨリ聞ク所ニヨルニ英ハ巨文嶋ヨリ退去セサルコトヲ決セリト云ヘリト申候處該

領事ノ云フ所ハ當ニハナラストノ趣相答候又右ニ付李ハ語ヲ繼キ

右ノ如ク余自ラ淸國ノ比斯馬克ナリト云ヒ又李鴻章之ヲ許サストヘルハ言甚タ驕豪ナルニ似タレトモ我屬國ヲ保護スルニハ亦タ自ラ任スル斯ノ如クセサルヘカラス是レ誠ニ已ムヲ得ザルニ出ツル者ナリ

曩キニ貴國外務卿榎本公使ニ訓令シテ朝鮮政府ヲ監視スルコトヲ余ニ任セシメントセリ是レ余ニ於テ甚タ同意スル所ナリ今回朝鮮政府ニ對シテ指命スル所モ亦タ此趣旨ヨリ出テタリ

余今回朝鮮國王ニ書ヲ贈リテ曩ニ浦鹽斯德ニ行キ露ト密約ヲ結フコトヲ企テタル者五名ヲ罰セシムルコトヲ勸告シタリ若シ此輩ヲ罰セザレハ露ノ迫リテ履約ヲ求ムルノ際何ノ辭柄ヲ以テ之ヲ拒ムヘキカ之レ余カ此事ヲ勸告シタル所以ナリ而シテ王ハ右ノ勸告ヲ用ヒ該罪犯者五名ヲ僻遠ノ海嶋ニ放チタル旨回答セリ

トノ趣ヲ相話候拙官ハ共同船所說ニ付キ李ノ意見問試度存候得共機會宜シカラス候ニ付是レニテ談話ヲ相停候右談話中正經ノ道ヲ守ラバ云々ト云ヒ交際ノ法則アリト云ヘル如キハ如何ニモ世界ノ事情ニ迂闊ナル樣ニ相聞ヘ候得共是レハ通辯ノ誤リニモ無之筆記ノ間違ニモ無之實ニ李ノ得意ニ講說致吳候儀ニ有之候

右具報ニ及候也

明治十八年九月七日　　天津

領事　波多野承五郎 (印)

外務卿伯爵　井 上　馨 殿

82

조선 문제에 대한 신중한 접근 촉구

井上馨 (1885. 9. 15) ➡ 波多野承五郎

九月十五日發

機密第四拾壹號

外　務　卿

波多野領事宛

機密第五拾貳號本月十三日接手致披見候吳太(*sic*)澂ニハ朝鮮永興港ヲ(各國共同ノ船所)[ニウトラールポールノ意歟]トナサントノ議貴官ニ揚々然トシテ談話候處貴官ニハ甚タ妙ナリト御稱贊相成候趣抑モ前ノ駐朝鮮獨乙理事官ゼンブス氏ノ案ノ如ク朝鮮全國ヲ擧テ中立國トスルカ如キハ彼ノ爲又亞洲全體ノ爲ニモ好策ト存候ヘ共唯永興港ヲ中立ノポルト致候共同タル效能モ無之ヨシヤ貴官ノ吳太澂ニ御話相成候如ク英米獨等ニ於テ之ニ贊成候共支那ヲ扶テ露國ニ備ヘシムルノミノ事ニ可有之シテ其效瑣少ナルノミナラズ却テ露國ノ忿怨ヲ招キ我ニ於テ不得策ト存候況ンヤ英米獨等ニ於テ之ニ同意スルハ決シテ可得ノコトニ無之候要之近來ハ朝鮮國ニ付テモ種々ノ關係相起リ決シテ三年前ノ該國ニ無之輕卒ニ手ヲ出ヘキ場合ニ無之ニ付我邦カ該國ニ對スル政略モ可成干涉ヲ避ケ唯注意以テ其國運ノ成行ヲ傍觀スル次第有之加之淸國官吏ノ如キハ表裏反覆毫モ信憑スヘキモノニ無之候條深ク御注意相成座話ノ際ト雖モ將來不都合相生候樣ノ御應答無之(樣脱カ)致希望候此段回答旁申進候也

明治十八年九月　日

83
李鴻章의 거문도 점령에 대한 견해

P. S. Popov (1885. 9. 20) ➡ N. K. Girs

AVPRI, F.150, Op.493, D.113, L.102-102ob.

Секретная телеграмма Действительного Статского Советника Попова, Пекин, 8-го Сентября 1885 года.

Передаю буквально следующее интересное сообщение, полученное мною из Тянь-Дзина от Шишмарева: Ли просил меня написать Вам, что все ходившие слухи о действиях Китая, направленных против России — неверны, что Китай никогда не соглашался на занятие Гамильтона англичанами, что, напротив, когда узнал об этом, — заявил протест, что никакого договора он не заключал с Японие й о совокупных действиях против России или, вообще, в защиту Кореи, что никаких особенных приготовлений не производилось и не производится на Уссурийской границе, что нет, по его мнению, причины к нарушению добрых отношений между Россией и Китаем. На вопрос мой, справедлив ли слух, будто в корейских водах находятся, по соглашению Китая с Японией, китайские и японские военные суда, — Ли отвечал, что подобного соглашения не было, но, что китайские суда плавают в тех водах для охраны острова. «Против кого эта охрана?» спросил я. Ли отвечал шутливо: «против русских». Защищать Корею, как страну, зависимую от Китая, он считает обязанностью последнего. Уважит ли Англия протест Китая и очистит ли Гамильтон, Ли не знает, но, воевать с ней из-за этого, говорит он — не стоит; надо уладить дело как-нибудь иначе. Он уверен, англичане оставят Гамильтон, если Россия обяжется не занимать его, так как занятием этого порта они хотели только предупредить русских. Таково сообщение Шишмарева. Надеюсь скоро иметь свидание с Ли, В Пекине, и тогда объяснюсь с ним, в смысле телеграммы Вашей 10 августа.

84
조·청 간의 전신선 가설 협정 체결에 대한 보고

A. P. Davydov (1885. 9. 27) ➡ A. Y. Vlangali

AVPRI, F. Glavnyi arkhiv U-Az, 1885 g, D.45, L.334-6.

Токио, 15/27 Сентября 1885 года.

Его Превосходительству А.Е. Влангали.

Милостивый Государь, Александр Егорович.

Имею честь препроводить при сем Вашему Превосходительству перевод на Английском языке телеграфной Конвенции, заключённой между Китаем и Кореей. Подлинная Конвенция на китайском языке, перевод же сделан здесь и за точность его я ручаться не могу. Японскому правительству удалось достать эту Конвенцию через одного из его тайных агентов, а мне же она была сообщена конфиденциально без ведома Министерства Иностранных Дел.

Сущность Конвенции состоит в следующем: Корейский Король ходатайствовал об учреждении телеграфного сообщения между Сеулом и Чемульпо с одной стороны и Сеулом и Gi-shiu с другой стороны, а оттуда с Но-чжоу. — Судя по карте Кореи, изданной Японским Генеральным Штабом, Gi-shiu (по китайски И-чжоу) есть, вероятно, пункт этого имени на западном конце корейско-китайской границы, недалеко от моря, а Но-чжоу, правильным должно быть, Но-о-чжоу (по китайски Фынъ-хуанъ-чэнъ) — у ветви Великой стены, на дороге из Gi-shiu.

Король просил в то же время, чтобы Китайское Правительство ссудило денежную сумму, необходимую на покрытие расходов по сему предприятию. По докладе сего ходатайства Ли-Хун-Чжаном Богдыхан приказал, чтобы

Китайская телеграфная администрация взяла на себя постройку означенных линий и отпустила сумму 100000 таелей, которая будет выплачена Корейским Правительством без процентов в 20 лет по пяти тысяч таелей в год. Корейское Правительство принимает на себя обязательство не допускать никакого вмешательства какого бы то ни было иностранного Правительства или Компании в ущерб Китайской телеграфной администрации и не дозволять в течение 25 лет постройки телеграфных линий вдоль берегов Кореи. Оно обязуется также обращаться к Китайской Администрации и приглашать служащих в ней, если окажется нужным, строить новые телеграфные линии.

На сообщенном мне в переводе документе не означено числа подписания оного, но, как меня уверяли, Конвенция заключена 4 месяца тому назад и уже приводится в исполнение.

Копию с Конвенции я передал нашему Поверенному в Делах в Сеуле.

С глубоким почтением и таковою же преданностью имею честь быть

Вашего Превосходительства
покорнейший слуга
А. Давыдов.

85
영국의 거문도 점령에 대한 각국의 입장

J. Sienkiewicz (1885. 10. 2) ➡ Ch. de Freycinet

Direction Politique
Sous-Direction de l'Extrême-Orient n. 113.

Tôkiô, le 2 Octobre, 1885

Monsieur le Ministre,

Le retour du Taï-in-Koun à Séoul, que j'indiquais comme, probable dans les derniers rapports que j'ai eu l'honneur d'adresser à Votre Excellence sur les affaires de Corée, est aujourd'hui un fait accompli. Ce personnage, d'après les informations que m'a données le Ministre des Affaires Etrangères du Mikado, se serait engagé à ne plus intervenir dans les questions politiques, à ne plus créer de troubles, à mener en un mot une existence calme et retirée. A-t-il réellement pris de pareils engagements? et, dans le cas où il l'aurait fait, le Comte Ino-ouyé est-il bien sincère en affectant de les considérer comme sérieux? Sur ces deux points j'ai plus que des doutes.

Je serais plutôt porté à voir dans le retour du Daï-in-Koun l'indice d'un accord intervenu entre le Japon et la Chine dans le but d'opposer une résistance énergique aux projets que les Russes peuvent avoir sur la Corée. Ce pays absolument pauvre, sans organisation aucune, incapable par lui-même de défendre son indépendance occupe néanmoins une situation géographique telle que la puissance européenne qui y exercerait une influence prépondérante pourrait sérieusement inquiéter les deux Empires de l'Extrême-Orient. Et c'est précisément parce qu'ils se rendent compte de l'importance de la Corée à ce point de vue spécial que les gouvernements de Pékin et de Tôkiô semblent avoir jugé nécessaire d'en confier le gouvernement à titre officiel ou officieux à un prince connu par son énergie et qui est appuyé par un parti puissant.

Il est vrai qu'il y a trois ans le Taï-in-Koun provoquait un mouvement contre les Japonais, faisait attaquer leur Légation à Séoul et qu'aujourd'hui encore il passe pour leur être profondément hostile. On peut donc, au premier abord, être quelque peu surpris de l'attitude que le gouvernement du Mikado a adoptée à son égard. Mais, outre que dans tout l'Orient l'amitié et la haine sont des sentiments absolument relatifs et n'ayant presque jamais cette ténacité qui les caractérise parfois en Occident, le Japon, éclairé par les expériences qu'il a faites en Corée notamment au mois de Décembre dernier, semble avoir renoncé d'une manière définitive à se porter en Corée comme le rival de la Chine. Et, d'ailleur, sans parler de l'action que très-certainement l'Angleterre exerce dans ce sens, la crainte de la Russie n'oblige-t-elle pas le Japon à vivre en bonne intelligence avec la Chine. Il y a donc une sorte d'évolution dans la politique japonaise et Votre Excellence verra, en prenant connaissance d'un article du "Japan Mail" qu'elle trouvera ci-joint, comment on cherche à l'expliquer et à la justifier.

Convaincu depuis longtemps de l'importance politique de la Corée, je m'étais d'autant plus attaché à suivre les événements qui s'y produisaient que les circonstances rendaient cette tâche très-difficile à notre représentant en Chine. Aujourd'hui que nos relations avec cet empire sont rétablies, notre Légation à Pékin sera en mesure de renseigner exactement Votre Excellence sur les affaires de Corée. Cependant une occasion de puiser à une source nouvelle des indications sur ce pays s'étant offerte ces jours derniers, je n'ai pas cru devoir la laisser échapper. Mgr. Blanc, vicaire apostolique de Corée venait d'arriver à Osaka pour sacrer un Evêque; mais de peur de se compromettre auprès des autorités de Séoul, il devait repartir immédiatement sans pousser jusqu'à Tôkiô. Je confiai donc à un interprète de la Légation le soin de poser diverses questions à ce prélat et de consigner dans un rapport les réponses qu'il pourrait obtenir.

Ce rapport a été fait et je m'empresse de le communiquer, ci-joint, à Votre Excellence à titre tout-à-fait confidentiel. Mgr. Blanc, comme il fallait s'y attendre, s'est placé dans les informations qu'il a données, au point de vue de la situation des missionnaires. Il a, dans tous les cas, le mérite de ne parler que de ce qu'il a lui-même vu ou entendu.

Il appréhende d'une manière particulière et cela se conçoit, le retour du

Taï-in-Koun. Mais à mon sens, il n'est pas absolumment certain que les événements justifient ses tristes prévisions. De même que la haine du Taï-in-Koun contre les Japonais n'a plus de raison de subsister du moment que ceux-ci ont renoncé à prétendre à la suprématie en Corée, de même est-il fort admissible que les sentiments hostiles qui l'animaient contre les chrétiens se modifient au milieu de circonstances qui lui font un devoir de concentrer ses efforts vers un but unique et ne lui permettent point de s'attirer par des persécutions contre les chrétiens, la réprobation des nations civilisées.

Parmi les informations d'ordre politique donnés par Mgr.Blanc, il en est une qui m'a causé quelque surprise. Les diplomates russes ne pêchent point, en général, par excès de naïveté. Comment expliquer, dès lors, que M. de Speyer ait confié à un évêque catholique des projets qui, s'ils eussent abouti, auraient activé d'une manière puissante la propagande orthodoxe. S'il y a là quelque finesse, j'avoue qu'elle m'échappe.

En ce qui concerne la question de Port Hamilton, Mgr. Blanc n'a su dire qu'une chose, c'est qu'on ne s'en préoccupait guère à Seöul. Il n'est pas impossible qu'il en soit réellement ainsi. Je ne puis, de mon côté, ajouter aux renseignements que j'ai déjà fait parvenir à Votre Excellence sur cette affaire, que quelques considérations générales émises par mon Collègue d'Angleterre au cours d'une conversation que j'ai eue dernièrement avec lui.

M. Plunkett n'admet pas un instant la supposition, émise par moi, et d'après laquelle Sir Harry Parkes en renonçant à son ancienne idée de négocier avec la Chine un traité de commerce relatif à la Corée et en se prononçant un faveur de l'indépendance de ce dernier pays aurait été guidée par le désir de faciliter l'occupation future de Port-Hamilton — "Sir Harry Parkes", m'a-t-il dit, "n'avait point de conceptions de cette nature et ne regardait pas si loin dans l'avenir. C'était un Anglais de la vieille école. S'il avait eu la conviction que Port-Hamilton pût nous être nécessaire il en aurait recommandé l'occupation sans se soucier même de savoir si cette île appartenait à la Corée, à la Chine ou au Japon. En ce qui me touche," continua-t-il, "je n'ai eu connaissance de l'occupation que lorsque elle est devenue un fait. J'en ai été fort surpris. L'Amiral Dowell n'était, d'ailleurs, point partisan de l'occupation. Il avait reçu des instructions cachetées et il n'a pu faire autrement que de les mettre à éxécution dès qu'il a pu en prendre connaissance. L'utilité de Port-Hamilton est l'objet de discussions entre nos marins; les avis sont partagés. Il est dans tous les cas positif que cette île ou ce groupe d'îles offre des inconvénients. les navires ancrés dans le port ne sont pas à l'abri des boulets ennemis; d'autre part, bien que la population indigène s'élève à 2000 âmes (on avait d'abord dit 700), il faut faire venir du dehors tous les vivres destinés aux Anglais qui s'y trouverait."

M. Plunkett aurait pu ajouter que des fièvres pernicieuses règnent dans ces îles. Ainsi, pour ne citer qu'un exemple, l'"audacious" a perdu trois officiers à son dernier retour de Port-Hamilton.

Quoi qu'il en soit, M. Plunkett sans se prononcer d'une manière absolue, laisse entendre, assez clairement, qu'il n'est point partisan de l'occupation de Port Hamilton. Il peut se faire qu'en s'exprimant de la sorte, il donne simplement son opinion personnelle, mais il est également admissible qu'il se propose avant tout de rassurer les Japonais dans la mesure de ses moyens. Et c'est sans doute après avoir eu à ce sujet des entretiens avec M. Plunkett et l'Amiral Dowell, que le Comte Ino-ouyé a pu me dire, comme je l'ai rapporté à Votre Excellence, que les Anglais étaient disposés à abandonner Port-Hamilton. Quelles que soient, d'ailleurs, les intentions réelles des Anglais, il est à présumer que ce ne sont pas les événements dont la Turquie d'Europe est actuellement le théâtre qui les déciderait à évacuer Port-Hamilton.

Je profite de cette occasion pour informer Votre Excellence que M.Cogordan vient d'arriver au Japon et que sous peu de jours il s'embarquera pour Shang-haï. Il a été reçu par les Ministres Japonais avec cette politesse exquise qu'on ne rencontre en aucun autre pays, et le Mikado auquel je l'ai présenté aujourd'hui lui a fait un très gracieux accueil.

J'ai, d'ailleurs cru devoir remettre à M. Cogordan une copie des notes sur la Corée qui accompagnent ce rapport.

Veuillez agréer, Monsieur le Ministre, les assurances de ma très-haute considération.

Sienkiewicz.

P. S. Il y a, à certains égards, beaucoup d'analogie entre la situation de la Corée et celle de l'Egypte. Aussi pour se faire une idée exacte de l'importance politique du retour du Taï-in-Koun à Séoul, et en admettant bien entendu que mes appréciations personnelles soient justes, faudrait-il supposer qu'Ismaïl-Pacha a été autorisé à revenir en Egypte.

Son Excellence
Monsieur de Freycinet
Ministre des Affaires Etrangères
à Paris

86
거문도 점령에 대한 조선의 반응 및 러시아의 계획
Mgr. Blanc (1885. 10. 2)

Annexe à la dépêche politique de Tôkiô n. 133 du 2 Octobre 1885

Mgr. Blanc

Très-Confidentiel

Notes sur la Corée fournies par Mgr. Blanc, vicaire apostolique de Corée, durant son séjour à Osaka, du 21 au 25 septembre 1885.

Situation des Chrétiens en Corée. — Ce fut vers la fin du siècle dernier que la religion chrétienne se répandit en Corée: les premiers habitants qui l'embrassèrent étaient nobles. Malgré les persécutions presque continuelles, auxquelles elle fut en butte, la société chrétienne de Corée comptait, avant 1866, plus de 25000 membres.

Mais cette année même, commençait une persécution d'une violence extrême et il ne reste plus aujourd'hui que 12.000 chrétiens environ. Ils sont disséminés dans le royaume, principalement dans les provinces du Centre, du Nord et de l'Ouest. Parfois ils sont groupés dans des villages au milieu des montagnes.

Les missionnaires vivent cachés. Cependant les autorités n'ignorent pas leur présence. mais actuellement elles leur ont fait savoir qu'ils ne seraient pas inquiétés aussi longtemps qu'ils s'abstiendraient de toute manifestation extérieure. Pour éviter les allées et les venues, les missionnaires laissent ignorer aux chrétiens les lieux de leur résidence. Les chefs seuls les connaissent. Pour remplir leur ministère, les missionnaires sortent en costume du pays, de préférence pendant la nuit, et prennent toutes les précautions pour n'éveiller aucune susceptibilité.

L'Evêque réside dans la capitale, où sa présence est connu des autorités coréennes. La maison qu'il occupe a pour propriétaire nominal un noble, qui habite avec lui et qui, en vertu de son titre, assure à cette habitation le privilège de l'inviolabilité de domicile. Lorsque son ministère est réclamé chez quelque chrétien, il se rend dans sa maison. Il y a un assez grand nombre de chrétiens dans la capitale. Il y a auprès de la reine quelques femmes chrétiennes. La Reine douainière a exprimé le désir d'être admise au baptême.

Au commencement de cette année (1885) un hopital pour recevoir des vieillards abandonnés a été élevé par les soins de l'Evêque. Les païens ont vu cet établissements de très bon oeil: la Reine elle-même a fait adresser des félicitations à l'Evêque.

Le Gouvernement Coréen qui a, de son côté, le projet d'établir un hopital, s'est adressé à l'Evêque, afin d'obtenir des soeurs de Charité pour le service des malades.

Etat politique de la Corée — Le Gouvernement de la Corée est la monarchie absolue. Mais le Roi est vassal de l'Empereur de la Chine, dont il reçoit l'investiture, et auquel il envoie chaque année une ambassade avec des présents. Cette ambassade reçoit, en retour, le calendrier; ce qui est le signe indéniable de la vassalité.

Le Roi appartient à la famille Ly; il est le fils du Taï-in-Kun. Le Roi précédent étant mort sans laisser d'enfant, la Reine, sa veuve, adopta ce fils du Taï-in-kun, alors âgé d'une dizaine d'années et le fit élever sur le trône. Quoique, en principe, il gouverne par lui-même, il est d'un caractère faible, si faible qu'il n'ose rien décider sans l'avis de l'agent Chinois à Séoul.

La Reine appartient à la famille Min et s'intéresse beaucoups aux affaires de l'Etat.

La Noblesse est très nombreuse et très puissante. Elle se répartit entre six grandes familles principales, qui se disputent le pouvoir. Ses privilège sont très étendus, et elle en abuse pour refuser de payer aucune taxe et pour arracher au peuple des sommes considérables. Elle n'a point recours à des moyens violents; mais elle emprunte, sans qu'il soit jamais question de restitution, du riz, des boeufs, de l'argent. Il est admis qu'on ne saurait leur opposer un refus. Les Gouverneurs et les mandarins n'essaient même pas d'intervenir.

L'esclavage existe en Corée. On devient esclave volontairement ou par le fait de la naissance. Tel individu se vend pour payer une dette; tel autre entre comme esclave dans une famille noble pour s'assurer des moyens d'existence. Les enfants des esclaves sont esclaves et appartiennent au maître. Quoique celui-ci ait droit de vie et de mort sur ses esclaves, il serait puni, d'après les moeurs actuelles, s'il usait de ce droit, sans s'adresser aux tribunaux. Il faut ajouter cependant que le nombre des esclaves diminue chaque année. On les trouve principalement chez les nobles.

Le Taï-in-kun qui est le père naturel du roi, s'était institué lui-même, de sa propre autorité, membre du Conseil de régence; ce conseil s'étant réuni, il s'y présenta sans y avoir été convoqué et aussitôt il mit la main sur le sceau royal. Il était parent éloigné du précédent roi. Le nom de Taï-in-kun est un titre ou une dignité et signifie: Seigneur de la grande chambre. Intelligent, ambitieux, ne reculant pas devant l'effusion du sang, il s'est créé une situation prépondérante, en abaissant toutes les familles nobles, à l'exception de la sienne qu'il s'efforça d'élever. Le peuple lui est dévoué et attend son retour avec joie. Le Taï-in-kun manifeste pour la reine la haine la plus profonde. Il a déjà essayé d'attenter à sa vie. On prétend qu'un de ses premiers actes, lorsqu'il sera rentré en Corée, sera de se débarrasser de la reine. Il est hostile aux Japonais et aux Chrétiens.

Un trait donne une idée de son caractère. En 1866, lors de la grande persécution contre les chrétiens, on mit la main sur une liste contenant les noms des personnes qui avaient contribué par leurs offrandes à l'entretien des missionnaires. On reprocha au Taï-in-kun que le nom de sa fille s'y trouvait inscrit. Aussitôt il la fait venir, lui demande si le fait est vrai, et, sur sa réponse affirmative, l'avertit qu'elle va mourir. Il fait apporter du poison, et, que par crainte révérencielle, elle ait pris elle-même le poison, ou qu'on l'ait forcée à l'avaler, le fait est qu'elle mourut aux pieds du Taï-in-kun, son père.

La chine a un agent à Séoul. Ce n'est qu'un fonctionnaire d'un rang inférieur appartenant à la Direction du Commerce. On dit même que c'est lui qui fait la première visite aux Consuls étrangers lorsque ceux-ci arrivent. C'est lui, néanmoins, qui dirige, en fait, les affaires du Pays. Le roi ne prend aucune décision sans le consulter.

Depuis les troubles du mois de décembre, les Japonais sont vus de très mauvais oeil. L'évêque de Corée qui, auparavant, avait eu avec eux quelques relations, a jugé prudent, dans ces derniers temps, d'user de la plus grande réserve à cet égard.

M. Mollendorf a joué un rôle important en Corée; mais depuis quelque temps il se plaint amèrement d'être tenu à l'écart. Ce changement qui s'est fait dans sa situation s'explique d'une manière toute naturelle. D'un caractère extrêmement mobile, il varie plusieurs fois par jour dans ses opinions, et n'hésite point parfois à prendre des engagements qu'il lui est impossible de tenir. Citons un exemple entr'autres. Il propose un jour à l'évêque de Corée d'assurer aux missionnaires catholiques le monopole de la propagande religieuse. Comme condition il demande que la Cour de Rome souscrive un emprunt de deux millions, garanti par le revenu des douanes. Il offre, en outre, aux missionnaires catholiques la direction de l'Université de Corée.

Mgr Blanc repoussa catégoriquement ces propositions matériellement irréalisables. M. Mollendorf n'en continua pas moins ses obsessions, réduisant ses prétentions, au point de ne plus demander que 500.000 francs. L'évêque ne voulut rien entendre.

Ces procédés inconsidérés sont assez familiers à M. Mollendorf. Aussi a-t-il perdu peu à peu la confiance des Coréens et celle aussi des étrangers.

Mission de M. de Speyer. — Pendant son séjour à Séoul, M. de Speyer, secrétaire de la Légation de Russie à Tôkiô, vint un jour trouver Mgr. Blanc et s'ouvrit à lui de la démarche qu'il venait d'entreprendre auprès du roi et qu'il exposa ainsi qu'il suit:

"M. de Mollendorf, lors de son voyage à Tôkiô, comme membre de l'ambassade envoyée, il y a quelques mois, au Japon par le Roi de Corée, a fait connaître au Ministre de Russie le désir du Gouvernement Coréen d'engager des officiers instructeurs russes pour organiser son armée. M. Davydov déclara que cette question ne le regardait point. Il promit néanmoins d'en référer à son gouvernement. Il eut soin, toutefois, en écrivant à Pétersbourg de faire observer que, la Corée étant un pays pauvre, le Gouvernement Coréen éprouverait probablement un grand embarras pour assurer les paiements de traitements convenables. Le

Gouvernement russe répondit à M. Davydov en l'autorisant à faire des démarches à Séoul dans le sens des intentions du Gouvernement Coréen; il se déclara même disposé à prendre à sa charge la moitié des traitements. Il prescrivit, en outre, à M. Davydov de négocier de manière à obtenir la direction des postes, des télégraphes et des mines. J'ai été chargé de cette double mission et je viens de faire connaître les intentions de mon gouvernement au roi, qui a paru les accueillir favorablement. Que pensez-vous du succès de ma démarche?"

"Si le roi, répondit Mgr Blanc, se décide à agir seul, s'il ne consulte point l'agent chinois et si l'affaire n'est pas ébruitée, il se peut que vous réussissiez. Mais, étant donnés le caractère et la situation du roi, les chances de succès me paraissent bien faibles. L'agent chinois sera inévitablement consulté et opposera son veto. D'autre part, il est bien difficile de compter sur la discrétion de l'entourage du roi, et d'empêcher que l'affaire ne vienne à la connaissance des autres agents étrangers qui ne manqueront pas de la faire avorter."

Huit jours après, M. de Speyer venait prendre congé de l'Evêque et lui disait que sa démarche avait échoué, le roi ayant commis la faute de consulter l'agent Chinois.

Relativement au protectorat ou à l'annexion, M. de Speyer affirma que son Gouvernement n'y songeait nullement, n'ayant point l'intention d'endosser une responsabilité qui l'amènerait, un jour ou l'autre, à avoir à nourrir les habitants de la Corée.

Traité avec la France. —Le Gouvernement Coréen a un très-vif désir de conclure un traité avec la France. Il l'a témoigné plusieurs fois déjà. Mais, en même temps, il s'attend à ce que le gouvernement français demande des compensations ou des indemnités pour le massacre des missionnaires français en 1866 et pour l'attaque contre les navires de guerre français, qui eut lieu à la même époque. Tout ce qui appartenait aux missionnaires fut pillé et les pertes subies par eux ont été d'autant plus considérables que Mgr. Berneux, en prévision de l'avenir, gardait en réserve les allocations de quelques années. Cet argent fut prix.

Lorsque, en 1801, le roi de Corée fit mettre à mort en haine du Christianisme le prêtre Thomas Tsiou, Chinois d'origine, il crut devoir aussitôt envoyer des excuses à l'Empereur de la Chine. Il prétendit que rien dans le langage ni dans les manières de ce chef de religion n'avait laissé deviner sa qualité d'étranger et qu'il avait été condamné comme sujet Coréen. Il avouait cependant que, en agissant avec plus d'affection, les juges auraient pu découvrir la vérité, mais il suppliait l'Empereur de tenir compte du danger dont le pays était menacé par l'introduction d'une doctrine perverse, et de pardonner une négligence causée par la précipitation. La lettre, qui contient ces excuses, est datée du 20e jour de la 10e lune de l'année KiaKing (25 novembre 1801). On assure qu'elle était accompagnée d'une grosse somme d'argent.

87
영흥만 중립에 관한 吳大澂과의 협의

波多野承五郎 (1885. 10. 17) ➡ 井上馨 (1885. 11. 5)

十一月五日接受

機密信第七二號

去八月廿五日付機密第五十二號ヲ以テ拙官吳太(*sic*)澂ト面話之際同氏ハ露國ヲシテ朝鮮ノ永興港ニ占據スルノ念ヲ斷タシメント欲セハ同港ヲ以テ各國共同ノ船所トナスヘシト物語候ニ付拙官之ヲ賛稱シテ甚タ妙ナリト申候趣具申ニ及候處去月十五日付機密第四十一號ヲ以テ懇ヽ御示論相成候儀敬承致候然ルニ拙官ニ於テ何故ニ甚タ妙ナリト賛稱致候歟ト云フニ共同船所トハ意味モ曖昧ニシテ解シ難キコトナレトモ兎ニ角吳太澂ニシテハ出來過タル考ニ有之候ニ付何歟由來スル所可有之而シテ之ヲ探出スル爲メ貴國ニテ之ヲ發議セラルレバ云々杯申候ニハ先ツ此議妙ナリト歟可ナリト歟多少ノ賛辭ヲ用ヒサレハ連續ヲナサズト相信ジ候儀ニ有之候且ツ其節ハ吳太澂カ酒抔ノ間ニ於テ得意談ヲナスノ最中ニ有之候ニ付多少ノ賛辭ヲ用ヒサレハ場合柄ニ於テモ都合宜シカラスト思考シ卽チ前顯甚タ妙ナリト申候又共同船所トハ ニユートラルポルト ノ義歟判然不致候得共吳太澂ハ國際上ノ事杯ニハ通セサル方ノ人物ニ有之候ニ付今精密ニ之ヲ推問スルモ無益ニ可有之他日此儀ニ關シ萬一御來示ヲ奉スルコトモアラハ其時ヲ俟テ始メテ之ニ付キ詳話可致其爲メノ餘地ヲ存候積リニ有之候又先般差出候機密第五十二號ニモ吳太澂一個ノ得意談ト御見倣可然歟ト具申致候通リ此共同船所說ハ左マデ效顯無之談話ト存候得共兼テ朝鮮中立ノコトニ付キテハ東京ニ於テ御面論之趣モ有之且ツ去七月十五日付機密第二十九號ヲ以テ御差越相成候近藤臨時代理公使ポルトハミルトン第六回報告中ニモ獨逸領事モ愈ヽ中立論ヲ金穆兩氏ニ勸告シ實行セシメ候樣相成モ難計トノ趣相見候ニ付旁ヽ幾分ノ御參考トモ可相成ト相心得縷々御報告ニ及候儀ニ有之候然レトモ今般ノ御示論ヲ接讀シ貴意了解致候ニ付向後ハ尙ホ一層ノ注意ヲ加ヘ言語應答相謹ミ候樣可致候唯タ機密第五十二號ニ於テ拙官ノ意旨未タ悉サザル所モ有之候ニ付此ニ事情開陳シ御賢察相祈候

右御回答旁旁具申致候也

明治十八年十月十七日　天津

領事　波多野承五郎 (印)

外務卿伯爵　井 上　馨 殿

下札

第六回報告ハ

英國軍艦朝鮮國巨文島占領及撤回ニ關スル件ト題スル書中ニアリ(編者附言)

88
거문도 점령 관련 영·청 간 거래 소문

V. K. Shneur (1885. 11. 17) ➡ Director of the Military-Scientific Committee of the General Staff

AVPRI, F.150, Op.493, D.113, L.104-104ob.

Копия с рапорта Военного Агента в Китае от 5-го Ноября 1885 года за № 35, Управляющему Делами Военно-ученого Комитета Главного Штаба.

Занятие англичанами порта Гамильтона без протеста со стороны Китая, который, казалось бы, ближе всего заинтересован был этим захватом, возбудило в свое время не малое удивление и факт этот тогда же объяснялся существованием особой тайной сделки между Англией и Китаем, хотя о характере этой сделки ничего достоверного не проникло ни в публику, ни в печать. Теперь на основании нескольких слов, сказанных в моем присутствии лицами близкими к Ли-хун-чану, можно заключить, что сделка состоит в том, что англичане занимают порт Гамильтон только на время войны с Россией и до тех пор укрепляют и устраивают его по своему усмотрению. По миновании же в нем надобности они обязались уступить его со всеми укреплениями и постройками китайцам, за денежное вознаграждение, равное произведенным или затратам. Насколько это объяснение отвечает истине, сказать трудно, но, во всяком случае, оно заслуживает внимания.

Подписал Полковник Шнеур.

89
청 總理衙門의 전신선 작동 여부 확인

N. R. O'Conor (1885. 12. 5) ➡ The Marquis of Salisbury (1886. 1. 26)

No. 5.

Mr. O'Conor to the Marquis of Salisbury.—(Received January 26, 1886.)

Foreign Office, February 3, 1885.

(Confidential.)

My Lord,

AT the interview which I had with the Prince and Ministers of the Tsung-li Yamên on the 4th instant, his Highness alluded to Port Hamilton, and inquired whether there were still any British ships there. I said, I thought so. One, perhaps, said his Highness. More than that, I imagined, but I had no direct news for a very long time.

His Highness also inquired whether it was true that the cable from North Saddle Island to Port Hamilton was broken, and that there was no intention of repairing it.

I replied that I had no information on the subject. I supposed some foreign Minister had been asking questions. His Highness smiled and said, "Yes;" they had been questioned as to how matters stood by the German Minister, M. von Brandt.

I took occasion to speak of the occupation of the Island I-na-sa by the Russians, alluded to in my despatch No. 477 of the 1st instant. The Ministers seemed pleased at the discovery, and one of them said he saw how it was the Russians had been pressing them to object to our occupation, while they were doing themselves exactly the thing they thought England should not do.

I have, &c.

(Signed) N. R. O'CONOR.

90
井上馨·徐承祖 회담

井上馨·徐承祖 (1885. 6. 15)

日清ノ両全權ガ天津ニ於テ專條ヲ訂立スル以前ニ於テ英露ノ兩國ハ阿富干ノ疆界案件ニテ相互ニ意見ヲ異ニセシ末或ハ和好モ破裂センカト人々ノ思考セシ折柄英國軍艦ハ露人ノ先鞭ヲ着ケ進ンデ朝鮮國ノ巨文島ヲ占據セシトコロ日清ノ天津ニ訂立セシ專條ノ第三款ニ將來朝鮮國若シ變亂重大ノ事件アリテ日中兩國或ハ一國兵ヲ派スルヲ要スルトキハ應ニ先ツ互ニ行文知照スベシ其ノ事定マルニ及テ仍卽チ撤回シ再タビ留防セズトアルヨリ推セバ隣國タル露政府モ亦朝鮮ニ出兵スルノ權利ヲ有スルモノナリト露人ニ主張スルモノアリ殊ニ李鴻章ノ拔擢シテ朝鮮ノ外國交涉顧問トセシ獨逸人モルレンドルフ氏ノ如キハ朝鮮ヲシテ露國ノ保護ヲ受ケシメント主張セシモノヽ一人ナリ國王ニ近侍セル內官等ト謀リ國王ニ勸メテ密使ヲ浦鹽斯德ニ派セシメタル報ガ在京城我臨時代理公使近藤眞鋤ヨリ到達スルニ及ビ井上外務卿ハ頗ル韓國ノ事ニ憂ヲ深フシ明治十八年六月十五日ヲ以テ淸國公使徐承祖ヲ其官邸ニ招キ應接スル如左

此 前日モ御話申候通朝鮮國王君臣ノ間政治ノ體其所爲殆ンド小兒ニ類スル者アリ從來貴我兩國彼ニ注ク所ノ精神ニ符セズ深ク憂慮致居候處昨日在韓我代理公使ヨリノ報告ニ據レバ該國王先般金鏞元外一名ヲ密使トシテ露國浦鹽斯德港地方官ト談事ノ上該地方官ヨリ朝鮮王ヘノ密書ヲ持歸リ鏞元等潛ニ國王ヘ面呈シ該政府諸重臣ハ素ヨリ王ガ何時密使ヲ出シ如何ナル返書ヲ得タル歟ヲ知ル者ナシトノ事ヲ探偵人ニ因テ之ヲ聞キシ後統理督辦金允植ヨリ近藤ノ舍ニ迄迆密ニ人ヲ以テ前段同樣ノ事情且其密書ハ祕シテ發セザル故未ダ之ヲ見ザレドモ文中ニハ日淸天津條約ニ兩國互ニ在韓ノ兵ヲ引佛フベシトアリテ第三款ニ至リ將來朝鮮ニ事アリ兩國或ハ一國ヨリ派兵スルナラバ互ニ先ツ通知スベシ云々是ニ由テ觀レバ我露モ日淸ト同ク貴國ニ隣邦タルヲ以テ日淸ト同樣ノ權利ヲ有スルハ勿論ナリ日淸條約批准ノ後ヲ俟テ我國ヨリ早速該兩政府ヘ右ノ段可申入ナド書シ有之候由洩レ聞キタリト內々報知セシ趣ニ有之因テ閣下ヲ御招キ致シ此報告書ヲ

御一覧ニ入ルヽト

近藤報告密信及ビ京城近況ノ二冊ヲ示ス

彼 前月朝鮮ヨリ派使來京ノ砌モルレンドフ等我公使館ニ參リ該國王ヨリ密使ヲ露領へ遣ハセシ事噂致候儘直ニ公信ヲ以テ李中堂ヘ及報告置候

此 風聞ハ疾クニ知リタレドモ確證ナキ故未ダ敢テ言ハザリシ今此報ヲ見テハ片時モ捨置可ラズ急ニ閣下ト面商シテ防阻ノ法ヲ謀ラザレバ該邦外交ノ拙ナキヨリシテ禍ヲ貴我兩國ニ惹キ及ボスハ旦夕ニ在リ我ガ所存ハ好ミテ該國ノ內事ニ干預スルニハ非ザレドモ方今英露ノ轇轕ニ付テモ東洋ニ幾多ノ影響ヲ來タシタルニ朝鮮ノ外交上ニ若シ失錯アリテ多國ヨリ攪擾セラルヽ如キ事出來セバ之ニ因リ貴我兩國ニ無數ノ障礙ヲ致シ恐クハ東洋ノ事復タ爲ス所無カラン故ニ朝鮮王ノ臨政ヲ少シク拘束シ外交上ニ妄爲ナカラシムヲ要ス如何ニ候哉

彼 御所存ハ可然事乍ラ朝鮮ノ內事外交共王ガ獨裁ニ成ル者ニ非ズ概ネ逼迫ニ出ル事多ク強ガチニ王ヲ責ム可ラザル歟故ニ之ヲ拘束セント云フハ甚ダ面倒ナラン其內事ニ干預スル嫌ヲ取ランヨリハ我等ノ國ニテ鯁直有爲ノ人物ヲ選抜シテ彼國ニ遣ハシ其君臣ノ間懇々說諭ヲ加ヘ自ラ改良スル所アラシムヲ佳トス如何

此 此策平素ニ在テハ佳トスベキモ方今ノ事勢ニ當リ恐クハ其効ナカラン今京城ノ近況ヲ聞クニ彼ノ六孽ト目セラレタル內官共ガ晝夜王側ニ昵近シテ朋比奸ヲ爲シタベニ其人ヲ薦ムレバ金玉均ト同罪タル尹雄烈ノ如キモ王猶ホ之ヲ擧テ重用シ朝タニ讒言ヲ進メテ金宏集ヲ冷曹ニ遠ケ魚允中ヲ庶人ニ放タシム僅ニ金允植一人位ヲ統理督辦ニ保チタルモ已ニ風前ノ燭ノ如シト云ヘリ然レバ此人アルモ亦タ無キニ等シク其爲ス可ラザルヲ知ル且拙者前日朝鮮ニテ王ト對顔ヲ得シトキ親シク風采ヲ窺フニ今年約ソ三十四五歳ト見ユ此年齢ニシテ其事ヲ處スル此ノ如ケレバ假令他ヨリ賢良ナル人ヲ送テ諄々ト勸諭スルトモ其進善去惡スル能ハザル事知ル可キナリ抑モ亦タ奸佞ナル六孽ノ爲メニ讒離セラレンノミ今貴國ノ邊疆露ト接壤スル者正ニ其幾萬里アルヲ知ラズ只黑龍江ノ下流ニ沿フ者ノミニシテ已ニ七百有餘里ニ亘ルモ彼レ猶ホ志ヲ逞スル事止マズ英ハ印度以東ニテ海上ノ權ヲ益々擴張シ卽チ英ガ軍艦ヲ巨文島ニ繫ゲバ露モ亦將サニ元山津カ或ハ釜山浦ヲ假ラントスルノ意アルカ如ク貴我兩國此東洋中ノ獨立ヲ鞏固ニセント勉勵ノ際ニ在テ我ガ事ヲ壞亂スルノ根源ハ此朝鮮ニ非ズシテ何ゾヤ我國ハ一ノ海島ニシテ他邦ハ聯接セズ且ツ褊小ナレバ外人ハ未ダ必ラズ垂涎セザルモ貴國

版圖ノ大ナル遥カニ歐洲ニ連リタレバ豈彼人ニ覬覦ナシト謂フヲ得ンヤ外人ノ講スル公法ハ恃ム可ラズ彼ハ利ヲ見テ義ヲ忘レ競テ人ノ物ヲ取ル此時ニ富リ我レ彼ノ公法ヲ論スルトモ彼ハ但ダ答フルニ腕力ヲ以テス我等ハ實ニ是レニ困却シタリ目今外人已デニ其色ヲ朝鮮ニ擧ルノ勢ヲ形ハシ貴我兩國ニ關繫スル所最モ大イナリ果シテ擾ヲ受ルノ日ニ至ラバ日淸韓ハ決シテ連合セズ只各其國利益ニ妨害アランヲ防ク爲メ銘々ニ外人ノ請ヒヲ拒ミ相離レテ談判スルヲ要トス譬ヘバ英人ガ巨文島ヲ佔據スルヲ貴國ヨリ開談センニハ只ダ切近ノ海境ニ據ラレテハ危害ヲ中國ノ利益ニ及ボサンヲ以テ拒絶ノ論柄ト爲シ若シ日本ニ對スル海境ニ據ル事アラバ我國モ亦之ヲ以テ拒絶ヲ爲シ而シテ朝鮮ヘモ此意ヲ相勸テ心得シメ只管ニ自國ノ利益ニ妨害アリト斷言セシメン事ヲ希望ス貴我兩國ヨリ或ハ朝鮮ノ爲メニ成リ替リテ之ヲ拒ム樣ノ姿ニ立至テハ節外生枝テ幾分カノ面倒ヲ負擔スルノ患アルベキガ如シ前日伊藤大使貴國コリ歸リシトキ我ニ告ルニ李中堂ガ東洋事機ニ注意セラレタル話ヲ以テス其旨趣正ニ我ガ今日ノ所見ト同ク彼此符節ヲ合セタル如シ故ニ閣下ニ因リ之ヲ李中堂ニ謀リ必ス中堂ノ明鑑ヲ以テ朝鮮政府大臣中ヨリ兩三名ノ賢良ナル有爲ノ人ヲ選マレ國王ニ令シテ之ヲ擧ゲ其倚畀ヲ重クシ外交軍事會計ノ事務ヲ委任シ之ト咨諏裁決シ別テ外國ト通使行文スル事ハ一々李中堂ヘ咨禀シテ批定ヲ請ヒ核准ノ上始テ之ヲ送リ之ヲ發シ決シテ私自妄爲ヲ許サズ且ツ戒飭ヲ加ヘ奸佞ノ徒ヲ遠ケ賢良ノ臣ヲ進メシムルニ於テハ外交上ニ大ナル失錯アルヲ免ルベシ若シ然カセズシテ今日ノ妄爲ニ任セ之ヲ匡正スルノ機ヲ失セバ大院君ガ歸國スルモ近キニ在リ草莽ノ橫議再ビ興リモルレンドルフガ事ヲ隣港ニ賣リ其身ニ利セントスル如キ總テ雇外國人ハ其之ヲ使フ人ノ忠奸ニ因テ反復無常ナリ苟モ時ノ乘ズベキアリ奸ノ與ミスベキヲ見レバ利ニ就キ義ヲ去ル事猶ホ敝屣ヲ棄ルガゴトシ何ゾ其主ヲ愛スル事之レアランヤ假令中堂モルレンドルノヲ退ケ別ニ其信用スル所ノ外人ヲ進ムルトモ今日ノ朝鮮ニ往テ事ヲ執ラシムルトキハ亦復如是ニ過ギズト思フ

事共粛牆ノ內ニ起リ爲メニ外患ヲ來タシテ禍ヲ貴我兩國ニ延カン事其レ旦夕ニ在ラン乎請フ此意ヲ中堂ニ達セヨ

彼 此報告書二冊ハ拜領シテ不苦候哉

大院君歸國云々ニ付テハ中國實ニ之ヲ放還スルカ未ダ確知セザルナリ

此 御持チ可被成

彼 漢文ヲ以テ之ヲ照譯セシメ御談話ノ旨趣ヲ逐一申添ヘ卽便中堂ニ飛報シテ返簡到
着次第早速報道可致候間東洋ノ爲メ御畫策ノフカキヲ始テ領略スルヲ得實以テ佩
服ノ至我不敏ト雖ドモ從今閣下ニ師事致度存候間以後萬端御敎示ヲ祈ル所ニ候

91

조선과 청국 간 전신망 연결 및 일본 정부의 부산과 나가사키 전신선 부설권 획득 보고

A. P. Davydov (1886. 1. 5) ➡ N. K. Girs

AVPRI, F. Glavnyi arkhiv U-Az, 1885 g, D.45, L.386-8.

Токио, 24 Декабря/5 Января 1885/1886 гг.

Его Высокопревосходительству Н. К. Гирсу.

Милостивый Государь, Николай Карлович.

Не так давно Китайское Правительство выговорило у Кореи право соединить Сеул телеграфною линией с сетью Китайских телеграфов, что уже и приведено в исполнение.

Японское Правительство протестовало в Сеуле против устройства этой линии, ссылаясь на право, выговоренное телеграфной Конвенцией в пользу Японии при проложении его из Нагасаки в Корейский порт Фузан кабеля.

Этой Конвенцией Корея действительно обязалась не устраивать ни с каким иностранным государством международной телеграфной линии, не согласившись предварительно с Японией.

Получив нынешний Японский протест, Корейское Правительство пыталось однако отговориться тем, что во-первых новая телеграфная линия соединила ее не с иностранным государством, а с Китаем, ее сюзереном, что во-вторых это даже и не соединение, так как телеграф от Сеула доведен только до реки, служащей границей между Китаем и Кореей и через речку не переходит, телеграммы же перевозятся на Китайскую сторону паромом и что наконец в третьих международного значения линия эта не имеет.

В конце концов однако Японскому Поверенному в Делах в Сеуле удалось добиться от корейцев подписания формального обещания соединить в 6-месячный срок Фузан, конечный термин Японского кабеля, с Сеулом и таким образом уравновесить выгоды в этом деле двух соседних с Кореей Империй.

Кроме этого, документ, подписанный 9/21 Декабря в Сеуле, содержит в себе обязательство Корейского Правительства применять в продолжение 25 лет к официальным Японским телеграммам половинный тариф, а также формальное обещание, что плата за телеграммы от Фузана до Сеула не будет превышать 8 центов за слово, взимаемых Корейским Правительством ныне за передачу депеш от Сеула до Китайской границы.

В настоящее время обнародовано было Японским Правительством запрещение принимать частные телеграммы в Сеул и передавать в Японии приходящие этим путем из Кореи снята и опубликована следующая такса для телеграмм, посылаемых из Шанхая в Корею: в Wi-ji — 44 цента за слово, Phyeng-an — 48 центов, в Сеул — 52 цента и Inchen (Чемульпо) — 56 центов. Телеграммы, отправляемые в Корею из Японии должны конечно сверх того уплатить пословную таксу из Японии в Шанхай.

Соединение Фузана с Сеулом является несомненно очень желательным. Оно во-первых удешевит телеграфные сношения Японии с Кореей и во-вторых установление этой второй линии гарантирует правильность этих сношений в будущем, на что трудно рассчитывать теперь, когда единственный телеграфный путь, связывающий Корею с Европой, находится в руках Китайцев.

С глубочайшим почтением и таковою же преданностью имею честь быть

Вашего Превосходительства
покорнейший слуга
Шпейер

92
거문도 전신선 관련 O'Conor 지시 내용 전달

Currie (1886. 2. 3) ➡ The Secretary to the Admiralty

No. 8.

Sir P. Currie to the Secretary to the Admiralty.

Foreign Office, February 3, 1886.

(Confidential.)

Sir,

WITH reference to your letter of the 27th ultimo, inclosing a Report from the Commander of Her Majesty's ship "Wanderer" with reference to the security of the telegraph cable at Port Hamilton, I am directed by the Marquis of Salisbury to state to you, for the information of the Lords Commissioners of the Admiralty, that it has been suggested to his Lordship that, in order to gain the good-will of the Chinese Government for the telegraph line and for the British occupation of Port Hamilton, it might be politic to send occasionally to them from that place telegraphic news of events in Corea. It is thought that they would then from time to time make use of the line for their own messages to Corea.

Her Majesty's Chargé d'Affaires at Peking has been instructed, if he thinks it worth while to do so, to suggest this course to the Admiral and to Her Majesty's Acting Consul-General in Corea.

I am, &c.

(Signed) P. CURRIE.

93
李鴻章에게 Denny의 거문도 문제 개입 차단 요청

N. R. O'Conor (1886. 3. 12) ➡ Earl of Rosebery (1886. 5. 3)

No. 28.

Mr. O'Conor to the Earl of Rosebery.—(Received May 3.)

Peking, March 12, 1886.

(No. 81.)

My Lord,

WITH reference to my despatch No. 491 of the 15th December last, I have the honour to report that Mr. Denny, who, as your Lordship is aware, has been engaged by the Viceroy Li Hung-chang for the post of Political Adviser to the Corean Government, rendered vacant by the dismissal of M.von Möllendorff has arrived at Tien-tsin. I have again privately urged upon the Viceroy the advisability of giving Mr. Denny strict instructions not to interfere in the question of Port Hamilton, as such interference would be likely to complicate the question without doing any good.

I have, &c.

(Signed) N. R. O'CONOR.

94

러시아의 영흥만 측량에 따른 영·러 간 알력

袁世凱 (1886. 5. 22 / 光緖十二年四月十九日) ➡ 李鴻章

十九日下午九點五分發計一百二十二字

中堂鈞鑒 密 俄船在永興測量已電稟今晤英貝云俄人或有意於永興不如英派船往守□云再如巨文斷不可行□將電請我政府派船往巡不須英船往萬一俄有他意或英派一二隻船泊元山藉名護商觀勢牽制斷不可遽赴永興致啓訟端英貝又云永興宜開口岸□將憲前電告之□稟豪卅一次

95
거문도 문제 관련 문건 작성에 袁世凱 개입

袁世凱 (1886. 6. 26 / 光緖十二年五月二十五日) ➡ 李鴻章

五月廿五日下午七點半發

中堂鈞鑒 密 韓廷索巨文島囑德尼繕文韓王甚嘉其文而外署徐相雨以其詞太激私來請改□恐韓廷方議自主將又加禍於徐細檢其最刺目處指示一二聽其自改俄約尚推未議允植雖復職韓廷未催任事尙在城外□稟蒸廿九次

96

전신선의 유지 여부 문의

J. Walsham (1886. 8. 15) ➡ Earl of Iddesleigh

관련문서 거문도 전신선의 유지 여부 해군성 문의

NO. 58.

Sir. J. Walsham to the Earl of Iddesleigh.—(Received August 15, 5·35 P. M.)

Peking, August 15, 1886, 5·15 P. M.

(No. 56.)
(Telegraphic.)
YOUR telegram No. 49.

China and Corea might each [? or jointly] offer guarantee, but it would be utterly worthless unless in combination with England, and this might, at any moment, prove embarrassing. It was on account of inability to devise a settlement of this kind that I suggested the plan of Treaty ports which. I think, would have support of Viceroy Li.

Before attempting it as a basis of arrangement, I should be glad to know what Her Majesty's Government would propose to do with the cable from Saddle Island, and also, whether they would wish to retain present [? trading] sites at Port Hamilton with the plots of ground already rented from inhabitants. Eastern Extension Company might, perhaps, be inclined to amalgamate cable and prolong it to Corean mainland. See Inclosure 1 in O'Conor's No. 144. and his No. 429 of last year.

Plan of Treaty ports, if accepted, might be granted by an Additional Article to our Corean Treaty, and any other details recorded in the form of a declaration.

If cholera is less prevalent, I propose to go to Corea in October to present credentials.

【관련문서】

No. 63.

Sir P. Currie to the Secretary to the Admiralty.

Foreign Office, August 17, 1886.

(Secret and Confidential.)

Sir,

I AM directed by the Earl of Iddesleigh to transmit to you, to be laid before the Lords Commissioners of the Admiralty, copies of telegraphic correspondence with Her Majesty's Minister at Peking in regard to Port Hamilton; and I am to request that you will move their Lordships to favour his Lordship with their opinion as to the answer that should be returned to Sir J. Walsham's inquiry in respect to the cable from Saddle Island to Port Hamilton, and the sites rented in the last mentioned place.

I am, &c.

(Signed) P. CURRIE.

97
거문도의 조약항 지정 방안

Earl of Iddesleigh (1886. 8. 18) ➡ J. Walsham

No. 64.

The Earl of Iddesleigh to Sir J. Walsham.

Foreign Office, August 18, 1886.

(No. 237. Ext. 53.)

Sir,

WITH reference to my telegram No. 52 of the 16th instant, I have to state to you that Her Majesty's Government would propose, in the event of Port Hamilton being made a Treaty port, to take up the cable connecting that place with Saddle Island, and sell it for what it is worth; they would have no wish to retain the sites rented from the inhabitants of Port Hamilton.

I have to request you to keep Her Majesty's Government informed as to the question of a Russian Protectorate over Corea.

I am, &c.

(Signed) IDDESLEIGH.

98
조선의 지위 관련 Denny · 李鴻章의 대담

G. C. Foulk (1886. 10. 14) ➡ T. F. Bayard

No. 13.

Oct. 14, 1886.

Secretary of State

Sir,

With reference to my despatch No. 3, dated September 8th ultimo, having for its subject the political disturbance in Söul of August last, I have now to report that Judge Denny has returned to Korea from Tientsin and has communicated to me at some length the substance of his interviews with the Viceroy Li Chung Fang. The information I have thus obtained is fully in harmony with the opinions expressed in my despatch — that the disturbance in Söul was created by the Chinese representative here in an attempt of China to suppress the independent sovereignty of this Kingdom, and that the attempt was frustrated by unexpected complications in Söul and the fight between sailors of the Chinese fleet at Nagasaki and the police and people at that place.

Judge Denny reports that in his earlier interviews, the Viceroy was disposed to defend the Chinese representative here — Mr. Yuan — against the charges vigorously brought against him by Judge Denny and Mr. H. F. Merrill, the American Chief Commissioner of Korean Customs. The chief charge was that Mr. Yuan had created copies of a purported agreement bearing the seal of the King of Korea by which Korea was turned into a protectorate of Russia; assuming that the announced existance of these copies would create the impression that a real agreement had been made, he believed that China's right to absorb Korea would be established. These copies were, however, denounced as forgeries from the beginning by Judge Denny, Mr. Merrill, and the several foreign representatives except the Consul General of England, and the two officers named brought these opinions to the attention of the Viceroy by telegrams and letters. The Viceroy and Peking government thus discovered that their ruse was detected; thus with the affair at Nagasaki, which foreboded difficulty with Japan, checked effectually the move intended.

Judge Denny states that while the Viceroy is charged with the control of Korean affairs for China, it was not at his original instance that Mr. Yuan made the attempt in Söul; that the scheme originated in the Peking government, which ordered the Viceroy to furnish ships of war and men necessary to Mr. Yuan to effect the suppression of Korea. The Viceroy conveyed the idea to Judge Denny that England through her representative at Peking has long been urgently pressing the government there to incorporate Korea into her own Empire out and out. The plan decided upon by China was to remove the King, Queen, and Crown Prince of Korea to China, place the Tai Wön Kun temporarily at the head of affairs in Korea (because of his popularity and power with the people), and finally to create out of her a new province of the Chinese Empire.

Judge Denny states that the Viceroy fully appreciate the inexpediency of the annexation of Korea, and realize that England is operating in relation to Korea, out of purely selfish motives; also that the Peking government has had its eyes opened to the fact that it has been handled as a tool by England at the risk of bringing grave trouble upon China. The English minister had just proposed to China the opening of Port Hamilton and had announced his intention of proceeding to Korea to effect the necessary arrangements. With regard to this, Judge Denny states he endeavored to satisfy the Viceroy with such a mission of the English minister would be useless — that Korea could not entertain the proposition, and that in view of the manner in which England had occupied the Port, Korea could only insist upon its release — and that it was China's plain duty to maintain Korea's stand in the matter. To these remarks the Viceroy gave his approval.

After considerable discussion as to the most feasible in which the inviolability of Korea could be preserved, it was finally decided upon that China should ask Russia to enter into an agreement providing for the neutrality of the Korean Peninsula, as regards to the two nations. The Russian minister at Peking was consulted in this connection by the Viceroy and by Judge Denny. Upon leaving Tientsin, Judge Denny was informed by the Viceroy that Russia had regarded the proposition favorably, and that the agreement would soon be effected.

At Nagasaki, the investigation of the affray there on August 15th by Chinese and Japanese officials, is being prolonged while there are as yet no evidences of a speedy satisfactory settlement. It is apparently the attitude of China which delays the proceedings. Japan evinces marked irritability over the affair, involving consideration of Korea. It is now reported on good authority that Mr. Takahira Kogoro, the present Chargé d'Affaires of Japan to Korea is about to be recalled and the impression is popular that Japan will place in his stead an official prepared to deal more summarily with questions involving Korea and Japan and China. In this connection I may quote from my dispatch No. 306, dated June 2, 1886—"Mr. Takahira impressed to me clearly that the attitude of China has reached a point at which the misunderstanding arrived at in the convention at Tientsin, in regard to Korea, has been departed from, and the interference by his government would seem to be imperatively necessary."

I beg to point out that in the above it is Judge Denny's account and opinion that I have given its relation to the intentions of the Viceroy with respect to Russia and Korea and England. I am not so sanguine that China and Russia will enter into a satisfactory agreement with regard to Korea, though this is to be hoped for, and is desireable to both these governments. England has already a strong hold upon the Peking government and will the more energetical endeavor to create Chinese suspicions of Russia's good faith. I regret to add also, that there is evidence to warrant the belief that Judge Denny has not the support and confidence of the Viceroy;—nor in view of his having been selected and summoned for service in Korea by China, has he the confidence of the progressive or anti-Chinese faction in Korea; thus far he has been permitted no confidential and active part in the affairs of Korea.

George C. Foulk.

99
거문도 전신선 처분 여부 결정 요청

Macgregor (1886. 12. 21) ➡ Currie

No. 132.

Sir. Macgregor to Sir. P. Currie.—(Received December 23.)

Admiralty, December 21, 1886.

(Confidential.)

Sir,

WITH reference to your letter of the 4th instant and the correspondence which ensued respecting the instructions to be sent to Her Majesty's Minister at Peking and to the Naval Commander-in-chief on the China Station with regard to the withdrawal of the British force from Port Hamilton, I am commanded by my Lords Commissioners of the Admiralty to request that you will state to the Earl of Iddesleigh that the ultimate disposal of the telegraph cable to Port Hamilton, which is Admiralty property, has engaged their Lordships attention.

2. My Lords desire me to suggest, for the consideration of the Secretary of State for Foreign Affairs, that the Port Hamilton cable might be offered to the Chinese Government, as it might suit them to continue it to Corea, a distance of about 30 miles, thus strengthening their own connection with that country.

3. My Lords desire me to state that the cable is believed to be a good one, and, although not at present in working order, the fault in it could be readily repaired. My Lords would be ready to dispose of the cable to the Chinese Government for 30,000*l*., which is much below half the cost of it, when laid down in 1885.

I am, &c.

(Signed) EVAN MACGREGOR.

100

청 정부의 거문도 전신선 구매 거절 결정

J. Walsham (1886. 3. 12) ➡ Earl of Iddesleigh (1886. 5. 3)

No. 2.

Sir J. Walsham to the Earl of Iddesleigh.—(Received January 5.)

Peking, January 5, 1887.

(No. 2.)

(Telegraphic.)

YOUR telegram No. 62. Chinese Government thank Her Majesty's Government for opportunity given of purchasing cable, but do not want it, having land line with Corea. This decision is taken after reference to the Viceroy Li, Superintendent of Telegraphs. No allusion made t6 conditions on which landing of cable on Saddle Island was allowed, but I venture to call attention to corres- pondence during 1885, especially to O'Conor's No. 256 and 279, 2nd and 10th June, in order to prevent questions respecting its removal from Chinese territory.

7-1.
영국 내 거문도 무용론과 철군 논의

101
거문도 점령의 경제적 이점

F. Plunkett (1885. 5. 25) ➡ E. Granville

No. 66.

Mr. Plunkett to Earl Granville.—(Received July 30.)

Tôkiô, May 25, 1885.

(No. 151. Very Confidential.)

My Lord,

YOUR Lordship can well understand that our "temporary" occupation of Port Hamilton is much discussed in these countries, and various opinions exist, as to whether, or not, it will now be to our interest to keep it.

The opinion is very generally expressed that its possession is not worth the excuse which it gives to other European nations, and especially to Russia, to go and do likewise; that it is too small to be self-supporting, and would therefore have to be fed at great expense from the main land; that the money which would be required for putting it in even a decent state of defence might be much more usefully employed in strengthening the fortifications of Singapore and Hong Kong; and that it would weaken our squadron in the East by the number of ships which would have to be detached for its protection.

I venture, however, to take a somewhat different view of the subject, and to urge that, the step of occupying it having been once taken, we should not be in a hurry to give up a position which may, I think, without much expense, be made of great political and commercial value to Great Britain.

Situated as Port Hamilton is, within about 100 miles from Tsushima and Fusan, 160 miles from Nagasaki, and under 300 from Shanghae, the provisioning of the islands, under ordinary circumstances, ought not to be more difficult than is that of Malta in the Mediterranean, or that of Syra in the Aegean; even if the neighbouring large Island of Quelpart did not, as would be probable, contribute to its support.

As I had the honour to report when I visited them in 1875, the configuration of the islands forming Port Hamilton is such that fortifications on a small scale ought to suffice for its defence, and the argument that, whatever they cost, the money might be better employed at Hong Kong, loses weight from the improbability that whatever might be saved, by not taking Port Hamilton, would be devoted to other military purposes in these quarters.

On the other hand, I consider a depôt for our trade, such as Port Hamilton might form if it were made a "free port" under the British flag, would be of the greatest possible benefit to English Trade in this part of the Far East.

I cannot help feeling that the days of "foreign Settlements" and "enforced Tariffs" are rapidly passing away, and that the small profits on which trade must now be carried on will make it every day more and more difficult for the English merchant to compete on the spot with the native, whom education and the telegraph are every day placing more on a par with him. If, therefore, our home manufacturers hope to force the sale of our goods on these Eastern nations, they will have to look to native agents to do it, or they will find themselves beaten out of the field by the Germans and other foreigners who work at lower rates than we do.

In view, therefore, of what I fear is the inevitably decreasing influence of the "Settlements," it would, I think, be of the utmost value to British commerce to have a depôt for our goods such as Port Hamilton might offer, and which, taken in connection with Singapore and Hong Kong, would give us a control over Eastern markets with which other nations will find it difficult to compete.

The early completion of the Trans-Canadian Railway is expected to lead to the establishment of a line of fast steamers from Canada to Shanghae to compete with the very inferior service now carried on from San Francisco to Yokohama, and whether those steamers should, as is proposed, pass by Hakodate and the Japan Sea (the route laid down in great circle sailing) or whether they should call at Yokohama, in either case would almost within sight of Port Hamilton, and thus, without any extra expense, bring it into the regular route of mail communication round the world.

There is also another reason for remaining at Port Hamilton, to which I would venture to call your Lordship's attention.

As long as we remain there these countries may have a sort of moral certainty that we shall not want anything else and that, in fact, they know the worst. If we leave it now, we shall certainly be understood to have retired merely in consequence of the representations made by China and Corea at the suggestion of Russia, and every time rumours arise of complications between Great Britain and Russia, these countries will have a constant fear of other temporary occupations by Great Britain for coaling purposes, and no professions on our part of future honesty are likely to counterbalance the arguments which Russia would certainly use against us. In fact, it would be our retirement which would be considered "temporary," and the "occupation" would again be expected whenever desirable.

Your Lordship will recollect that in my despatch No. 249, Secret, of the 22nd December, I expressed the opinion that it might suit Japan to connive at Russia taking some part in Corea in order to have a greater security for her not coveting any part of this Empire, and my reasoning in that case applies with equal force to the occupation of Port Hamilton by England.

I believe, moreover, that it would not at present be very difficult to reconcile China, Corea, and Japan to the notion of Great Britain remaining at Port Hamilton. They have, as yet, only thought of the political value of it to us against Russia, and have not yet appreciated the commercial value it might be, as a depôt for goods, in future years when higher Tariffs come to been forced in China and Japan, and the Russian ports become more populated.

I have, &c.
(Signed) F. R. PLUNKETT.

102

무역항으로서의 거문도의 가치를 다룬 Plunkett 보고서

Currie (1885. 7. 4) ➡ Furrer

No. 69.

Mr. Currie to Sir T. Furrer.

Foreign Office. July 4, 1885.

(Very Confidential.)

Sir,

I AM directed by the Marquis of Salisbury to transmit to you, very confidentially, the accompanying copy of a despatch from Her Majesty's Minister at Tôkiô, expressing his views as to the retention of Port Hamilton and its importance to this country; and I am to request that in laying this letter before the Lords of the Committee of Privy Council for Trade, you will move their Lordships to favour Lord Salisbury at their early convenience with opinion as to the value of the place in question as a commercial port.

I am, &c.

(Signed) P. CURRIE.

103
해군 기지로서 거문도의 적합성 검토

The Secretary to the Admiralty (1885. 9. 15) ➡ Hamilton

No. 44.

The Secretary to the Admiralty to Vice-Admiral Hamilton.

Admiralty, September 15, 1885.

Sir,

MY Lords Commissioners of the Admiralty having had under their consideration Reports in regard to the recent occupation of Port Hamilton, and the value of that island as a naval station, I am commanded by their Lordships to signify their direction to you take an early opportunity, after assuming command of the China Station, to investigate and report upon the capabilities of Port Hamilton as a coaling-station and naval station.

My Lords also desire that you will give your opinion as to whether or not, in time of war, the occupation of Port Hamilton would be a source of weakness, or strength, to the cruizing power of the squadron in the China command.

I am, &c.
(Signed) EVAN MACGREGOR.

104
거문도 주둔 해군 상황 보고

The Secretary to the Admiralty (1886. 1. 20) ➡ Currie (1886. 1. 21)

No. 2.

The Secretary to the Admiralty to Sir P. Currie.—*(Received January 21.)*

Admiralty, January 20, 1886.

(Confidential.)

Sir,

WITH reference to Admiralty letter of the 6th October last, respecting the purchase of Port Hamilton, as suggested by Mr. Aston, Acting British Consul in the Corea, in which it was stated that Vice-Admiral Hamilton had been instructed to report upon the occupation of this island, I am now commanded by my Lords Commissioners of the Admiralty to transmit to you, for the perusal of the Marquis of Salisbury, the Report received from Vice-Admiral Hamilton, Commander-in-chief on the China Station, dated the 7th December, respecting Port Hamilton, together with the Report made by his predccessor, Admiral Sir William Dowell.

Admiral Sir George Willes, who was Commander-in-chief on the same station previous to Sir William Dowell, thoroughly concurs in these Reports.

2. My Lords consider that the opinion of these officers should carry great weight from a naval point of view. They all agree, after a careful local investigation, in considering that it is not desirable to hold Port Hamilton, and that, until it is made a first-class fortress, it would be a source of weakness, in war time, to the cruizing power of the squadron in the China command.

3. My Lords desire to add that these views meet with their entire approval.

4. Port Hamilton is at the present moment occupied by a body of marines, and there are, in addition, considerable expenses connected with the temporary retention of the island.

5. The cable laid between Port Hamilton and Saddle Island (Shanghae) requires repair, but my Lords have declined to sanction the large outlay necessary to restore it to working order until they are in possession of the definite views of the Foreign Office.

6. Their Lordships would, therefore, impress upon the Secretary of State for Foreign Affairs the advisability of an early decision upon the subject.

I am, &c.
(Signed) EVAN MACGREGOR.

Inclosure 1 in No. 2.

Vice-Admiral Hamilton to the Secretary to the Admiralty.

"Audacious," at Hong Kong, December 7, 1885.

(Confidential.)

Sir,

IN compliance with the directions contained in your letter of the 15th September last, Confidential, I have the honour to report, for the information of the Lords Commissioners of the Admiralty, that having attentively perused and carefully considered the documents, plans, &c., in my Office, on the subject of the occupation of Port Hamilton, and having also consulted several of the Senior Officers of the squadron, I have arrived at the same conclusion as my predecessor has so ably expressed in his letter of the 28th May last, and, therefore, have nothing further to say on that head, beyond observing that a harbour, with three entrances as now exists, while admirably adapted for flight, is not as well adapted for permanent defence as is a harbour with a single entrance, on which all the defensive powers can be concentrated, instead of, as in the case of Port Hamilton, being scattered over three entrances.

2. I also entirely concur with my predecessor's views of the inadequacy of the fortifications proposed by the War Office, as stated in his letter of the 19th June

7 last.

Captain Long, of the "Agamemnon," in writing of Port Hamilton to the Commander-in-chief in May last, says, "It must be observed, if the place is to be a base for, and not to be a tax upon, the navy, it will require a garrison and fortifications. At present it requires the constant presence of a large proportion of the naval force on the station to preserve the flag from insult in the event of war."

I commend the portions under lined to their Lordships' special notice; I entirely concur in them; a base for the navy must be one in which they can find themselves defended when unable, from any cause, to keep the sea, which is their proper place, and to protect our commerce by driving the enemy's ships from the sea, as we have done in all previous wars, but which cannot be done if the navy is condemned to the defensive, to remain in port, guarding its own base.

3. Captain Maclear, of the "Flying Fish," in a very able Memorandum on the defences of Port Hamilton, observes: "To defend it against the attack of two corvettes, three sloops and a gun-boat would be required," and on the main point I agree with him.

4. The Port Hamilton force now consists of six vessels, three of which are always to be there, on which point I see no reason at present to modify my predecessor's views. It must be remembered, owing to past neglect, Hong Kong and Singapore, with their immense trade, are at the present moment defenceless, as far as the War Office is concerned; and the Naval Commander-in-chief is hampered in the disposal of his squadron to guard "our ocean highways" by the necessity of protecting these important ports.

5. Considering that military defence is still a work of time, it cannot be expected Port Hamilton can become, as Sir Cooper Key considered necessary, a first-class fortress, for many years. Its defence must therefore, till then, devolve on the navy. Until it is Northern Division, and under whom the continuity of the necessary works to make it an efficient coaling station would be better carried out than under merely temporary Senior Officers, as is now the case; there having been four since its occupation, and who would also better be able to place our relations with the natives on a friendly and permanent footing.

It should be garrisoned mainly by marines; and amongst the clever officers of the Royal Marine Artillery an efficient one could be found to superintend the fortifications it may be decided to erect. By this plan those curses of the natives in new Settlements — sutlers — (already application by foreigners to set up stores has been made and refused) — would be avoided; and should it be deemed necessary at any time to give it up, there would be no traders' interests to be considered, and if it seems likely to become in the future an important trading place, as the sanguine expect, there would be no difficulty in transferring it to the Civil Power, and no interests to be considered.

13. In recommending Port Hamilton being placed on the same footing as Ascension, I would beg to point out that it would place an additional force at the disposal of the Commander-in-chief for the attack on Vladivostock, who, being equally responsible for the defence of Port Hamilton, would be sure not to unduly weaken its garrison until well assured no hostile attack was probable.

14. I would further observe, the naval reserves of this station are not to be considered with reference to the naval force on the station alone. It can be very considerably supplemented by the very fine fleet of steamers engaged in commerce, sailing from this port, if naval officers could be found to man them. There would be little difficulty in finding transport for coal, stores, or men, which would, of course, have to be highly paid for.

I have, &c.

(Signed) R. VESEY HAMILTON.

105
거문도 매입 관련 해군성 입장

The Secretary to the Admiralty (1886. 1. 25) ➡ Currie (1886. 1. 26)

No. 6.

The Secretary to the Admiralty to Sir P. Currie.—(Received January 26.)

Admiralty, January 25, 1886.

(Confidential.)

Sir,

REFERRING to your letter of the 20th instant, forwarding de cypher of a telegram dated 18th instant from Her Majesty's Consul at Söul, on the subject of the retention of Port Hamilton, I am commanded by my Lords Commissioners of the Admiralty to request that you will state to the Marquis of Salisbury that they do not observe any material difference between the last telegram from Mr. O'Conor and that forwarded with your letter of the 6th October, 1885, which stated that Port Hamilton may, perhaps, be purchased for 500,000 dollars, and which proposal the Secretary of State did not consider satisfactory, as it would not give Her Majesty's Government a proper title to the place.

I am, &c.

(Signed) EVAN MACGREGOR.

106
원산항에 대한 Hertslet 각서

E. Hertslet (1886. 2. 4)

No. 9.

Memorandum by Sir E. Hertslet.

PORT LAZAREFF was visited among other places by Mr. Spence when he accompanied the Duke of Genoa to the Corea in 1880, and in his description of it he said it was one of the points which the Russians were supposed to have designs upon, as a basis of operations against China; that it was one of the finest harbours in the world, perfectly land-locked, with waters as unruffled as a lake, and with a practically infinite space of good holding-ground in from 8 to 10 fathoms of water; and that, though fringed with ice round the shores, the harbour was open in winter.

Mr. Spence again alluded to Port Lazareff in his Report to Sir T. Wade of August 1882. He said the well-known harbour of Port Lazareff was only a few miles off Gensan, and he attached to his Report a rough map of the Corean coast near Gensan, showing their relative position.

In 1868 it was very generally believed that Russia contemplated, as time and opportunity might serve, to absorb Corea and obtain a port or ports further south than Papiette, which was liable to be frozen over in severe winter.

(Signed) E. HERTSLET.

Foreign Office, February 4, 1886.

107
예상되는 청의 부정적인 견해에 대한 보고

N. R. O'Conor (1886. 3. 6) ➡ Earl of Rosebery

No. 27.

Mr. O'Conor to the Earl of Rosebery.—(Received May 3.)

Peking, March 6, 1886.

(No. 74 Confidential.)

My Lord,

WITH reference to my despatch No. 49 of the 18th ultimo, inclosing a copy of a note from the President of the Corean Foreign Office in regard to Port Hamilton, I now do myself the honour to transmit to your Lordship a copy of the reply which I have addressed to his Excellency Kim Yun-sik.

In this despatch I have stated that I have referred his communication for your Lordship's consideration, and that, though not unmindful of the position in which he is placed. I feel assured the friendly relations existing between the two Governments will enable an understanding to be come to which will not in any way prejudice the dignity or welfare of the King or of His Majesty's Government.

I have already had the honour to state to your Lordship that there was good reason to believe that the present note was written in consequence of the remonstrances of M. Waeber, the Russian Chargé d'Affaires at Söul, but, in spite of its emphatic style, which is the common characteristic of Corean State papers, Mr. Baber seems to consider that it is a mere formal communication, which does not require more than a formal reply, couched in friendly and sympathetic terms, provided that some suitable reply is returned in due course by your Lordship, so that the feelings of the Corean Government shall not be hurt by seeming disregard of their communications.

From confidential information which has lately reached me, it appears that the influence of M. Waeber at Söul has been supported by very strong remonstrances to the Viceroy Li Hung-chang against the partiality shown by China in consenting to our occupation without demur or protest.

I also hear that the Russian Consul at Tien-tsin has told the Viceroy that it is impossible for Russia to allow herself to be shut out from the China Seas by the occupation by Great Britain of islands which, in case of war, would virtually bar the passage south to her ships of war and commerce, and that if China and Corea will not insist on the evacuation of Port Hamilton, Russia will occupy Port Lazareff, or some other station, as a counterbalance to the British occupation.

The Chinese Government seems determined to resist the execution of these threats by force of arms if necessary, but, at the same time, they are watching with considerable uneasiness the extensive armaments reported as going on at Vladivostock. They perfectly understand and silently approve the reasons of the occupation of Port Hamilton, and in their language to me during the late Russian difficulty I have found no trace of suspicion in regard to our action. It is even evident that they would have recognized our occupation officially, did it not involve the risk of a serious difference with Russia.

Somewhat similar feelings are entertained by the Corean Government, but, being weaker, they stand in more dread of their powerful neighbour, and try to justify themselves in her eyes by fitful notes and threatened protests.

Under such circumstances, China will not be likely to recognize in a formal manner our occupation, except on the condition of Her Majesty's Government joining her in a guarantee to protect Corean territory against any act of Russian aggression arising out of this question. They would certainly be unwilling to bear alone the responsibility of our occupation if Russia persists in her present policy of opposition, or to involve themselves in difficulties which they believe to be mainly owing to our action.

The interests of China later on will perhaps lead to a protest for form's sake against our occupation. In such a contingency the Chinese Government will be placed in a dilemma by renewing the proposal of Lord Salisbury to ask them whether, if we withdraw from Port Hamilton, China would undertake that it should not be occupied by another foreign Power.

Meantime, the financial straits of the Corean Government will favour a solution on the lines proposed by Her Majesty's Government; and as I understand from Mr. Baber that the Chinese Commissioner has lately received instructions not to press this matter in opposition to the views of Her Majesty's Consul-General, I do not anticipate much danger of the question being immediately brought to a crisis.

I have, &c.

(Signed) N. R. O'CONOR.

108
거문도 점령 유지에 관한 해군성의 의견

The Secretary to the Admiralty (1886. 3. 19) ➡ Currie (1886. 3. 20)

No. 19.

The Secretary to the Admiralty to Sir P. Currie.—(Received March 20.)

Admiralty, March 19, 1886.

(Confidential.)

Sir,

I HAVE received and laid before my Lords Commissioners of the Admiralty your letter of the 11th instant, requesting to be favoured with their Lordships' views in regard to the occupation of Port Hamilton.

2. On this subject my Lords have already expressed their concurrence with the Reports of the present and late Commanders-in-chief on the China Station, which were forwarded to you in my letter of the 20th January last.

3. In reply to your present letter, my Lords desire me to acquaint you, for the information of the Earl of Rosebery, that, unless it be the intention of Her Majesty's Government to fortify and garrison the island, so as to place it in a proper condition of defence to resist the attack of iron-clads, their Lordships are decidedly of opinion that it is not advisable to retain possession of Port Hamilton.

4. It is impossible, however, to overlook the fact, that if Her Majesty's Government is prepared to incur the expense of placing the island in an efficient state of defence its possession might prove valuable to the squadron in the China Seas.

5. On this point my Lords desire me to observe that if it is proposed that naval votes are to be chargeable with the cost of the necessary defence works, their Lordships would not hesitate to decide against the retention of the island.

6. They desire me further to observe that the cost of the retention of Port

Hamilton is now being defrayed out of the Vote of Credit, but that after the 31st instant all expenses will have to be defrayed out of naval votes.

7. Certain ground has been taken up on lease at a yearly rental, payable in advance; and although all progress is stopped, and no new works are being undertaken at present, a daily expenditure for absolutely necessary work is being incurred.

8. Moreover, the Commander-in-chief is obliged to keep two or three ships at the port, and it is therefore at present a source of weakness to the cruizing power of the squadron on the China Station.

9. In view of these circumstances, and of the opinion expressed in the earlier part of this letter, my Lords request that you will point out to the Earl of Rosebery the desirability of obtaining an early decision on this important question.

I am, &c.

(Signed) EVAN MACGREGOR.

109
거문도 철수의 조건

Earl of Rosebery (1886. 4. 30) ➡ N. R. O'Conor

No. 26.

The Earl of Rosebery to Mr. O'Conor.

Foreign Office, April 30, 1886.

(No. 113.)

Sir,

I HAVE received your despatch No. 49 of the 18th February, inclosing copy of a note addressed to you by the President of the Corean Foreign Office on the subject of Port Hamilton.

I have to acquaint you that the substance of this communication has been made known to. the Marquis Tsêng, who has been informed that; in view of the request of the Corean Government for the restoration of Port Hamilton, I should be glad to know the opinion of the Chinese Government on the suggestion made to the Chinese Minister as to obtaining an international guarantee for Corea, including Port Hamilton.

A copy of the Memorandum embodying this suggestion was sent to you with my despatch No. 99, Confidential, of the 15th instant.

I am, &c.

(Signed) ROSEBERY.

110
정부 결정에 대한 신속한 통보 요청

The Secretary to the Admiralty (1886. 5. 19) ➡ Currie (1886. 5. 20)

관련문서 Currie의 답신 (1886. 5. 22)

No. 32.

The Secretary to the Admiralty to Sir P. Currie.—(Received May 20.)

Admiralty, May 19, 1886.

Sir,

WITH reference to your letters of the 11th instant, I am commanded by my Lords Commissioners of the Admiralty to request that you will move the Earl of Rosebery to cause my Lords to be informed, as soon as possible, of the decision of Her Majesty's Government relative to the retention of Port Hamilton.

2. I am to add that, pending this, decision, there are many matters connected with the naval occupation of the island on which action has been suspended, but which press for an early decision.

I am, &c.
(Signed) EVAN MACGREGOR.

【관련문서】

No. 33.

Sir P. Currie to the Secretary to the Admiralty.

Foreign Office, May 22, 1886.

(Confidential.)

Sir,

WITH reference to the letters from this Office of the 11th instant on the subject of Port Hamilton, and to your communication of the 19th instant, I am directed by the Earl of Rosebery to transmit to you copies of a Memorandum giving the substance of a communication made on the 11th March last by Sir H. Macartney by direction of the Marquis. Tsêng, and of a Memorandum in reply thereto, which was communicated to Sir H. Macartney on the 14th ultimo, giving the views of Her Majesty's Government with regard to this question.

I am to request that, in laying these papers before the Lords Commissioners of the Admiralty, you will inform their Lordships that Lord Rosebery is still awaiting an answer to this last communication, and that the Chinese Government will be pressed for a reply. In the meanwhile it would not, in his Lordship's opinion, be advisable to take any steps for the termination of the occupation.

I am, &c.

(Signed) P. CURRIE.

111
거문도 점령에 대한 Hamilton의 부정적 견해

The Secretary to the Admiralty (1886. 7. 17) ➡ Currie (1886. 7. 19)

No. 45.

The Secretary to the Admiralty to Sir P. Currie.—(Received July 19.)

Admiralty, July 17, 1886.

Sir,

WITH reference to previous correspondence respecting the occupation of Port Hamilton, I am commanded by my Lords Commissioners of the Admiralty to transmit to you, for the perusal of the Earl of Rosebery, copy of a letter from Vice-Admiral Hamilton, the Commander-in-chief on the China Station, dated the 1st June, respecting the inexpediency of retaining this island as a naval station.

I am, &c.
(Signed) EVAN MACGREGOR.

Inclosure in No. 45.

Vice-Admiral Hamilton to the Secretary to the Admiralty.

"Audacious," at Nagasaki, June 1, 1886.

Sir,

IN continuation of previous correspondence on the subject of the occupation of Port Hamilton, I request you will inform the Lords Commissioners of the Admiralty that I have just spent two days there, and am the more strongly convinced of the inexpediency of retaining it as a naval station; in point of fact,

I do not see a single point in its favour, and very many objections against it.

Unless it is strongly fortified, there are several points from which the ships laying in the harbour can be shelled by a smart hostile cruizer with impunity, or tremendously harassed by a ship passing to and fro the entrances (three in number) at night, and firing into the harbour.

2. Sir Geoffrey P. Hornby's remarks on Berehaven, in his General Memorandum of the 1st July, 1885, exactly express the state of affairs at Port Hamilton) on a smaller scale. Its retention weakens the naval force on the station very materially; but little protection can be afforded to our commerce to Japan from it, and none too much to our North China trade; no probable enemy could harass either unless China and Japan afforded them coaling facilities, which would, of course, also be afforded to us.

3. As a base of operations against Vladivostock it is useless from its distance. In the war against China in 1860 Hope Sound, about 100 miles from the mouth of the Peiho, was seized on as the rendezvous for our transports, colliers, and victuallers. Vladivostock is 660 miles from Port Hamilton; our gun-boats would exhaust all their coal in steaming to and fro to replenish. Moreover, the facilities of moving ships, stores from Hong Kong would now be as great or greater to Vladivostock as it was in 1860 to Hope Sound, the distance being 1,700 miles now against 1,300 then, and there are good harbours, easily defended, within a short distance of Vladivostock that could be seized on as a base, and given up when no longer of use.

4. Our Minister at Peking attaches an importance to Russia seizing Port Hamilton if we leave it; I confess I do not participate in it. The knowledge that they intended to do so would quicken my departure, as I consider nothing could more conduce to our interests than their doing so, or more suicidal to their own; but I do not believe for one moment they would commit so gross an act of folly. Lord Collingwood, in a letter of the 25th July, 1808, to Lord Castlereagh, says: "A small garrison could not protect itself in any of the large islands (of the Greek Archipelago), and would exhaust the produce of the small ones; and, in a state of war, it would require a squadron t6 protect it. The Russians had a good castle at Tenedos, but when the Turkish fleet came out Admiral Siniavin discovered he must

either continue in the road to protect his garrison, or, by going to sea, subject it to capture, and he took the first opportunity to withdraw his men and blow up the fort." (And, it is to be remembered, the Russians had then no commerce to protect.)

5. The latter sentence expresses precisely what I should do if acting on my own responsibility with regard to Port Hamilton in the event of a war with France or Russia.

6. The documents already at the Admiralty will show their Lordships that the greater portion of this squadron, that should have been at sea protecting commerce, were employed trying to render this port secure against a hostile attack during the war scare of last year. To fortify it efficiently great expense must be incurred, or if defended by the navy still greater. It has already cost 300,000*l.* or 400,000*l.*, if in that sum is included, as. ought to be the case, the expense of the large squadron constantly kept there to protect the ninety-five marines forming the garrison.

7. If retained, the inhabitants must be deported, a proceeding that would do an immense harm amongst the Corean and Northern Chinese. As it is, the justice with which they have been treated, the high rent paid for land occupied by us, and also for wages for those employed, and the respect paid to their customs, has raised our national character, not only in the islands, but has spread to the mainland and doubtless to North China. The villages of the inhabitants occupy the only really available ground for commercial settlements; they are a lazy, filthy race, do no fishing, which is carried on by Japanese, and not more agriculture than they are obliged to do to raise money to pay the taxes. The women do all the hard work in the field except the very primitive ploughing, which is done by the men. At the approach of a European the women all hide themselves, whether fearing the evil eye or from having been. maltreated by Europeans in the past is not known; but it is a curious fact that although these islands have been in our possession a year, there has been no sexual communication between our men and the native women.

8. In my submission of the 21st April last, on Captain Powlett's letter of the 7th April, I have raised the question as to my right to keep people out. The subject has again cropped up, as their Lordships will see in my submission of the 31st May it is a subject that requires a speedy decision and explicit instructions, or we may find ourselves involved in unpleasant correspondence with some foreign 682 British

Diplomatic Archives nation.

9. I can quite understand the heavy sea that sets in with a south-easterly gale, as mentioned by Captain Powlett, as even in the fine weather we had a slight ground swell set in.

10. To sum up. As a naval station it is decidedly a very bad one; an indifferent anchorage in many parts. In loa-king over the Senior Officer's journal I see repeated instances of ships dragging; an anchorage that cannot be made secure from a hostile force except by an extensive system of land forts, which must be widely scattered, consequently necessitating a much larger force to defend it than if it only had one entrance. If command of the sea is lost, it must fall by blockade alone, and the Power possessing the command of the sea can take it at any time if likely to be of use.

Commercially, I was assured by a merchant at Chefoo, one of the strong advocates for taking it, it is valueless; and as our Colonies have as a rule grown up and flourished best when unfettered, he is probably right. It would be going to the French system of settling a Government first, hoping commerce may follow, instead of adhering to our own of the Government establishment being made when commerce has developed.

I cannot of course give any opinion on its political importance with regard to the future of Vancouver, owing to the opening of the Canadian Pacific Railway. The steamship route from there to China can be ascertained from the Hydrographer; if, as I imagine will be the case, it passes south of Japan, Port Hamilton will be 200 or 250 miles out of their way; if they pass between Yesso and Niphon it may be useful; but as the Straits of Sangar are directly opposite Vladivostock, and only 300 miles from it, while Port Hamilton is over 600 miles off, the advantages would be greatly on the Russians side for harassing our commerce over ours for protection.

11. Moreover, as at present Singapore and Hong Kong cannot for some time be left without naval protection, it is evident Port Hamilton cannot be either. Unless the naval squadron out here is very materially increased in war-time, so as to have a strong movable force, having it so scattered renders it liable to be cut up in detail. It is no use having such a possession and thinking it will not be a costly one.

I have, &c.

(Signed) R. VESEY HAMILTON.

112

O'Conor의 원산항 개방안 동의

The Secretary to the Admiralty (1886. 7. 10) ➡ Currie (1886. 7. 12)

No. 44.

The Secretary to the Admiralty to Sir P. Currie.—(Received July 12.)

Admiralty, July 10, 1886.

(Confidential.)

Sir,

REFERRING to your letter of the 29th ultimo, inclosing a copy of a despatch from Her Majesty's Chargé d'Affaires at Peking on the subject of Port Lazareff, I am commanded by my Lords Commissioners of the Admiralty to acquaint you that they concur in Mr. O'Conor's views as to the desirability of inducing the Corean Government to declare Port Lazareff an open port.

I am, &c.

(Signed) EVAN MACGREGOR.

113
거문도와 원산항

E. C. Baber (1886. 7. 14) ➡ J. Walsham

No. 28.

Her Consulate General.
Hanyang, July 14, 1886.

Sir,

I have the honour to enclose a note on the subject of Port Hamilton, with translation by M. Scott, which the acting President of The Corean Foreign office has requested us to forward to you, for representation to Her Majesty's Government. With regard to the last passage in the note, "begging for an early reply,'' I find myself unable to judge from the tenour of Her Original document, whether the intention of the writer was to request reply on the general question, or elect an answer from Her Majesty's Government. But in either case it seems to us — I write with deference and diffidence — that a courteous acknowledgement from yourself, and a statement that the note has been forwarded, will for the moment suffice.

A question about your official style and title, which had been hostile and incorrectly received into Chinese Characters by Mr. Denny, the Foreign Advisor to the Corean Government, gave me the opportunity of taking the note back to the Corean Foreign Office for alteration, and thereby of judging from his demeanour and conversation of His Ministers whether they regarded her evacuation of Port Hamilton as a matter of urgent and imminent consequence. It is remarkable that they said working whatever about the merits of the question, and I still believe that their persistence in demonstrating is little more than a formality. But at the same time I would respectfully beg you to remember that Mr. Waeber, the Russian Minister is continually urging the Corean Foreign Office to insist upon the evacuation; and is way to with a view to her furtherance of this end that Russian men-of-war have been lately. Visiting and surveying Port Lazareff, as a hint to the Corean Government that, if they accept the occupation of Port Hamilton, Russia is not unlikely to compensate herself by the occupation of a convenient harbour.

The suspected Russian designs on Port Lazareff are ultimately connected to the Corean mind with the Port Hamilton question, and I therefore beg to enclose a copy of a letter which I have written to Admiral Hamilton on the subject of Port Lazareff I showed not have done so, fearing to infringe the etiquette of the service, had I just received a telegram from Captain Bromley of H. M. S. Swift, inquiring if I had any information for the Admiral. I took this as an indication that Admiral Hamilton required some information from one which I might be expected to flourish.

I may add that I learned on the 12th instance that another Russian men of war has visited Port Lazareff.

I have the honour to be,
Sir,
Your most obedient,
Humble servant
(Signature) Baber.

114

거문도 점령 종료 논의

The Secretary to the Admiralty (1886. 7. 21) ➡ Currie

No. 46.

The Secretary to the Admiralty to Sir. P. Currie.—(Received July 22.)

Admiralty, July 21, 1886.

(Sccret.)

Sir,

WITH reference to your letter of the 22nd May last, communicating to my Lords Commissioners of the Admiralty the opinion of the Secretary of State that it was not advisable to take any steps for the termination of the occupation of Port Hamilton, I am commanded by mv Lords Commissioners of the Admiralty to transmit herewith, for the information of the Earl of Rosebery, copies of three Reports from Vice-Admiral Hamilton:—

I. Dated the 31st May, 1886, in regard to the manner in which settlers in the vicinity are to be dealt with, and the responsibility which devolves upon the naval authorities in connection with the deportation of undesirable persons, looking to the fact that discipline cannot be maintained if wine and women ad libitum are easily accessible to the garrison,

II. Dated the 1st June, 1886, urging the inexpediency, from almost every point of view, of retaining Port Hamilton as a naval station.

III. Dated the 2nd June, 1886, pointing out the expense which it will be absolutely necessary to incur if Port Hamilton is retained through another winter.

2. in laying the above Reports before Lord Rosebery, my Lords request that you will call his attention to the opinions expressed in their letters of the 20th January and 19th March last, which their Lordships see no reason to alter; and they further request to be informed what instructions should be sent to the

Commander-in-chief as to the position to be maintained by the occupying force, both towards the natives and towards foreigners.

I am, &c.

(Signed) EVAN MACGREGOR.

Inclosure 1 in No. 46.

Vice-Admiral Hamilton to the Secretary to the Admiralty.

"Audacious," at Nagasaki, May 31, 1886.

FORWARDED for consideration, observing that, while approving of the course adopted by Lieutenant and Commander Adams, of the "Espoir," of ordering these people from the island, as being a very strong necessity for the preservation of discipline. I have ordered that in future, if any settlements are made on the island, the Corean village to whom the land belongs on which the settlement is made will be fined if immediate information is not given.

2. I cannot conceal from myself that nothing in the Admiralty instructions for taking possession of Port Hamilton legally justifies my ordering settlers off the island. I can only wonder it has hitherto been submitted to so quietly.

3. In my submission of the 21st April, 1886, on Captain Powlett's letter of the 7th April, have already pointed out our anomalous position there.

4. At present a very unfair responsibility is placed on the Senior Officer at Port Hamilton, who must either run the risk of legal proceedings for deporting people, or find it impossible to maintain discipline if wine and women are allowed *ad libitum*.

(Signed) R. VESEY HAMILTON.

Inclosure 2 in No. 46.

Lieutenant-Commander Adams to Vice-Admiral Hamilton.

"Espoir," at Port Hamilton, May 21, 1886.

Sir,

IN forwarding the inclosed letter from Captain Gordon, R. M. L. I., commanding the detachment on shore. I have the honour to inform you that upon Captain Gordon reporting on Monday, the 17th, that three marines had broken out of the camp on the previous day, I sent the interpreter for a Japanese who had, unknown to me, established himself on shore for the ostensible purpose of drying fish, and warned him to clear out.

2. On Tuesday, the 18th. I ascertained that the cause of attraction to the marines was that five Japanese women had arrived on Saturday night; I sent again for the man, and told him to go, and to take his women away as soon as possible.

3. At 10·40 P. M. on Tuesday night cries were beard of men in the water. I sent two boats away, and saw marines' dingy also going to assist; I also sent to warn Captain Gordon, Lieutenant de Robeck, with our boats, saw some marines disembarking from one boat and escaping into the bush, but saw no men in the water, nor did he hear any cries for assistance. He then took possession of all boats afloat. Afterwards five marines, returning to back of Observatory Island in a Corean boat, were cut off by our boats and brought alongside. They were all wet, and I asked if they were all there, to which they replied in the affirmative. I sent them in as prisoners to Captain Gordon Captain Gordon then came off, and I agreed to go with him next morning and see these Japanese out of it.

4. In the forenoon of. Wednesday Captain Gordon signalled that Private Peter Ward. was missing, and he feared that he was drowned; I sent boats away to drag for the body, and offered a reward of 5 dollars for its recovery.

5. Accompanied by Captain Gordon I visited the bay opposite the camp, and found a rough shanty erected in the bush. Ordered Japanese to leave the island at once, and at 5 P. M. on revisiting the spot, found shanty demolished and their gear

removed. I am still dragging for the body.

I have, &c.
(Signed) HORACE R. ADAMS.

Inclosure 3 in No. 46.

Captain Gordon, R. M. L. I., to Lieutenant-Commander Adams.

Port Hamilton, May 19, 1886.

Sir,

IN connection with the case of three marines of the detachment under my command breaking out of the camp and island on the forenoon of Sunday, the 16th instant, which resulted in my doubling the guard and sentries, and your ordering away some Japanese, including females, who were afterwards ascertained to have apparent intentions of settling on the shore of the bay opposite Observatory Island, I have the honour to acquaint you that last night, about 10·40 P. M., when the officer of the day, Lieutenant Trotter, R. M. A., was visiting the sentries, he was attracted by a cry for help, and voices in English, which came from the water near the opposite shore. Before he could reach the guard-room, the sergeant of the guard had dispatched one of the boats in the direction of the cries, and Lieutenant Trotter directed the detachment, to be mustered, informing me of what had occurred. Twelve men were found to be absent from the huts, although at tattoo at 9·15 P. M. all were mustered and reported present.

A petty officer from Her Majesty's Ship "Espoir," now landed and informed me that some marines were out in Japanese boats, that one of these had been upset, and that boats from the "Espoir" had been sent, after them.

Shortly afterwards the detachment boat returned, bringing, by order of the First Lieutenant of the "Espoir," a Japanese boat which had been found in the bay opposite, and which I directed to be searched, but without any result. One of the

"Espoir's" boats now came in, with five marines, as prisoners, who had been attempting to return this side in a Corean boat.

They were wet through, stating that they had been upset, but that all who had been in the boat were there. Six out of the remaining seven absentees came in at intervals, having landed apparently at a point to the southward of the camp on the alarm having been given.

This morning the five men who had been upset made a statement that a sixth man had been in the boat (named in the margin[1]), that he could not swim, and that he had a considerable weight of silver dollars in his pocket. One of these men added that he had stripped and searched for his missing comrade without avail; but no mention of this occurrence was made last night.

I fear that there can be but little doubt that this man has been drowned, and I have the honour to request that you will be good enough to offer a reward to any Coreans who may find the body, and give such directions as you may deem expedient for instituting a search.

I have, &c.

(Signed) C. G. W. GORDON.

Inclosure 4 in No. 46.

Vice-Admiral Hamilton to the Secretary to the Admiralty.

"Audacious," at Nagasaki, June 1, 1886.

Sir,

IN continuation of previous correspondence on the subject of the occupation of Port Hamilton, I request you will inform the Lords Commissioners of the Admiralty that I have just spent two days there, and am the more strongly convinced of the inexpediency of retaining it as a naval station; in point of fact,

1) Private Peter Ward, R. M. L. I.

I do not see a single point in its favour, and very many objections against it. Unless it is strongly fortified, there are several points from which the ships lying in the harbour can be shelled by a smart hostile cruizer with impunity, or tremendously harassed by a ship passing to and fro the entrances (three in number) at night and firing into the harbour.

2. Sir Geoffrey P. Hornby's remarks on Berehaven, in his General Memorandum of the 1st July, 1885, exactly express the state of affairs at Port Hamilton on a smaller scale. Its retention weakens the naval force on the station very materially; but little protection can be afforded to our commerce to Japan from it, and none too much to our North China trade; no probable enemy could harass either unless China ani Japan afforded them coaling facilities, which would of course also be afforded to us.

3. As a base of operations against Vladivostock, it is useless from its distance. In the war against China in 1860 Hope Sound, about 100 miles from the mouth of the Peiho, was seized on as the rendezvous for our transports, colliers, and victuallers. Vladivostock is 660 miles from Port Hamilton; our gun-boats would exhaust all their coal in steaming to and fro to replenish. Moreover, the facilities of moving ships, stores from Hong Kong would now be as great (or greater) to Vladivostock as it was in 1860 to Hope Sound, the distance being 1,700 miles now against 1,300 then; and there are good harbours, easily defended, within a short distance of Vladivostock that could be seized on as a base, and given up when no longer of use.

4. Our Minister at Peking attaches an importance to Russia seizing Port Hamilton if we leave it; I confess I do not participate in it. The knowledge that they intended to do so would quicken my departure, as I consider nothing could more conduce to our interests than their so doing, or more suicidal to their own. but I do not believe for one moment they would commit so gross an act of folly.

5. Lord Collingwood. in a letter of the 25th July, 1808, to Lord Castlereagh, says: "A small garrison could not protect itself in any of the large islands" (of the Greek Archipelago), "and would exhaust the produce of the small ones;" "and in a state of war it would require as squadron to protect it." "The Russians had a good castle at Tenedos, but when the Turkish fleet came out Admiral Siniavin discovered

he must either continue in the road to protect his garrison, or by going to sea subject it to capture, and he took the first opportunity to withdraw his men and blow up the fort." (And it is to be remembered the Russians had then no commerce to protect.) The latter sentence expresses precisely what I should do, if acting on my own responsibility, with regard to Port Hamilton, in the event of a war with France or Russia.

6. The documents already at the Admiralty will show their Lordships that the greater portion of this squadron, that should have been at sea protecting commerce, were employed trying to render this port secure against a hostile attack during the war scare of last year.

To fortify it efficiently great expense must be incurred, or if defended by the navy still greater. It has already cost 300,000*l*. or 400.000*l*., if in that sum is included, as ought to be the case, the expense of the large squadron constantly kept there to protcct the ninety-five marines forming the garrison.

7. If retained, the inhabitants must be deported, a proceeding that would do an immense harm amongst the Corean and Northern Chinese. As it is, the justice with which they have been treated, the high rent paid for land occupied by us, and also for wages for those employed, and the respect paid to their customs, has raised our national character, not only in the islands, but has spread to the mainland, and doubtless to North China.

The villages of the inhabitants occupy the only really available ground for commercial settlements; they are a lazy, filthy race, do no fishing, which is carried on by Japanese, and not more agriculture than they are obliged to do to raise money to pay the taxes. The women do all the hard work in the field, except the very primitive ploughing, which is done by the men. At the approach of a European the women all hide themselves, whether fearing the evil eye, or from having been maltreated by Europeans in the past, is not known; but it is a curious fact that, although these islands have been in our possession a year, there has been no sexual communication between our men and the native women.

8. In my submission of the 21st April last on Captain Powlett's letter of the 7th April, I have raised the question as to my right to keep people out. The subject has again cropped up, as their Lordships will see in my submission of the 31st

May. It is a subject that requires a speedy decision and explicit instructions, or we may find ourselves involved in unpleasant correspondence with some foreign nation.

9. I can quite understand the heavy sea that sets in with a south-easterly gale, as mentioned by Captain Powlett, as even in the fine weather we had a slight ground-swell set in.

10. To sum up. As a naval station, it is decidedly a very bad one; an indifferent anchorage in many parts. In looking over the Senior Officer's journal I see repeated instances of ships dragging; an anchorage that cannot be made secure from a hostile force, except by an extensive system of land forts, which must be widely scattered, consequently necessitating a much larger force to defend it than if it only had one entrance. If command of the sea is lost it must fall by blockade alone, and the Power possessing the command of the sea can take it at any time if likely to be of use. Commercially, I was assured by a merchant at Chefoo, one of the strong advocates for taking it, it is valueless; and as our Colonies have, as a rule, grown up and flourished best when unfettered, he is probably right. It would be going to the French system of settling a Government first, hoping commerce may follow, instead of adhering to our own, of the Government establishment being made when commerce has developed. I cannot, of course, give any opinion on its political importance with regard to the future of Vancouver, owing to the opening of the Canadian Pacific Railway. The steam-ship route from there to China can be ascertained from the Hydrographer. If, as I imagine will be the case, it passes south of Japan, Port Hamilton will be 200 or 250 miles out of their way. If they pass between Yeddo and Niphon it may be useful, but as the Straits of Sangar are directly opposite Vladivostock, and only 300 miles from it, while Port Hamilton is over 600 miles off, the advantages would be greatly on the Russian side for harassing our commerce over ours for protection.

11. Moreover, as at present Singapore and Hong Kong cannot for some time be left without naval protection, it is evident Port Hamilton cannot be either. Unless the naval squadron out here is very materially increased in war-time, so as to have a strong movable force, having it so scattered renders it liable to be cut up in detail. It is no use having such a possession and thinking it will not be a costly one.

I have, &c.

(Signed) R. VESEY HAMILTON.

Doc. 286 (Inclosure in Doc. 281.)

Vice-Admiral Hamilton to the Secretary to the Admiralty,

"Audacious," at Nagasaki, June 2, 1886.

Sir,

I REQUEST you will inform the Lords Commissioners of the Admiralty that on the 28th ultimo I inspected the Royal Marine Detachment stationed on shore at Port Hamilton, together with the officers' and men's huts, hospital. &c., and the works that have been performed since this place has been in our possession, and beg to make the following Report: —

2. The detachment, consisting of four officers and ninety-one men, were drawn up on the ground which has been levelled as a parade-ground, and I minutely inspected them; they are a fine body of men, well hardened by the winter they have just gone through, and appeared to be well cared for, drilled, and in a very creditable state.

3. The men's huts were clean and well kept, and comfortable as long as the fine weather we are experiencing exists; but it would not be advisable, nor would it be right, to allow either officers or men to be exposed to another winter, especially the officers, whose huts are on a higher level and consequently colder, without means being taken to make all the huts both air-tight and water-tight; and I propose, should it be decided to retain Port Hamilton, to submit estimates for their Lordships' approval with a view to making the huts warm and comfortable, as the stores they have at present produce no heat, and the officers and men lived completely in their great coats to keep themselves warm and dry. The inside of the huts should be chinamed or lined with fearnought.

4. The hospital was clean and of sufficient size for the number of men, but

the same applies to it as to the officers' and men's huts.

5. The cooking-house is a temporary building, and a new stove large enough to cook for 100 men is required, as the present one is too small and really belongs to the telegraph operators who left it behind. I propose directing Commodore Morant to procure a suitable stove, together with thirty of Hinx's paraffin lamps for lighting the huts, the Service lanterns being of no use.

6. The means of supplying water are bad; a gun-boat stationed off Observatory Island has to be continually condensing, as the water on the island, although plentiful, was condemned, in my predecessor's time, by the medical officers of the fleet, as unsafe for drinking purposes. Several large tanks were brought up in the "Audacious," this time, and will be set up and filled, in case it should be necessary for the gun-boat to be withdrawn for any length of time; but the great difficulty is getting the water from the landing-place to the huts; the elevation and state of the road [__] rendering it impossible to drag the water-cart (supplied from Hong Kong, which is much too heavy and large) up the incline. I propose, in the event of the "Midge" taking the place of the "Opossum" (contagious hospital ship at Hong Kong), to have her condensers sent up there, where they could be fitted for a trifling expense, and, with Crease's or other filters, would render the detachment, as far as water was concerned, quite independent.

7. In the event of fire occurring the only thing to do would be to pull the huts down, as of course it would be impossible to get sufficient water up in time. I have directed the Commodore to procure and forward hand-grenades for extinguishing fire.

8. In the event of it being found necessary to increase the force or to fill up vacancies, 1 request that the men chosen may be artificers, especially carpenters, as there is always sufficient work for that kind of trade.

9. I cannot bring too strongly to the notice of my Lords the existing arrangements for the charge of valuable stores at present on shore at this place. During the nine months that the place has been in our possession, there have been six Senior Officers, exclusive of the time my predecessor was there, consequently the stores have been constantly transferred at short notice from one set of departmental officers to another, and I consider it quite impossible for those officers to

be responsible for the loss or damage of any of these stores; and to avoid this in future, I have ordered careful surveys to be made, the several departmental stores to be tallied and restowed in separate places, and I propose, with their Lordships' approval, to hand over all these stores to one of the subalterns of Royal Marines stationed on shore, and request that a suitable allowance may be made to this officer.

10. With reference to my submission of the 12th April, 1886, forwarding estimates and plan for an infectious diseases hospital, at a cost of 700*l*., to be erected at Port Hamilton, I request that, in the event of the place being retained by the English Government, their Lordships' approval of the same may be telegraphed to me as soon as possible, as it is a necessity owing to the prevalence of small-pox at Nagasaki, the mail and leave port.

I am, &c.

(Signed) R. VESEY HAMILTON.

115
해군성의 거문도 철수 주장
The Secretary to the Admiralty (1886. 8. 18) ➡ Currie

No. 66.

The Secretary to the Admiralty to Sir P. Currie.—(Received August 20.)

Admiralty, August 18, 1886.

(Extract.)

WITH reference to the retention of Port Hamilton generally, my Lords desire to repeat the opinion which has been expressed by two previous Boards of Admiralty, that from a naval point of view Port Hamilton, unless fortified and garrisoned, must be a source of weakness instead of strength to British naval forces on the China Station, that it is of no value to the navy as a coaling-station, and that, provided its occupation by another Power can be guarded against, the sooner it is given up the better.

116

거문도 방어의 어려움 통지

The Secretary to the Admiralty (1886. 11. 10) ➡ Currie

No. 106.

The Secretary to the Admiralty to Sir P. Currie.—(Received November 11.)

Admiralty, November 10, 1886.

Sir,

I AM commanded by my Lords Commissioners of the Admiralty to transmit herewith, for the perusal of the Earl of Iddesleigh, copy of a joint Report which has been received from the officers commanding Her Majesty's ships "Leander," "Constance," and "Linnet," dated the 30th July last, together with a copy of Admiral Hamilton's remarks thereon, respecting the present defenceless state of Port Hamilton, the facility with which shipping there could be destroyed by an enemy's cruizer, and forwarding a plan of the proposed defences of that place.

2. My Lords are of opinion that, in its present unfortified state, Port Hamilton would be a source of weakness to the Naval Commander-in-chief in China in time of war, as it would necessitate the presence of at least two of his vessels to protect it, and that unless it should be decided to fortify and garrison the place-a proceeding which their Lordships do not advocate-it would be better not to retain it.

3. I am to request that the plan of the proposed defences, with the explanatory sheet, which are in original, may be returned when no longer required, together with the cuttings from the Charts illustrating the respective positions of Port Hamilton and Centre Harbour.

I am, &c.

(Signed) EVAN MACGREGOR.

Inclosure in No. 106.

Vice-Admiral Hamilton to the Secretary to the Admiralty.

"Audacious," at Fusan, Corea, August 6, 1886.

SUBMITTED, observing that I specially selected these officers as not having been at Port Hamilton before, so there would be no bias on their part.

Practically this Report amounts to this: —

1. The harbour, except at a great expense, is defenceless against a superior force.

2. Even an enterprising inferior enemy could neutralize its value as a depot, or base of operations, by passing it at various times by night and day, and firing into the crowded anchorage, through the entrance channels, over the gaps between Triangle Peak and Sodo Island, also by firing over the low neck of land to the north of Sodo Island; and, as we proved in the "leander," when I went out in her for target practice, at 1 mile or further from the neck of land, 280 feet high, between Sharp and Hamilton Hills, with 7 degrees elevation, a shot could be pitched into the middle of the harbour, or, in all, five places from which the anchorage could be shelled — a harassing warfare against which the only remedy would be having two or three ships always outside.

3. In a naval point of view I am most strongly against its retention. If, as hitherto has been the case, the navy are to be employed doing military duty by garrisoning it, it will be a great source of weakness to the Naval Commander-in-chief in war time, as at least six ships must be diverted from their proper duty of protecting commerce at sea, and the naval Commander-in-chief, instead of devoting his sole attention to that most important duty, will find Port Hamilton a serious addition to his anxieties.

4. If decided to retain it, a Fortification Committee should be sent out at once to decide on the proper places for permanent fortifications, which is not one to be dealt with by the navy.

5. And as it will be a necessity to deport the natives, who have cholera or small-pox almost constantly in their villages, a Civil Commissioner should be sent

to decide on the best method of so doing (some of the Corean Consular officers would be the best for this purpose). They cannot remain except under the present strict, almost non-intercourse, system, which can only be enforced while in purely naval occupation, and even then I have my doubts as to its continuance.

(Signed) R. VESEY HAMILTON.

Captains Dunlop, Dacres, and Marrack to Vice-Adimral Hamilton.

"Leander," at Port Hamilton, July 30, 1886.

Sir,

In compliance with your Memorandum of the 9th instant, we have the honour to report as follows: —

Q. 1. As to whether Port Hamilton is, in our opinion, open to an attack from sea? — A. We consider that it is open to an attack of any kind from sea.

Q. 2. The points that would be most accessible? — A. It is accessible from any direction; the westward, where the coast is more or less bold and precipitous, being less so than by other parts.

It is easily accessible to attack by the three entrances, and tolerably so from the several bays on the north and east sides, more particularly so from the bay immediately to westward of the northern entrance, where a ship could come and fire over the low neck separating the bay from the harbour. The same may be said of the small bay between Triangle Hill and the remainder of Sodo Island.

Q. 3. How, in the event of Port Hamilton being retained as an English Settlement, we should propose to defend it by forts, batteries, and torpedoes? — A. In reply to this question, we consider at least six forts are necessary. We have, however, so little experience on this subject that we approach it with diffidence, and have not ventured into many details, leaving them to experts. We believe that six forts would give a good defence; but we are alive to the benefit of detached guns, "particularly with the formation of Port Hamilton, accessible from so many points," and, but that we believe it would be more expensive and require more men, we should be inclined to suggest a larger number of small forts or batteries.

The main entrance between Sumbodo and Observatory islands has water for the largest iron-clads, and is remarkably easy of access. A spit runs out from Sumbodo towards the centre of passage, and on it we should place a strong armoured fort to defend the main channel principally, but having fire also to northward of Observatory Island, in the event of the passage on the other side of that island being forced. With this fort we should combine a Whitehead battery and some observation mines, together with a search light. It would also be well to fill up by a breakwater or sunken vessels the space between Sumbodo Island and fort. The entrance to westward of Observatory Island we should defend by a properly constructed mining-field and booms, covered by two forts, one on Observatory Island with fire to seaward, and on both this and main entrances, and another on Sodo Island. In both these forts, being at some elevation, we should place machine as well as larger guns, and also in one a search light.

(This entrance has 32 feet at high-water spring, and 27 feet high-water neap tides.)

Triangle Peak is steep to outside, and difficult of access. Its inner slope would be well commanded by forts on Observatory and Sodo Islands, and if the fort on the former were far enough out, there would be little shelter behind Triangle Hill for a ship.

Sharp Peak is very small, and masked by hills to north and south-east. It is, however, the highest point, and would be of use for outside defence, viz., to prevent ships approaching near enough to shell anchorage, and to cover other forts.

We have not, however, included it here, preferring to fortify Hamilton Hill, of nearly the same height, immediately to northward.

This fort would fire in almost any direction. Shambles Peak, 760 feet in Sodo Island, would give fire along weak part of west coast and defend northern entrance and Torpedo and Tea Bays.

(The northern entrance has a depth of 20 feet at high-water springs and 15 feet at high-water neaps.)

There are strong tides, making it more difficult of access. We should partly obstruct it, place a boom across the so narrowed entrance and some mechanical mines. And on Pegasus Peninsula place a fort for its special defence.

In conclusion, we offer the following general remarks: —

Port Hamilton could not, in our opinion, be successfully defended against an enterprising enemy by ships alone, unless they landed their guns and placed them in batteries as shown. Further, they would want more mines, more electrical stores, electric lights fitted to land and work under cover for the protection of mines and booms; and though the entrance were efficiently protected by mines, booms, &c., there is no part of the harbour where the ships would not be exposed to fire from one or more of the entrances, there being deep water close to, every where, and we feel sure a superior force could, without attempting to enter the harbour, destroy the ships inside from the entrances. Here we would draw attention to the fact that mines and booms are of little or no use unless protected by guns, and the electric light by night. It would take several ships to watch the entrances, and they could be terribly harassed by even one fast ship.

We are certain, therefore, that if Port Hamilton is to be retained it must be fortified and made self-defending, so as to be a shelter for our ships, for if it is to depend on the navy for defence, it must greatly cripple the action of the Naval Commander-in-chief.

In considering the nature of defence, we have held in view such foreign ships as are now on this station. The Coreans must be deported, so as to remove an element of weakness and to give a suitable and sheltered position for settlement.

We recommend quick-firing guns in forts, for the protection of mining-fields, and an electric light for each entrance; and if Sharp Peak is to be held, it would be easy to do so with few men, by having only 6-pounder quick-firing guns.

We have, &c.

(Signed) M. J. DUNLOP, Captain of H. M. S. "Leander."

S. H. P. DACRES, Captain of H. M. S. "Constance."

W. MARRACK, Commander, H. M. S. "Linnet."

7-2.
이홍장 · 라디젠스키 회담과 각국의 철군 교섭

117
거문도 임대에 대한 李鴻章의 부정적인 견해

N. R. O'Conor (1885. 10. 14) ➡ The Marquis of Salisbury (1885. 11. 30)

No. 203.

Mr. O'Conor to the Marquis of Salisbury.—(Received Novermber 30.)

Peking, October 14, 1885.

(No. 429. Confidential.)

My Lord,

I HAVE the honour to inform your Lordship that I called by appointment upon the Grand Secretary Li Hung-chang yesterday morning, accompanied by Mr. Hillier, Assistant Chinese Secretary.

After some conversation on other subject, his Excellency asked what Her Majesty's Government intended doing about Port Hamilton. The Russian question had now been settled, and it was time that the British Government did something to put an end to the present unsatisfactory state of things, which placed the Chinese Government in a very unpleasant position vis-a-vis to other Powers, and especially Russia, and if continued, was even calculated to mar the friendship between England and China. The question was a very grave one, and ought not to be allowed to drag on in this unsatisfactory way.

Corea had declined, and he now thought rightly so, to part with any of her territory, and he could assure me, as a fact within his own positive knowledge, that if the Corean Government accepted to rent the island, a demand would be presented from another quarter within ten days for the cession of other territory on the same terms.

I remarked that as a rule I did not think that foreign Governments were inclined to pay ten times the territorial value of land, and that the possession of a neighbouring island by that other foreign Power would scarcely be worth the large expenditure so long as we occupied Port Hamilton.

His Excellency dwelt much on the necessity of coming to a practical and acceptable arrangement in the matter, and proposed that we should take down the British flag, remove the ostentatious military shanties which had been erected, and extend the cable to Chemulpo, where it could be connected with the Corean land-line, thus rendering it useful to both Governments.

We could maintain a coaling depot and keep a gun-boat always there, so as to be able at short notice to reoccupy the island, should such a course be rendered advisable hereafter. He hoped, however, that I would ask Her Majesty's Government to consider this question at once, and to come to an understanding with China in the way he had suggested.

I replied that the moment was inopportune for putting a question of this sort before your Lordship, as elections were impending in England, and that, until they were over, Her Majesty's Government would probably be unwilling to consider any proposals in this matter.

His Excellency appeared satisfied with this explanation, but said that the Chinese Government would expect a decision by the end of the year, and that he hoped I would not forget to communicate what he had said to your Lordship, as the subject was within his official province.

It is possible, and even probable, that in the remarks made by the Grand Secretary his Excellency exaggerated the pressure put upon him by Russia to induce the Chinese Government to call upon England to withdraw from Port Hamilton; but I have no doubt all the same that this pressure was at the bottom of his remarks.

The feelings and position of the Chinese Government have shifted and changed a good deal since the first mention of this subject, in part owing to a feeling of disappointment at the settlement of the Afghan question, and in part engendered by the frame of mind left by the settlement of the difficulty with France. The continued pressure of Russia, and the fear of displeasing her may possibly lead to strong remonstrances being ultimately made respecting our occupation which, if ignored, would, perhaps, leave something of the soreness in the relations of the two countries hinted at by the Grand Secretary.

I have, &c.

(Signed) N. R. O'CONOR.

118
李鴻章의 거문도를 담보로 한 차관 제안

N. R. O'Conor (1885. 11. 17) ➡ The Marquis of Salisbury (1886. 1. 12)

No. 1.

Mr. O'Conor to the Marquis of Salisbury.—*(Received January 12, 1886.)*

Peking, November 17, 1885.

(No. 457.)

My Lord,

IN my despatch No. 451 of the 8th instant I had the honour to transmit to your Lordship a copy of a despatch from Mr. Baber, Acting Consul-General at Söul; stating that, by order of the King, the President of the Foreign Office called on Mr. Aston on the eve of his departure and had inquired whether any answer had been received from Her Majesty's Government to the note from the Corean Government respecting Port Hamilton, of which a copy was inclosed in Mr. Aston's No. 81 of the 10th July, and forwarded by him direct to the Foreign Office.

I reported to your Lordship in an earlier despatch that on the occasion of Li Hung-chang's visit to Peking his Excellency referred to this question, and begged me to inform Her Majesty's Government that some understanding should be come to with regard to the British occupation of Port Hamilton.

Since then his Excellency has on two occasions alluded to the same subject in conversation with Mr. Brenan, and a few days ago repeated his request that some definite understanding should be come to in the matter, for as long as it remained open it gave Russia a pretext for threatening Corea. He proposed at the same time that Her Majesty's Government should lend Corea 1,000,000 taels (about 250,000*l.*) on mortgage, taking the Islands of Port Hamilton as security. At any time that England wished to hand back the islands, Corea would have to pay back the money. His Excellency talked of drawing up an Agreement with Corea, and concluded by saying that, unless a settlement was arrived at, China would have to protest. against a state of things which threatened to involve her in difficulties.

Exorbitant as is the proposal of the Viceroy, it shows that he is not altogether opposed in principle to the arrangement offered by Her Majesty's Government, though differing largely as to the amount. It may also be interpreted to mean that he would only favour an Agreement which would allow China to take up the mortgage his case circumstances should hereafter lead to the complete annexation of Corea.

The insistance with which the Viceroy recurs to this question gives reason to suppose that the Tsung-li Yamên may possibly be induced to make representations to Her Majesty's Government in the same sense. At all events, I consider it worth while to bring his remarks again to the notice of your Lordship, particularly as he very explicitly declared in Peking that some definite arrangement should be come to before the close of the current year.

I have, &c.

(Signed) N. R. O'CONOR.

119
李鴻章에게 거문도의 타 열강 점령 방지 가능 여부 확인 지시

The Marquis of Salisbury (1885. 12. 12) ➡ N. R. O'Conor

관련문서 (1) 李鴻章에게 거문도의 타 열강 점령 방지 가능 여부 타진에 대한 의견
(2) 李鴻章에게 거문도의 타 열강 점령 방지 가능 여부 타진에 동의

No. 208.

The Marquis of Salisbury to Mr. O'Conor.

Foreign Office, December 12, 1885.

(No. 316. Confidential. Ext. 59.)

Sir,

IN reply to your despatch No. 429, Confidential, of the 14th October last, reporting the views of Li Hung-chang on the question of Port Hamilton, I have to request you, in case the question is again raised by his Excellency, to ascertain from him whether, if Her Majesty's Government withdrew from the islands, the Chinese Government would undertake that it should not be occupied by any other foreign country.

The substance of the above was sent to you this day by telegraph.

I am, &c.
(Signed) SALISBURY.

【관련문서 1】

No. 206.

Sir P. Currie to the Secretary to the Admiralty.

Foreign Office, December 8, 1885.

(Confidential.)

Sir,

REFERRING to your letter of the 10th October last, and to previous correspondence relative to the occupation of Port Hamilton by Her Majesty's Government, I am directed by the Marquis of Salisbury to transmit to you, to be laid before the Lords Commissioners of the Admiralty, a copy of a despatch from Mr. O'Conor, Her Majesty's Chargé d'Affaires at Peking, giving the substance of a conversation he has had on the subject with the Viceroy Li Hung-chang.

In reply to this despatch, Lord Salisbury proposes to instruct Mr. O'Conor, by telegraph, that if the question of Port Hamilton is again raised by the Viceroy, he should ask his Excellency whether, if we withdrew from the islands, China would undertake that they should not be occupied by any other foreign Power.

I am to request that, in laying this letter before the Lords Commissioners of the Admiralty, you will move them to inform Lord Salisbury whether they concur in the proposed instruction.

I am, &c.

(Signed) P. CURRIE.

【관련문서 2】

No. 207.

The Secretary to the Admiralty to Sir. P. Currie.—(Received December 11.)

Admiralty, December 10, 1885.

(Secret.)

Sir,

IN reply to your letter of the 8th instant, on the subject of the interview which had taken place between Her Majesty's Chargé d'Affaires at Peking and the Grand Secretary relative to the occupation of Port Hamilton by Her Majesty's Government, am commanded by my Lords Commissioners of the Admiralty to request that you will inform the Marquis of Salisbury that they concur in the terms of the telegram which it is proposed to send to Mr. O'Conor, viz., that if the question is again raised by the Grand Secretary Li Hung-chang, he should be asked whether, if we withdrew from the islands, China would undertake that they should not be occupicd by any other foreign Power.

I am, &c.

(Signed) EVAN MACGREGOR.

120
러시아의 전략에 대한 Detring의 보고 전달

李鴻章 (1885. 12. 12 / 光緒十一年十一月十六日) ➡ 總署

奇譯署

光緒十一年十一月十六日午刻

頃德璀琳密告 聞俄廷定議 現英踞朝鮮巨文島 如中國不催退還 俄亦必奪據朝鮮口岸一處 倘朝有事 中國派兵往扎 俄亦卽派兵往云云 據云此信甚確謹電聞 鴻

121
영국의 거문도 철수 여부 탐문 지시

李鴻章 (1886. 1. 4 / 光緖十一年十一月三十日) ➡ 袁世凱

寄漢城袁道

光緖十一年十一月三十日申刻

總署本日來電 英果否退巨文島 希電袁探 復云前電稱貝使謂英政府尙未定局 半月後可定巨文事 現英廷定議若何 望傳總署諭催詢爲要 鴻

122
청 總理衙門에게 거문도의 타 열강 점령 방지 가능 여부 확인 지시

N. R. O'Conor (1886. 1. 7) ➡ The Marquis of Salisbury (1886. 3. 9)

No. 16.

Mr. O'Conor to the Marquis of Salisbury.—(Received March 9.)

Peking, January 7, 1886.

(No. 4. Very Confidential.)

My Lord,

IN the course of a conversation with the Ministers of the Tsung-li Yamên on the 6th instant, their Excellencies informed me that they had heard a report that the British fleet had evacuated Port Hamilton, and inquired if it were true.

I said I would reply to their question by asking another, and that was whether, in the event of the British Government evacuating Port Hamilton, the Chinese Government were prepared to occupy it themselves, or to give us a guarantee that it would not be occupied by any other European Power.

The Ministers replied that the territory was Corean, and that it was not the practice of China to occupy her vassals' territory, and that they did not see how they could undertake that the islands would not be occupied by any other foreign Power, and that such an undertaking was not a matter of immediate concern, whereas the continued occupation by Great Britain had made Russia, as they lately heard, intimate to Corea that she would have to take another island off Corea if England remained in possession of Port Hamilton.

I said that it seemed to me a matter of immediate concern, inasmuch as it was neither agreeable for me to report nor for Her Majesty's Government to hear the carping remarks which a high Chinese functionary indulged in from time to time respecting our occupation, and this, while I was as sure as I well could be, that China no less than Corea was glad to see Her Majesty's fleet in occupation of the islands, though they were willing that we should bear the obloquy while acting in their interests as much as in our own. I thought the report they had mentioned, that Russia was looking out for another island off Corea, would in itself be ample proof of the danger of their occupying Port Hamilton if vacated by us. As we were now engaged in friendly conversation on this subject, I would mention privately that I had heard the other day that the Russian Agent at Söul was very anxious to find out whether the King of Corea had recognized our occupation, as, if not, the Russian Government would be glad to have the island.

So far as I was able to judge the occupation was a costly business, and I thought it unfair that the Chinese Government should have even the appearance of finding fault with Her Majesty's Government for a policy which the Ministers had not concealed was in their interests. More than this I expected, and I thought I had a right to expect, to have been able to report to Her Majesty's Government that our occupation was fully recognized by the Chinese Government.

The Ministers left me under the impression that they pretty well agreed with what I had said, and begged to assure me that they had no wish to reproach Her Majesty's Government with the occupation of Port Hamilton.

I was glad of this opportunity to avail myself of the instructions contained in your Lordship's telegram No. 59 of the 12th December last, and I hope it will have the effect of removing from the minds of the Ministers of the Yamên any unpleasant feeling respecting our occupation, and of preventing the Viceroy Li from recurring to the subject in an unpleasant and fault-finding manner.

I have, &c.
(Signed) N. R. O'CONOR.

123

Currie · Macartney 회담

Currie · Macartney (1886. 3. 11 / 光緒十二年三月六日)

一千八百十六年三月十一日 馬格里與外部侍郎克蕾面談節略 馬格里云 駐紮北京俄國公使近者屢向總理衙門催問英軍佔據巨文島之意 並云倘英軍佔據此島係屬永遠佔據 則俄廷亦欲於高麗地方佔據一地 我奉 曾侯之命來問英廷前佔據巨文島 本稱暫爲佔據 刻下仍佔據未退 未悉何意 允齊答云 伊當將此事轉詢外部尙書 尙書自能將此意告知曾候 克蕾又云 李中堂及總理衙門曾與英國駐京署理公使歐憝訥言及英軍退出巨文島之事 歐憝訥曾問李中堂云 倘英軍遠出巨文島 中朝能否據保必無歐洲別國佔據該處

124
李鴻章 · O'Conor 회담

N. R. O'Conor (1886. 3. 27) ➡ Earl of Rosebery (1886. 5. 17)

No. 31.

Mr. O'Conor to the Earl of Rosebery.—(Received May 17.)

Peking, March 27, 1886.

(No. 109. Confidential.)

My Lord,

IN conversation with the Viceroy Li Hung-chang this morning, his Excellency inquired whether Her Majesty's Government had come to any decision about Port Hamilton, or fixed a time for our occupation to cease. He had been harassed and worried in the matter by Russia, and would be again, but if he could ask Russia whether she would give a written engagement not to take Port Hamilton if Her Majesty's Government abandoned the islands, he would be able to stop further annoyance. He could not do this, however, unless he was sure beforehand that on his getting this engagement from Russia we would give it up. In any case, if he got this undertaking from Russia, China would have no excuse for not formally requesting us to leave. Sooner or later the question would have to come to an issue, and, meantime, China was placed in a very awkward position.

I said that this was a question on which I was not authorized to make any communication at the present moment, but, speaking privately, I thought that China, unless herself prepared to take over the islands, would make a mistake if she exercised any pressure on Her Majesty's Government in the matter. In all probability Port Hamilton would not have been occupied by us if we had not been more or less assured that we were acting in accordance with the wishes of China, and pretty certain of her assent. The possession was not, so far as I could see, either lucrative or very valuable, but having occupied it, we could not now let it fall into the hands of another foreign Power. The Coreans feared that Germany intended to take it, the Chinese feared Russia, and the self-denying promises of to-day might be rendered nugatory to-morrow by what was called force *majeure.* In any case, I thought he would do well to wait and see how things turned in the near future.

His Excellency was, however, energetic in his views, and declared that China could not get into trouble with Russia about a matter that concerned only England's interests. If Russia, as certainly would happen, pressed the matter again, China would have to decide to take over the place herself if necessary, and in course of time she would be able to fortify it and turn it into a naval and commercial station. If Russia then tried to take it, she would have to do so in spite of China. He was anxious to be relieved from the anxiety of this question, and hoped Her Majesty's Government would now vacate the islands.

I think it well to add that the Tsung-li Yamên have been particularly reticent in this matter for some months, and that the observations of the Viceroy are altogether founded on his fear of entanglements with Russia arising out of this question. He is also, no doubt, aiming at a joint guarantee for the protection and integrity of Corean territory as against Russia.

I have, &c.

(Signed) N. R. O'CONOR.

125
주청 러시아 공사의 청 정부에 대한 압력 행사

Earl of Rosebery (1886. 4. 1) ➡ N. R. O'Conor

No. 22.

The Earl of Rosebery to Mr. O'Conor.

Foreign Office, April 1, 1886.

(No. 79.)

Sir,

THE following communication was made by Sir Halliday Macartney on the 11th ultimo, by direction of the Marquis Tsêng: – He stated that "the Russian Minister at Peking has on several occasions urged the Chinese Government to obtain the withdrawal of the British force from the islands forming Port Hamilton; and has stated that, in the event of the British occupation being continued, Russia would feel obliged to occupy some place in Corea."

Under these circumstances, Sir H. Macartney was instructed to ask what were the intentions of Her Majesty's Government with regard to the prolongation of the occupation of Port Hamilton, which it was understood, at the time it was made, was to be only of a temporary nature.

I am, &c.

(Signed) ROSEBERY.

126
청의 조선 영토 보장 시 철수 단행 통지
Currie (1886. 4. 14) ➡ Macartney

No. 23.
Sir P. Currie to Sir H. Macartney.

Foreign Office, April 14, 1886.

Dear Sir Halliday,

I INCLOSE a Memorandum of the answer which I have been instructed to give to the communication which you made to me, on behalf of the Chinese Minister, on the 11th ultimo, respecting Port Hamilton.

Yours, &c.
(Signed) P. CURRIE.

Inclosure in No. 23.
Memorandum of proposed Answer to the Communication made by Sir H. Macartney on the 11th March with regard to Port Hamilton.

THE communication respecting Port Hamilton, made on the 11th March by Sir H. Macartney on behalf of the Marquis Tsêng, has been laid before Her Majesty's Government.

Her Majesty's Government have no desire to prolong the occupation of Port Hamilton in opposition to the wishes of the Chinese Government, but it appears to them that it would be against the interests both of China and England if it were to be occupied by another European Power.

If the Chinese Government are prepared to guarantee that no such occupation shall take place, one of the chief objects which Her Majesty's Government had in view in taking possession of Port Hamilton would be accomplished.

Should the Chinese Government be unwilling to undertake such a responsibility, Her Majesty's Government would suggest that China should propose to Russia and to the other Powers interested to enter into an international arrangement guaranteeing the integrity of Corea. If this proposal is accepted, Her Majesty's Government would be ready to become parties to the arrangement, and to retire at once from Port Hamilton on the understanding that it should be recognized as forming part of the guaranteed territory of Corea.

Foreign Office, April 14, 1886.

【漢譯文】

英外部侍郎克蕾致馬格里函

御賜寶呈馬大人閣下 前月十一日 閣下代中國出使大臣傳說巨文島一事 玆將覆文節畧一件附呈 卽乞察收 須候□祺 馬格里於三月十一日代 曾候傳說巨文島之事 英廷業已知悉 倘中朝不願英廷久佔巨文島 英廷亦不願久佔此口 但恐若被別國佔去 則必有損中英兩國之利 □中朝□保無人來佔此口 則英廷可以放心 而英廷所以佔據此口之本意 亦無所失矣 倘中朝不肯擔保此等責任 英廷欲勸中朝請俄國及別國會商 公訂一約 擔保不取高麗之地 倘中朝以此辦法爲然 英廷甚願入會簽名於條約內 并願立卽退出巨文島 各國應知巨文島係經各國所保之高麗地方也

127
거문도 철수 관련 영국 정부의 제안

曾紀澤 (1886. 4. 17 / 光緒十二年三月十四日) ➡ 總署

使英曾紀澤致總署英人謂如各國不佔韓地英還巨文島電

英答澤云華請俄日及各西國公訂約不佔高麗地英卽還巨文島 三月十四日

128

거문도 철수 관련 영국의 추가 입장

曾紀澤 (1886. 4. 25 / 光緒十二年三月二十二日) ➡ 總署

附 曾侯寄譯署

光緒十二年三月二十二日巳刻到

高催英退安島 英侯接華覆語乃覆高 澤交卸英事後 擬現各廠局 侯劉遞國書乃同赴俄

交卸 個

129

거문도 점령 보고 및 정부의 추가 지시 요청

The Secretary to the Admiralty (1886. 6. 4) ➡ Currie

No. 36.

The Secretary to the Admiralty to Sir P. Currie.—(Received June 7.)

Admiralty, June 4, 1886.

(Confidential.)

Sir,

IN reference to your letters of the 11th March last and 22nd ultimo in regard to Port Hamilton, I am commanded by my Lords Commissioners of the Admiralty to transmit, for the information of the Secretary of State, a Report from Vice Admiral Vesey Hamilton, dated the 21st April, 1886, inclosing the opinion of Captain Powlett, of Her Majesty's ship "Champion," who has been stationed as Senior Officer at that place for about eight months.

2. My Lords desire me to point out that it appears to them absolutely necessary that they should be enabled to give some instructions at once by telegraph to the Commander-in-chief, to the effect that the occupation of Port Hamilton is to be provided for six months or a year longer.

3. My Lords would wish to be informed, at an early date, if such instructions may be sent, observing, however, that they adhere to the opinions which. were expressed in their letter of the 19th March last as to the unadvisability of retaining Port Hamilton.

I am, &c.

(Signed) EVAN MACGREGOR.

Inclosure in No. 36.

Report on Port Hamilton by Captain Powlett, R. N., Her Majesty's ship "Champion," April 7, 1886.

Remarks of Vice-Admiral Hamilton on forwarding above Report.

"Audacious." Hong Kong.

SUBMITTED with reference to my letter of the 7th December, 1885, observing that I wrote a private note to Captain Powlett, of the "Champion," who had been Senior Officer at Port Hamilton for about eight months, asking for his opinion on the place.

2. His hydrographical remarks are very valuable. It is not a good typhoon harbour, which must be a very important consideration for a naval station. Captain Long, who had much experience of Port Hamilton both in the "Agamemnon" (and "Curacoa?"), agrees in the main with Captain Powlett; he is now in England, and can give valuable information.

3. Paragraphs 5 and 6, particularly the latter, are very important. At present a gun-boat is stationed at Observatory Island to condense water for the marine detachment. It is scarcely necessary to remark on the very unsatisfactory and expensive nature of this proceeding; moreover, it will be necessary to lay down moorings for that gun-boat in the typhoon season, as the anchorage between Observatory Island and Sodo Island is then unsafe, and this must be done at the latest by August, so I wish to have speedy instructions on that head.

4. The want of water is a serious objection also to forming a settlement: I cannot, however, but think that ought to be got over, either by sinking wells, or, if that fails, rain water must be collected, as at Bermuda, where there are no springs.

5. On the main points Captain Powlett's views confirm those already sent to their Lordship's in my predecessor's letter of the 28th May, 1885, and my above-quoted letter.

6. Paragraphs 14 and 15 I particularly commend to their Lordship's attention. My predecessor refused to allow a German settler to settle there. I have had another application of a similar nature, which I have refused, from a British subject. If Port

Hamilton is British territory, have I any right to do so? I presume there is some special Act or Order in.'Council putting Ascension under the Admiralty.

By paragraph 15 it will be seen Corea levies taxes as usual, and an attempt was made to arrest a Corean interpreter, a clashing of jurisdiction that may some day lead to unpleasant complications. It would be awkward if Corea gave permission to foreigners to settle there.

7. I cannot speak too highly of the tact and judgment that has been displayed by the senior' officers, officers, and men stationed there during the last year. Not only has there been no violation of native habits and customs, but the Chief some time ago thanked Captain Powlett for it, asking at the same time for more work.

8. I cannot express my own views too strongly against its retention on naval grounds, as it would require a considerable part of the naval force out here for its' protection. If retained for colonial, commercial, or other purposes, I hope their Lord-ships will not consent to its being defended by the navy.

9. Such old and valuable settlements as Singapore and Hong Kong are still undefended. It is very certain for the next twenty years Port Hamilton will be also undefended, and the navy, instead of finding it a port of refuge to refit and recruit and prepare for sea, its proper' place in war time, will have to be shut up there doing other people's work.

10. Two other points their Lordships will note, the remark relative to deportation of the natives arid the necessity of building a breakwater. It will be an expensive port to retain.

(Signed) R. VESEY HAMILTON. Vice-Admiral.
The Secretary of the Admiralty.

Captain Powlett to Vice-Admiral Hamilton.

"Champion," at Kobé, April 7, 1886.

Sir,

IN compliance with your directions, I have the honour to make the following observations on Port Hamilton: —

1. Port Hamilton is a fairly good anchorage in all winds except those from the south-east, and then, in order to avoid the sea the wind brings from that quarter, it is necessary to get Shoal Point to bear about S. S. E., and the anchorage then available is very circumscribed. This is best seen by reference to the accompanying plan, drawn by Lieutenant Roughton, of this ship. To the north-east of the red line is a well sheltered anchorage from all winds. Although it is open to the north entrance, no sea comes in there worth mentioning.

2. In north-east winds, which are frequent in the summer months, the harbour is unsafe for boats under sail, owing to the whirlwinds that are produced, even in a moderate north-east breeze.

3. The holding-ground is undoubtedly good, and when the anchor has been down for a week or two it is not easy to get it. The best holding-ground is in the north-east corner of the anchorage.

4. Two or three large vessels might find shelter in a typhoon by anchoring to the north-east of the red line, but anyone going here for shelter from a typhoon should make up his mind to give his ship plenty of cable at once, so that with the wind at northeast, which is probably the quarter from which typhoon winds begin in this neighbourhood, she should not start her anchor, as if she does so she drags out of the safe part of the anchorage, and exposes herself to the wind and sea when the shift to the south-east takes place.

No rule can be given as to which anchor to let go first, as until the first shift takes place no opinion can be formed as to which side of you the centre will pass. This is not the place for a dissertation on typhoons, but I should like to add a warning to the younger members of my profession not to hold a typhoon too cheap in consequence of having passed several years in the China Seas without having witnessed a severe one. "Precaution" and "fear" are not synonymous terms.

5. As regards supplies, none can be depended upon on the spot. The natives grow nothing except for their own consumption, and until our arrival at Port Hamilton in April 1885 they had not even any poultry. Sheep will not live on the islands, as they abound in bam boo grass.

Cattle there were a few, but not purchasable; there is, however, no reason why many more should not be introduced. Supplies of all kinds can, however, be obtained from Shanghae and Nagasaki; the former is the better, though the more distant market.

6. There are many small streams of water that find their way into the sea, and several springs inland that are used by the natives, but such of these as were analyzed were all more or less impure, and the supply of water from those running into the harbour fails after two or three weeks of dry weather.

7. Before either of the islands forming the harbour of Port Hamilton could be used as a settlement for foreigners it would, I think, be necessary to deport the natives from that island at least. Their filthy habits and thieving propensities would make this a necessity. It is a place where, emphatically, there is not room for civilization and barbarism to exist side by side.

8. The soil, where it is free from stones, appears to be rich, as two crops — viz., one of barley and one of millet — are grown annually, and capital crops, too; but the patches so cultivated have been made of use by dint of great labour probably, namely, in removing the stones, which are built up into walls at the sides of the fields.

9. There are tracks (mere foot-paths) connecting the villages which might be widened into roads without great labour, as in most places it is but a question of digging out the side of the hill, the surface being generally debris; one rarely finds the parent rock projecting. I do not think there would be much difficulty in making an artillery road to the peaks, on which it would be necessary to put guns to hold the place, as its weakness is not only due to its three entrances, but to other gaps through which ships inside might be shelled from the outside.

10. The surface of these islands is one confused mass of boulders and debris, here and, there covered with soil, and occasionally with small trees and undergrowth. The nearest approach to a flat surface anywhere has been obtained by artificial terracing.

11. If the settlement is ever formed, it will, I suppose, be on the eastern island, as on that alone could wharves of sufficient strength to resist a typhoon be formed. In course of time the harbour face of this island would probably be

"bunded" with occasional cambers for boats, similar to the "bund" and "hatobas" at Yokohama, but the work would have to be of the most solid description. I do not think that Port Hamilton can be called a harbour until a breakwater 500 yards long is thrown out from Shoal Point.

12. I am aware that there 8.fe those who believe that the days of resident foreign traders in Japan are numbered; on this I am not competent to give an opinion, but if our trade in the future with Japan is to be done not on the spot, but by means of depots, Port Hamilton might be of some value. I understand, however, that the Foreign Office officials, who should be the best judges, have no wish to retain the place. From a naval point of view, it is quite worthless. No one can hold it who has not the command of the seas, and if you have command of the seas, of what good is it? You must detach a division of your squadron to protect it: with what object?

13. The establishing of huge steamers makes a fixed secondary depot for a naval force no longer of the same consequence as was formerly the case, as all coals, provisions, &c., necessary will in all future naval expeditions, I apprehend, be carried in large steamers wherever the expedition goes; thus, secondary depots are no longer required. Port Hamilton is, however, too far from any possible objective point to be of use as a base of operations.

14. If, however, it is determined not to give it up, the necessity of at once establishing some duly authorized person as Governor is obvious. It is, indeed, remarkable that no difficulties have already occurred for the want of some law; complications have been avoided, however, by preventing foreigners from settling on the islands, and that is a state of things that it is scarcely desirable should continue.

15. Corea levies taxes as usual (I am inclined to think rather more than usual, owing to the money that we have distributed in wages), and on Sundays the Union Jack is displayed, or on the approach of a foreign man-of-war. On one occasion, when I was at Port Hamilton, an attempt was made to arrest our Corean interpreter on the warrant of an official on the mainland whilst he was in the company of the Commander of the "Pegasus," pointing to a not unnatural confusion of ideas as to sovereignty not to be wondered at under existing circumstances.

16. There is but a very small supply of water on Observatory Island, on which our establishments were erected for the following reasons: – 1st. Observatory Island is the only place in the harbour where boats can boats can be kept in all weathers. 2nd. Torpedo work could be more secretly carried on there than elsewhere. 3rd. It is the most convenient place for the telegraph station. 4th. No natives reside on the island, probably owing to the scarcity of water.

I have, &c.

(Signed) A. T. POWLETT.

130
청 정부로부터의 답신 대기 중

Currie (1886. 6. 12) ➡ The Secretary to the Admiralty

No. 38.

Sir, P. Currie to the Secretary to the Admiralty.

Foreign Office, June 12, 1886.

(Confidential.)

Sir,

I AM directed by the Earl of Rosebery to acknowledge the receipt of your letter of the 4th instant relative to Port Hamilton.

In reply, I am to request that you will state to the Lords Commissioners of the Admiralty that no answer has yet been received from the Chinese Government to the proposal that an international guarantee should be obtained for Corea, including Port Hamilton, communicated to you in the letters from this Office of the 11th and 22nd Ultimo.

Under these circumstances, his Lordship regrets that it will be necessary to make provision for the occupation of Port Hamilton for a further period, and I am to request that you will move their Lordships to make arrangements accordingly.

I am, &c.

(Signed) P. CURRIE.

131
거문도 철수 관련 영국의 공식 제안

曾紀澤 ➡ 總署 (1886. 6. 13 / 光緒十二年五月十二日)

五月十二日 出使大臣曾紀澤文稱 竊照英國 佔據朝鮮濟洲東北之安島卽巨文島一案 上年經本爵大臣與英外部爭論數次 嗣據該外部前任尙書伯爵葛蘭斐爾密咨 欲與中國相商立約 不損中國上邦權利等語 比將往來照會於上年春間先後錄稿咨呈在案 近接北洋爵閣大臣 因外部尙書勞偲伯力每日在上議政院議事甚忙 難以隨時會晤 是以遣派參贊官馬格里前往外部與侍郎克蕾提論此事 旋准英外部侍郎克蕾西應四月十四日覆函幷具節畧一件 聲明英廷不欲久佔此島 但恐別國佔去則損中英兩國之利 中朝如能擔保無人來佔此島 則英廷可以放心 佔中朝不願如此擔保 英廷欲勸中朝請俄羅斯日本及別國會商 公訂一約 擔保不取高麗之地 英國甚願入會簽名 幷願立卽退出此島 緣如此辦理 則各國應知巨文島係經各國所公保之高麗地方 不至再佔等情 查英國佔據巨文島係與俄國相爭 現欲俟各國見有公約乃退巨文島 仍係預防俄國佔據 在我應如何請各國會議訂約方爲盡善 除於十三日摘要電陳外 合將本爵大臣派馬格里前往外部與侍郎克蕾面談節略一件 及克蕾覆函節畧各一件 先行譯漢咨呈貴衙門 謹請察閱

132

영국의 제안에 대한 청 總理衙門의 동향

J. Walsham (1886. 7. 27) ➡ Earl of Rosebery (1886. 7. 27)

No. 51.

Sir J. Walsham to the Earl of Rosebery.—(Received July 27, 3 P. M.)

Peking, July 27, 1886, 8 A. M.

(No. 52.)

(Telegraphic.)

YOUR telegram No. 46.

Yamên professed at first to be ignorant of proposal, but eventually said that they did not consider it [__] basis for settlement of Port Hamilton question, and evidently are not intending to send any reply.

Further formal representation [__] to me from the Corean Government [__] is on its way.

Would Her Majesty's Government consider it [__] a solution if Port Hamilton and Port Lazareff could be made Treaty Ports.

133
거문도·원산항의 조약항 지정 방안 제안

J. Walsham (1886. 7. 31) ➡ Earl of Rosebery (1886. 7. 31)

No. 52.

Sir J. Walsham to the Earl of Rosebery.—(Received July 31, 3:35 P. M.)

Peking, July 31, 1886, 2:55 P. M.

(No. 53.)

(Telegraphic.)

YOUR Lordship's telegram No. 47.

Two last paragraphs are:—

"Further formal representation to me from Corean Government is on its way.
"Would Her Majesty's Government consider it a solution if Port Hamilton and Port Lazareff could be made Treaty ports?"

I received the Corean note last night. It states that prolonged occupation of Port Hamilton is not consistent with promise of it being only temporary, and is very embarrassing to Corea, who wants some definits answer from Her Majesty's Government.

I shall merely acknowledge receipt, and say I have forwarded it.

The King is reported to have quite recently asked for protection of Russia, and the Russian Agent to have said that request must be in writing. The Viceroy Li has telegraphed to Corea to prevent written request at all costs.

134

러시아의 원산항 조약항 지정 요구의 군사적 의미

W. Parker (1886. 8. 4) ➡ T. F. Bayard

No. 24.

Aug. 4, 1886.

Secretary of State

Sir,

Mr. Waeber, Russian Chargé d'Affaires — in Söul, is making application to the Foreign Office to have established a Trading Post in Korea 100 ri (about 35 mi.) from the Russian border of the N. E. province and also to assent to Russian soldiers, armed, &c., travelling freely to the post.

This request has not yet been formally considered, but I am advised will not be granted. The advisers of the govt. suggest that the most that can be given to Russia is a Trading Post on the border to correspond to Aichu (Ichu) on the Yalu river — the trading border post of China & Korea which is accessable to light draught vessels from the sea & by the favored nation clause open to all powers in treaty with Korea.

The Dept. is no doubt aware of the fact that the Russians have made Vladivostok their chief naval station on the Pacific — this port, however, in latitude 43° is closed by the ice for three months of the year & it is feared by some here that Russia is looking to obtaining possession of Port Lazaret in lat. 39° on Broughton Bay (the seizure of Port Hamilton by Great Britain having established a precedent).

I think this very probable and would bring them within 115 miles of Söul & Chemulpho.

In the case of war between Russia & China, Russia would undoubtedly seize upon Korea — a single regiment could do the work — and then make Chemulpho the base of operations against Peking — the possession of Korea, then, by any other power could not be permitted by China as it is necessary to the safety of its capital, and I should suppose the Monroe Doctrine would apply?

Of course Great Britain would interfere as she could not permit her enormous China trade to be interrupted, but it would look somewhat as though Mr. Waeber's request was tending to a further step in this direction — ie. to the ultimate possession of Port Lazaret.

Mr. Youen, Chinese Minister, with whom I am on very good terms informs me that the Chinese Squadron is now on the east coast of Korea in the neighborhood of Gensan (Wonshan)!

Wm. H. Parker.

135
거문도·원산항의 조약항 지정 협상 지시

Earl of Iddesleigh (1886. 8. 12) ➡ J. Walsham

No. 55.

The Earl of Iddesleigh to Sir J. Walsham.

Foreign Office, August 12, 1886, 3:30 P. M.

(No. 49.)

(Telegraphic.)

YOUR telegram No. 53.

We approve suggestion for making Port Lazareff and Port Hamilton Treaty ports.

You may discuss this confidentially as a basis for an arrangement to be made on our quitting Port Hamilton. You can assure Chinese Government that Her Majesty's Government wish to deal with the question in the manner most conformable to the interests of China.

(Confidential.)

As the Admirals' Reports show that Port Hamilton is of no value to us, we should be willing to leave it at once, if any suitable arrangement could be made securing that neither it nor Port Lazareff shall pass into hostile hands. Let me know if any such seems to you possible.

136
거문도·원산항의 조약항 지정 협상 진행 상황

J. Walsham (1886. 8. 25) ➡ Earl of Iddesleigh (1886. 10. 19)

No. 99.

Sir J. Walsham to the Earl of Iddesleigh.—(Received October 19.)

Peking, August 25, 1886.

(No. 26L Confidential. Ext 58.)

My Lord,

I HAVE the honour to inform your Lordship that, in consequence of the telegraphic wire having been broken between Peking and Tien-tsin, all messages to and from the coast have, during several days past, been greatly delayed, and some confusion has occurred in the order of their dispatch from the port.

For instance, although I received your Lordship's telegram No. 53 of the 18th August on the 23rd instant, the two earlier ones of the 16th, to which it referred, did not reach me until to-day.

This will explain why I left the question addressed to me in the telegrams of the 16th instant so long unanswered.

I have now the honour to state that the information as to Corea having actually asked for a Russian Protectorate, and to the probability of her obtaining it, which the Marquis Tsêng, who is at present in St. Petersburgh, gave confidentially to Her Majesty's Ambassador, should in my opinion, be accepted with caution.

I am inclined to regard it as being exaggerated. The Marquis Tsêng, if not an intimate friend of the Grand Secretary Li, is known to be in constant communication with him; and I do not think it at all improbable that the news about the Protectorate, which, from the circumstance of the Marquis Tsêng, being at St. Petersburgh, would have the appearance of being obtained on the spot, was in reality sent by the Grand Secretary, and not procured in Russia.

The Viceroy Li professes to credit the report that the King of Corea has Russian proclivities, and may have been expressing himself in favour of a Russian Protectorate; and Yuan, the Viceroy's Agent in Corea, who also professed a short time ago to take a similar view of the matter, and who may have had his personal reasons for doing so, is not likely to have underrated the importance of this political movement in his communications with Li, so that it is not absolutely necessary to place implicit faith in the detailed statement made to Sir Robert Morier.

Information I have just received from Corea leads me to believe that, although the rumour about a Protectorate scheme is not positively without foundation, there is good ground for supposing that, for the time being at all events, no great importance need be attached to the plan. Even Yuan, the Chinese Commissioner, while still professing anxiety, seems willing now to admit that it has been concocted by a few uninfluential and insignificant individuals, and that nobody of position or of official standing has had any hand in it.

As yet, therefore, I can see no valid reason for hesitating about proceeding with the suggestion for having Port Hamilton and Port Lazareff opened as Treaty ports, and I shall take an opportunity of sounding the Ministers of the Tsung-li Yamên on the subject. My chief difficulty will consist in the mode of carrying on the negotiations, as nothing can be kept secret here, and if the Corean Government discovered that I had been arranging matters here before consulting them, they would probably oppose the plan. On the other hand, I feel sure that were I to try and find out first of all what the views of the Corean Government were, every official in Söul, and every foreign Representative, with the exception, perhaps, of the Chinese Commissioner, would be publicly asked to give his opinion.

I have, &c.

(Signed) JOHN WALSHAM.

137

Ladygensky · 李鴻章, Brenan · 李鴻章 회담

李鴻章 (1886. 8. 30 / 光緒十二年八月二日) ➡ 總署

寄譯署

光緒十二年八月初二日

俄廷迭有電致拉使 頃俄使來談 外部欲結好於華 約明俄國以後永遠不取朝鮮之地 中國亦不取其地 先互換照會爲憑 如另立條約 俟新使到仍按照會語意續訂亦可 拉謂我兩國旣經約定 英 日必不敢生心 巨文亦當自退 幷免旁人誑惑離間 意頗眞切 此與英外部節略內各國會商擔保稍異 但韓後慮實在俄 日 於他國無涉 俄旣與我約明 日必縮手 無須與彼會商 鴻令拉使先將照會稿開閱 妥與商定 再電聞 又 璧利南今早來詢華爾身巨文 永興作通商口岸之說 鴻直告以我可擔保 俄不占此島 英須早退 若欲借通商爲轉場地步 則只論巨文 勿提永興 璧云華使不日將往朝鮮 署內接晤可否照此回答 又 圖們江口行船一節 俄使允告外部 據稱將來可在天津定議 祈代奏

138

영국과 러시아 동향 관련 吳大澂의 보고

李鴻章 ➡ 總署 (1886. 9. 7 / 光緒十二年八月十日)

直督李鴻章致總署據吳大澂報俄無佔巨文島意電

頃來電甫通吳欽差七月二十八日來電二十六日抵□杵河與巴使倫巨文島事俄人實無佔意如英艦退出□保俄人必不效尤事竣回津過此島時可與英將一晤英有棄志無須立約澂以一言爲信等語又袁世凱初人來電韓廷因俄來催陸路通商金允植甫回外署未便遠離擬另派員齎咨云 八月初十日

139
Ladygensky · 李鴻章 회담(1)

李鴻章 · V. Ladygensky (1886. 9. 12 / 光緖十二年八月十五日)

附 與俄使拉德仁問答節略

光緖十二年八月十五日

十五日下午四點鐘　署理俄國公使拉德仁帶同翻譯四達爾祚福來見　寒暄畢　李云這幾天接到貴國駐扎朝鮮總領事韋貝來信否　接到貴國家電信否　拉云韋貝未有信來　本國外部由海道來電　命我來津會李中堂議事　其所應議之事由陸路發電詳告　此電須由恰克圖專送　再遲五六天卽可接到　李云我們議事總須開誠布公　不要說一句假話　拉云甚是　中堂分付的話　我自己辦得到的　卽自己辦了　辦不到的　應請國家示　李云我們要議的卽英據巨文島一事　從前汝前任公使博柏福與我說起　請我勸英國不要據此島　隨後我見英國歐署使　幷其新派公使華爾身　均已詰問　曾侯亦以此事詰問倫敦外部　拉云英據巨文島　係由俄　英在阿富汗爭界　一事而起　英據此島之後　俄國從未過問　因此事與中國有關係　與俄國無關係　李云汝們可不問此事　不管此事麽　拉云此係中國的事　俄國本可不問　惟中國如與我商議　我亦可相商　李云我以此事詰問英國　他說我本不要此島　因恐爲俄所據　故以先占爲主　今一退出　則必爲俄有　拉云我們幷沒有占過別人地方　英國何得如此措辭　李云他說中國如能保別人不來據　他卽退出　拉云這個話可以信得麽　李云可信不可信這也難說　惟彼以此借口　俄國如可保　我卽可保　英國自必語塞　拉云論此事　不要提起俄國名字　李云他只要中國能保　他卽退出　他意中係指俄國　文中只說他國　拉云自始迄今　俄國彷彿不理此事　英國侵占此地時說怕我們　今不肯退亦說怕我們　無非因我們力大　李云我們兩國請他退出可乎　拉云我們與英國不和氣時　旣未提起此語　如今和了　更不便說　朝鮮係歸中國管理　巨文島又係中國戶庭　此事自應由中國專辦　中國地大力强　不借他國之力　能令英國退出　豈不更爲露臉　李云英國退出　俄國永遠不要此地麽　拉云爲什麽怕我們　我們幷沒有占過你們的地　李云英國怕你英國對我如此說　我不能不問俄國　拉云英國商務甚盛　占據此地是其本意　推諉俄國不過借口之辭　李云你給我一實在不占憑據　我便可令英國退出　拉云中國本不應疑俄國　譬如有一體面之人　不能預疑其行竊　李云英國外部復曾侯節略　我可鈔一分給你看　請

不要泄漏 拉云我聞英國海部中人願將巨文島退出者止一小半 其不願者竟有一大半中國如令退出 即要辦到底 如旣令其退出 彼竟不退 更爲有碍 李云先將英國節略鈔出給你細看後再談 拉云好極 俄國并無疑慮中國之處 盡可放心 近日朝鮮有何新聞李云你們諒必亦有所聞 拉云外間謡言太多 李云謡言未必無因 朝鮮國王過於長厚 沒有好主意 朝廷中有一輩小人 說如歸俄國保護 卽與各國平行 不作中華屬邦 拉云俄國國家主意我很明白 此事與俄國主意不對 李云我一聞外間有此謠言 卽令劉欽差面詢俄國外部 據外部侍郎倭良嘎里說 實在沒有此事 卽有此事亦當將其文牘作爲廢紙拉云恐怕從中有人要離間我兩國交情 李云我於此事辦得光明正大 一聞此語卽問俄國外部 外部旣云沒有此事 我卽不能不相信 拉云我亦接外部電告相同 但此事總是有人要想離間我兩國交情 如彼此兩國以後相信不疑 此等謠言卽無從而起 李云其文牘據朝鮮國王說係小人揑造 朝鮮國王實無此心 俄國外部旣說實無其事更好 拉云揑造文牘之小人果係何人 總要查出 李云朝鮮國臣子亂得很 此等小人一經查出 總要重辦拉云朝鮮係極貧之國 無甚出産 如欲占此地 第一要經費 第二要兵力 第三必至與中國 日本失和 俄國家斷無此意 恐是中間有人要離間我兩國 李云英國說俄國遲早總要此地 我本不信 俄國得了我黑龍江 吉林一帶荒地 花錢不少 若更要朝鮮荒地 離本國太遠 恐費力不討好 拉云中堂料事極明 英國已取緬甸 是其好占人地之據 并要進窺西藏 嗣聞總理衙門不准前往 已作罷論 大臣謀國 本應如此 李云英國自己有私心 偏要說別人有私心 拉云以後我兩國無論何事 無論有何等謠言 只要彼此開心見誠細說自可明白 請中堂轉達總署 大家皆照此辦法 必不至起爭端 李云當函達總署 這英國節略中有兩層辦法 請拉大人細看哪一層好 拉云俟恰克圖陸路電報來時 再訂期面商遂別去

140
Ladygensky와의 회담 요지 보고

李鴻章 (1886. 9.15 / 光緒十二年八月十八日) ➡ 總署

致總署 論俄日窺韓

光緒十二年八月十八日

朝鮮監國之擧 局外每持是論 鈞意未肯率爲附和 深識遠慮 敬佩曷任 査元朝曾屢派員往監國政 卒釀禍變而止 其時尙無各國通商之事 今則牽掣更多 俄固不願 猶可以口舌爭 日初與立約 卽認朝鮮爲自主獨立之國 明係不讓他人干預 蓋日韓中隔小海交界最近 元初 三道出師征倭 有一大軍由韓取道 渡對馬島而人倭 幾受創 玆明知我屬而認爲自主 一防我掠地侵逼 一利韓貧弱爲他日幷呑地步 意極狠惡 若遽派員監國無論韓君臣觀望反側 操縱輕重之間難得妥洽 日人必先決裂 陰嗾各國連合阻撓 恐有進退維谷之時 且不擁虛名眞有鎭壓實效者 環顧京外 實難其選 所謂言易而行難者此類是已 去秋李昰應回時 力請監國大員 今閔泳翊私發送俄印函 抵烟台後亦有書來請派兵保護防俄 定朝鮮治國好法 其言似爲大局起見 然各有私心 是應欲借我力去王妃 泳翊欲借我力去小人 又與是應世仇 恐奪政柄 而不顧我之挑釁日 俄也 目下時局艱難 須先自治而後治人 韓雖可慮 有俄在旁 日斷不遽生心 我當一意聯絡俄人 使不侵占韓地 則日亦必縮手 似只有練兵儲餉 見症治症 未便輕擧妄動 以致一發難收 循繹來示 正與鄙見相同 連日俄署使拉德仁奉其國電命來津會商韓事 昨將曾劼剛咨送英外部議復巨文島辦法節略交閱 彼已電請該國示遵 玆先將閔英翊稟函 十五日與拉使晤談節略 照鈔奉覽 可否轉交總署閱看 俟拉使復議若何 當再緘達總署 轉陳核辦巨文 永興作通商口岸之說 尙未便與拉使議及 昆明湖習水操 創學堂 以漸開風氣 經費暫由練餉內設法挹注 恭讀奏稿 仰見牖民覺世 培植根本將材 一片婆心 欽仰奚似俟續奉牘示 隨時督飭局員妥細籌商 盡力協助 海軍餉需日增 重費藎畵 同深焦悚 英德四艦明夏卽須來華 沿途雇送盤費及到防後薪粮一切 實愧綿力無可供支 務乞豫籌及之

141

Ladygensky · 李鴻章 회담(2)

李鴻章 · V. Ladygensky (1886. 9. 24 / 光緒十二年八月二十八日)

附 與俄使問答節略

光緒十二年八月二十八日

光緒十二年八月二十八日下午三點鐘 署理俄國公使拉德仁帶同繙譯四達爾祚福來見 李問 貴國電信到否 拉 本國外部有電信 令我對中堂說 朝鮮謠言全無其事 縱使日後果有此事 亦必作爲不算 李 如今放心了 旁人再造謠言 我們可以不聽 倫敦電報說俄國調兵一千五百人往海參崴 有此事否 拉 實有其事 此不過是換班的 幷無添兵 英國電報將調回的全不提起 將調來的故作危辭 無非欲使中國疑慮俄國 李 拉大人所見不錯 前次拉大人說彼此以後全說實話 我已將此語告知醇王爺幷總署矣 拉 現在朝鮮平靜否 李 現都平靜 韋貝有來信否 拉 下次日本信船來時當有信 李 貴國與朝鮮有何貨物通商 買朝鮮金砂否 拉 本國與朝鮮無甚買賣 不過買牛羊而已 至金砂一節 俄國北境出產甚旺 向來不向外國收買 俄境開礦所得金砂由官收買 熔鑄金錢 松花江通商一節 中 俄條約內有的何以不行 李 中國疑慮俄國想要此地 所以不願通商 拉 俄人絶無要占地方之意 此是華官誤會 松花江所出糧食麥子甚多 民食之外尙多羨餘 隣近俄境毫無出產 所有糧食均從本國運來 道途太遠 何如彼此通商 華民旣可得利 俄民復可得食 中國日後必當准辦 蓋華境內所出麥子過多 須售與俄人 方有銷場 李 新授黑龍江恭將軍昨過天津 托我對俄國公使說 甚願與俄國邊界大員和衷辦事 他若不欺負我 我絶不想欺負他 黑龍江內惟中 俄兩國可以行舟 其江口距海參崴有若干里 江中水路深淺如何 拉 光緒七年俄都所立條約 每條曾侯另有注解 此注解係曾侯一面之辭 幷未經兩國大臣畫押 總署竟將此項注解刊印成帙 頒發邊疆大吏 該大吏竟以此注解與條約幷重 遇有交涉事件 竟以曾侯之注解爲斷 俄國則指爲一面之辭 此爭端所以日多也 鄙意欲使彼此邊吏和衷 必先將曾侯條約之注解除去 方臻妥叶 黑龍江內惟有中 俄兩國可以行舟 別國輪船皆不准入口 其江口距海參崴約計五千里 水深處約七尺 淺處不及三尺 李 條約注解之是非 曾侯自有定論 俟其回京時 拉大人可與細談 英國電報說 俄國將取布加利亞國 有此事否 拉 實無其事 此又係英國編造謠言 李

巨文島事前次面交英國節略一分　拉大人帶回譯出細看後有何主意　拉　奉到本國國家電諭　飭向中堂擔保　俄國國家幷無欲取巨文島或朝鮮他處地方之意　李　拉大人說得結實　可將此番議論寫一節略麽　拉　擔保一節　只能當面應承　不便再具公文　因向來俄國幷無侵占中國土地　何必具此文牘　李　中國絶無疑慮俄國之意　惟英國借辭於彼退則俄取　拉大人何妨具一節略　擔保俄國必不侵占朝鮮口岸　我卽能杜英人之口　拉　俄　英同爲自主之邦　一切平行　安能令我無故出一保結　如英國令我出結　何不令法國　德國先出此結　李　英國願請中國擔保　中國不得不問俄國　英國節略內云　英退恐他國來取　所謂他國　實指俄國而言　不指旁國也　拉　俄國只能向中國擔保　不能向英國擔保　李　俄國向中國擔保　中國卽可向英國說明　令其退出　拉　俄國只向中國擔保　至中國如何辦法　非俄國所敢過問　李　中國素信俄國　俄國旣如此結實擔保　我亦不疑　但英人每謂俄國卽具文牘亦靠不往　從前各國與俄國公立黑海之約　不久俄卽背約了　拉　黑海之約俄國遵行　直至十七年後　因歐洲大局變更　該約窒碍難行　故不得不變通辦理　非背約也　英國在中國通商之利甚大　必不願以巨文島一事與中國失和　中國如認眞令其退出　彼不能不照辦　至於借口俄國以飾其非　非實語也　李　前　日我遣兵船巡視巨文島　見英國只有兵船一只停泊該處　一切炮台等件全未布置　料其似有去志　彼又謂可將巨文島幷永興灣均作爲各國通商口岸　他便退出　你意以爲何如　拉　朝鮮能添口岸　與俄國無所損益　李　英國必以永興灣與巨文島相持幷論者　係恐俄國有侵占永興之意　惟該處與元山相距二十餘里　似不必另開口岸　巨文爲海中孤島　旣無出産　卽無可通商　我以其主意幷不見佳　尙未向朝鮮國王提及　巴蘭德昨密談　作爲通商口岸　若無人前往做生意有事仍可强占　似作通商口岸亦非防患之策　拉　俄實無窺占永興之意　中國但令其退出巨文　英國勢所必從　中堂勛業最隆　今若令英國退巨文　聲名更大　各國尤加敬重　無色已晩　改日再談　遂別去

142

거문도·원산항의 조약항 지정에 대한 청 總理衙門의 입장

J. Walsham (1886. 9. 27) ➡ Earl of Iddesleigh (1886. 11. 18)

No. 107.

Sir J. Walsham to the Earl of Iddesleigh. — *(Received November 18.)*

Peking, September 27, 1886.

(No. 279. Confidential. Ext. 62.)

My Lord,

WITH reference to my despatch No. 268, Confidential, of the 7th instant, and to previous correspondence on the subject of the recent excitement in the Corean capital on account of a project said to have been set on foot for obtaining a Russian Protectorate, I have now the honour to state that I have excellent reasons for believing the report to have been absolutely without foundation, and to have been fabricated for the sole purpose of undermining the influence which certain subordinate Corean officials were supposed to enjoy at the Palace, and of which the Chinese Commissioner, Yuan, was jealous.

I have in my possession a copy of the letter alleged to have been addressed by these same officials to the Russian Agent at Söul, asking for the protection of Russia, but there does not now seem to be any doubt that this document was a forgery.

Under these circumstances it can scarcely be wondered at that Russia may have felt irritated at the accusation brought against her Representative of having been party to a Russian Protectorate intrigue, and she may, of course, be insisting on some kind of satisfaction.

When I was lately at the Tsung-li Yamên, I incidentally alluded to the plan of making Ports Hamilton and Lazareff Treaty or open ports, as a possible solution of the difficulty arising out of our continued occupation of Port Hamilton.

The Ministers seemed disposed to look upon it with favour, but said that they would like to think over it before giving a decided opinion. Some days have passed since my interview, and I have not yet heard from them again. It is not improbable that they may be disinclined to compromise themselves by giving any very decided opinion on the merits of the project; and so long as they do not seek to minimize the sense of their qualified approval, it will be sufficient for all my purposes.

But should I, apart from this, have good grounds for supposing that Russia, in consequence of the late occurrences in Corea, is endeavouring, quite independently of our presence at Port Hamilton, to obtain by way of satisfaction a permanent standing within Corean territory, I should certainly hold that it would be inexpedient for Her Majesty's Government to withdraw from Port Hamilton yet awhile, and I should not push on the plan further for the moment.

If, on the contrary, I ascertain that Russia is not putting forward any such pretension, and I hope shortly to be in a position for getting at the truth, I shall proceed to Corea next month with the object of presenting my letters of credence to the King, and at the same time of submitting the plan for opening the two ports. The substance of this despatch was telegraphed to your Lordship.

I have, &c.
(Signed) JOHN WALSHAM.

143
Ladygensky · 李鴻章 회담(3)

李鴻章 · V. Ladygensky (1886. 9. 29 / 光緒十二年九月二日)

附 與俄國拉使問答節略

光緒十二年九月初二日

光緒十二年九月初二日下午三點半鐘　署俄國公使拉德仁帶同繙譯四達爾祚福來見　拉 近日朝鮮有何新聞　李云　朝鮮平靜如常　拉　朝鮮介在中　俄　日三國之間　無論何國要取其地　其餘兩國必不答應　李云　朝鮮如永遠遵守屬邦名分　中朝斷無侵占其地之理 所恐俄國有此意耳　俄國若無此意　則朝鮮必無旁人敢來侵占　俄國能否與我立一密約 拉云　此約乃俄國所願立　外部來電有此意　惟此約之格式不一　或彼此照會定案　或立條約兩三款　均無不可　李云　可先照會　其大意當說明朝鮮係中華屬邦　又爲俄羅斯隣境　今俄國情願擔保　以後永遠不占朝鮮土地; 中國亦照覆聲明　絶無占取朝鮮土地之意 彼此便可盡釋嫌疑　他人亦不能造言離間　拉　前次會商時　中堂令出擔保不取巨文島節略　俄國本無此意　英人現暫占踞　俄國不便出結　今不侵占土地之約係指朝鮮全境而言 卽巨文島亦包在內　互換後　我將中國照會送呈俄國家　中堂亦將俄國照會送呈中國朝廷　如須另立密約　將來新使到後　卽仍用原照會語意立兩三條畫押亦可　李云　照會一經互換　我卽可緊催英國將巨文島退出　今早英使華爾身派璧利南來探巨文島事　我說俄國已說明可以擔保無侵占之意　渠說總須公牘方可爲憑　貴國照會應先將稿子擬出與我看　斟酌定後照辦　拉云　中堂照復底子亦先給我看　李云　彼此一樣辦理　惟我有辦理朝鮮事宜之權　不知汝有代俄國國家畫押之權否　拉云　俄國國家已給我此權　李云　中俄交好最久　本無疑慮俄國之意　惟近來旁人屢從中煽惑　望其失和　今若立此約　旁人卽編造謠言　亦無人肯信　兩國邦交從此益睦矣　拉云　日本伊藤告我東京駐使云　中國近有廢朝鮮爲郡縣之意　俄國何不先發制人　李云　伊藤告我們駐扎東京公使云　俄有侵占朝鮮土地之意　中國宜先下手　似此看來　無非唆使兩國相爭　以冀從中得利　日本慣有此等小伎倆　拉云　兩國共保不占取此地　日本自無從施其伎倆　亦不敢望分占其地 李云　朝鮮係中國屬邦　中國自有保護之權　其於俄羅斯爲通商平行之國　自無保護之權 只由俄國具一擔保不侵占其土地之明文　拉云　英國窺伺巨文島已十餘年　乘俄　英在阿

富汗有事乃攫取之 無非借口於俄以便其私 李云 英人之初探得巨文島者名哈來頓 英國卽以是名其島 固知處心積慮之已久 前英占此島 卽告中國云 此地不爲英據必爲俄有 英據巨文不惟英國之利 亦中國之利等語 當時中國卽加駁斥 不爲所動 否則今日必不能令其退出矣 今早璧利南來談 華使欲將巨文島 永興灣均作通商口岸 我謂俄實無據永興灣之說 英據巨文島乃已然之事 二者豈容相提幷論 已將永興灣撇開 中 俄兩國互換照會之後 我必催英國退出巨文島 更爲有辭 拉云 英國自知理屈 不能不退 又恐爲人所非笑 故有請作通商口岸之語 以求自全其體面 李云 吳欽差與貴國巴大人分界大致已定 惟吉林邊界據圖們江之上流 離海尙有二十里 左爲俄境 右爲朝鮮境 朝爲我屬 中國船只應有出入江口之權 吳欽差以是相商 巴大人已電致外部 一時尙無回信 吳欽差亟欲辦竣此事 回津求我轉詢拉大人俄國家之意如何 外部能否速復定局 拉云 國家之意未知如何 我可轉告外部 但有益兩國之擧俄國無不願辦 現近封河 恐必延至來春 吳欽差如欲速回 卽在天津由中堂與新任俄國欽差商辦 李云 新任公使已由彼得堡起程否 拉云 未有來電 想尙未起程 李云 照會照復稿子擬就 彼此再商 拉遂別去

144
Ladygensky와의 회담 요지 보고

李鴻章 (1886. 9. 29 / 光緖十二年九月二日) ➡ 總署

寄譯署

光緖十二年九月初二日酉刻

連日電局密報 俄廷迭有電致拉使 頃拉來談 外部欲結好於華 約明俄國以後永遠不取朝鮮之地 中國亦不取其地 先互換照會爲憑 如另立密約 俟新使到 仍按照會語意續訂亦可 拉謂我兩國旣經約定 日 英必不敢生心 巨文亦當自退 且免旁人謠惑離間 意頗眞誠 此與英外部節略內各國會商擔保稍異 但韓後慮實在俄 日 於他國無涉 俄旣與我約明 日必縮手 無須與彼商會 鴻令拉先將照會稿送閱 妥與酌定 再電聞 又 璧利南今早來詢華爾身巨文 永興作通商口岸之說 鴻直告以我可擔保 俄不占此島 英須早退 若欲借通商口爲轉場地步 則只論巨文 勿提永興 璧云華使不日將往朝鮮 署內接晤 可否照此回答 又 圖們江口行船一節 拉允告外部 據稱將來可在天津定議 請先代奏 鴻

145

Ladygensky와의 교섭 경과 보고

李鴻章 (1886. 10. 1 / 光緒十二年九月四日) ➡ 總署

覆總署 請英退巨文島

光緒十二年九月初四日

敬密覆者 前奉八月十六日公函 以英使商及巨文島 永興灣作通商口岸 屬爲籌酌等因 旣擬作各國通商口 自不妨遇便告知各使 前巴蘭德在津敍及 謂該口等無生意可做 終是虛名 若他國有事 仍可强占 俄署使拉德仁來議韓事 亦不以巨文作通商爲善策 但未下斷語 九月初二日曾將與拉使商議互送照會并英使派員來詢大略電奏 奉初三日電復 俄旣允立約 不取韓地 通商碼頭一節可作罷論 允爲直截了當 祈鈞署接晤英使時以此諷之 催其早退 敝處亦必遇便轉致也 玆將八月二十八 九月初二日與俄使問答節略鈔呈□察 俟其照會稿送到酌定 再行電聞 專泐密復 敬頌中堂王爺大人鈞祺 李鴻章謹復 直字四百六十七號 計抄冊

146
Ladygensky의 조회문 초고

V. Ladygensky ➡ 李鴻章 (1886. 10. 1 / 光緒十二年九月四日)

附 照譯俄國署使拉德仁面交法文照會底稿

光緒十二年九月初四日到

遵照俄羅斯向來願保和局之主意 惟望朝鮮境內永遠平靜 朝鮮爲俄之隣邦 於俄國既有關係 願守事宜計有三節如左

一 朝鮮與中國及朝鮮與各國之交際保無更變

二 朝鮮全境土地遵守完全

三 朝鮮國王應有自主之權并保其平安 俾能遵行有益於百姓之事 在朝鮮境內如將現時所有情形干預更改變換 於俄國在朝鮮境內應有之權利有碍 致生事端 卽與俄國情願隣邦平靜之意相悖 如後來有難於預料之事與朝鮮大有關係 致使朝鮮必行變法 中俄兩國或由彼此政府或由彼此駐韓大員公同商定辦法 以免誤會 如有改變朝鮮現時所有情形之事 彼此兩國必不擅自辦理 以爲中 俄兩國願守敦睦和好之據 中 俄駐韓兩國大員均應奉有訓條 飭其於朝鮮國王臣工應辦事宜 無論有何緣由 均不得與聞 誤會之事如不速定 日後所生事端難於預料 中國東三省吉林與朝鮮邊界 應請早日秉公劃定

147
영국에 거문도 철수 촉구 지시

光緖帝 (1886. 10. 2 / 光緖十二年九月五日)

諭軍機大臣等 電寄李鴻章 英議將巨文作爲通商碼頭 本以防俄占踞藉口 今俄旣允立約 不取韓地 則英更無他慮 正可藉此轉圜 應勸令速還朝鮮 以全睦誼 其通商碼頭一說 可作罷論

148

러시아의 對 조선 방침에 대한 李鴻章의 발언

J. Walsham (1886. 10. 6) ➡ Earl of Iddesleigh

No. 91.

Sir. J. Walsham to the Earl of Iddesleigh.—(Received October 6.)

Peking, October 6, 1886.

(No. 63.)

(Telegraphic.)

MY telegram No. 62.

Following confidential statement by the Viceroy Li to Her Majest's Consul:—

Russia, through Representative here, who went to Tien-tsin to treat with his Excellency, has solemnly denied having mad or received overtures in respect to Corea or having designs in that direction.

She has, moreover, given solemn pledge to Great Britain that if we leave Port Hamilton she will not, under any circumstances, occupy Corean territory. The Viceroy insisted on this, and warned the Russian Chargé d'Affaires that a breach of this engagement would lead to a rupture.

As the Chargé d'Affaires declined to give his assurances in writing, as calling in question his honesty, and as the Viceroy's statement was verbal, I have suggested to the latter that the Yamên, as an inducement for our speedy withdrawal, should record in a note for publication, in case of need only, the Russian pledge, for communication to Her Majesty's Government.

I imagine that Her Majesty's government would then deem it sufficient to assign publicly, as the grounds for our retiring, that the special motive for our occupation had happily ceased.

If the written record should be refused, I should propose, as a reply to their protests, to write to the Corean Government suggesting plan of Treaty ports, to which the Viceroy pretends to be less well disposed, especially as regards Port Lazareff, since he took upon himself to consult German Minister and Russian Chargé d'Affaires.

Or, if her Majesty's Government are content with the verbal assurances of the Viceroy, in order to avoid delay, we could still retire now in the manner I have indicated, and I could personally negotiate next spring with Corea about opening the ports.

I have decided, in any case, not to go to Corea this year.

149

이홍장·Brenan 회담(1)

J. Walsham (1886. 10. 6) ➡ Earl of Iddesleigh

No. 111.

Sir. J. Walsham to the Earl of Iddesleigh.—(Received November 30.)

Peking, October 6, 1886.

(No. 285. Very Confidential.)
(Telegraphic.)

IN continuation of my immediately preceding despatch of this date, I have the honour to transmit herewith to your Lordship a copy of Mr. Consul Brenan's account of what passed at his interview with the Grand Secretary Li, when he called upon his Excellency in accordance with my instructions to discuss confidentially various matters connected with our occupation of Port Hamilton, respecting which I was anxious to obtain information.

Should the Grand Secretary Lave faithfully recounted to Mr. Brenan the incidents of his negotiations with the Russian Chargé d'Affaires, M. Ladygensky, there would be good grounds for believing not only that the late report of Russian intrigues in Corea, to which I have had occasion to allude in previous despatches, was unfounded, but also that, in the event of our retiring from Port Hamilton, Russia is prepared to give a solemn pledge to China, as the Suzerain Power, that she will not under any circumstances occupy Corean territory.

This statement as regards the rumours of a Russian Protectorate tallies with the interesting details of the recent crisis in the Corean capital, recorded in the despatch from Her Majesty's Acting Consul-General which accompanied my despatch No. 280 of the 27th ultimo; and the pledge that Russia is reported as willing to give in respect of her future action in Corea would, I cannot help thinking, be the kind of guarantee against a possible Russian occupation of Port

Hamilton after our departure, which has more than once suggested itself to Her Majesty's Government.

Hitherto I have taken the liberty of stating that I did not conceive Her Majesty's Government would have been justified in retiring from Port Hamilton on an ordinary assurance from the Chinese Government that if we left nobody else would take our place.

I do not suppose I should have had any difficulty in obtaining such a guarantee as this, which, however, I should have regarded as absolutely worthless; but, always, of course, supposing the Viceroy Li's story to be authentic, the guarantee now exacted by his Excellency, and accepted by the Russian Representative, bears a different character.

The Viceroy seems to have plainly indicated to M. Ladygensky that until he were placed in the position of being able positively to assure Her Majesty's Government of a disinterested policy on the part of Russia with regard to Corea, he could not himself offer any pledge to them in the matter of the Port Hamilton question, and although the Russian Chargé d'Affaires hesitated to comply with the Viceroy's wish, that the engagement should be a written one, he is said to have reiterated the promise in the most formal manner, whereupon the Viceroy, on his own part, warned 31. Ladygensky that should there be any breach thereof in the future, it would lead to a rupture.

We therefore have here, without the asking for it, precisely the guarantee which, if it be genuine, would allow of Her Majesty's Government availing themselves of it as a basis for our withdrawal from Corean territory. It would be, as it were, a double guarantee, to which Russia and China were equally parties.

But then comes the question of its genuineness. The Viceroy, it will be observed, undertook, upon M. Ladygensky renewing his assurance of Russia's good faith, to submit to Her Majesty's Government the conditions of the Russian pledge; but it should be remembered that, although his Excellency directs affairs between China and Corea, he cannot take the place of the Chinese Government so far as to enter into direct communication with a foreign Government on an international question;. and besides this, it is unlikely that the Viceroy would himself consent to repeat in writing what he said to Mr. Brenan.

I have therefore ventured on the adoption of the somewhat unusual plan of drawing up and privately submitting to him such a note as, under the circumstances, the Chinese Ministers might address to me for communication to Her Majesty's Government.

Your Lordship would naturally be entitled to ask me why I took such a roundabout way of performing a very simple operation, as I had nothing to do but make a similar proposal to the Yamên myself.

In the first place, I should have been obliged to explain how I had come into possession of the results of the Viceroy's discussions with the Russian Chargé d'Affaires and my reasons for being indirect communication with his Excellency, a course which would probably have given offence to both the Viceroy and the Ministers. In the second place, had I thought it prudent to speak to the Chinese Ministers, apart from the Viceroy, I could scarcely have done more than suggest the propriety of their furnishing me with a note. I could not well have proposed to them the terms of that note, and the chances would have been in favour of their introducing into it language with respect to our occupation of Port Hamilton and to our withdrawal which might have been highly objectionable.

Whereas with the Viceroy I was on somewhat safer ground. He had answered my appeal for information about Russia and Corea by giving me a detailed version of his negotiations with the Russian Representative, and by leading me to suppose that I could communicate it to your Lordship; so that, when thanking him for his statement, I had an opportunity of begging him to go a step further, and take the initiative in recommending to the Tsung-li Yamên the advantage to be derived from my being made acquainted at once with the Russian assurances as to the non-occupation of Port Hamilton after our departure.

In the case of the Viceroy, the fact of my accompanying my suggestion with a sketch of such a note as I thought might properly be addressed to me by the Yamên was not likely to give rise to the same inconvenience as might have been created by my advising the Chinese Ministers themselves as to the tenour of their communication, and I was at the same time equally anxious that, his Excellency should not be intrusted with the framing of the note, as he too would have been quite capable of saying things about our presence at Port Hamilton which would be better left unsaid.

I have the honour to inclose a copy of my draft note, and also a copy of the despatch which I addressed to Mr. Brenan when I instructed him to lay it privately before the Viceroy.

Should his Excellency agree to my suggestion, and should the Tsung-li Yamên write to me more or less in the sense I have proposed. I do not suppose that Her Majesty's Government would be otherwise than disposed to acquiesce in the invitation of the Chinese Government to relieve them of the embarrassing position in which they are placed by our continuing to occupy Port Hamilton; nor do I imagine that Her Majesty's Government would be unwilling to give as a reason for our withdrawal that the special grounds which led to the temporary occupation had happily ceased to exist.

Such a statement would, I presume, be gratifying to the three States principally concerned, and it would render unnecessary, except in the case of Russia breaking her engagement, the publication of the Chinese note in which the Russian guarantee would have been recorded.

But I confess I shall be disappointed if the Viceroy Li should decline to have anything put down on paper in connection with the Russian assurances, all the more so because it would then look as if he had not been quite straightforward in his communications to Mr. Brenan; and the modified views that his Excellency now professes to hold on the Treaty port scheme, which he had previously approved, and was prepared to uphold, might then have some significance, especially as he lays stress on the importance he attaches to his idea of excluding Port Lazareff from the plan.

In spite of this change in the Viceroy's views, I should, in the event of my being unable to obtain a written record from the Chinese Government, still be of opinion that it would be advisable to submit the Treaty port project to the Corean Government.

We ought not, I should say, to leave them much longer without a definite reply of some sort to their protests against our continuance at Port Hamilton, and even if they did not agree to the project, they could not complain, as they are now doing, that Her Majesty's Government are disregarding the various representations they have made.

No doubt the course I am proposing might entail delay in the settlement of the Port Hamilton question; but unless Her Majesty's Government were prepared to accept as sufficient the unwritten statements of the Viceroy with a view to enabling our naval force to retire before the winter sets in, I do not see what other course I could with propriety suggest, having regard to our present position in respect of the occupation.

I have, &c.

(Signed) JOHN WALSHAM.

150

Ladygensky의 수정 조회문

V. Ladygensky ➡ 李鴻章 (1886. 10. 6 / 光緖十二年九月九日)

附 譯俄使續交改訂照會內三條

光緖十二年九月初九日到

一 中 俄兩國爲捐除彼此誤會起見 議明朝鮮一切情形 以後無有更變 均照歷來及現在辦法 所有一切變法與朝鮮現在情形有碍 或生出轇轕枝節 卽與中 俄兩國願共保有平靜之意不符

二 俄國除擔保太平外 并無他意 不願取朝鮮土地 中國亦自不行如此之事

三 日後如有意外難於預料之事 與朝鮮現在情形大有關係 或與俄國在朝鮮之利益有碍 致使不得不變朝鮮現在情形 中 俄兩國或由彼此政府或由彼此駐韓大員公同商定辦法

151

조회문의 재수정 요구 사실 보고

李鴻章 (1886. 10. 7 / 光緒十二年九月十日) ➡ 總署

寄譯署

光緒十二年九月初十日戌刻

連日俄拉使商敍照會稿 內有幾條語多枝節 再四駁改未定 頃令另具簡明照會 聲明俄國日後不取朝鮮土地 正義已足 俟定稿再電聞 昨璧利南又來密送華使代鈞署擬照會英文稿 詳言俄使在津議明不占巨文 不提作通商口之語 容譯出函達 但須俄使文到署方可照催晤華 乞勿先道破 鴻

152
러·청 간 교섭 경과(1)

J. Walsham (1886. 10. 8) ➡ Earl of Iddesleigh

No. 112.

Sir. J. Walsham to the Earl of Iddesleigh.—(Received November 30.)

Peking, October 8, 1886.

(No. 286. Confidential. Ext. 64.)

My Lord,

WITH reference to my telegram No. 63 of the 6th instant, I have now the honour to report to your Lordship that, in compliance with my wishes, the Grand Secretary Li has expressed himself as ready to invite the Tsung-li Yamên to communicate to me, in an official note, the assurances which have been formally given to him by the Russian Chargé d'Affaires, M. Ladygensky, to the effect that, in the event of our withdrawing our naval force from Port Hamilton, Russia will undertake not to occupy Corean territory under any circumstances.

His Excellency has, at the same time, given me to understand that he will not be able to take this step for a few days, as, with a view to obtain from the Russian Representative something more substantial, in the shape of a guarantee, than mere verbal assurances, he is now occupied with M. Ladygensky in drafting what he calls a "Secret Treaty," in virtue of which China and Russia Trill pledge themselves to respect the integrity of Corea; and to protect her from aggression on the part of any other Power.

So soon as these negotiations shall have been concluded, the Grand Secretary he says, be prepared to arrange with the Tsung-li Yamên about the note to me,

His Excellency's modified views in respect of the Treaty port scheme which he had previously favoured, arise from the fact that the Russian assurances will, he considers, effect all that such a project was intended to insure, and that, consequently, it is no longer necessary.

If I am furnished with a copy of the instrument negotiated by the Grand Secretary and M. Ladygensky, and should I see no reason to be dissatisfied with the Chinese statement when it reaches me, I should suggest to your Lordship the propriety of my withdrawing altogether the plan for opening Ports Lazareff and Hamilton.

Concurrently with the note from the Yamên, the Chinese Minister in London will be instructed by telegraph to offer to your Lordship the assurances which it will contain.

I have reported the above by telegraph.

I have, &c.

(Signed) JOHN WALSHAM.

153
조회문 작성 관련 Ladygensky와의 교섭 경과

李鴻章(1886. 10. 8 / 光緒十二年九月十一日) ➡ 總署(1886. 10. 11 / 光緒十二年九月十四日)

致總署 駁俄照會幷議巨文島

光緒十二年九月十一日

敬啓者 連日與俄署使拉德仁商叙照會稿 大略情形昨已電陳在案 九月初四日 該使送來照會法文底 令委員譯出 詞意含混 枝節頗多 鴻章面告該使 以朝鮮係我屬邦 向來自有辦法 與俄僅隣境通商大區別 汝意或爲韋貝所聳動 欲以牽制中國 萬不准行 必須另改 初九日 該使覆另換三條送閱 雖較前稿稍爲明淨 亦間有語病 彼意第三節爲防范日後他國或有侵奪韓境之事 欲隱指日本 又不肯說明 恐有窒碍 初十日下午 該使來署 辨論至晩 鴻章屬令另擬簡明照會 專以第二條俄國日後不取朝鮮土地爲正義 其餘枝節均應刪除 免致後來轇轕 該使允可照辦 俟其送稿商定後 幷將照復稿大意再行電呈 請旨核定 以便互換 玆先將俄使兩次送來照會稿譯寄備查 英領事璧利南初九日來言 華爾身接彼轉致信後 巨文島作通商口岸之說可作罷論 因代擬貴署致該使照會英文底稿 屬卽密寄尊處酌辦 彼謂恐措詞過於嚴峻 使英廷不能轉場 故但叙前後原委 照催伊卽電請該國回示 冀早日退出巨文 共敦睦誼 鴻章與譯員詳細推敲 該使原稿於英外部前給曾侯節略要語未提 後於鴻章與俄使議商各節有過火語 因照譯出 酌加刪潤 是否有當 謹將英使洋文底幷譯稿奉呈核辦 璧領事謂華使擬旬日內起程往朝鮮 鴻章屬其轉致稍緩 巨文事非與中朝議辦 難得妥協 請俟此事辦定後再行 未知果否 想鈞署須待俄使照會互送方能照催英使也 再 前致朝鮮王函交徐相雨齎回 謹鈔函稿奉閱 專肅縷布 敬頌中堂王爺大人鈞福 李鴻章謹啓 直字四百六十八號 計抄三冊 又洋文一件

154
러·청 간 교섭 경과(2)

J. Walsham (1886. 10. 9) ➡ Earl of Iddesleigh

No 113.

Sir. J. Walsham to the Earl of Iddesleigh.—(Received November 30.)

Peking, October 9, 1886.

(No. 287. Confidential.)

My Lord,

IN continuation of my despatch No. 285 of the 6th instant, I have the honour to forward herewith to your Lordship a copy of a despatch from Mr. Brenan, Her Majesty's Consul at Tien-tsin, in which he reports the details of a further confidential conversation with the Grand Secretary Li on the subject of our retention of Port Hamilton, and of the assurances given by Russia that she will not occupy Corean territory if we withdraw.

The principal object of Mr. Brenan's visit was to lay before the Grand Secretary my views with regard to the negotiations now going on between his Excellency and the Russian Chargé d'Affaires. Those views were recorded in my despatch to Mr, Brenan of the 2nd instant, a copy of which accompanied my above-mentioned No. 285.

It will be seen that the Grand Secretary, on being made acquainted with the tenour of the draft note, which I had suggested might be adopted by the Tsung-li Yamên when communicating to me the conditions of the Russian guarantee, expressed his concurrence, and said he was himself ready at once to give Mr. Brenan a note based on my draft.

But on Mr. Brenan pointing out to him that such a note should more properly come from the Tsung-li Yamên, his Excellency remarked that his only reason for having made the offer was a desire to avoid delay, adding that he now would arrange with the Yamên about the note. There would, however, be a short delay, as he was desirous of obtaining from Russia a more substantial guarantee than a verbal assurance, and was then engaged in drafting, with the Russian Chargé d'Affaires, what he termed a "Secret Treaty," according to which China and Russia would pledge themselves to respect the integrity of Corea, and to protect her against encroachment at the hands of other Powers.

This communication was made by the Grand Secretary in strict confidence, and in making it his Excellency seems to have alluded to a Memorandum connected with the Port Hamilton question, which, he told Mr. Brenan, had been submitted to the Chinese Minister in London by Her Majesty's Secretary of State for Foreign Affairs.

This Memorandum can, I imagine, be no other than the one which was inclosed in the Earl of Rosebery's No. 99, Confidential, of the 15th April last.

It was given to Sir Halliday Macartney as a reply to a representation he had made in the name of the Marquis Tsêng on the 11th March, and contained the views of Her Majesty's Government on the point of our withdrawal from Port Hamilton.

The Memorandum explained that, although Her Majesty's Government had no desire to prolong the occupation of a portion of Corean territory in opposition to the wishes of the Chinese Government, they were of opinion that, in the interest of both China and England, Port Hamilton should not be occupied by another European Power; and they would be prepared to retire if China would guarantee that no such occupation should take place, or should China be unwilling to undertake such a responsibility. Her Majesty's Government would be no less ready to withdraw if Russia and the other Powers interested would, on the initiative of China, enter into an international arrangement guaranteeing the integrity of Corea, including, of course, Port Hamilton.

No answer having been returned by the Chinese Government to these proposals, I was instructed by Lord Rosebery to ascertain from the Tsung-li Yamên whether it was intended to act upon the suggestion of Her Majesty's Government, who were anxious to know, without further delay, if there was any likelihood of its being entertained; and in my telegram No. 52 of the 27th July, I informed his

Lordship that the Chinese Ministers were evidently disinclined to regard as feasible the proposed solution of the pending difficulty.

It was then that I ventured to submit the plan of converting Ports Lazareff and Hamilton into Treaty ports. The scheme was, I am aware, unpretending enough, nor had it any special merit beyond, perhaps, that of being fairly easy of execution, while it would have enabled Her Majesty's Government to return some kind of definite reply to the Corean protests, and would have afforded a slightly greater if not positive security against either of the two ports being occupied by another Power after our departure from Port Hamilton.

It seems pretty clear that the Grand Secretary's plan for obtaining a written guarantee from Russia is founded on the principle indicated in the Memorandum submitted to Sir Halliday Macartney, and so long as what his Excellency calls a "Secret Treaty" is restricted to an engagement on the part of the two Signatories to respect the integrity of Corea. I do not suppose that Her Majesty's Government would see anything objectionable in this modification of their own proposals.

I doubt very much whether the more comprehensive scheme, which would have included other Powers besides China and Russia, could be carried out just at present. One of those Powers must necessarily have been Japan, and for the moment, at least, there is unfortunately a certain amount of unpleasantness apparent in the relations between Japan and China, due to the recent rather serious occurrences at Nagasaki, which, as Sir Francis Plunkett will have informed your Lordship, originated in a squabble between some sailors from Chinese men-of-war and the Japanese police. There were a good many lives lost on both sides, and the two Governments are taking the matter up with more warmth than the affair really merited.

I daresay means can and will be found for arriving at a satisfactory settlement, but for the time being China would certainly not admit Japan as one of the Guaranteeing Powers.

When the Grand Secretary mentioned to Mr. Brenan the nature of the joint pledge which he was endeavouring to obtain in respect of Corea, the latter asked him whether Japan would be asked to become a party to it. whereupon the Grand Secretary spoke very bitterly against that Power, and intimated that if she attempted to more in Corea, she would be crushed between Russia and China.

In answering Mr. Brenan's despatch I have begged him, as the inclosed copy of my reply will show, to suggest to the Grand Secretary that the note which the Tsung-li Yamên will write to me on the conclusion of his negotiations with the Russian Chargé d'Affaires, should contain a copy of whatever engagement may have been signed, as when I forwarded to his Excellency the draft of such a note as I thought the Yamên could properly address to me, I was under the impression that the Russian Representative had declined to record his promises in Writing.

I have, &c.

(Signed) JOHN WALSHAM.

155

조회문 재수정 지시

光緒帝 (1886. 10. 11 / 光緒十二年九月十四日)

諭軍機大臣等　電寄李鴻章　酉電並由總理衙門進呈該督信函鈔冊均悉　俄使擬改照會有兩國政府約明不改變朝鮮現在情形之語 仍是隱寓保護之意 於將來措置屬國事宜恐多牽掣 必須刪去此語方妥 所有擬改照會字句 著李鴻章詳細斟酌 勿令一字含混仍錄稿請旨 再與定議 電寄

156
조회문 재수정 지시 이행 상황 보고

李鴻章 (1886. 10. 11 / 光緒十二年九月十四日) ➡ 總署

寄譯署

光緒十二年九月十四日申刻

本日電旨謹悉 俄使惑於浮議 慮我將來改變朝鮮爲郡縣 或派大員監國 故歷擬照會稿皆力持不改變之說 韓爲我屬邦 俄乃通商隣邦 卽係現在情形 似彼無保護意在內 前已囑將此語刪去 彼堅不允 此係彼之照會稿也 鴻擬於我照覆稿內聲明 朝鮮爲中國屬藩 歷來辦法皆爲保護平安 玆來文云云 與中國歷來辦法相符 似已補足正義 將來措置屬國 若改郡縣 派監國兩層恐辦不到 其他平亂等事宜當無掣肘 是否有當 請酌核代奏 查電局報 拉使旬餘無電 昨忽電俄廷三百四十九字 必係此事 俟其接復電來商再遵旨商令刪去不改變情形一語 能否照辦 再電聞 鴻

九月十四日奉旨 李鴻章酉電悉 俄使擬改照會有兩國政府約明不改變朝鮮現在情形之語 仍是隱寓保護之意 於將來措置屬國事宜恐多牽制 必須刪去此語方妥 所有擬改照會字句 着李鴻章詳加斟酌 勿令一字含混 仍錄稿請旨 再與定議

157
영국의 거문도 철수 관련 내용 보고

李鴻章 (1886. 10. 13 / 光緒十二年九月十六日) ➡ 總署

寄譯署

光緒十二年九月十六日申刻

頃璧利南來傳華使語 暫緩赴朝鮮 俟俄使照會定議 祈由總署摘錄文內 不占據朝鮮境內土地 要語 或文移 或函示 彼即電請英廷退巨文島 前送擬稿可酌改云 鴻

158
조회문 수정의 방침 지시

慈喜太后 (1886. 10. 14 / 光緒十二年九月十七日)

丁未 欽奉 慈禧端佑康頤昭豫莊誠皇太後懿旨 本日據軍機大臣呈進醇親王信函 內稱中俄因韓立約原恐俄懷他意 若因此被俄牽制 轉不如不約爲愈 蓋俄不侵韓 乃其本分應爾 安能 與我爲上國者相提並論 牽就立約 無論郡縣監國 本不欲辦 亦辦不到 恐如此次責問之類 亦做不到矣 得具文一時之虛名 失全韓日後之通局 履霜冰至 諒公議亦同此情 法之於越 英之於緬 倭之於球 皆自彼發難 中國多事之秋 興滅繼絕 力有未逮 尙不足爲可恥 若俄約則無中生有 自我發端 而乃墮其術中 自貽伊戚 豈不貽後人之訾乎 無已 或酌添數語 大致謂韓爲華屬 保全周至 苟非干名犯義 斷不別有措置 俄與韓修睦通商 亦斷無侵擾之心云云 似名分疆界 尙覺清楚等語 所論切中窾要著李鴻章詳審酌度 照此定議 免貽後患 將此由五百里 密論知之

159
거문도·원산항의 조약항 지정 관련 중국 주둔 해군과의 협의

J. Walsham (1886. 10. 22) ➡ Earl of Iddesleigh (1886. 12. 13)

Doc. 322.

Sir. J. Walsham to the Earl of Iddesleigh.—(Received December 13.)

Peking, October 22, 1886.

(No. 290. Confidential.)

My Lord,

AT the time I thought of going to the Corea in order to take advantage of the occasion of presenting my letters of credence for discussing the plan of opening Ports Hamilton and Lazareff to trade, to which I have had the honour of referring in previous correspondence, I telegraphed to Admiral Hamilton to ascertain his views with regard to it, and also with the object of learning whether his objections to a continuance of our occupation of Port Hamilton remained unaltered.

From the telegram of which a copy is inclosed I gathered that, while the Admiral still maintained his objections to the occupation from a naval point of view, he had no opinion to offer on the subject of the Treaty port scheme.

The telegram at the same time stated that Captain Powlett, commanding Her Majesty's ship "Champion," would be at Chefoo towards the middle of this month, and prepared to give me detailed information on all matters relating to Port Hamilton, as he was thoroughly conversant with the question.

Shortly after receiving Admiral Hamilton's telegram I became aware of the negotiations between the Grand Secretary Li and M. Ladygensky, the Russian Chargé d'Affaires, which I have reported to your Lordship.

These negotiations, although the direct outcome of the late so-called crisis in Corea, which was due to the alleged project for a Russian Protectorate, were very intimately connected with our occupation of Port Hamilton. I therefore determined to postpone my journey till the spring of next, year, as the season was already almost too far advanced for me to undertake it this year, even if I had not waited for the result of M. Ladygensky's discussions with the Grand Secretary at Tien-tsin.

Under these circumstances, I acquainted Captain Powlett, by telegraph, with my decision not to go to the Corea in case he might have been coming to Chefoo solely on my account, but I subsequently learnt that it was his intention to be there at the date originally named by the Admiral.

I was glad to hear this, as in the event of my having to take any action with respect to the Port Hamilton question it would have been a great convenience to have so distinguished an officer as Captain Powlett within communicating distance, seeing that the direct telegraphic line with the Corean capital is still interrupted.

At the same time, it occurred to me that Captain Powlett, when he did arrive at Chefoo, should not he left in complete ignorance of the possibility there was of an arrangement being effected in connection with our presence at Port Hamilton, and as I was unable myself to proceed to Chefoo. I requested Mr. Hillier to undertake the duty of seeing the Commander of the "Champion," and of personally explaining to him in confidence how matters at present stood.

I have the honour to lay before your Lordship a copy of my instructions to Mr. Hillier, and of the letter I sent to Captain Powlett by him, as well as of the reply I have received from this officer.

When I wrote to him I did not imagine, as he seems to have gathered from my letter, that without orders from the Admiral he could have acted on his own responsibility in carrying out any measures which Her Majesty's Government might have directed me to adopt under certain contingencies.

What I wished Captain Powlett to understand was that it was very satisfactory for me to have him so comparatively near at hand, as with his knowledge and experience of all questions concerning Port Hamilton he could render me invaluable service at a moment's notice by assisting me in giving effect to any instructions your Lordship might send me, and the carrying out of which would necessarily in the present case require the co-operation of the naval authorities on the station.

I have heard from Mr. Hillier, who tells me that Captain Powllet will not want his services, and that he therefore intends to return to Peking at once.

The accompanying copy of a confidential despatch from Admiral Hamilton, bearing upon his telegram of the 29th ultimo (Inclosure 1), gives his reasons for believing that even if Russia were desirous of annexing any portion of Corean territory, she is at present too weak in this part of the world, and likely to be so for some time to come, to allow of her carrying out any such project.

The Admiral's despatch is all the mere interesting because the information it contains is founded on the results of what he personally heard and saw during the recent cruize of the fleet in the Sea of Japan, when he had an opportunity of visiting both Corean and Russian ports.

Reports which have reached me through other independent sources would certainly tend to corroborate the accuracy of Admiral Hamilton's view of the relative strength of China and Russia in their frontier provinces.

I have, &c.

(Signed) JOHN WALSHAM.

P. S. — A copy of my reply to Admiral Hamilton's despatch is also here with inclosed.

J. W.

160
조회문 수정 요청에 대한 Ladygensky의 반응

李鴻章 (1886. 10. 22 / 光緖十二年九月二十五日) ➡ 總署 (1886.10. 23 / 光緖十二年九月二十六日)

致總署 論删改俄照會

光緖十二年九月二十五日

密啓者 前奉九月初五日電示 袁世凱十款四條到時錄寄 以便進呈等因 頃接袁世凱來稟 將八月十一日以後情形辦理各節 九月初三日上朝鮮國王書 譬喩時弊各條款及是日與國王筆談 十二日國王覆書幷示韓臣籌擬朝鮮大局論其抄五折 謹將原折轉寄察核應否另繕進呈 恭候酌裁 又奉十四日電旨後 卽派譯員羅豐祿往俄署使處 告以必須删去不改變朝鮮現在情形一語 拉使謂 俄廷覆電若專提不占據土地字樣 本無此心而憑空出此甘結 如人本不爲盜賊 必要具一文結 有傷大國體面 且所謂不改變者係約明不改兩國朝鮮現在名分也 俄實無干預朝鮮政權之意 斷斷力持不允 今已旬日 該使不再來商 鴻章亦置不問 昨知該使又密電俄國 俟其晤談若何情形當再電聞 英使頃遣禧在明來詢 何時可給照會 鴻章謂如俄有照會 自當請總署備文催退巨文 否則我必據俄使面允不占據朝鮮土地之說 咨請總署轉行照會 禧云亦可行 華使專候此文 電達本國又 伍廷芳擬議長崎兵 捕互斗案辦法 頗有條理 已鈔寄徐公使酌辦 專肅密布 敬頌中堂王爺大人鈞祺 李鴻章謹上 直字四百六十九號 計五折一册

161

Ladygensky · 李鴻章 회담(4)

李鴻章 · V. Ladygensky (1886. 10. 24 / 光緒十二年九月二十七日)

附 與拉署使問答節略

光緒十二年九月二十七日

光緒十二年九月二十七日下午三點鐘 署俄國公使拉德仁隨帶翻譯王厚 四達爾祚福來見 寒暄畢 李 汝所擬照會底稿內云 兩國政府約明不改變朝鮮現在情形一句 殊有語病 將來中國辦理屬藩事宜 誠恐俄國誤會 借此牽掣 是以朝廷命我與拉大人商議 刪去此句 前已屬羅翻譯傳知 貴國可否照辦 拉 昨得國家回電 命我照所議底稿畫押互換 不便再改 查此次國家派我來津 與中堂商議朝鮮事宜 足爲俄國與中國願敦和好之據 彼此會商多次 知無不言 盡釋疑慮 卽不換照會 亦可執面訂之語爲憑 從前議換照會 本爲捐除誤會起見 今因照會底稿措辭而轉生誤會 竊謂貴國疑慮過多 查約明不改變朝鮮現在情形一句 卽中國向來辦法皆在不改變之列 何必有牽掣之慮 李 朝鮮爲中國藩屬 中國有保護之責 如有內亂 中國不能不派兵前往 亂平之後 卽仍撤回 如俄國以改變情形爲辭 豈無牽掣之慮乎 拉 俄國惟以朝鮮平靜爲願 如有內亂 中國發兵平定 亦俄國之利 俄國必不過問 何牽掣之有 俄國惟願朝鮮平靜之外 幷不想得別項便宜 我所擬底稿 無論交與何人閱看 必不能指出俄國別有私意 李 拉大人第一次 第二次所擬底稿 措辭多有過當處 我鈔寄政府合看前兩次之稿 不能無疑 拉 從前寫的 中堂說不妥 我卽改擬 今又說不妥 我實無法 我政府以專說不占據朝鮮土地太突 上添一語 以足其意 兩句仍作一氣看 李 論朝鮮事 我兩國不便相提幷說 拉 中 俄兩大國本是平行 約明兩國不改變現在情形 內含有中國屬邦 俄國隣邦之意 未可顯分高下 我所已說明者 皆代傳俄國政府之語 非我私言也 李 我將拉大人所說不占據朝鮮土地寫一照會 催英國退出巨文島 言我擔保俄國必不來占此地 拉大人可將此意告明貴國將來萬不可使我爲難 拉 俄廷如有侵占朝鮮土地之心 此次必不派我來津與中堂商議有此一番議論 英國不久必將巨文島退出 惟此次互換照會 不專爲巨文島一事 實爲將來他人謠惑 杜絶後患起見 今已將成議 又復中止 恐俄國國家必疑中國日後或改變朝鮮辦法 李 朝鮮不干名犯義 中國卽不改變向來辦法 請轉告國家勿疑 拉 我到此與中

堂商議月餘 朝鮮卽晏然無事 如互換照會 更可長保平靜 外人亦不敢生心 今說不成 朝鮮官員躁競者多 每思有以自見 而外國人從中附和 誠恐復生事端 李 只要韋貝不出來附和 朝鮮必不至復生事端 拉 韋貝之外 尙有別人 李 汝指袁世凱乎 袁世凱本非生事之人 韋貝如不附和朝鮮小人 我看將來不至生事 拉 駐朝鮮各國人多出主意所怕者 中 俄兩大國耳 現在中國政府不換照會 恐後來有變亂事又想換了 李 朝廷幷非不換照會 因拉大人所擬之稿措辭有語病 將語病去了 改寫明白 卽可互換 拉 我看無語病 現在俄國政府肯換 中國政府不肯換 只恐後來中國政府肯換 俄國政府又不肯換 李 語病不去 不改寫明白 日後反致誤會 不如不換了 所喜者 拉大人所述俄國政府之語 雖不換照會仍可爲憑 我卽可據此語而催英國退出巨文島 拉 我所已說之話足爲憑據 我在天津月餘 與中堂面談多次 於兩國敦睦之誼殊大有益 惟新疆邊界交涉案件 中國官待俄商多無情理 牘已盈尺 我亟須回京商辦 明日行李收拾淸楚 由水路進京 卽告辭了

162
李鴻章 · Brenan 회담(2)

J. Walsham (1886. 10. 25) ➡ Earl of Iddesleigh (1886. 12. 13)

No. 123.

Sir J. Walsham to the Earl of Iddesleigh.—(Received December 13.)

Peking, October 25, 1886.

(No. 292. Confidential.)

My Lord,

IN continuation of my despatch No. 287 of the 9th instant, I have the honour to transmit to your Lordship a copy of a despatch from Mr. Brenan, Her Majesty's Consul at Tien-tsin, in which he gives the details of a further confidential conversation with the Grand Secretary Li, on the subject of his Excellency's pending negotiations with the Russian Chargé d'Affaires respecting Corean affairs.

I did not think it necessary to telegraph to your Lordship about the further progress of these negotiations, as, until some definite issue has been arrived at, I could not pretend to give any assurances to Her Majesty's Government in the matter of the guarantee for the integrity of Corea.

Whatever the hitch may be, to which the Grand Secretary alluded, I have thought it best to let the matter rest for the moment, as I am unwilling to give his Excellency any occasion for thinking that Her Majesty's Government are seeking for a pretext to leave Port Hamilton.

I have, &c.

(Signed) JOHN WALSHAM.

Inclosure in No. 123.

Consul Brenan to Sir J. Walsham.

Tien-tsin, October 13, 1886.

(Confidential.)

Sir,

I HAVE the honour to report that the Viceroy Li received me this morning, and that I took the opportunity of explaining to his Excellency that the draft of the note I had left with him on the 6th instant was intended by you to suggest the terms in which, the Tsung-li Yamên might communicate to you the verbal assurances received from the Russian Chargé d'Affaires regarding the integrity of Corea. At the time you prepared this draft you had been led to believe that the Russian Government would confine itself to verbal assurances, but now that you understood that an Instrument was about to be drawn up by Russia and China guaranteeing the integrity of Corea, you thought that in the note which it had been proposed the Tsung-li Yamên should send you, instead of laying stress on the verbal assurances of Russia, it would now be more reassuring were the Yamên to state that such an Instrument had been drawn up and communicate to you a copy.

The Viceroy stated that he had already sent a translation of the draft note, with a few alterations, to the Yamên, but he thought that it might be supplemented with a copy of the joint Agreement when the conditions had been settled. His Excellency gave me to understand that the Agreement would be in the form of an exchange of notes between himself and M. Ladygensky. There was at present a slight difficulty in the way of a settlement. As the Viceroy had told me before, M. Ladygensky had pointed out that self-respect alone would make it impossible for Russia to give a bare bond undertaking to keep her hands off Corea. It had been necessary to import other matters so that the Self-denying Clause might be decently brought in, and it was the discussion of these other matters that caused delay. There was one point which M. Ladygensky refused to yield, and he was now awaiting the instructions of his Government.

What this point was the Viceroy would not tell me, although he assured me it was distinct from the Corean question. On the other hand, M. Ladygensky wished to introduce a stipulation, that the intervention of China in Corean affairs should never be more active than at present. So far as he was concerned, his Excellency said, he would have been willing to agree to this, but the Chinese Court was unwilling to pledge China.

Before leaving I repeated to the Viceroy that you wished to be able to inform Her Majesty's Government of the nature of the joint Agreement between China and Russia, and his Excellency promised that when he had come to an understanding with the Russian Chargé d'Affaires, he would request the Yamên to bring the Agreement to your knowledge.

I have, &c.
(Signed) BYRON BRENAN.

163
러시아 측의 조회문 수정 거절에 따른 대책 제시

李鴻章 (1886. 10. 25 / 光緒十二年九月二十八日) ➡ 總署

寄譯署

光緒十二年九月二十八日辰刻

前奉十四電旨 令刪去不改變朝鮮現在情形之語 當卽傳知俄使 據稱電告該國 電復以此語無碍中國辦法 俄日後亦不致干預保護 與下文兩句一氣 必不允刪 拉使昨來辭行謂雖不遽換照會 而所已說明者均係傳達俄國家之意 絶無更改 鴻奉十七日密旨 飭酌添數語 較原文更淸楚 但原文旣不肯改 卽不再商 現擬據俄使面允不占據朝鮮土地之說 咨請總署照會英使 催退巨文島 以完此案 拉使卽日回京云 新疆交涉案積壓甚多須趕辦 乞代奏 鴻

164
러시아 측과의 교섭 중단 사실 보고

李鴻章 (1886. 10. 26 / 光緖十二年九月二十九日) ➡ 總署 (1886. 10. 27 / 光緖十二年十月一日)

致總署 論俄牘未定催英退島

光緖十二年九月二十九日

密啓者 俄國拉署使不願刪改照會底稿 卽日回京 昨已電聞在案 玆將九月二十七日問答節略鈔呈鑑核 前欽奉九月十七日懿旨 若被俄牽制 轉不如不約爲愈等因 今拉使電告該國政府旣不肯刪去不改變現在情形之語 若另商添改亦必不允 自不如暫緩互換照會爲愈 惟該使恐其政府因此生疑 仍盼回京後續商 應由鈞署隨時相機核辦 拉使已於二十八晩起程回京矣 至日後不占據朝鮮土地一節 俄國已切實應允 我自應據此語照催英國速退巨文島 以了此案而免後患 謹就華爾身送來英文底稿酌加修改 繕文咨呈冰案 以憑照催 禧在明前日來詢 已與言明 幸勿遲廷爲禱 專泐密布 敬頌中堂王爺大人鈞福 李鴻章謹啓 直字四百七十號 計抄冊

165
영국 측에 거문도 철수 조회 발송 요청

李鴻章 (1886. 10. 26 / 光緒十二年九月二十九日) ➡ 總署 (1886. 10. 27 / 光緒十二年十月一日)

爲咨明事　竊照英國占據朝鮮巨文島一事　當經貴衙門面商駐京歐署使　幷由曾大臣知照英國政府　此事於中國屬邦甚有關係　旋准英外部覆稱　據守該島不過暫時之計　幷無圖損中國及中國屬藩體制權利之意　英廷亦不欲久占此島　但恐若被別國占去　則必損中英兩國之利　中朝如能擔保無人來占此島　卽英廷可以放心云云　迄今爲時已久　英兵船仍在該島踞守　由此局外遂生爲難之事　卽如近日朝鮮傳言　有俄國干預我藩邦之說　中國因詰問俄國有無其事　俄外部向我出使劉大臣輸誠相告　言俄廷絶無此意　幷准飭派駐京之拉署使前赴天津　與本大臣晤談數次　又將前答劉大臣之語重爲剖白　幷云俄廷誠心允許　如英國將巨文島退出　無論如何情形　俄國決不占據朝鮮土地等語　本大臣告以英國恐兵船退後該島爲別國續占　必須俄國擔保日後不占該島　中國方可據以催令英國迅行退出　旋准拉署使遵照本國訓條　切實擔保　言明俄國日後不取朝鮮土地　中國自可據俄國所擔保者向英國擔保　應請貴衙門將以上情節速卽照會英國駐京華公使傳達英國政府　速飭兵船退出巨文島　以爲愿敦和睦之據　相應咨會貴衙門　請煩查照核辦施行　須至咨者　右咨欽命總理各國事務衙門

166
청 總理衙門의 철수 요청 조회

總署 (1886. 10. 31 / 光緒十二年十月五日) ➡ J. Walsham

관련문서 Walsham의 답신(1886. 11. 10)

十月初五日 給英國公使華爾身照會稱 業查朝鮮巨文島一案 前經本衙門面商歐署大臣 並由曾大臣知照貴國政府 此事於中國屬邦甚有關係 旋准貴外部覆稱 據守該島不過暫時之計 並無圖損中國及中國屬藩體制權利之意 亦不欲久佔此島 但恐若被別國佔去 則必損中英兩國之利 中國如能擔保無人來佔此島 則英廷可以放心等語 迄今爲時已久 貴國兵船仍在該島踞守 由此局外遂生爲難之事 卽如近日朝鮮傳言有俄國干預我藩邦之說 中國因詰問俄國有無其事 旋據俄外部向我出使劉大臣輸誠相告 言俄廷絶無此意 並准飭派駐京之拉署大臣前赴天津 與北洋李中堂晤談數次 又將前答劉大臣之語重爲剖白 並云 俄廷誠心允許 如貴國將巨文島退出 無論如何情形 俄國决不佔據朝鮮土地等語 復經北洋李中堂告以恐貴國兵船退後 該島爲別國續佔 必須俄國擔保日後不佔該島中國卽可據以照催貴國退行退出 旋准拉署大臣遵照俄國訓條切署擔保 言明俄國日後不取朝鮮土地 中國自可據俄國所擔保者向貴國擔保 卽希貴大臣將以上情節速遠貴國政府 卽飭兵船退出巨文島 以敦睦誼爲要 相應照會貴大臣查照可也

【英譯文】

No. 134.

Sir J. Walsham to the Earl of Iddesleigh.—(Received December 27.)

Peking, November 5, 1886.

(No. 298. Confidential.)

My Lord,

WITH reference to previous correspondence, 1 have the honour to transmit to your Lordship herewith a translation of a note which has been addressed to me by the Minister of the Tsung-li Yamên, in which his Highness the president and their Excellencies his colleagues state their grounds for hoping that the moment may have arrived for the withdrawal of Her Majesty's ships from Port Hamilton.

Allusion is made to the temporary character that it was always intended to give to the English occupation of the group of islands in which Port Hamilton is situated and, speaking in the name of the suzerain State, the Chinese Ministers point to the embarrassing situation created by our continued presence on Corean territory, citing as an instance the recent troubles in the Core an capital on account of rumours to the effect that a Russian Protectorate was imminent.

An official representation being made at St. Peters burgh, the Russian Government not only frankly disavowed to the Chinese Minister any such designs on the part of Russia, but authorized the Russian Chargé d'Affaires at Peking, M. Ladygensky, to repeat personally these assurances to the Grand Secretary Li, Minister Superintendent of Northern Trade, who is charged with the direction of affairs between China and Corea.

In carrying out his instructions, M. Ladygensky had also been empowered to offer the additional assurance that, in the event of the English occupation of Port Hamilton ceasing, Russia would undertake not to interfere with Corean territory under any circumstances.

Several interviews had taken place between the Russian Chargé d'Affaires and the Grand Secretary, who had impressed upon M. Ladygensky the importance of such a guarantee being furnished by Russia, as it would enable China on her side to give a similar pledge to Her Majesty's Government officially.

M. Ladygensky having now, therefore, in virtue of instructions from St. Petersburgh, explicitly declared that Russia would not hereafter meddle with territory belonging to Corea, the Chinese Government naturally felt themselves in a position to assure Her Majesty's Government, on the faith of the Russian guarantee, that the temporary occupation of Port Hamilton could be relinquished without risk as regards the future, and they trusted, under these circumstances, that the evacuation might be effected, so that the friendly relations between Great Britain and China might be still further consolidated, this being a matter to which the Chinese Government attached importance.

The substance of this despatch has been telegraphed to your Lordship.

I have, &c.

(Signed) JOHN WALSHAM.

Inclosure in No. 134.

The Tsung-li Yamên to Sir J. Walsham.

Peking, October 31, 1886.

(Translation.)

THE Prince and Ministers of the Tsung-Ii Yamên have the honour to refer Her Britannic Majesty's Minister to the personal consultations which have. earlier taken, place between Mr. O'Conor, Chargé d'Affaires, and the Yamên on the subject of the Corean islands of Port Hamilton; also to the communications of his Excellency Tsêng to Her Majesty's Government, who were informed by him that this matter was one that greatly concerned a tributary State of China.

In due course a reply was received from. Her Majesty's Foreign Office, to the effect that the occupation of the islands in question was a messure of a temporary nature, and that it carried with it no intention whatsoever of doing anything injurious to the prestige, rights, and interests of either China or her vassal. State. Further, that there was no desire to occupy these islands for any length of time, but that it was feared that, if they were taken possession of by another Power, it must infallibly be injurious to the interests both of England and of China. If China could guarantee that no onc would come and take these islands, the British Government could feel reassured.

A long time has now elapsed, and British vessels of war continue to hold these islands, thus giving rise to embarrassing questions from without.

For instance, rumours have recently been disseminated from Corea that Russia was interfering with China's feudatory. The Chinese Government accordingly demanded an explanation from Russia as to the existence or otherwise of this fact, and in due course the Russian Foreign Office gave the Chinese Minister Lin the most frank assurances that the Russian Government had absolutely no such intentions. M. Ladygensky, the Russian Chargé d'Affaires at Peking, further went to Tien-tsin at the orders of the Russian Foreign Office, and had several personal conversations with the Grand Secretary Li, Minister Superintendent of Northern Trade, to whom he repeated and enlarged upon the answer earlier given to the Minister Liu. He also stated that the Russian Government gave a sincere promise that if the British would evacuate Port Hamilton, the Russian Government would not occupy Corean territory under any circumstances whatsoever.

The Grand Secretary Li, Minister Superintendent of Northern Trade, then told M. Ladygensky that what was feared was that after the British vessels of war had retired from these islands they would be again taken possession of by some other Power. Russia, therefore, must guarantee that she would not hereafter seize these islands, and on the faith of this guarantee China could officially address the British Government, and urge their speedy evacuation.

In course of time M. Ladygensky, in obedience to instructions from the Russian Government, gave a most, explicit guarantee, distinctly declaring that in the future Russia would not take Corean territory.

The Chinese Government is therefore naturally in a position, on the faith of the guarantee of the Russian Government, to give a guarantee to the British Government, and in making this communication, as is their bounden duty, to Her Britannic Majesty's Minister, they would express a hope that he will lose no time in communicating the above particulars to Her Majesty's Government, with a view to the issue of orders for the evacuation of Port Hamilton by their vessels of war, so that friendly relations may thereby be consolidated, this being a matter to which importance is attached.

【관련문서】

十月十五日　英國公使華爾身照會稱　光緒十二年十月初五日　接准來文內開巨文島一事俱已閱悉 業由奉大臣將文內各節大旨電咨本國查核矣　相應照覆查照可也 爲此照覆

167
러·청 협상 결렬

J. Walsham (1886. 11. 5) ➡ Earl of Iddesleigh (1886. 11. 5)

No. 102.

Sir J. Walsham to the Earl of Iddesleigh.—(Received by telegraph, November 5.)

Peking, November 5, 1886.

(No. 297. Confidential. Ext. 65.)

My Lord,

WITH reference to the further steps which, as recorded in my telegram No. 64 of the 8th ultimo, the Grand Secretary Li was taking to obtain from M. Ladygensky, the Russian Chargé d'Affaires, a written statement of Russia's promise to respect the integrity of Corean territory in the event of our retiring from Port Hamilton, I have the honour to inform your Lordship that his Excellency's efforts were unsuccessful, and that the negotiations have terminated without any agreement having been signed. Reciprocal verbal assurances have been given.

The difficulty apparently arose as to the precise wording of the formal letters which it was proposed to exchange.

A note which I have received from the Ministers of the Tsung-li Yamên refers in courteous terms to the embarrassing position created by our continuous occupation of Port Hamilton, and it at the. same time notifies the denial which has been officially given by the Russian Government to the recent rumour of a scheme having been set on foot for a Russian Protectorate in the Corea, as well as their distinct promise that Russia will not occupy Corean territory under any circumstances after our evacuation of Port Hamilton.

The note goes on to say that the Chinese Government insisted upon this guarantee during the negotiations, and that, on the faith of it, they are now able, on the part of China, to give a guarantee to Her Majesty's Government, who, it is therefore hoped, will shortly be able to arrange for the cessation of the temporary occupation of Port Hamilton.

I should state that no mention is made in the note of China having, equally with Russia, pledged herself to abstain from seizing territory belonging to Corea, but I cannot help thinking that this omission would not prove disadvantageous for England and China in any possible eventualities, and I doubt whether a more favourable occasion for our withdrawal from Port Hamilton is likely to present itself. I have telegraphed to your Lordship the substance of this despatch.

I have, &c.

(Signed) JOHN WALSHAM.

168
러·청 협상의 타결 가능성

J. Walsham (1886. 11. 5) ➡ Earl of Iddesleigh (1886. 12. 27)

No. 135.

Sir J. Walsham to the Earl of Iddesleigh.—(Received December 27.)

Peking, November 5, 1886.

(No. 299. Confidential.)

My Lord,

IN my immediately preceding despatch of this date I have purposely avoided commenting upon the note from the Tsung-li Yamên , of which a translation was inclosed, and which relates to the pledge obtained from Russia by China not to occupy Corean territory in the event of our retiring from Port Hamilton, because Her Majesty's Government may some day wish to have it in their power to publish this communication, and it appeared to me that, in that case, they would probably prefer the covering despatch being free from observations on my part.

It will however, be necessary for me to make a few remarks on the Chinese note, which is a fairly honest reproduction of the draft I had submitted to the Grand Secretary Li, as stated in my No. 285 of the 6th ultimo.

When I prepared that draft I had reason to believe that his Excellency had given up all idea of pressing the Russian Chargé d'Affaires, M. Ladygensky, for a written record of the guarantee he had been authorized to offer, that Russia would not interfere with Corean territory.

In letting me know confidentially that he would suggest to the Ministers the propriety of their addressing to me, for communication to your Lordship, a note embodying the Russian assurances, the Grand Secretary also informed me that he had renewed his negotiations with the Russian Chargé d'Affaires in the hope of being able to induce him to consent to a written Agreement, and it was then I gave his Excellency to understand that were his efforts successful, I should naturally expect to be placed by the Chinese Ministers in a position to acquaint Her Majesty's Government with the provisions of such an Agreement.

In reply, the Grand Secretary said that, if any formal Instrument were signed, he would do his utmost to furnish me with a copy of it.

My telegram No. 64 of the 8th ultimo explained the nature of the concession which China was willing to make if Russia would give a written guarantee. It was to the effect that China, also, would pledge herself to respect the integrity of Corea, and would undertake with Russia to see that it was respected.

The Russian Chargé d'Affaires, however, raised difficulties, alleging that he had pledged the word of the Russian Government, and that it was unfair to call in question the validity of such a promise because it happened to be verbal; but on the invitation of the Grand Secretary, M. Ladygensky telegraphed to St. Petersburgh for further instructions.

It is to be presumed that they did not admit of his signing an Agreement in the terms proposed by his Excellency, seeing that the negotiations were apparently concluded without any official record of the proceedings, as stated in my telegram No. 65 of this date.

When I received the Chinese note of the 31st ultimo I was not aware of this fact. I therefore telegraphed to Mr. Brenan, Her Majesty's Consul at Tien-tsin, and asked him to tell the Grand Secretary that the Ministers of the Yamên had written to me more or less in the sense of my draft, but that no mention was made by them of any written Agreement, and that, consequently, I was desirous of ascertaining how matters stood.

The accompanying extract from Mr. Brenan's Report of his interview will inform your Lordship that, according to the Grand Secretary's account, he and M. Ladygensky could not come to an understanding as to the precise wording of the letters which were to be exchanged, this being the form it was proposed to assign to the reciprocal guarantee, and that the question of an exchange of notes was to be left for future discussion, Russia and China in the meantime mutually pledging themselves not to take possession of Corean territory.

The difference between the present verbal arrangement and the one which existed at the time I laid my draft before the Grand Secretary is, that in the latter case the guarantee was on the side of Russia alone, whereas now the pledge, although still verbal, is equally applicable to China.

This does not appear in the Yamên note, and I am inclined to think that the omission, as well as the absence of a more formal Agreement between China and Russia, may, not be altogether disadvantageous, as is shown by the Grand Secretary's observation to Mr. Brenan on the merits of verbal bargains, which were not meant to last indefinitely. For instance, said his Excellency, should England and Russia go to war at any time, China would have no objection to seeing England again make temporary use of Port Hamilton, although China would also again expect her to retire from the Corean Islands as soon as the necessity for their occupation should have ceased to exist.

On the whole, therefore, I look upon the outcome of these negotiations as satisfactory. They originated in events connected with Corea that directly concerned China and Russia, and the circumstance of China having called upon the Russian Government to say categorically whether or not there was any truth in the rumours of. a Russian Protectorate proves that, as regards Corea, she would not quietly submit to any interference with the vassal State on the part of her powerful neighbour. The question of our presence at Port Hamilton came to be discussed on the initiative of the Grand Secretary himself, and it was in consequence of his spontaneous pressure that Russia undertook not to meddle in any way with Corea if we withdrew from Port Hamilton.

Her Majesty's Government have thus been spared the inconvenient task of having it her to demand a guarantee as a condition of their evacuating Port Hamilton, or to take part in the discussions which led up to the result that has been obtained; and I cannot help thinking that, inasmuch as a purely naval occupation of Port Hamilton seems to be open to serious objections, it would be almost a pity to lose so favourable a chance of performing an act which, while it would be agreeable to both China and Corea, would likewise afford relief from what must daily become a more embarrassing position for Her Majesty's Government, unless it were determined to incur the expense of fortifying the islands permanently, and perhaps even then on account of the compromising situation that we should create for

China.

I have, &c.
(Signed) JOHN WALSHAM.

Inclosure in No. 135.
Mr. Brenan to Sir J. Walsham.

Tien-tsin, November 3, 1886.

(Confidential.)
(Extract.)

AS directed by your telegram of the 1st instant, I called on the Viceroy Li Hung-chang this morning to make inquiries as to the issue of his Excellency's negotiations with the Russian Chargé d'Affaires respecting Corea.

At the outset I informed the Viceroy that the Tsung-li Yamên had addressed to you a note much in the language of the draft I had several days ago given his Excellency from you, and I added that no reference had been made to the written pledge which you had understood from me was about to be given by the Russian Chargé d'Affaires.

The Viceroy informed me that the exchange of letters which it had been intended should be made between himself and M. Ladygensky had not taken place.

The negotiators had failed to agree upon the wording of the notes. China wished the Russian note to state that Corea was China's vassal State. This admission the Russian Government would not consent to make, although M. Ladygensky had no objection to the assertion being made in the Chinese note. As China seemed disinclined to accept a note not containing the admission, M. Ladygensky informed the Viceroy that pressing business called him back to Peking, and that, the verbal assurance of his Government being of the same value as a written document, the matter had better be so settled for the present, and the question of an exchange of notes he left to be discussed between M. Ladygensky and the Tsung-li Yamên at some future time.

Upon my asking the Viceroy what the verbal bargain amounted to, his Excellency said that Russia pledged herself to China, and China to Russia, not to seize any portion of Corean territory. His Excellency them ed me whether a verbal pledge was to be relied upon. I said that it might be kept for a year or two, but asked what evidence of the pledge there would be in twenty years. His Excellency said that bargains of this nature were not meant to last so long; "sufficient unto the day" was the maxim he was guided by. For example, his Excellency said, should England and Russia go to war at any time, China would have no objection to seeing England again make temporary use of Port Hamilton, but China would again expect England to retire from the islands as soon as the necessity for their occupation has ceased to exist.

In leaving, the Viceroy requested me to convey to you a message to this effect: That having, at your request, suggested to the Yamên the form in which the assurances of Russia should be communicated to you for the satisfaction of Her Majesty's Government, and having overcome the Yamên's objections by urging that such a communication to Her Majesty's Minister was a necessary preliminary to the evacuation of Port Hamilton, his Excellency trusted you would now tele- graph to Her Majesty's Government that you had received satisfactory assurances, and recommend that the British ships and garrison be forthwith withdrawn.

169
조선 문제에 대한 李鴻章과 Ladygensky의 회담 내용 보고

Ladygensky (1886. 11. 7)

관련문서 Li-Ladygensky 구두 협약

RGAVMF, F.417, Op.1, D.312, L.7-11ob.

Выписка из донесения Поверенного в Делах в Пекине, коллежского асессора Ладыженского от 26 октября 1886 года

Первой заботой нашего поверенного в делах в Пекине, по прибытии его в Тянь-Цзин для объяснений с канцлером Ли-Хун-Чжаном по корейским делам, было удержать сановника этого от принятия крайних и немедленных мер по отношению к Корее, каковые меры поставили бы нас в самое щекотливое положение.

Продолжительные беседы, кои коллежский асессор Ладыженский имел с канцлером, выяснили ему, насколько наши недоброжелатели, преимущественно английские агенты, успели воспользоваться присущей китайцам подозрительностью, что бы возбудить опасения китайских сановников, а через них и пекинского двора, относительно наших завоевательных намерений в Корее.

Немало усилий потребовалось со стороны нашего поверенного в делах, чтобы разъяснить Ли-Хун-Чжану всю неосновательность таких опасений правителей империи и, чтобы при посредстве канцлера, заставить министров Богдохана и двор отказаться от мысли о свержении с престола корейского короля за его стремление к сближению с Россией.

С неподдельной радостью сообщил потом нашему представителю об успокоении возбуждения высших правительственных сфер в Пекине. Ли-Хун-

Чжан неоднократно просил коллежского асессора Ладыженского принести Императорскому министерству глубокую признательность китайского правительства за данное ему, г-ну Ладыженскому, разрешение приехать в Тянь-Цзин для разъяснения наших видов на Корею.

Безусловно, подтвердив имевшиеся у нас сведения о полученных им от отца Богдохана приказаний занять Корею и сослать королевскую семью в город Бао-Дин-Фу, канцлер подробно рассказал нашему поверенному в делах о той борьбе, которую он должен был вести с враждебными ему влияниями для того, чтобы предотвратить военную оккупацию королевства. Он высказал, между прочим, что пекинский двор, увлеченный успехами Китая в войне с французами и окруженный неопытными советниками, смотрит на Корею, как на нераздельную часть владений Богдохана, и, не сознавая достаточно могущества других держав, всегда готов придать всякому недоразумению острое направление и решиться на принятие крайних мер.

По словам Ли-Хун-Чжана, кроме непосредственных приказаний отца Богдохана, он был осаждаем предложениями относительно Кореи со стороны некоторых иностранных представителей. Так великобританский посланник в Пекине убеждал его воспользоваться содействием Англии и немедленно занять Корею, дабы навсегда прекратить там русские происки. В тоже время японское правительство, через китайского посланника в Токио, предлагало ему, для прекращения недоразумений в будущем, разрешить теперь уже всегда угрожающий мирным отношениям Китая и Японии корейский вопрос, произведя полюбовный раздел Кореи, при чем Китай получил бы северную, а Япония южную ее часть.

Беседуя с Ли-Хун-Чжаном, коллежский асессор Ладыженский счел нужным категорически заявить ему, что мы вовсе не имеем желания занимать Корею или лишать ее независимости, если нас не принудят к этому нанесением ущерба нашим собственным интересам, но что в тоже время мы не можем допустить в Сеуле исключительного преобладания какой-либо другой державы, что, несомненно, нарушило бы мир, страхами коего мы всегда были.

Канцлер ответил на это, что именно подобный взгляд русского правительства на корейский вопрос, он остановился от принятия энергичных мер на полуострове и что примирение наших взглядов с взглядами пекинского правительства в данном вопросе всегда будет его особенной заботой. При всем том, сказал Ли-Хун-Чжан, в виду возможности нового развития корейского вопроса и тех увлечений, которым пекинский двор может вновь отдаться и которые он, канцлер, быть может не в силах будет вторично сдержать, лучше всего было бы письменным соглашением установить тот порядок, коего оба правительства должны придерживаться по отношению к Корее.

В силу полученных от Министерства иностранных дел инструкций, наш поверенный в делах изъявил Ли-Хун-Чжану согласие на составлением такого документа и, после продолжительных переговоров относительно редакции, он и согласились обменяться тождественными нотами, в силу коих как Россия, так и Китай одинаково обязывались бы охранять настоящее положение в Корее и воздерживаться от занятия ее территории.

Проект означенной ноты при сем прилагается.

По сообщении канцлером проекта сего соглашения в Пекине отец Богдохана выразил желание, чтобы в оном было упомянуто о вассальных отношениях Кореи к Китаю и об особых обязанностях китайского правительства к корейскому.

Запросив мнение Императорского министерства по предмету означенного желания отца Богдохана и получив от оного предписание не допускать никакого изменения в тексте нот, коллежский асессор Ладыженский заявил канцлеру, что, если правительство Богдохана не отступит от своей новой претензии, то он полагает ограничиться одним словесным соглашением.

Как узнал наш поверенных в делах от лиц, близко стоящих к Ли-Хун-Чжану, сановник этот намерен напрягать все усилия к тому, чтобы привести пекинский двор к полному одобрению его соображений по корейским делам, и даже предполагает объявить, что, если ему не будет предоставлена полная свобода в направлении корейских дел, он сложит с себя всякую ответственность за последствия.

Перед отъездом коллежского асессора Ладыженского из Тянь-Цзина, канцлер обещал ему никогда не изменять своему слову и всегда руководствоваться состоявшимся между ними, пока только на словах, соглашением.

Наш поверенных в делах полагает, что свидание его с Ли-Хун-Чжаном, выяснив нам взгляд китайцев на Корею, надо нам вместе с возможность высказать Китаю откровенно наши виды на это Королевство и успокоить Пекинское Правительство на счет наших завоевательных планов на Дальнем Востоке.

【관련문서】

RGAVMF, F.417, Op.1, D.312, L.6.

Перевод с китайского текста

Китай и Россия желают действительно спокойствия в Корее, для этого и для устранения недоразумений оба Правительства уговариваются не применять нынешнего положения Кореи и никогда не присваивать себе земель, входящих в пределы Кореи.

170

거문도 철수 이후의 협의 사항 지시

Earl of Iddesleigh (1886. 11. 19) ➡ J. Walsham

No. 108.

The Earl of Iddesleigh to Sir J. Walsham.

Foreign Office, November 19, 1886, 5:45 P. M.

(No. 57.)

(Telegraphic.)

YOUR telegram No. 65.

You may read the following to the Yamên as the reply of Her Majesty's Government to their note: —

"Her Majesty's Government have learnt from your telegram of the 5th instant that the Chinese Government have informed you officially that they are prepared, in the event of Her Majesty's Government terminating the occupation of Port Hamilton, to guarantee that no part of the territory of Corea, including Port Hamilton, will be occupied by a foreign Power. Her Majesty's Government are prepared, on the faith of this guarantee, to comply with the wishes of the Chinese Government, which have now been officially formulated."

You are authorized to discuss with the Yamên how this decision can best be carried into effect in the interests of China and England, which we regard as identical in this matter.

171
철수 이후 청의 조선 영토 보장 문서화 지시

Earl of Iddesleigh (1886. 12. 10) ➡ J. Walsham

No. 120.

The Earl of Iddesleigh to Sir J. Walsham.

Foreign Office, December 10, 1886.

(No. 318. Ext. 60.)

Sir,

I HAVE to inform you that you are authorized. to address notes on the subject of Port Hamilton to the Governments of China and Corea, as proposed in your telegram No. 69 of the 1st instant, but before doing so, you should obtain from the Tsung-li Yamên a note, suitable for publication, in case of need, guaranteeing that no part of the territory of Corea will be occupied by any foreign Power.

The Commander-In-chief on the China Station has been instructed to place himself in communication with you in regard to the manner in which the withdrawal of the British force from Port Hamilton is to be carried out.

I am, &c.

(Signed) IDDESLEIGH.

172
청에 거문도 권리 양여에 대한 일본 정부의 우려

F. Plunkett (1886. 12. 18) ➡ Earl of Iddesleigh (1886. 12. 18)

No. 126.

Sir F. Plunkett to the Earl of Iddesleigh.—(Received December 18.)

Tôkiô, December 18, 1886.

(No. 22.)

(Telegraphic.)

PRIME MINISTER and Minister for Foreign Affairs spoke to me separately yesterday about Port Hamilton.

Minister for Foreign Affairs says that if England abandons it she should return it to Corea, but he would now prefer to see England remain there.

Cession to China at present will cause great outcry here, and further complicate Chinese question.

(Confidential.)

He says Russian Minister has made private advances, and suggested co-operation with Russia in case of trouble with China Minister for Foreign Affairs much disturbed by the excessive honour shown at St. Petersburgh to General Kuroda, and fears he may be gained over by Russia.

173
Li-Ladygensky 협약에 대한 Girs의 견해

N. K. Girs (1887. 1. 20) ➡ I. A. Shestakov

RGAVMF, F.417, Op.1, D.312, L.1-5.

Министр иностранных дел
8 января 1887 года

Секретно

Его Превосходительству И.А. Шестакову

Милостивый государь, Иван Алексеевич,

Во всеподданнейшей записке о наших прибрежьях в Восточном океане Ваше Превосходительство изволили высказать убеждение, что для нас не представляется никакой необходимости добиваться расширения владений наших в этих краях, и что усилия наши должны быть направлены к установлению тесных отношений к двум нашим соседям: Китаю и Японии.

Взгляд этот вполне совпадает с тем, которым вверенное мне Министерство неуклонно руководилось до сих пор во всех вопросах, касающихся нашего положения на Крайнем Востоке.

Особую для нас важность представляют, конечно, отношения наши к Китаю в виду того, что территория наша соприкасается со страною этою на расстоянии нескольких тысяч верст, что благодаря своим естественным условиям, Китай предназначен играть видную роль в этой части света, и что результаты его недавнего столкновения с Франциею пробудили в Китайском Правительстве совершенно чуждую ему в прежнее время самоуверенность.

Последнее обстоятельство не замедлившее отразиться на отношениях означенного правительства к иностранным государствам, едва не повело к весьма серьезным осложнениям между нами и Китаем по поводу Кореи.

Тяготясь постоянным вмешательством в эти дела своей страны, как Китайских, так и Японских Агентов, Корейский Король, со времени заключения с нами договора, возымел мысль обеспечить себя от гнета названных Агентов при помощи протектората России. Находя неудобным предрешать вопроса о наших будущих отношениях к Корее, о которой мы весьма мало знали, мы не сочли возможным принять предложение короля, но, с другой стороны, не видели и необходимости решительно отклонять эти предложения. Мы выразили готовность оказывать ему, возможное с нашей стороны, содействие, но в тоже время передали ему, через нашего Поверенного в делах в Сеуле, совет тщательно воздерживаться от всяких действий, способных осложнить его положение относительно наиболее могущественного из его соседей — Китая.

При всей нашей осторожности обращения Корейского Короля к нам, не остались в тайне. Слухи о них не замедлили дойти до Пекина и Китайское Правительство под влиянием подстрекательств Англичан, заподозрило нас в намерении, если не разом завладеть Кореею, то захватить на первый раз порт Лазарев. Следствием этих подозрений было сосредоточение значительных китайских сил на сухопутной границе Кореи и появление китайской эскадры в корейских водах. Из достоверных источников нам сделалось известным, что Пекинское Правительство не думало ограничиться одними демонстрациями план его заключался в низложении короля, как неблагонадежного вассала Китая, и в замещении его отцом, Тай-Ин-Куном, за несколько лет перед тем удаленного из Кореи.

Дабы отвратить эти осложнения, которые могли выпудить и нас к вмешательству, признано было полезным разрешить нашему Поверенному в делах в Пекине отправиться в Тянь-цзинь для личного объяснения с Ли-Хун-Чжаном, который всегда отличался умеренностью своих политических взглядов и признавал необходимость поддержания отношений доброго соседства с Россиею.

Из прилагаемой у сего выписки из донессния Коллежского Асессора Ладыженского Вы изволите усмотреть, что, благодаря объяснениям его с Ли-Хун-Чжаном, было устранено китайское вмешательство в дела Кореи, что между ними состоялось соглашение относительно обеспечения неприкосновенности и status quo Кореи и что предложенное самим китайским Сановником письменное соглашение в том же смысле не могло состояться только вследствие предъявленного из Пекина требования, чтобы в соглашении этом было упомянуто и о вассальных отношениях Кореи к Китаю. Несмотря на издревле существующие между этими двумя странами связи, мы не сочли возможным согласиться на означенное требование, так как, во всяком случае, необходимо было предварительно выяснить, как понимается в Пекине выражение «вассальные отношения», а вступать в переговоры по этому предмету нам казалось несвоевременным.

Полагая, за всем этим, что заключение соглашения в означенном смысле было бы лучшим средством к отстранению честолюбивых замыслов Китайцев на Корею, я не могу упустить из виду, что, согласно всеподданнейшему отчету Вашему, находящийся близ корейского берега остров Шим-по (Гончарова) может иметь весьма важное для нас значение или как зимняя угольная станция или как продовольственный склад для армии, двигающейся вдоль берега от Тюмень-Улы, и что со временем он может перейти в неприязненные нам руки.

Мне кажется, что соображения эти нисколько не ослабляют значения соглашения, переговоры о котором были возложены на г-на Ладыженского, так как соглашение это может до известной степени служить гарантиею против возможности покушений на неприкосновенность корейской территории со стороны не только Китая, но и других держав, для которых было бы невыгодно входить в столкновения с последним. При всем том, для меня как нельзя более важно было бы знать: представляется ли, по мнению Вашему, возможным в видах устранения поводов к недоразумениям между нами и Китаем, отказаться с нашей стороны от всяких предприятий, касающихся острова Шим-по, хотя бы то было устройство зимней угольной станции. Не подлежит ни малейшему сомнению, что всякое подобное предприятие послужит в глазах Китайского Правительства подтверждением наших замыслов на Корею и повредит нашим к ним сношениям, и мне кажется, что предстоящее в скором времени очищение Англичанами Порта Гамильтона дозволяет нам ограничиться пока заботами об упрочении международного положения Кореи.

Примите, Милостивый Государь, уверение в отличном моем почтении и совершенной преданности.

Н. Гирс.

174
타 열강의 거문도 점령 방지에 대한 청국 신문기사

K. I. Veber (1887. 3. 6) ➡ I. A. Zinoviev

AVPRI, F.150, Op.493, D.113, L.143a-143ob.

Императорская Российская Миссия в Корее
24-го февраля 1887 года

Его Превосходительству И. Зиновьеву

Милостивый Государь Иван Алексеевич,

Имею честь препроводить при сем к Вашему Превосходительству перевод статьи, появившейся недавно в одной из главных китайских газет, издающихся в Шанхае, Шэнь-бао, об очищении порта Гамильтона и необходимости для Китая принять, совместно с англичанами, меры против завладения оным другою Державою.

Помимо того, что в этой статье отражаются китайская спесь и смутные понятия о международных политических отношениях, рассуждения эти интересны для нас еще в том отношении, что в них высказываются воззрения местной прессы на положение Кореи по отношению к Китаю. О корейцах говорится не иначе как о подвластных Китаю варварах, страна которых составляет лишь часть китайской территории. Почти та же идея пропагандируется в здешней английской печати. Так, новая тяньцзиньская газета «Chinese Times» старается убедить китайцев в том, что интересы Китая в Корее весьма существенны, и не договоры ее с другими государствами, ни академические рассуждения о том, что такое сюзеренитет и чем оправдываются претензии Китая на подобные исключительные права, не в состоянии устранить необходимость для него овладеть Кореею. Для Китая весьма опасно будет, если Корея сделается достоянием другого государства, например, России. Корейский вопрос, поэтому, вопрос жизни и смерти для Китая, который во что бы ни стало должен стремиться к окончательному, если нужно, то и насильному, занятию полуострова.

Нельзя отрицать того влияния, которым пользуется на «юный Китай» здешняя английская печать, систематично и упорно преследующая намеченную цель. Подобная пропаганда, направленная против нас и ежедневно из года в год действующая на китайское общественное мнение, тем более может быть опасна, что на Востоке не издаются, за исключением небольшого немецкого листка (с октября прошлого года), газеты других направлений, поставившие себе задачею разоблачать английские интриги. Как удалось англичанам уверить китайцев в наших замыслах на Порт Лазарев, так им удастся убедить их в необходимости завладения Кореею.

Примите, Милостивый Государь, уверение в отличном моем почтении и совершенной преданности.

Вебер.

7-3.
철군과 사후 처리

175
조선 정부에 거문도 철수 통보 예정

J. Walsham (1886. 12. 1) ➡ Earl of Iddesleigh (1886. 12. 3)

No. 114.

Sir J. Walsham to the Earl of Iddesleigh.—(Received December 3, 9:30 A. M.)

Peking, December 1, 1886, 4:50 P. M.

(No. 69.)

(Telegraphic.)

YAMÊN propose that I should answer their note in the sense of second and third paragraphs of your telegram No. 57, and that I should officially inform Corea that Her Majesty's Government are now prepared to terminate occupation because the circumstances which led to it are happily over, and because their decision has been strengthened by the formal guarantee given by China.

Does your Lordship approve? and if so, shall I communicate direct with the Admiral respecting formality of the evacuation?

176
거문도 철수 통지
Currie (1886. 12. 3) ➡ Macgregor

No. 115.

Sir P. Currie to Mr. Macgregor.

Foreign Office. December 3, 1886.

(Confidential.)

[Transmits copy of Sir J. Walsham's No. 268, Confidential, of September 7, 1886: ante, No. 100.]

177

중국 주둔 영국 해군에 철수 결정 통보

Macgregor (1886. 12. 7) ➡ Currie (1886. 12. 8)

No. 118.

Mr. Macgregor to Sir P. Currie.—(Received December 8.)

Admiralty December 7, 1886.

(Confidential.)

Sir,

WITH reference to your letter of the 4th instant, forwarding copies of telegraphic communications which have passed between the Secretary of State for Foreign Affairs and Her Majesty's Minister in Peking in regard to the withdrawal of the British force from Port Hamilton, I am commanded by my Lords Commissioners of the Admiralty to transmit herewith, for the concurrence of the Earl of Iddesleigh, the decypher of a telegram which they propose to send to the Commander-in-chief on the China Station, and my Lords will be glad if you will favour them with as early a reply as possible to this letter.

I am, &c.

(Signed) EVAN MACGREGOR.

Inclosure in No. 118.

Draft Telegram to the Commander-in-chief on the China Station.

HER Majesty's Government has decided to withdraw from Port Hamilton. Consult with British Minister Peking, and arrange for withdrawal of garrison, stores,

&c., and terminate leases. Report arrangements by telegraph.

A separate communication will be made as to submarine cable.

178
거문도 점령에 대한 영국, 청국, 일본의 입장과 영국의 거문도 철수에 관한 보고

P. S. Popov (1886. 12. 7) ➡ N. K. Girs

AVPRI, F.150, Op.493, D.113, L.113-114ob.

Копия с депеши Посланника в Пекине от 25 Ноября 1886 года.

Секретную телеграмму Вашего Высокопревосходительства от 21 Ноября старого стиля я имел честь получить только после полудня 24 числа сего месяца а, потому, только сегодня утром мог ответить на нее. В этом ответе я счел долгом представить в самой сжатой форме сущность сведений, изложенных в весьма важном и любопытном донесении Коллежского Асессора Ладыженского от 26 Октября сего года, за № 32 (которое полагаю, не замедлит достигнуть Санкт Петербурга), проверив насколько было возможно и настоящее положение дела.

Из вышеозначенного донесения Вы, Милостивый Государь, изволите усмотреть, что мысль о занятии Кореи китайскими войсками была внушена летом нынешнего года, Канцлеру Ли-хун-чжану Англиею, обещавшею свое к тому содействие. В замене его она, очевидно, со своей стороны рассчитывала окончательно закрепить его за собою остров Гамильтон. Почти одновременно, Япония предлагала Китаю полюбовно разделить с нею Корейский полуостров. Вследствие происходивших в Тянь-цзине переговоров оба эти предложения были категорически отвергнуты. Вместе с тем, Корейское Правительство потребовало от Английского Посланника очищения острова Гамильтона.

Что дело остается и поныне в том же положении, я имел случай удостовериться, разумеется, насколько заслуживают доверия заявления китайских сановников, незадолго до получения вышеозначенной телеграммы Вашего Высокопревосходительства. Дня за три до того, здесь была распространена телеграмма Рейтера следующего содержания: «London, 28 November 1886. Negociations are proceeding between England and China about the cession of Port Hamilton.(Remainder of clause[ ])»

Я поручил Коллежскому Советнику Подер[ ], то содержание этой телеграммы, осведомиться в Цзунг-ли-ямыне как следует понимать употребленное в ней слово «cession», в смысле ли возврата острова Гамильтона его законным владельцам или же в смысле окончательного признания ими самовольного захвата его англичанами. Сановники отозвались, что вообще о новых, каких-либо переговорах по этому вопросу им ничего неизвестно и что он остается в прежнем положении, обусловленном недавно заявленным Англией требованием очищения острова. Конечно, этот отзыв не внушил бы мне сам по себе полного доверия, если бы он не подтверждался до некоторой степени и другими данными.

Так, не далее как вчера Японский Посланник говорил мне, что о каких-либо новых переговорах или постановке дела он ничего не знает, хотя за всем, что касается до Кореи и Гамильтона, следит с особенным вниманием и старается добывать самые точные сведения. В этом же смысле высказался и Английский Посланник в разговоре с Первым Секретарем Императорской Миссии, после обеда, данного вчера в честь мою Германским Посланником. К этому Сэр Донан Чольнан добавил, что до сих пор не получил еще от своего Правительства никаких новых указаний и что известие о более или менее близком очищении острова Гамильтона продолжает казаться ему наиболее вероятным.

По этому то, сопоставляя вышеприведенные признаки, я и принял смелость выразить Вашему Высокопревосходительству по телеграфу убеждение, что благосклонно сообщенные мне Императорским Министерством доверительные сведения едва ли можно считать соответствующими настоящему положению дела, каковым оно, по крайней мере, представляется здесь.

Тем не менее, я буду продолжать местные наблюдения и разведки, и о последующем, если представится надобность, не премину донести.

С отличным уважением и прочее.

179
Walsham의 보고 전까지 철수 준비 보류
Currie (1886. 12. 11) ➡ Macgregor

No. 121.

Sir P. Currie to Mr. Macgregor.

Foreign Office, December 11, 1886.

(Confidential.)

Sir,

IN reply to your letter of the 7th instant, I am directed by the Earl of Iddesleigh to state, for the information of the Lords Commissioners of the Admiralty, that his Lordship concurs In the terms of the telegram which it is proposed to address to the Commander-in-chief on the China Station with regard to the withdrawal of the British force from Port Hamilton.

His Lordship would suggest, however, that the Admiral should be instructed to take no step before he has communicated with Her Majesty's Minister at Peking.

I am, &c.

(Signed) P. CURRIE.

180
중국 주둔 영국 해군에 Currie의 전신 통보

Macgregor (1886. 12. 11) ➡ Currie (1886. 12. 13)

No. 124.

Mr. Macgregor to Sir P. Currie.—(Received December 13.)

Admiralty, December 11, 1886.

(Confidential.)

REFERRING to your letters of the 4th and 11th and to mine of the 7th instant, I am commanded by my Lords Commissioners of the Admiralty to acquaint you, for the information of the Secretary of State for Foreign Affairs, that a telegram, of which the following is the decypher, has this day been sent to the Commander-in-chief on the China Station, viz.:—

"Her Majesty's Government has decided to withdraw from Port Hamilton. Consult with British Minister at Peking, and arrange for withdrawal of garrison, stores, &c., and terminate leases. Report by telegram what arrangements have been made, but take no steps before communicating with British Minister at Peking.
"Separate message will be sent as to submarine cable."

I am, &c.
(Signed) EVAN MACGREGOR.

181
영국군 거문도 철수 결정 통보

J. Walsham (1886. 12. 23 / 高宗二十三年十一月二十八日) ➡ 金允植

大英欽差駐箚朝鮮便宜行事大臣華　爲照會事　前准光緒十二年六月初三日來文　論及暫行據守巨文島一事　當由本大臣照囑　將文內各節逐一轉咨我國查核　并於七月初六日　先行照覆在案　玆准咨覆　以當日據守該島非常之故幸已無存　我國現可按照原意將據居巨文島之事停止等語　理合遵囑卽行奉達　查此事現經中國公行擔保　以倘能將暫行據守之事停止　中國亦可擔保別國不取巨文島及貴國他處土地之語　是本國退出巨文島之意藉以益固　如本大臣能將此事面向貴督辦陳述　方愜素心　奈因時令日已滿　未克如願　惟有將親赴貴國之行展至明春爲是　至退出巨文島之期　應候本國水師軍門將撤船時日　轉由本國駐紮貴國總領事官自行奉布　合幷聲明　爲此備文照會貴督辦　請煩查照　須至照會者

右照會
大朝鮮督辦交涉通商事務 金
一千八百八十七年正月二十日 戊戌十二月二十七日

【俄譯文】

AVPRI, F.150, Op.493, D.113, L.134-135ob.

Перевод с китайского текста официального сообщения великобританского Посланника сэр Джон Вольшем (Walsham) Президенту корейской Коллегии Иностранных Дел, от 11/23 декабря, 1886-го года.

Бумагою от 3-го числа 6-ой луны 12-го года Правления Гуань-сюй (22 июня/4 июля 1886-го года) по делу о временном занятии Порта Гамильтон, Вам угодно было предложить мне содержание этой бумаги с точностью изложить и представить моему Правительству на рассмотрение и, вслед за тем, 7-ой луны 6-го числа (25 июля/6-го августа) уже было отправлено ответное сообщение на означенную бумагу. Теперь получено разъяснение, из которого явствует, что экстраординарные причины, побудившие некогда к занятию Порта Гамильтон, в настоящее время, к счастью, более не существуют, и мое Правительство согласно прекратить дело о завладении островами, что мне, и поручено безотлагательно разъяснить Вам. Теперь китайское Правительство возлагает на себя тяжесть охранения и, таким образом, является возможность прекратить дело о временном занятии. Китайское Правительство также принимает на себя поручительство в том, что никакая другая Держава не завладеет Портом Гамильтон, а равно какою-либо другою частью корейской территории, и это обстоятельство еще более побудило мое Правительство выдать остров. Для вашего убеждения в этом, предполагалось, чтобы я лично разъяснил Вам это дело и тем устранил опасения, но в то время случились разные обстоятельства, которые воспрепятствовали моей поездке, а в настоящее время уже поздно, нельзя исполнить этого желания, так что я могу прибыть только по наступлении будущей весны.

Что же касается до срока выдачи Порта Гамильтон, то следует подождать, когда, Командующий эскадрою, Адмирал окончательно отзовет суда оттуда, о чем будет доведено до сведения, проживающего в Корее, английского Генерального Консула, для сообщения об этом Вам.

Перевел ______этом Вам.

Перевел ______

182
영국 정부의 거문도 철수 통보

J. Walsham ➡ 總署 (1886. 12. 24 / 光緖十二年十一月十九日)

十一月二十九日 英國公使華爾身照會稱 光緖十二年十月初五日接准來文 均已閱悉 因內敍各節 知本國日前暫行據守巨文島一事如能罷議 貴國現可擔保日後別國不取巨文島 及朝鮮他處土地 卽希英國兵船退出巨文島云云 當由本大臣將文內大旨電咨我國查核去後 玆准電復內開 我國現以貴國公文所擔保者爲據 亦可照文內之意辦理等語囑爲轉致前來 除將知照朝鮮同回之文抄錄送閱外 合卽備文照覆查照可也 爲此照覆

183
청과 조선 정부에 거문도 철수 통보

J. Walsham (1886. 12. 25) ➡ Earl of Iddesleigh

No. 80.

Sir J. Walsham to the Earl of Iddesleigh.—(Received February 21, 1887.)

Peking, December 25, 1886.

My Lord.

I HAVE the honour to report that I went by appointment yesterday afternoon to the Tsung-li Yamên accompanied by Mr. Hillier and Mr. Bullock, and placed in the hands of his Highness the President and their Excellencies the Ministers the note of which I beg leave to transmit to your Lordship a copy.

It is the reply which, by your Lordship's instructions, has been returned to the official communication from the Tsung-li Yamên of the 31st October last, placing on record the circumstances that have enabled the Chinese Government to guarantee the future integrity of Corean territory in the event of Her Majesty's Government being prepared to terminate the temporary occupation of Port Hamilton. A translation of this communication accompanied my despatch of the 5th ultimo.

The Prince and his colleagues having each read the note, expressed their high appreciation of the loyal manner in which Her Majesty's Government had fulfilled their promise with regard to the duration of the occupation.

His Highness and their Excellencies at the same time thanked me for having given them an opportunity of seeing the note which I had addressed to the Government of His Corean majesty for the purpose of notifying to them the decision of Her Majesty's Government, and they added that the mention in it of the formal guarantee offered by China caused them great satisfaction, because they thought it important for Corea to know that she could depend in future upon this pledge, which would strengthen her position.

I explained to the Prince and Ministers that, in consequence of there being no regular communication between China and Corea during the winter, my note to the Corean Government would be taken to Chemulpo by one of Her Majesty's vessels of war, and would probably reach its destination within a fortnight or three weeks.

The substance of this despatch will be telegraphed to your Lordship.

I have, &c.
(Signed) JOHN WALSHAM.

Inclosure 1

Sir J. Walsham to the Tsung-li Yamên.

Peking, December 23, 1886.

IN a note dated the 19th ultimo, his Highness the President and their Excellencies the Ministers of the Tsung-li Yamên notified to Her Britannie Majesty's Minister that the Imperial Government of China, for the special reasons recorded in the note, were in a position to guarantee that in the event of Her Majesty's Government terminating the temporary occupation of Port Hamilton, neither the group of Corean Islands in which Port Hamilton is situated, nor any part of Corean territory, should be occupied by another Power, and a hope was expressed that the British naval force might therefore be withdrawn.

The substance of this note was at once telegraphed to Her Majesty's Government, and Her Majesty's Minister has been instructed to make known to his Highness and their Excellencies that on the faith of this guarantee Her Majesty's Government will be prepared to comply with the wishes of the Chinese Government, which have now been officially formulated.

Her Majesty's Minister has the honour to inclose, for the information of the Prince and Ministers, a copy of the note which he has addressed to the Government of His Corean Majesty for the purpose of intimating to them this decision on the part of

Her Majesty's Government, and he avails himself, &c.
(Signed) JOHN WALSHAM.

Inclosure 2

Sir J. Walsham to the President of the Corean Council.

Peking, December 23, 1886.

M. le President,

IN compliance with the wish expressed by the Government of His Corean Majesty in the note which they did me the honour to address me on the 4th July, I communicated to Her Majesty's Government, as in my reply of the 5th August I stated I would do, the observations contained in that note with regard to the temporary occupation of Port Hamilton, and, in obedience to instructions from Her Majesty's Government, I now hasten to inform your Excellency that the exceptional circumstances which led to the occupation having happily ceased, Her Majesty's Government will be prepared to terminate it conformably to their original intentions.

This decision has been strengthened by a formal guarantee given to them by the Imperial Chinese Government, that in the event of the temporary occupation ceasing, neither the group of islands in which Port Hamilton is situated nor any part of Corean territory shall be occupied by another Power.

I should have been glad to have had it in my power to make this communication personally to your Excellency, but the lateness of the season will oblige me to defer my visit to Corea till the spring of next year.

His Excellency the Commander-in-chief of Her Majesty's Naval Forces will let your Excellency know, through Her Majesty's Consul-General at Söul, the date of his having withdrawn the ships from Port Hamilton.

I avail, &c.

(Signed) JOHN WALSHAM.

184
거문도 철수 결정에 따른 후속 조치 이행 계획

J. Walsham (1886. 12. 27) ➡ Earl of Iddesleigh (1886. 12. 28)

No. 138.

Sir J. Walsham to the Earl of Jddesleigh. —(Received December 28, 11:30 A. M.)

Peking, December 27, 1886, 12:20 P. M.

(No. 73.)

(Telegraphic.)

YOUR Lordship's telegram No. 60.

I have addressed notes to Chinese and Corean Governments. Former have expressed high appreciation of loyalty shown by Her Majesty's Government, and have no objection to publication, in case of need, of their guaranteeing note of the 31st October, with my reply, dated the 24th instant, which includes copy of my note to Corean Government. The latter should reach its destination in about three weeks. I have arranged with Admiral that he can prepare to withdraw about that date, and have asked him to notify the act itself to the Corean Government through Consul-General. He thinks a fortnight will suffice for operation of leaving.

185
조선에 영국의 거문도 철수 사실 통고 지시

李鴻章(1886. 12. 29 / 光緒十二年十二月五日) ➡ 袁世凱

寄漢城袁道

光緒十二年十二月初五日申刻

鴻商總署 照會英使 擔保日後別國不取巨文島及朝鮮他處土地 請英船退出巨文島 昨英覆總署 照議辦理 華使另致韓外署文云 退出巨文之期 候提督將撤船時日由駐韓英總領事自行奉布 望密告韓政府 靜候英使文件 勿先宣露 似須密派妥員赴巨文 預備接收 以禮相待

186
거문도 주둔군에 철수 관련 지침 통보

Admiralty (1887. 1. 3) ➡ Foreign Office (1887. 1. 4)

No. 1.

Admiralty to Foreign Office.—(Received January 4.)

Admiralty, January 3, 1887.

(Confidential.)

Sir,

REFERRING to your letter of the 29th ultimo, and to previous correspondence respecting the withdrawal of the British force from Port Hamilton, I am commanded by my Lords Commissioners of the Admiralty to transmit herewith, for the perusal of the Earl of Iddesleigh, decyphers of two telegrams which have been received from the Commander-in-chief on the China Station on this subject. 2. As Her Majesty's ship "Himalaya" is due at Hong Kong about the first week in February, my Lords propose to employ her in removing the stores and marines, and they request that you will signify Lord Iddesleigh's concurrence in this arrangement as soon as possible, in order that the necessary telegraphic communication may be sent to the Commander-in-chief in China.

lam, &c.

(Signed) EVAN MACGREGOR.

Inclosure 1 in No. 1.

Vice-Admiral Hamilton to Admiralty.

Hong Kong, December 27, 1886.

(Telegraphic.)

HAVE communicated with British Minister at Peking, who informed me that negotiations with Government of Corea will take some time. Propose to withdraw detachment of Royal Marines and stores before winter sets in, leaving a ship till negotiations are complete, as we merely hoisted flag. Think it unlooked-for termination haul flag down and withdraw, leaving place in possession of Corea Chief.

Inclosure 2 in No. 1.

Vice-Admiral Hamilton to Admiralty.

Hong Kong, December 29, 1886.

(Telegraphic.)

SUBMIT sending "Himalaya" Port Hamilton to bring detachment of Royal Marines and stores to Hong Kong. Would occupy her about a fortnight.

187
영국의 거문도 철수 사실 상주

總署 ➡ 光緒帝 (1887. 1. 3 / 光緒十二年十二月十日)

總署奏英人退還朝鮮巨文島片 附照會

奕劻等片 再英人佔據朝鮮巨文島一事疊經臣等與英國前署使臣歐格訥並由臣曾紀澤與英外部辯論經年迄無成議本年三月間臣曾紀澤復派英文參贊馬格里與英之外部侍郎克□往返籌商旋准函覆並繕其節略聲稱據守該島係屬暫時之擧並無圖損中國及屬邦體制權利之意英廷亦不欲久佔此島但恐他國來佔則損中英兩國之利欲請中國擔保或請中國與俄日各國會商訂約不取朝鮮土地英願立卽退出等語其言雖似近情但訂立公約豈易就我範圍且以中國屬邦必賴各國公保立言亦難得體是其籍詞廷宕意已顯露因函致北洋大臣李鴻章並鈔寄馬格里與克□談論各節密屬其隨時妥籌辦法籍可轉圜嗣於本年九月間先後准李鴻章函電內稱俄國使臣拉德仁面稱伊外部欲結好於華約明俄國以後永遠不取朝鮮之地中國亦不取其地先互換照會爲憑旋准該使臣送來照會底稿詞意含混枝節頗多再四駁改囑其另其簡明照會聲明日後不取朝鮮土地一語已足其餘枝節槪可刪除乃該使臣電告伊國外部堅持不允刪去不改朝鮮現在情形之語著另議添改牽制愈多自不如暫緩互換照會至日後不佔據朝鮮土地一節在彼現已切實應允自可據此一語照催英國退出巨文島似更直捷了當各等因業經臣等隨時恭呈御覽並於本年十月間照會英國駐京使臣華爾身轉達英國政府卽飭兵船退出巨文島以敦睦誼去後玆於十一月二十九日准英國使臣華爾身來署面稱現接本國電信巨文島事允卽退讓並面交照會一件片附鈔致朝鮮公文一件臣等公同檢閱文內語意亦尙明晰除密致北洋大臣妥爲辦理外謹鈔錄往來照會各件該使臣致朝鮮公文一件恭呈御覽謹奏光緒十二年十一月初十日奉旨知道了

188
조선 정부에 대한 거문도 철수 통지 일정
Admiralty (1887. 1. 7) ➡ Foreign Office

No. 3.

Foreign Office to Admiralty.

Foreign Office, January 7, 1887.

(Confidential.)

I LAID before the Earl of Iddesleigh your letter of the 3rd instant, relative to the steps to be taken for the withdrawal of the British force from Port Hamilton; and I am directed by his Lordship to request that you will inform the Lords Commissioners of the Admiralty that he concurs in the arrangements which are proposed for the purpose in your letter. I am also to request that you will remind their Lordships, with reference to Vice-Admiral Hamilton's telegram of the 27th ultimo as to the negotiations with the Corean Government, that Her Majesty's Minister at Peking, in his telegram of that date, of which a copy was sent to you on the 29th ultimo, stated that his communication to the Corean Government would probably reach its destination in about three weeks' time from the date of his telegram.

I am, &c.

(Signed) P. CURRIE.

189
미국의 거문도 임대 가능성 타진

W. W. Rockhill (1887. 1. 13) ➡ T. F. Bayard

No. 47.

Jan. 13, 1887.
Secretary of State

Sir,

The question of the evacuation of Port Hamilton by Great Britain, or as it is frequently called, its cession to China, has of late taken some definite form, and it is generally believed in China, Japan, and Korea that the present occupation of the island will shortly cease.

It has been frequently stated of late in the english press, with what authority I know not, that England would cede Port Hamilton to China if that power would guarantee its neutrality. My knowledge of the policy adopted by Great Britain in China in regard to Korea, tends to convince me that, as a matter of fact, Great Britain would be pleased to dispose of the question in this manner. But on the other hand, it is equally well known that Japan cannot admit of a new settlement of the question which would give China a naval station on her very coast, or which, admitting that the latter power did not make a permanent establishment on the island, would give it a vantage ground in case of warlike operations against Japan. I gather from a recent number of the Japanese newspaper that the mere rumor of such a settlement has been deemed sufficient ground for the Japanese government to order the immediate return to Japan of General Saigo, the Minister of the Navy, who is now on a voyage around the world.

This mode of settlement appears therefore impracticable, and a simple evacuation of the islands by Great Britain and their return to Korea either directly or through China, is the solution which is naturally forced upon us as the only feasible one.

The Korean Government, which is well aware of the present state of the question, has not, however, any definite plan as to the course it will pursue in the event of the evacuation of Port Hamilton. It is its intention to send an official to reside there, but it feels that his presence or even that of a body of Korean troops cannot guarantee the future inviolability of the islands, and that the reoccupation of the group by some power, in case it deems it necessary, is a step beyond its power to prevent.

China on its side, while it cannot, as I have stated, occupy the islands without gravely offending Japan, fears, in case they are abandoned, their occupation by some power which would constitute a grave menace against its northern coast.

The question is therefore reduced to this, Great Britain for reasons of her own will no longer hold the islands, China cannot take them and Korea would not be able to keep them.

There appears another solution to the question which would, I think, unquestionably meet not only with the consent but with the approval of all the powers interested in the question, and that is, as soon as the group is returned to Korea, for that power to lease it to a power at once friendly and entirely disinterested in the questions which make occupation by China, Great Britain, Japan or Korea impossible.

The attention of the Department of State and of the Navy has frequently been called to the desirability of the United States leasing Port Hamilton as a coaling station for our fleet on this station, and the Secretary of the Navy in his Annual Report for 1884 (p. 41) strongly recommended such a measure.

I believe that the Korean Government could without much difficulty be prevailed upon to lease these islands for the purpose above mentioned for any length of time which might be thought advisable, and thus dispose of a most troublesome question in a dignified and advantageous way. $6,000 a year (the amount which our Government has until recently paid for the naval depot at Nagasaki) would be gladly accepted by Korea.

I have deemed it my duty to submit the above suggestions to your consideration, and I have no doubt that the negotiations could be successfully conducted to this end should the plan meet with your approval.

W. W. Rockhill.

190
거문도 사후 처리를 둘러싼 조선 내의 동향

李鴻章(1887. 1. 21 / 光緒十二年十二月二十八日) ➡ 總署

寄譯署

光緒十二年十二月二十八日巳刻

袁世凱二十七來電 英總領事昨來漢城 據金允植函稱 英送文外署 言明巨文島中國擔保他國不占 故退還 至水師撤期候再告等語 倭使來探巨文事 告以由英退還 華不代守 蓋有人謠言華允代守 倭頗驚疑云 鴻

191
영국의 거문도 철수 통보

W. W. Rockhill (1887. 1. 22) ➡ T. F. Bayard

No. 50.

Jan. 22, 1887.
Secretary of State

Sir,

I have the honor to inform you that yesterday Mr. Watters, H. B. M.'s Acting Consul General at Söul, handed to the President of the Foreign Office a despatch from Sir John Walsham, H. M.'s Minister at Peking. the substance of which is as follows: In a former despatch from this legation, it was stated that annexation was not (as Your Excellency had implied) intended when a naval force was stationed at Port Hamilton, but that the action of H. B. M.'s government was simply to guard these islands when they were exposed to seizure at a critical time. It was also stated that when the necessity of keeping guard should have passed, the temporary occupation would cease. This time would appear to have been reached, and the British forces will be withdrawn from the islands. To effect this, an agreement has been made by which the government of China guarantees the security of the islands from seizure by any other power. British forces will be withdrawn in the spring and when the evacuation takes place, Your Excellency will be informed of it by the Admiral Commanding our naval forces through the Consul General at Söul. It was my intention, adds Sir John, to visit Korea a short time ago to inform you of these facts in person, but circumstances having prevented it, I have addressed you this communication.

I have been informed from another source that the Chinese government has offered Korea three of its ships of war, manned of course with Chinese crews, to assist in protecting these islands. The Korean government has also appointed an official to reside on the islands which will also be garrisoned with troops.

It will be I think a most unfortunate circumstance if Korea is obliged to accept China's profered aid in this affair, as each step of such a nature greatly decreases what little liberty of action is left this country in its relations with China.

W. W. Rockhill.

192
영국의 거문도 철수 및 반환에 대한 보고

K. I. Veber (1887. 1. 23) ➡ N. K. Girs

AVPRI, F.150, Op.493, D.113, L.126-126ob.

Сеул 11-го Января 1887 года.

Его Высокопревосходительству Н. К. Гирсу.

Милостивый Государь, Николай Карлович,

Телеграммою от 9-го числа сего месяца я имел честь донести Вашему Высокопревосходительству об официальном заявлении Англиею здешнему Правительству об очищении порта Гамильтона.

При первом представлении своем президенту корейской Коллегии Иностранных Дел, 8-го числа сего месяца, вновь назначенный сюда великобританский Генеральный Консул, господин Watters передал ноту своего Посланника в Пекин, Sir John Walsham, в которой он заявляет, что вследствие минования того политического положения, побудившего его Правительство временно занять порт Гамильтон, он имеет честь уведомить о выдаче оного обратно Корейскому Правительству. Фактическая передача состоится, как скоро Командующий английскою эскадрою в китайских и японских морях, Вице-адмирал Гамильтон окончит очищение порта.

С отличным почтением и совершенною преданностью имею честь быть Вашего Высокопревосходительства покорнейшим слугою.

Вебер.

193
영국의 거문도 철수에 대한 도쿄 주재 러시아 공사의 보고

A. P. Davydow (1887. 1. 24) ➡ N. K. Girs

AVPRI, F.150, Op.493, D.113, L.129-129ob.

Копия с донесения Посланника в Токио от 12/24 января 1887 года, за № 6.

В дополнение к донесению моему от 4/16 сего января № 4, имею честь уведомить, что по полученным Графом Иноуе сведениям английский Представитель в Корее сделал корейскому Правительству официальное заявление оп предстоящем оставлении англичанами Порта Гамильтона, который был занят только временно и покидается ныне вследствие минования в нем надобности.

В заключение английское заявление уведомляет корейское Правительство, что ему ничего опасаться впредь занятия Порта Гамильтона какою-либо другою Державою.

Я имел честь довести об этом до сведения Вашего Высокопревосходительства моею сегодняшнею телеграммою.

С глубоким почтением и прочее.

194
거문도 철수에 대한 사은 조회의 북경 전달 요청

金允植 (1887. 1. 26 / 高宗二十四年一月三日) ➡ J. Walsham

관련문서 거문도 철수에 대한 사은 조회

逕啓者 上年十二月二十七日 接到貴國公使華大臣照會 知貴國深以友誼爲重 將敝邦之巨文島已准退出 奉閱之下 不勝欣幸 玆派本衙門主事朴準禹齎復前往 面交貴總領事 請煩查收 轉送北京貴國公館 仍望代致感謝之意 禱切盼切 藉請大安

丁亥元月初三日 金允植

【관련문서】

大朝鮮督辦交涉通商事務金 爲照覆事 接准上年十一[二]月二十七日貴照會內開 云云見上等因 查貴國將巨文島暫行據守 諒非本意 終能顧念友誼 決然退出 可見貴國政府之意 重在友誼 昭守信義 從此兩國敦睦之情愈益鞏固 人無間言 渙然釋疑 豈惟吾兩國之幸 抑亦爲天下人之所稱揚 本大臣實深欽佩 至撤船之期 應俟嗣音 再由我政府派員前往如禮相送 並商接收 明春貴大臣東轅有光本國 方切翹企之至 爲此照覆須至照覆者

右照覆

大英欽差駐劄朝鮮便宜行事大臣 華

丁亥正月初三日

195
조선 정부의 거문도 점령 반대 성명서 및 영국의 거문도 철수 통첩 번역문 송부

K. I. Veber (1887. 2. 1) ➡ N. K. Girs

AVPRI, F.150, Op.493, D.113, L.132-133ob.

Сеул 20-го января, 1887-го года.

Его Высокопревосходительству, Н. К. Гирсу

Милостивый Государь Николай Карлович,

Телеграммою от 9-го и донесением своим от 11-го числа сего месяца я имел честь донести Вашему Высокопревосходительству об официальном заявлении великобританского Правительства об очищении порта Гамильтона. При сем позволяю себе приложить перевод последнего протеста корейского Правительства против завладения Гамильтоном и перевод ноты великобританского Посланника Сэр Джон Вольшем, в которой он сообщает Президенту здешней Коллегии Иностранных Дел о предстоящем очищении острова.

Протест редактирован советником здешнего Правительства, господином Денни, которому, как я имел честь довести до сведения Вашего Высокопревосходительства, Король, при первой аудиенции, внушил, что главным делом, о котором он имеет озаботиться, —это вопрос о Гамильтоне. Что касается принятых Китаем на себя обязательств, упомянутых в ноте Посланника Вольшем, то я позволяю себе заметить, что последнее соглашение между нами и Канцлером Ли Хун-чжаном дало возможность Богдыханскому Правительству устранить мнения опасения англичан относительно покушений России на неприкосновенность Кореи.

С отличным почтением и совершенною преданностью имею честь быть

Вашего Высокопревосходительства покорнейшим слугою.

Вебер.

196
영국 의회 질의, 응답
(1887. 2. 2 ~ 2. 3)

No. 10.

Question asked in the House of Commons, February 2, 1887; and Answer.

PORT HAMILTON.

Mr. Bryce asked the Under-Secretary of State for Foreign Affairs whether it was the fact that Port Hamilton was to be shortly evacuated by Her Majesty's forces, and, if so, what arrangements had been made with the Chinese or any other Government regarding its future custody.

Sir J. Fergusson.-With the permission of the honourable Member for Christchurch, I will answer his question at the same time; and I am also requested by the Secretary of State for the Colonies to answer that of the honourable Member for the Eye Division of Suffolk. Port Hamilton will shortly be evacuated by Her Majesty's forces. No arrangements have been made respecting its future custody; but it is understood that a Corean official will be present at the time of the departure of the British ships. No conditions have been made with the Corean Government, but Her Majesty's Government did not determine to retire from Port Hamilton till they had received a guarantee from the Chinese Government that no part of Corea, including Port Hamilton, will be occupied by any foreign Power.

Her Majesty's Government acted under naval advice when they decided to leave Port Hamilton. Papers on the subject will shortly be presented to Parliament.

No. 11.

Question asked in the House of Commons, February 3, 1887; and Answer.

PORT HAMILTON.

Captain Colomb asked whether the late Government, responsible for the occupation of Port Hamilton, acted upon naval advice; and, if so, what had been the expenditure from Imperial funds incurred from the date of occupation down to the present time at Port Hamilton.

Lord G. Hamilton. Sir William Dowell, the Naval Commander-in-chief, was directed by the Admiralty to occupy Port Hamilton in May 1885. A change of Government took place, and shortly afterwards a Report was received from Sir W. Dowell in which he pointed out that it was unsuitable for the purposes for which it had been temporarily occupied, and he advocated its abandonment. I was then at the Admiralty, and I found that both the Naval Members of the Board and Sir George Willes, who had preceded Sir William Dowell as Commander-in-chief in Chinese waters, was strongly of the same opinion. Admiral Hamilton, who succeeded Sir William Dowell in the autumn of 1885, was specially instructed to report upon the whole matter, and he has sent in a series of Reports to the effect that the retention of the place is a waste of money in time of peace and a source of weakness in time of war. These papers will be laid before Parliament.

The main evil of occupation has been the laying down of a cable between Port Hamilton and Hong Kong, and a certain sum has been spent in building huts for stores and marines. The total direct expenditure has not yet been brought to account; I cannot, therefore, state the approximate amount.

197
거문도에 영국이 설치한 시설물 철거 관련 보고

V. Kostylev (1887. 2. 8) ➡ 외무부 아시아국

AVPRI, F.150, Op.493, D.113, L.130-131ob.

Российско-императорское консульство в Нагасаки
27 января 1887 года

В Азиатский Департамент.

Имею честь донести, что, в ответе на сделанное 31 прошлого декабря, по распоряжению английских властей, стоявшим здесь командиром английского корвета Констанс предложение купить все выстроенные англичанами в порте Гамильтона здания и находившийся там английский казенный лес, с тем, чтобы, как можно скорее окончательно снести здания и вывезти их, вместе с лесом, из порта Гамильтон, не явилось покупателей. В виду этого, 19/31 сего января стоявшим здесь командиром английской канонерской лодки Фаир-брандт сделано было новое объявление, что находящийся в порте Гамильтон лес и большая часть построенных там зданий уже готовы к погрузке на судно, а остальная часть зданий будет готова к погрузке 18/20 будущего февраля месяца, и что канонерская лодка Фаир-брандт останется в порте Гамильтон до тех пор, пока не будет все убрано оттуда. Желающим купить здания и лес предоставлено было право проезда в порт Гамильтон на лодке Фаир-брандт.

На днях нашелся покупатель на английские здания и лес в порте Гамильтон здешний плотник китаец Тали, который предложил за все здания и лес в порте Гамильтон 250 долларов, но с тем, чтобы судно, на котором он повезет лес, было пробуксировано лодкою Фаир-брандт до порта Гамильтон и обратно. Хотя буксировка стоит гораздо дороже 250 долларов и одни здания для порта

Гамильтон, построенные летом 1885 года в Гонконге, без доставки в порт Гамильтон, стоили более 20.000 долларов, англичане приняли предложение китайца Та-ли, и вчера лодка Фаир-брандт увела на буксире в порт Гамильтон нанятую китайцем Та-ли, для перевозки из порта Гамильтон сюда купленного им английского казенного леса и разобранных зданий, английскую шхуну «Dorothy», с тем, чтобы к концу следующей недели окончательно очистить порт Гамильтон от английских зданий и леса.

В настоящее время, кроме лодки Фаир-брант, в порте Гамильтон стоит английский корвет Констанс, но послезавтра он ожидается здесь.

Консул В. Костылов.

198
거문도 방어를 위한 진영 건설 제안

內務府 (1887. 2. 10 / 高宗二十四年一月十八日) ➡ 高宗

內務府啓曰 海路要衝 置鎭設防 所以備瞭望而戒陰雨者也 巨文島之未遑固圉 極其疎虞 不宜一向延拖 漢城判尹李元會 經略使差下 另該曹口傳下批 使之斯速下往 相其形止 看其事力 設鎭方略 論理登聞後稟處何如 傳曰允

199
거문도 철수를 조선, 청국에 통보한 내용 승인

The Marquis of Salisbury (1887. 2. 25) ➡ J. Walsham

No. 81.

The Marquis of Salisbury to Sir J. Walsham.

Foreign Office, February 25, 1887.

Sir,

I HAVE received your despatch of the 25th December last, inclosing copies of the notes which you addressed on the previous day to the Tsung-li Yamên and to the President of the Corean Council, announcing the intention of Her Majesty's Government to withdraw their forces from Port Hamilton, and placing on record the circumstances which have induced them to terminate the temporary occupation of the islands forming that port.

I have to inform you that Her Majesty's Government approve the terms of your two notes and your communication to the Tsung-li Yamên of the note which you had addressed to the Corean Government.

I am, &c.
(Signed) SALISBURY.

200
녹둔도 일대를 조선이 청국에 양여한다는 소문 보고

杉村濬 (1887. 2. 28) ➡ 井上馨 (1887. 3. 11)

관련문서 청국 정부가 鹿屯島를 점령했다고 하는 풍설 보고(杉村濬 ➡ 井上馨, 1886. 11. 15)

三月十一日接受

(朱書)
「機密第二十七號」

俄韓境界ノ一帶ヲ淸國ニ讓與スル風說

俄韓交界ノ鹿屯島ヲ淸國政府ニテ占領セントスル風說ニ關シ客年機密第百五十八號信ヲ以テ探聞ノ槪略及具報候處今般德源府使李重夒氏ハ土門又圖們勘界使ト爲リ陰曆三月任所ヨリ發程シテ該境ニ赴キ踏勘ノ上該境一帶ノ地ヲ割テ淸國ニ讓與スルトノ風說有之候此說果シテ事實ニ候ハハ多分俄韓ノ關係ヲ薄フセントスル淸政府ノ考案ニ出デタル者ト被推測候客年春巳來俄韓兩國間ニ屢々ノ協議ヲ重ネタル陸路通商ノ條約ハ今日迄未ダ結約ニ至ラザルヲ見テモ前說ノ益々事實ニ近カルベキヲ被疑候猶ホ本件ニ付探問ノ上具報可仕候

右及具報候敬具

明治二十年二月二十八日

在朝鮮

臨時代理公使　杉　村　　濬(印)

外務大臣伯爵井　上　　馨 殿

【관련문서】

十一月二十六日接受

「(朱書)機密第百五十八號」

鹿屯島ノ事

先便機密第百五十五號追書ヲ以テ清國政府ハ俄韓交界ニ在ル鹿屯島占領ノ義風說ノ儘御報申上候處其後種々探偵ヲ盡シ候得共于今確說ヲ得兼居候尤モ朝鮮探偵人ヨリハ別紙寫ノ通「今般朝鮮政府ヨリ俄公使ニ向ヒ該島ノ返遷ヲ要求セシ事ハ有之トイヘトモ清國ニハ毫モ關係セサル旨」報道有之候左スレバ清國占領ノ風說ハ或ハ虛傳ニ屬スルカト被愚考候別紙相添此段及御報道候敬具

明治十九年十一月十五日

在朝鮮

臨時代理公使　杉　村　　濬(印)

外務大臣　伯爵　井　上　　馨 殿

(附記附屬書)

「(朱書)別紙」

鹿屯島本是我地而年前水道改出島入水外故俄人奪之我民亦爲所奪今番陸路通商之後俄公使亦言及此而金替辨曰旣定好約之後此島須遷於我爲宜也俄公使曰諾(或云俄使言當議于俄政府後從之云云)如此而已情人初無所關於此地也外間多有此等浮說誤傳俱不足信也若已有之則豈有尙今不傳之理乎

201
2월 27일부로 거문도 철수 완료

Admiralty (1887. 2. 28) ➔ Foreign Office (1887. 3. 1)

No. 18.

Admiralty to Foreign Office — (Received March 1.)

Admiralty, February 28, 1887.

(Confidential.)

Sir,

I AM commanded by my Lords Commissioners of the Admiralty to transmit, for the information of the Secretary of State for Foreign Affairs, copy of a telegram dated the 28th instant from the Commander-in-chief on the China Station.

I am, &c.

(Signed) EVAN MACGREGOR.

Inclosure in No. 18.

Vice-Admiral Hamilton to Admiralty.

Hong Kong, February 28, 1887, 6:10 P. M.

(Telegraphic.)

FLAG hauled down Port Hamilton 27th. Cable under charge of Chief.

202
영국군 거문도 철수 통보

Watters (1887. 3. 1 / 高宗二十四年二月七日) ➡ 金允植

大英欽命駐劄朝鮮統理各口交涉通商事務署理總領事官倭 爲照會事 照得 昨夜接准電報內開 本國暫守巨文島之師艦 已奉我國水師提督札調撤退 軍械旗幟亦併盡撤 仍歸原舊模式等因 本署總領事官閱之 不勝欣喜 用特備文照會貴督辦 請煩查照 轉於貴國大君主陛下啓奏 巨文島所有本國師艦以及軍械旗幟并已盡行撤去 一切仍歸貴國版與舊制 永久完全 爲此照會 須至照會者

右照會

大朝鮮督辦交涉通商事務大臣 金

一千八百八十七年三月初一日 丁亥二月初七日

203
철수 통보에 대한 조선 정부의 회답

J. Walsham (1887. 3. 2) ➡ The Marquis of Salisbury (1887. 3. 2)

No. 20.

Sir J. Walsham to the Marquis of Salisbury.—(Received March 2, 4:40 P. M.)

Peking, March 2, 1887.

(No. 8.)

(Telegraphic.)

MY despatch No. 318 of 25th December.

Admiral telegraphs that flag was hauled down at Port Hamilton on the' 27th February.

I have just received reply of Corean Government to my notification of withdrawal. It records belief that Her Majesty's Government did not originally intend to occupy place, and testifies to their good faith and friendship in evacuating it altogether. It holds that relations between the two countries will therefore be stronger than ever, and that the action of Her Majesty's Government is highly appreciated.

In any public explanation respecting evacuation I think it would be as well not to ignore Corea entirely. The Government and people are most susceptible regarding their position towards China.

204
조선의 거문도 사후 처리에 관한 袁世凱의 보고 전달

李鴻章 ➡ 總署 (1887. 3. 4 / 光緒十三年二月十日)

二月初十日 北洋大臣李鴻章文稱 駐紮朝鮮總理交涉通商事宜幷用道補用知府袁世凱稟稱 竊照去冬英總領事倭妥瑪至韓 卽將其駐華公使照會韓外署退還巨文島公文 送投外署 當卽電稟憲核各在案 此事韓君臣頜深感激 擬俟派員接收後 再行派員赴都津申謝 聞韓王意 待閔泳翊回國 卽行派赴巨文接收 並經營一切 特恐泳翊未必願往 巨文水線 韓廷意欲購買 派員來商 當卽告以如無水師防守 則水線無用 且價値必昂 韓力難辦 不如不買 韓廷諾之 謹將英使來文及外署復文抄呈鈞鑒等情到本閣 爵大臣據此 相應咨明貴衙門 請煩查照 照錄顧摺 謹將駐華使及韓外署往來照會二件鈔摺恭呈憲鑒

205
영국의 거문도 철수에 관한 나가사키 주재 러시아 영사의 보고

V. Kostylev (1887. 3. 5) ➡ 외무부 아시아국

AVPRI, F.150, Op.493, D.113, L.142-142ob.

Российско-императорское Консульство в Нагасаки.
21 февраля 1887 года

В Азиатский Департамент.

Имею честь донести, что, по полученным мною частным путем сведениям, на прошлой неделе англичане окончательно очистили порт Гамильтон. Те морские солдаты, которые оставались в порте Гамильтон, на частном пароходе отвезены в Гонконг. Здания казарм, складов, телеграфной станции и прочее снесены, заграждения, сделанные в одном из входов в порт, сняты, и ни одного англичанина в порте Гамильтоне не осталось. Телеграфный кабель, соединявший порт Гамильтон с островом Saddle Island, около Шанхая, и с Гонконгом порванный еще в прошлом году, остается не убранным до сих пор, и насколько мне неизвестно, англичане не имеют в виду убирать этот кабель, а предпочитают бросить его. На днях мне случайно пришлось слышать объяснение этого факта одним из пришедших из порта Гамильтон командиров английских военных судов. По его словам, кабель, порванный еще в прошлом году, остается не убранным по той причине, что уборка его стоит дороже, чем сам он.

Консул В. Костылев.

206
영국군의 거문도 철수에 대한 조선 정부의 사은 조회

金允植 (1887. 3. 5 / 高宗二十四年二月十一日) ➡ Watters

관련문서 Watters의 답신(1887. 4. 6)

大朝鮮督辦交涉通商事務金 爲照覆事 貴曆一千八百八十七年三月初一日敝曆丁亥二月初七日 准貴署總領事內開 見上云云等因 准此 查前准貴國欽差大臣華照開 還退巨文島一案 當即由本大臣奏達我大君主 我大君主面詔 巨文島係本國土地 載在版圖前貴國事起倉卒 不得已而暫爲據守 亦一時權宜之計也 或有未悉貴政府之意者 不無疑議 今果還退在即 足見貴政府不失信義於天下 不遺口寔於當時 我兩國之交誼益敦而天下之紛議頓息 又豈但予一人之所深幸也 本大臣聞命之下 不勝欣佩 玆又准前因則貴國之始終信義 果踐前言 有如符契 我大君主宸悅豫倍加傾嚮 敝邦之人無不服貴國之高義 本大臣職忝交涉 亦與有榮焉 惟貴國師艦久處荒島 勞苦可知 本欲派員前往 以禮相送 妥爲接收 奈聞音遲後 未及往勞 遂闕東道之誼 本大臣竊有憾焉 相應備文照覆 請煩貴總領事查照 轉達貴國欽差大臣華 代致謝悃可也 須至照會者

右照覆

大英欽命駐劄朝鮮統理各口交涉通商事務署理總領事官 倭

丁亥二月十一日

【관련문서】

大英欽差駐劄朝鮮便宜行事大臣華 爲照覆事 照得 巨文島一事 本大臣 於上年十一月二十八日備文照會 旋於本年正月初三日 接准覆文 聆悉一切 查來文所云 顧念友誼 決然退出 可見英國政府重在友誼 昭守信義等語 素譜我國總理各國事務丞相 亦以顧全兩國睦誼爲重 與貴大臣同此襟懷 是以欣然轉行照電矣 來文又云 至撤船之期應俟嗣音 由貴政府派員前往 如禮相送 并商接收等語 凡以德音實深欽佩 合行奉知

惟因撤船之期 本國水師軍門 未能預先確訂 故於前文內聲明 退出巨文島之期 應候本國水師軍門將撤船時日 轉由本國駐劄貴國總領事官自行奉布 特恐有勞展轉故耳 現在惜已不及 未能轉咨本國水師軍門 拜領盛情 然本國一聞貴國將有派員如禮相送之意 事雖不行 其銘泐之忱自無少減 惟冀不日能將此情面爲奉達 始遂微衷也 爲此照覆 須至照會者

右

大朝鮮督辦交涉通商事務大臣 金

一千八百八十七年四月初六日 丁亥三月十三日

207
영국군의 거문도 철수에 관한 Veber의 전문

K. I. Veber (1887. 3. 28) ➡ I. A. Zinoviev

AVPRI, F.150, Op.493, D.113, L.149-150ob.

Императорская Российская Миссия в Корее
Сеул 16-го Марта 1887 года

Его Превосходительству И.А. Зиновьеву.

Милостивый Государь Иван Алексеевич,

В дополнение к телеграмме от 11-го и 20-го числа того же месяца, за №№ 8 и 12, в которых я донес Министерству о сделанном здешнему Правительству официальном заявлении английского Посланника, сэр Джон Уольшен, касательно очищения Порта Гамильтон, я имею честь сообщить, что окончательное очищение состоялось, и английский Генеральный Консул известил о том корейскую Коллегию Иностранных Дел.

Вашему Превосходительству известно, какой шум поднялся в конце прошлого года в английской прессе, когда известия о нерешимости великобританского Правительства относительно удержания или выдачи этого порта стали проникать в публику, и с каким усердием «Times» и, в особенности, газеты, посвященные более интересам крайнего Востока, восстали против очищения его. Прекращением работ на острове Гамильтон, произведенных японскими рабочими из Нагасаки, и, наконец, объявлениями о продаже с публичного торга, выстроенных на нем, бараков, — решение, принятое английским Правительством по этому предмету, стало известным в Японии даже ранее официального заявления сэр Джона. Выдача порта объясняется теперь тою же прессою громадными издержками, которых потребовало бы укрепление его и разными недостатками его в военно-морском отношении. Притом, нисколько не стесняясь, утешают самолюбие и патриотизм англичан тем, что, в случае надобности, то есть при столкновении Англии с Россиею, всегда можно будет снова занять Порт Гамильтон и воспользоваться им как станциею и угольным складом для флота. Возможные сомнения публики в нравственности подобной затеи стараются теперь же устранить заявлением о состоявшемся, будто бы, соглашении с Китаем, вследствие которого последнее государство не только дало гарантию, что никакая другая Держава не посягнет на целость Кореи, но и признало, выговоренное Англиею, право занятия Гамильтона в случае необходимости в будущем.

Мне кажется, что английское Правительство убедилось, что постоянное охранение этого порта было бы лишнею обузою, так как оно, без всякого серьезного сопротивления с чьей бы то ни было стороны, может во всякое время вновь занять остров, не нуждающиеся, при могуществе англичан на море, в укреплениях и превратить его в опорный пункт не только против нас, но и против Китая или Японии. Следует полагать, что лишь подобные расчеты, а не зазрения политической совести, побудили англичан в настоящее время к выдаче порта.

Здешнее Правительство, понимая предстоящую Корее в будущем опасность новой агитации, выразило намерение устроить на острове укрепленный лагерь, но насколько это предохранительное средство, если и будет приведено в исполнение, поможет, покажет будущее.

Примите, Милостивый Государь, уверение в отличном моем почтении и совершенной преданности.

Вебер.

208

거문도 유자리에 진영 설치 제안

內務府 (1887. 4. 10 / 高宗二十四年三月十七日) ➡ 高宗

內務府啓曰 卽見經略使李元會別單 則巨文島袖子里 可合鎭基 而設鎭措劃等節 惟在廟堂稟處爲辭矣 本島以海門要衝 不容不設鎭置將 然後乃可爲禦邊固之圖 該島僉使令該曹口傳差出 催促下送 而以邊地窠施行 瓜限三十朔爲定 凡所課歲廩費 公廨創建兵艦軍器措置之方 爛漫講究 論理登聞後裁處事 分付該道道臣何如 傳曰允

209
長淵府使 申錫孝의 巨文島僉使 임명

高宗 (1887. 4. 18 / 高宗二十四年三月二十五日)

傳曰 巨文島僉使有闕闕代 長淵府使申錫孝除授 長淵府使之代 平山府使吳順泳除授 平山府使之代 豊德府使韓聖根除授

210

거문도 사건 해결에 대해 청국에 사의 표시 제안

議政府 (1887. 5. 9 / 高宗二十四年四月十七日) ➡ 高宗

관련문서 거문도 사건 해결에 대해 청 정부에 보낸 사은 자문

議政府啓 巨文島占據之英國人 今已撤退云 不容無稱謝之擧 前頭使行 具方物奉表之意 令文任撰出 先通咨文於北京禮部 而付之今番別使之行何如 允之

【관련문서】

咨文內開巨文島永完事 敝邦巨文島 英人佔據 積爲三載之久 督其退迸 專事推宕 擬向各與國 確要辨理調停 慮或拂他如好 反致滋事 荏苒姑忍 削弱是恥 特蒙天朝視同內服一日據理而責非 則彼乃師艦言旋 場屋載撤 缺者完而欹者整 嗣後別國不敢規占 曷任感戴 爲此備咨

211
조선 국왕의 사은 상주 요청 자문 통보

禮部 ➡ 總署 (1887. 7. 9 / 光緒十三年五月二十九日)

五月二十九日 禮部文稱 本年五月二十六日 朝鮮國慶賀皇上親政正副使到京 賫到該國王移咨本部 及總理各國事務衙門 並北洋大臣咨文各一件 係因該國巨文島前被英人佔據 今師船撤歸 該國王感激天恩 咨請本部代爲韓奏等因 除由本部另行辦理外 應將分咨總理各國事務衙門咨文韓送查照可也

212

거문진 설치 문제에 대해 전라감사의 재조사 보고를 청하는 啓

內務府 (1887. 7. 13 / 高宗二十四年五月二十三日) ➡ 高宗

內務府啓曰 以巨文島設鎭 措劃講究登聞之意 啓稟行會矣 卽見該道臣李憲稙狀啓 則枚擧水營本縣所報 以爲羅牧屬鎭 恐合事宜 而繼是創革 請令廟堂稟處矣 今此所陳 只擧梱邑報辭 而謄啓而已 初無道臣之具意見論理者 有欠體段 況此牧場變通 多有窒礙 更爲從他爛商 斯速馳聞事 知委何如 傳曰允

213

청 禮部의 조선 국왕 사은 대주

禮部 (1887. 7. 28 / 光緒十三年六月八日)

甲午 禮部奏 朝鮮國王以該國巨文島 被英人占據三年 蒙天朝理責 今已收復 咨請轉奏謝恩 下總理各國事務衙門知之 摺包

214
청산진을 혁파하고 거문진의 설치를 청하는 啓

內務府 (1887. 9. 2 / 高宗二十四年七月十五日) ➡ 高宗

內務府啓曰 巨文島設鎭事 更爲爛商馳聞之意 覆啓行會矣 卽見該道臣李憲稙狀啓 則該島處在重溟之外 壤地狹窄人戶鮮少 劃付土地後 乃可成樣 而靑山島水路來往 不過三百里 兩鎭對峙 不無相妨 公廨軍器官廩吏況與諸般措施 雖不新備 移彼屬此 事半功倍 而係是創革 請令該府稟處矣 巨文一島 乃是南沿要衝 而不容不設鎭於此 則靑山鎭之對峙 便歸不緊 該僉使減下 凡廨舍軍物歲入廩備等節 竝依狀請移屬何如 傳曰允

215

거문도진 水軍僉節制使를 거문도진 水軍僉節制使兼守防將으로 변경을 청하는 啓

兵曹 (1887. 9. 6 / 高宗二十四年七月十九日) ➡ 高宗

兵曹啓曰 因內務部草記 靑山島革付巨文島事 允下矣 巨文島鎭水軍僉節制使 改以巨文島鎭水軍僉節制使兼守防將下批 靑山島之鎭管 古今島薪智島 改以巨文島鎭管下批之意敢啓 傳曰知道

216
거문진의 방어 강화 요청 승인

高宗 (1888. 7. 16 / 高宗二十五年六月八日) ➡ 內務府

內務府啓曰 卽見全羅監司李憲稙所報 則枚擧巨文島僉使申錫孝牒呈 以爲本島與靑山島 分設捍禦 而兩鎭相距 水路絶遠 公牒來往 每患愆滯 且靑山設鎭之初 旣有隣島付屬之例 長興府生日島平日島 興陽縣草島 竝屬之巨文鎭爲辭矣 當初靑山鎭創設之時 旣有隣島許屬之事 而況三島之於本鎭 所管甚緊且要 依道臣報請 竝付之巨文鎭 俾重海防何如 傳曰允

217
거문도 실상 조사와 방비 보강에 대한 의견

李鶴圭 (1890. 4.00 / 高宗二十七年三月)

臣與前主事臣成翊永本月十五日酉時昇海龍船十六日卯時由仁川港發錨前往因舟輕風烈未便疾馳十七日酉時到泊於古今島載量汲水十八日卯初拔錨同日午初始抵巨門島卽爲上陸僉使臣李宗鎬時在青山鎭故臣等暫曁吏廳招致鎭校二人問外國軍艦停泊與否則以爲九月十九日英國軍艦一隻來泊二十三日還發同月二十日又有英國軍艦兩隻來泊二十四日還發同月二十一日又有英國軍艦一隻來泊二十五日還發同月二十四日又有英國軍艦一隻來泊二十七日還發而最初一次問情則以爲適因巡海到此而別無他故云其後則因僉使不在更不問情云而十月十三日夜外國軍艦一隻來泊於倭島前洋十四日早朝還發因晩泊早發未詳何國軍艦云故問其前後來艦搭載人員上陸與否則以爲或三或五上山獵鳥旋卽等艦別無他事云是齊

7-4.
철군 이후 러시아의 극동 군사정책

218
조선에서의 정치적 영향력 유지를 위한 러시아 함대의 제물포 파견 요청

N. K. Girs (1887. 6. 8) ➡ Ansdreyev

RGAVMF, F.417, Op.1, D.312, L.13-5.

Министр Иностранных Дел
27 Мая 1887 года

Его Превосходительству Н. Н. Андрееву

Милостивый Государь, Николай Николаевич.

Положение дела в Корее, которое, благодаря соседству своему с нашею Тихоокеанскою окраиною, представляет для нас живой интерес, заслуживает с некоторого времени особого внимания в виду обнаруживаемых Китайским Правительством стремлений приобрести исключительное влияние на ход дела в стране этой. Как ни трудно, в виду тесных исторических связей, соединяющих Корею с Китаем, открыто противодействовать этим стремлениям, тем не менее, нельзя нам также относиться к обстоятельству этому с безучастием, в каковом Китайское Правительство может усмотреть лишь поощрение своим замыслам.

Самым естественным проявлением нашего внимания к положению Кореи должно служить появление русского военного флота в Корейских водах. Между тем, так явствует из донесения нашего Поверенного в Делах в Сеуле, с Ноября 1885 года ни одно из судов наших не показывалось в порте Чемульпо, ближайшем к Корейской столице, тогда как порт этот весьма часто посещается эскадрами других Держав, вследствие чего в краях этих распространяется убеждение, что будто бы мы не имеем права посылать суда наши в Корейские воды или же чего-то опасаемся. Так как главное назначение Тихоокеанской эскадры нашей заключается в поддержании нашего политического значения, то, признавая распространение означенных толко в крайне неудобным, я почитаю долгом обратиться к Вашему Превосходительству с покорнейшею просьбою благоволить по телеграфу предписать командующему нашею эскадрою, чтобы суда наши, в составе одного или двух, по возможности, чаще заходили в означенный Корейский порт. Сколько мне известно, моряки наши считают Чемульпо неудобною стоянкою, но, так как неудобство это не мешает посещению порта этого судами других наций, то мне кажется, что и нам не следует из-за этого соображения уклоняться от появления нашего флага близ Корейских берегов.

Считаю не лишним присовокупить к этому, что Корейское Правительство рассчитывает найти в нас опору против чинолюбивых замыслов Китая, но что мы не в каком случае не должны поощрять этих расчетов, почему командирам судов наших во время пребывания их в Корейских водах следует тщательно воздерживаться от всякого участия в местных событиях. В случаях же особой важности, они могут входить в соглашение с нашим Поверенным в Делах в Сеуле, Статским Советником Вебером.

Примите, Милостивый Государь, уверение в отличном моем почтении и совершенной преданности.

Н. Гирс.

219
러시아 군함의 제물포 파견 지시에 대한 보고

I. A. Shestakov (1887. 7. 5) ➡ N. K. Girs

RGAVMF, F.417, Op.1, D.312, L.17-17ob.

23 Июня 1887 года

Его Высокопревосходительству Н. Г. Гирсу.

Милостивый Государь, Николай Карлович.

В ответ на письмо Вашего Высокопревосходительства от 22 сего Июня, № 92, имею честь уведомить, что тотчас же после получения Вашего доверительного письма от 27 Мая сего года, было передано по телеграфу приказание Командующему отрядом судов Тихого Океана Контр-адмиралу Корнилову посылать каждый месяц одно из судов отряда в Чемульпо и в дополнение этой телеграммы было сообщено почтою тому же Адмиралу о порядке сношений с местными властями, который Ваше Высокопревосходительство сочли нужным указать, присовокупляя при сем, что по донесениям Контр-адмирала Корнилова, клипер «Вестник», в начале Мая сего года, посетил Чемульпо, а в конце того же месяца канонерская лодка «Бобр» — Фузан и Лазарев.

Прошу принять, Милостивый Государь, уверение в моем совершенном к Вам уважении и таковой же преданности.

Подписал: И. Шестаков.

220
러시아 군함의 제물포 입항 보고

A. Y. Vlangali (1887. 7. 12) ➡ I. A. Shestakov

관련문서 러시아 군함 '베스트닉'호 함장의 高宗 알현(1887. 6. 2)

RGAVMF, F.417, Op.1, D.312, L.19-19ob.

31 Июня 1887 года

Его Превосходительству И. А. Шестакову

Милостивый Государь, Иван Алексеевич.

Имею честь препроводить при сем к Вашему Превосходительству копию с донесения Поверенного в Делах и Генерального Консула нашего в Сеуле, от 21 Мая сего года, за № 64, о приходе Клипера «Вестник» в Чемульпо и о посещении Командиром Клипера и шестью офицерами Корейской столицы.

Примите, Милостивый Государь, уверение в отличном моем почтении и совершенной преданности.

А. Влангали.

【관련문서】

RGAVMF, F.417, Op.1, D.312, L.20-20ob.

Копия с донесения Поверенного в Делах и Генерального Консула в Корее Начальнику Азиатского Департамента от 21 Мая 1887 года.

Имею честь сообщить Вашему Превосходительству, что по приходе 9-го числа сего месяца Клипера «Вестник» в Чемульпо, Командир оного, Капитан 1-го ранга Ланг, посетил на другой день Сеул. Я поместил его и прибывших с ним офицеров в некоторых, наскоро отделанных для них домах Миссии.

По моей просьбе Король и Наследник соизволили назначить 13 числа особую аудиенцию, в которой участвовали, кроме Секретаря Миссии и меня, Командир Ланг и шесть офицеров. Король выразил свою признательность по случаю прибытия Русского военного судна, видя в этом доказательство участия и дружеского расположения России к Корее. Узнав потом о скором уходе Клипера, Его Величество высказали, вместе с сожалением своим, надежду на скорое возвращение Командира или приход другого судна. После представления нам показывали Королевский парк и некоторые здания и киоски в нем, и моряки наши остались весьма довольными оказанным им любезным приемом. Вообще произвел Сеул на них очень приятное впечатление.

14-го числа наши гости оставили нас опять и 15-го Клипер «Вестник» снялся с якоря и ушел в Нагасаки, чтобы соединиться там с отрядом судов Тихого Океана Контр-адмирала Корнилова.

Примите и прочее.

221
‘드미트리 돈스코이’호의 제물포 입항 관련 보고

Dmitry Donskoy 함장(1888. 4. 20) ➡ V. P. Shmidt

RGAVMF, F.417, Op.1, D.363, L.27-9.

Командир фрегата «Дмитрий Донской»
Нагасаки
8 Апреля 1888 года

Начальнику эскадры в Тихом Океане

Рапорт

15 марта, в 5 часов вечера, имея пары в трех котлах, снялся с якоря для следования в Чемульпо.

С 6 часов вечера ветер начал свежеть, меняясь в направлении от NtO к SO, установившись на этом последнем румбе, к 10 часам вечера, ветер засвежел до 10 баллов с порывами до 11 баллов, волнение 6-7 баллов. При курсе SW 65’ фрегат с 48 оборотами машины имел 10 узлов ходу, боковые размахи от 15’ до 22’ и от 14 до 16 раз в минуту, качка плавная.

Имея в батарее дополнительный запас угля в мешках количсством до 2000 пудов, счел более благоразумным закрепить стоявшие до этого времени фок и фока стаксель, уменьшить ход до 4 узлов (38 обор. Машины) и привести три румба от ветра. Без этого груза фрегат мог бы смело идти по курсу и нести фока стаксель и зарифленный фок.

Идя, против довольно крупной волны, фрегат всходил на нее легко, не принимая полубоком воды, килевые размахи до 4 1/2’ и до 7 раз в минуту.

Крепление всего по походному оказалось вполне надежным.

В 3 часа ветер стих, лег на курс.

18 марта с рассветом открылись острова Клиффорд в желаемом направлении и согласно счислениям.

Того же дня в 3 часа дня встал фертоинг на рейд порта Чемульпо.

Весь переход в 605 миль сделан в 70 часов со средней скоростью 8.5 узлов в час.

Здесь застал военных станционеров: Американский авизо Pallos, Японский корвет Ватуо и Китайский пароход Гси-ап (Командир — англичанин).

Для входа в Чемульпо на фрегате имелась карта №1258 и извлечение из донесения командира клипера «Крейсер» от 4 декабря 1885 года, помещенные в записках по Гидрографии 1887 года, 2й выпуск.

Но последнее заключает для плавания только краткое изложение прохода Flying-Fish-Channel, подробно начерченного на вышеозначенной карте и не может служить руководством для плавания, так как никаких описаний створов, берегов и островов ни рисунков или фотографий, никаких объяснений опасности в нем нет.

Благодаря любезности командира флагманского Французского броненосца «Jurenne» давшему на одни сутки свою лоцию и планы последней Французской съемки рек «Salli» и Seul, на фрегате имелись возможно подробные и новые сведения для этого плавания.

На Германском флагманском корвете Saphie карт и лоции не оказалось.

В отпущенной на фрегат английской лоции «The China sea Directory» 1874 года, Чемульпо и близлежащие места не помещены.

Оба прохода в Чемульпо, как Flying Fish так и южный, по своей широте, глубине и множеству разнообразных довольно типичных островов, дающих возможность ориентироваться во всякий момент, в ясную погоду не представляют затруднений для прохода судов, даже самых больших размеров. Проход Flying Fish для судов, идущих в первый раз в этих местах, имеет то преимущество, что в нем приходится проходить самые узкие и опасные места по створа, хотя и естественным, но настолько типичны, что ошибаться в них очень трудно.

В южном же проходе при совершенно таком же характере опасностей, нет такой наглядной проверки безопасности своего положения и правильности курсов. Для судов идущих от островов Клиффорд южный проход сокращает путь на одну милю, но главное преимущество что течения в этом проходе, не так быстры, и только в сидигии достигает 3 узлов, тогда как в проходе Flying Fish особенно у камня Button, встречаются сулои; и течение при вышесказанных условиях достигает 5 узлов.

В пасмурную погоду идти этими проходами для лиц, не бывавших в этих местах, довольно рискованно, в этом случае можно отдать предпочтение южному проходу, так как, пользуясь им, можно большую часть прохода определяться по высоким камням и островам, удаленным один от другого не более 1 1/2 миль.

Для входа на рейд следует, пройдя остров Ydolmi, курс к якорному месту держать на небольшую группу деревьев находящихся на горе острова Roze.

Лучшая якорная стоянка в Чемульпо для судов больших размеров в 2 1/4 милях от каменной пристани на SO 37, грунт старый ил.

Приливы и отливы здесь очень сильные, почему рекомендую всем судам без исключения становиться фертоинг, бросая один якорь на NO, а другой на SW, канатов иметь по 50 сажень (4 смычки) каждого.

На третий день после сидигии разница в уровнях большой и малой воды, измеренная ручным лотом была 32 фута, после же квадратуры она была 26 фут. Глубина в самую малую воду 81/2 сажень. Приливное течение на NO, а отливное на SW со скоростью до 31/2 узлов.

В Чемульпо имеется каменная насыпь, к которой шлюпки с рейда могут подходить во всякую воду. Для прохода шлюпкам и мелким судам к небольшому рейду между Чемульпо и островом Roze, имеются два створа: 1й на острове Srotion из белых знаков, с него переходят на створ из черных знаков на восточной оконечности берега Чемульпо.

Во время стоянки на якоре в Чемульпо, при чистом небе ветер первые два дня был NW до 6 баллов, чрезвычайно сухой, быстро высушивавший мокрое белье. Барометр стоял на 30.3. Температура воздуха ночью доходила до нуля, днем подымалась до 5’ и 6’, редко до 8’R. Температура воды была 5’R.

(подпись)

222
1888년 러시아 태평양 함대 극동 해역 순항 보고서

V. P. Shmidt (1888. 5. 18) ➡ N. M. Chikhachev

RGAVMF, F.417, Op.1, D.572, L.27-30.

Отчет
Пребывание эскадры Тихого Океана
в наших водах
в 1888 году

Приход судов эскадры во Владивосток.

Перед уходом во Владивосток, на Нагасакском рейде находились следующие суда, вверенной мне эскадры: фрегат «Дмитрий Донской», корвет «Витязь» и Канонерские лодки «Кореец» и «Бобр».

В рапорте от 22 мая за №349, была выяснена причина ухода из Нагасаки только 6 мая, а также донесено о назначении лодки «Бобр» на станцию в Чемульпо и разрешении катеру «Наездник» уйти 7-го апреля, для посещения некоторых Японских портов.

Фрегат «Дмитрий Донской» прибыл на Владивостокский рейд 9 мая, где застал уже лодку «Кореец», ушедшею днем раньше и пришедшей накануне Корвет «Витязь», вышедший одновременно с фрегатом, отдалился в тот же день для исполнения данного ему поручения, определить по пути астрономически положение острова Дажелет, и ширину теплого течения в Корейском проливе, вследствие чего пришел во Владивосток 17-го, а клипер «Наездник» 14 мая.

Корвет «Ренда» с Его Высочеством Великим Князем Александром Михайловичем прибыл из Австралии в Нагасаки с поврежденным приводом для поворота лопастей гребного винта; корвет «Витязь» был послан в Нагасаки

25 мая, согласно телеграммы, для сопровождения его до Владивостока, куда и прибыли 8 июня, а клипер «Разбойник» 18-го.

Таким образом, эскадра в полном своем составе, кроме лодки «Бобр», собрались на Владивостокском рейде только во второй половине июня месяца.

Портовые, дефектные и судовые работы.

Согласно резолюции Вашего Высокопревосходительства, положенной на рапорт моего предместника, от 22 декабря 1887 года за №814, 12-го мая в сопровождении Старшего помощника Командира порта Капитана 2 ранга Лаврова, Старшего артиллериста и минера порта Капитана 2 ранга Такаревского, Командира фрегата «Дмитрий Донской» и других лиц отправился на Эгершельд, чтобы лично убедиться в состоянии артиллерийского масла на судах французской эскадры в Тихом Океане, сообщенные флагманским Инженер Механиком Г. Edmond Mercier.

Посещение Владивостока иностранными военными судами.

Военные суда иностранных держав, плавая по преимуществу летом в северных морях, заходят ежегодно во Владивосток. Первым пришел 5 июля Американский корвет «Essex», простоявший до 11 июля; затем, через месяц, пришел французский крейсер «Primauguet» и лодка «Aspic» (10 августа), а 13 августа пришла английская лодка Linnet, Командир которой передал мне, что вновь назначенный Начальник Английской эскадры, сэр Novel Salmon, имеет намерение посетить Владивосток и, что он, имея флаг на вновь пришедший крейсер «Imperieuse», плавать с эскадрою из 12 судов вдоль нашего Уссурийского берега, адмирал находился при уходе лодки в Императорской гавани. Через два дня лодка «Linnet» ушла в море на соединение с эскадрою.

20 августа на рейд пришел под вице-адмиральским флагом крейсер «Imperieuse», в сопровождении авизо-яхты «Alacrity»; в тот же день в Амурский залив стали под Южным берегом остальные суда английской эскадры.

Тотчас по приходе на рейд, английский адмирал салютовал моему флагу по уставу и получил равное число выстрелов в ответ. Салют нации произведен английским адмиралом, проходя батарею Голдобина. В тот же день английский адмирал сделал мне визит, а также и визит Командиру порта, —я отдал визит тотчас, как адмирал вернулся от Контр Адмирала Ермолова.

22 августа сделал на фрегате обед для английского адмирала, к которому пригласил Штаб его, Командиров судов «Imperieuse» и «Linnet» («Alacrity» - в тот день ушел и его заменила лодка «Linnet») и Командира лодки «Aspic», вечером в тот же день был концерт в частном помещении, на который также пригласили ехать бывших у меня гостей; предложение мое было принято с видимым удовольствием, и адмирал Salmon оставался до конца.

На другой день английские суда ушли в море, а суда этой эскадры, стоявшие в Амурском заливе, ушли накануне.

В день ухода из Владивостока адмирал Salmon в 8 часов утра сделал мне прощальный визит. Желая ответить на его любезность, послал шлюпки с эскадры под парусами сопровождать фрегат «Imperieuse» при выходе с рейда.

25 августа на рейд пришел французский контр-адмирал Layrle, на броненосце «Jurenne», французский адмирал простоял на рейде до 6-го сентября. Стоявшая на рейде лодка «Aspic» заменялась последовательно «Vipere» и авизо «Parseval», последние простоял до 13 сентября. Командующий отрядом судов французской республики уже был в прошлом году во Владивостоке и видимо был чрезвычайно рад снова быть здесь. 30 августа суда его отряда «Jurenne» и «Vipere» приняли участие в празднестве дня тезоименитства Государя Императора.

Будучи извещен нашим посланником в Токио телеграммою, что в Владивосток отправился Председатель Верховного Совета Граф Ито и Морской Министр Граф Сайго, ожидал их со дня на день, но как оказалось впоследствии, Японская эскадра из 6 судов, проходя внутренним Японским морем, посетила некоторые порта Китая и Кореи и только 12 сентября пришла во Владивосток. На рейд вошли два судна: новый крейсер «Nanira» и броненосец «Fuso»; проходя Голдобинскую батарею, «Fuso» салютовал нам по сигналу с крейсера «Naniva», шедшим передовым, и как только суда эти стали на якорь, «Naniva-Kan» салютовал моему флагу. Почти в одно время остальные суда Японской эскадры под флагом контр-адмирала Ito Yuno, дойдя до Босфора, стали там на якорь.

На другой день Контр-Адмирал Ито и все Командиры сделали мне визит; в 11 часов утра я со своим Штабом и Командирами судов сделал визит Японским Министрам, а 14-го утром отвечал Контр Адмиралу Ито и Командирам судов.

Пребывание здесь Японских гостей совпало с прибытием 11-го сентября Генерал Губернатора Генерал Адьютанта Барона Корфа, которому Министры, адмирал и Командиры 13-го сделали визиты и Барон Корф лично всем ответил.

14-го я сделал на фрегате обед, на который были приглашены Японские гости, Командиры судов их и нашей эскадр, Генерал Губернатор, представители порта, крепостных войск, а также и города.

Я предложил тост в честь Японского Императора, и Граф Ито, на французском языке, предложил тост в честь Государя Императора. Граф Ито и Граф Сайго были во фраках с лентами Белого Орла, у остальных офицеров я заметил также русские ордена, некоторые из них были в Петербурге с Графом Сайго.

Начальник Штаба Японского флота Вице Адмирал Visconte Nire, прибыв в свите Графа Сайго, был не здоров, и я его не видел.

15-го по соглашению с портовым Начальством в нашем собрании был устроен концерт и после него вечер с ужином по подписке, что привлекало массу публики; вечер этот вышел очень удачен. По приходе в Йокогаму посланник наш Действительный Статский Советник Шевич благодарил меня за оказанный Японским Сановникам прием, которые, по его же словам, остались в высшей степени довольны радушием и гостеприимством чинов эскадры и местных властей.

16-го утром все суда ушли к берегам Японии, они предполагали обойти западный берег и внутренним морем вернуться в Йокогаму.

По газетам я ожидал в октябре еще прихода Начальника отряда судов Соединенных Штатов Контр-Адмирала Chandler, но в виду позднего времени года, посещение это вероятно было отменено.

В заключении считаю долгом доложить Вашему Высокопревосходительству, что, несмотря на не вполне благополучные климатические условия, в особенности в начале и в конце пребывания вверенной мне эскадры в наших водах, но благодаря заботливости флагманского доктора Действительного Статского

Советника Смирнова и судовых врачей, состояние здоровья команды весьма удовлетворительно.

Начальник эскадры
в Тихом Океане, Вице-адмирал Шмидт

223
영국의 거문도 재점령 가능성에 대한 정보 보고
V. P. Shmidt (1889. 1. 11) ➡ N. M. Chikhachev

RGAVMF, F.417, Op.1, D.572, L.51-51ob.

Ваше Превосходительство, Николай Матвеевич

Бывший с фрегатом «Дмитрий Донской» прошлого ноября в Йокогаме, посланник наш Д.Е. Шевич сообщил мне на словах, совершенно частным образом, как ему, что англичане снова заняли порт «Гамильтон».

Отправляя корвет «Витязь» в обратное плавание, я воспользовался этим случаем, чтобы, по пути из Нагасаки в «Рейгон», он зашел в бухту «Гамильтон», хотя бы для производства там практической пальбы из орудий, что Англичане часто делают.

В настоящее время я уже получил уведомление от Командира «Витязь» флигель адъютанта Макарова, что в этом порте, со времени оставления его Англичанами, никаких перемен не произошло!

Считаю своим долгом сообщить Вашему Превосходительству об этом на тот случай, если подобный слух, как это было в Йокогаме дойдет и до Петербурга!

Вместе с этим имею честь сообщить Вашему Превосходительству, что я предполагаю, идя из Сингапура в Нагасаки, побывать в Маниле, что заставит сделать лишние 200 миль от прямого пути.

Затем, если обстоятельства позволят, то я предполагаю продолжить плавание мое из Манилы через Фугао в «Чи-фу» на крейсере «Нахимов», а отсюда на коммерческом пароходе в Тьен-зинь и если ничто не помешает, то и далее до Пекина, о чем мною сообщено нашему посланнику А.М. Кумани.

Возвратившись в Чи-фу на крейсер «Нахимова», я предполагаю идти в Нагасаки с заходом в Чимульпо, где и предполагаю быть в начале будущего апреля. В половине же марта пошлю в Чимульпо лодку «Кореец»,- где и будет оставаться до нового распоряжения. Что же касается до клипера «Разбойник», то он так же много плавал, что не лишним будет постоять ему два-три месяца в Нагасаки в полной готовности идти по назначение, куда надобность укажет. В половине января «Кореец» войдет в док в Йокогаме для окраски подводной части, что требуется на основании приказа Управления Морского Министерства от 14-го мая за № 72.

Примите уверение в совершенной моей преданности и уважени.

Владимир Шмидт

«Нагасаки», 30-го декабря 1888 года

224
‘코레예츠’호의 블라디보스토크 하계 훈련 참가 계획

V. P. Shmidt (1889. 7. 10) ➡ A. A. Peshchurov

RGAVMF, F.417, Op.1, D.572, L.122-3.

Начальник Эскадры в Тихом Океане.
Владивосток
29 июня 1889г.
№ 303
Управляющему Морским Министерством.

Рапорт

Крейсер «Адмирал Нахимов» под моим флагом, снялся с якоря из Нагасаки 9-го мая; На пути следования предполагалось зайти в порт Лазарева, куда выслал лодку «Манджур» накануне моего ухода.

Догнав на пути эту лодку, сигналом показал рандеву вышеназванный порт, а 11-го мая в 8 ½ час утра встал на якорь в южной части бухты, против города Генсан, куда лодка «Манджур» пришла через 2 ½ часа.

Город Генсан или по-корейски Вонсан, растянут около мили в длину по Южному берегу бухты и состоит из небольших Корейских домиков, с весьма бедной обстановкой.

Японцы, поселившиеся здесь, составляют отдельный квартал, довольно благоустроенный; в особенности же отличатся дома Японского Консула и пароходной компании Nippon Yusen, которая держит правильное сообщение, каждые три недели, между Нагасаки, Корейскими портами и Владивостоком.

В тот же день в 3 ½ часа снялся с якоря и обошел только бухту Лазарева.

В ½ 7 часа утра 13-го мая встал на бочку на рейде Владивостока; лодка

«Манджур» пришла в 10 часов. Копия рапорта о переходе лодки во Владивосток, при сем представляю. Об этой лодке считаю доложить Вашему Превосходительству, что по произведенному смотру, я нашел ее в отличном состоянии и порядке.

Канонерскую лодку «Кореец» оставил в Нагасаки, в полной готовности идти в Корею по требованию нашего поверенного в делах в Сеуле; время, однако, проходило в Нагасаки бесполезно для летних занятий, и потому для выполнения их вытребовал 28-го мая «Кореец» во Владивосток, без замены ее лодкой «Манджур»; в тоже время просил телеграммой г. Вебера в случае надобности вызвать лодку из Владивостока. До настоящего времени надобности вероятно никакой не было; что дало возможность лодки исполнить вполне программы по Минной и Артиллерийской частям и уйти 22 июня из Владивостока к Южной части Сахалина, куда согласно приказания Ваше Превосходительства одно из судов Эскадры должно было быть послано, с Начальником отдельной съемки, для выполнения Гидрографических работ. Сделав хронометрическую связь Корсаковского поста с Владивостоком, лодка должна была вернуться около 10-го июля, и затем снова идти, но получив приказание окончить кампанию 31-го июля, предполагаю послать для этой цели лодку «Манджур», если к тому времени придет клипер «Крейсер».

Из данного поручения клиперу «Разбойник» в Южном Тихом Океане, согласно письма Начальника Главного Морского Штаба, от 23-го декабря пришлого 1888 года за №63, он не выполнил касающиеся острова Биллин [ ].

關係資料

1
거문도 사건 전말

英吉利國人來據巨文島 是時英吉利國 與俄羅斯國 以中央亞細亞境界有紛議 將以干戈相見 於攻守上爲有關係 突然派艦隊 占領我巨文島 築砲臺 盖恐俄人由東洋經朝鮮海邊 而窺印度也 我政府不發一言 惟俄國問其許否於淸國 淸廷卽使北洋海軍提督丁汝昌 率軍艦三隻 往日本長崎島 見英國艦隊司令長官詰責之 英廷遂許還 淸廷又向俄國 約以他日 俄亦不得占據該島之意 以其約示英 乃於二十四年丁亥 英罷占據之計 而還於我 巨文島屬全羅道興陽縣 距距全羅道樂安郡距沿岸約三百里 北緯三十四度一分至五分東經百二十七度六分至八十二分成以三箇島嶼 故亦稱以三山島 西曰西島 有長·德二村 東曰東島 有柚·竹二村兩島相抱 自南延北爲一峽 其南端更有倭島成海灣 灣內水深自八十尺至一百二十尺 可泊十餘軍艦 英人稱曰哈密爾敦港 實爲戰略上要衝之海島 又爲俄人航通西比利亞俄國領地之要路 故世人皆注目於此 英人所築波市(止)場與廢垣·殘壘之遺跡 至今尙存 近日英艦及各國軍艦每年數次來泊

2
영국의 거문도 점거 및 러시아의 대마도 점거 시도

對馬島紀事

對馬島는古者의我國所屬이라地辟俗陋ᄒᆞᆫ故로歷世의棄而不治러니맛ᄎᆞᆷ내日本管轄이된지數百年에人口와物産이至今토록繁盛치못ᄒᆞ나그地利를議論ᄒᆞ면海軍屯營處는甚宜ᄒᆞ다ᄒᆞ고ᄯᅩ該島南北은頗長ᄒᆞ고東西는最狹ᄒᆞ되西北은朝鮮釜山으로相對ᄒᆞ야人烟을可히通ᄒᆞᆯ너라分ᄒᆞ야두리되니一名은上島니稍大ᄒᆞ고一名은下島니稍小ᄒᆞ고ᄯᅩ數十小島잇고上下島間에一大灣이잇ᄡᅳ니名曰淺港이라ᄌᆞ못碇泊의甚便ᄒᆞᆫ고로數十年前의俄國이南岸地를來占ᄒᆞᄂᆞ未幾에自退ᄒᆞ더니近日各國新報의論說ᄒᆞ되俄國이英國으로더부러形勢를互爭ᄒᆞ다가英國이我國巨文島를先據ᄒᆞᆫ故로俄國이ᄯᅩᄒᆞᆫ傍近一島를佔據코ᄌᆞᄒᆞ야我國濟州에有意ᄒᆞ야該島險阻崎嶇를詳細히採探ᄒᆞ되結船키어려운고로俄國이ᄯᅩᄒᆞᆫ對馬島를다시佔據코ᄌᆞᄒᆞᆫ다ᄒᆞ고或云俄國政府에셔日本政府에致書ᄒᆞ야其意를告示ᄒᆞᆫ故로日本政府에셔深以爲憂ᄒᆞ야數月前에이믜陸兵八十人을對馬島의派送ᄒᆞ여防守ᄒᆞ라ᄒᆞ고ᄯᅩ沿海南岸地에장찻海防을設ᄒᆞᆫ다ᄒᆞ더라

3
열강의 약소국 침략 형세와 영국의 거문도 점거

論天下時局

天下大勢治則亂危則安治亂在於世運安危係乎人心然亦不無大小貧富衆寡强弱之勢焉今地球九洲星羅萬國而歐洲列國獨擅富强五洲萬國將不免被其凌夷其或世運之興替歟抑亦人心之存亡歟誠天下治亂安危之一大變局也試思亞非利加及阿西亞尼亞兩洲概歸歐洲各國之所呑噬復無所謂獨立國者南北亞米利加兩洲現有二十餘國獨美利堅爲一大强國與歐洲各國相頡頑然亦爲歐人之來侵鑿殺土民自成一國者也若其土人則山陬巖僻僅有遺類惟我亞細亞一洲鴻蒙肇闢聖人首出禮樂法度衣冠文物井井有圖治策安之具爲萬國之所嚮慕矣廼玆氣運變否北半失於俄羅斯西疆喪於土耳古南徼亦被英法人占據間有暹羅波斯等國尙保獨立而其勢岌岌乎旣濱滅亡矣然則五洲之大萬國之衆槪已臣服於歐洲各國而獨能自守者我國及中國日本而已爲此三國者將何以獨立自强永保無虞乎見今東西各國互相講疑結有條約交有通商輒據公法定議批准然噫彼各國一見利已則背公法而不畏棄條約而不媿終致大之抑小强之凌弱更無和疑之存其間者悲夫昔者西班牙遣使於呂宋請以牛皮一張大之地曰將築一室焉王許之西人扯裂牛皮細如綫相繼爲數萬尺繞占一方曰如約焉王雖大駭亦難强辨於是西人建厦於其地募兵於其地終襲王城俘其王而墟其國永爲其屬縣近聞法人密使於馬島與其叛徒締約曰爾若得志割地與法其徒終不得志而誅絶焉法人求遂其約於馬島政府而不聽廼執此啓衅攻陷馬島遂爲其保護國甚矣兩國之逞詐謀而行不義也彼全歐列邦專尙詐力互相侵伐甲起乙仆殆無甯歲將未知周烏之止誰屋秦鹿之死誰手此非惟人心之尙詐好利職由天下一亂之運也歟又査各國新報有可窺察天下時局者焉往年正月中法開衅從事詰戎法據台灣安南迭爲輸贏英人假兵於埃及以鎭內亂戡之不克伊國亦侵抹索華以爲其屬二月俄英互爭阿非干之境將啓兵端三月英人要占我巨文島俄人亦求對馬島於日本意其艦隊所經形勢必爭故也噫禍基於泰西兩國而將恐延及我東洋此亦有志者所可另籌也五月中法續和法兵撤還而安南終屬於法我亞洲旣失一大國也九月英俄幸保舊盟不至尋衅而德西兩國又爭加羅拉仁一島未卽整頓是月英緬有事十月英兵入緬境又塞爾維與伯布里搆衅東歐各國調兵而護其境泰西卽皆派使土京謀其平而未成十一月英兵擒緬王夷其宗祀我亞洲又失一大國也是時馬島亦歸

法人之保護十二月德西始和而德人更據大洋一島英俄復爭形勢於亞非利加埃及叛徒纔失其勢再爲猖獗故英又發兵而住□焉嗚呼一年之間天下事變如此況我亞洲實失兩大國乎東洋各國當道之所宜審愼而綢繆於未雨者也事變之來□智人達士未可以逆覩豫算然國勢之强弱不在乎兵卒之衆募(*sic*)國計之貧富無關乎版圖之大小惟是君民之心力籌富强圖安於未危制治於未亂內無渙散乖隔之憂外得兩國結托之援雖百萬歐人不能窺覦其隙寔所以應天下時局也切願時務君子留心熟籌於治安之方焉

4
李元會의 巨門島經略使 임명

經理疆場

同月二十六日漢城判尹李元會經略使興陽巨文島出去

5
영국군의 거문도 철수 현황(申報 기사)

譯日報紀巨文島事

二月十五日申報云英人歸還巨文島一事本報已屢次譯登玆閱東報□言尙有瑣屑情形爲從前所未錄者因再譯列左方據云英國政府所借朝鮮巨文島業已歸還刻下□軍所用一切物件拍買已畢房屋亦折毁無遺惟當時田該島架至上海之電線費至英金七萬磅合日本銀四十二萬九千一百圓□云早經收拾尙存線頭在島上交高麗人暫行看管海口□置鉄條三根五千餘碼需英金四十餘磅備放水雷之用刻下竟如海底撈針杳不可得回亦托高麗人打撈不准被他人所竊約本月三號統領船到時載運回國其房料與外面所打之梅花樁經長崎華商王大利以二百五十元買去□云此本應値五千元惜乎載運多費水脚耳守島英兵一百名先於上月二十三日搬運重具附兵船至香港矣

6

거문도 경략사 부임 보고

巨文島經略使狀啓

同日全羅道興陽縣巨文島經略使李元會謄報謹依傳敎臣於二月二十六日辭陛二十七日到仁川港二十九日辰時乘中國泰安兵船三十日酉時到泊於巨文島日暮仍宿船中本月初一日早朝下陸留二日東西南三島周察形止初三日卯時還乘泰安兵船初四日申時回泊於仁川港下陸量度事力□理方略臣才質魯鈍見識淺薄不能對揚萬一悸懼悚懔罔知攸達巨文島內事實一從聞見謹具別單以備乙覽緣由馳啓

7
영국 하원의 거문도 관련 논의(滬報 기사)

英員問答

西曆二月初一日英國下議院開門聚會時有院員數人詢問巨文島一事略謂該處所駐英兵是否將行撤退若果撤退該島將來如何處置未知英廷與中朝或別國立有合約否也大臣花加臣答曰外部大臣命於轉告諸君云巨文島之英兵將行撤退至於該島將何處置并未立有合約惟聞高麗將委官到該島以□英軍船之撤退與否然英廷雖未與高廷立約而已得中朝□允將來不准別國佔距是□及高麗地方也我英廷之所以撤兵者係據水師官員繼陳而後爲之初英踞是島時乃在一千八百八十五年是年水師提督杜威奉水師府之命於五月派船往佔既佔之後杜軍門察其形勢知非用武之地□□於英廷當棄之而莫取時有數水師大員亦謂此島無濟於事合棄地也至是年秋聞杜軍門□往別嚴察其缺者□水師提督咸美頓奉命査究是島之情形詳晰稟覆英廷亦謂是島非關緊要踞之□於事一無裨益若於太平時踞之則徒費餉項若於有戰務時踞之不□無益且□□以□弱以此之改英廷□□計棄之□□踞巨文而後已經置有電線由香港以達該島復在該島支架板屋以居兵士以貯軍需其所費餉項若干則未得而知也右係滬報

8
러시아와 영국의 군사 갈등 전망

擬設雷船

申報云當英俄齟齬之時有英人查理士馬雲者一新論刊布其新報略謂若英國與俄國從事疆場則英國戰艦當波羅的海及黑海兩口嚴爲巡緝以扼俄人之吭又當攻取琿春黑龍江及西伯利濱海一帶地方云云俄人見之甚爲震動俄廷卽決意製造淺水砲船一隊以駐守黑龍江以防敵人進攻查黑龍江地面俄國居民不過十萬之衆駐紮琿春之俄兵亦不過五千名且此兵原設以防華人若英軍一至恐俄人未易固守俄人運兵遲緩英軍則迅速從事俄國添兵赴西伯利濱海地方必須半年可到而英國則由美洲之北根拿地宴巴思佛火車路經過祇二十六日卽可駛抵琿春矣俄廷知琿春黑龍江爲英國所必爭之地是以加意整頓刻雖與英相安無事仍在他國定造砲船六艘以資守護云此係去年十二月念四日記載

9
러시아의 싱가포르 정탐(滬報 기사)

俄人圖英

正月念六日滬報云去月下旬有俄國大鐵甲戰船來抵叻中少爲停泊□□赴麻六甲海而約遊數日即復回叻現該船已□回俄國矣查該船前日泊於叻海時其管駕官乘坐小輪船在叻港四行遊玩據知者看俄船此次出巡幷非爲遊玩計當該管駕遊叻之際已將叻地新築各砲臺幷爲繪出圖形携回船中即鼓輪疾駛而去觀此則俄人之叵測不已可見耶夫英俄去歲已伏隱嫌今俄人之擧□如斯英亦不可不防其漸也

10
영국의 러시아 고립 외교(滬報 기사)

電報補譯

七月初九日英京發來電報云德國及奧國兩皇相見以通好間而俄皇不與其列由此觀之則俄皇與德奧交好之意不免有囿矣又云英國外務大臣照會俄廷言俄國在巴度暗地方所有設施英國槪不潤洽右係滬報

11

러시아 견제를 위한 영·중 연대 제안(*Times* 기사)

英報偉論

英京大晤士日報云現中國日形强盛振興之圖正未可量在英務宜加意與□□好得以合力同心併抵俄人呑噬之始有補於大局也該報之言如此所見殊大奚譯而登之

12
러시아의 불가리아 진출에 대한 영국의 대응책 고민(1)(滬報 기사)

英電彙譯

滬報云西曆九月念三號倫敦路透局來電云阿而倫之勃而番斯地方近有揭□之亂由兵捕協力卽行解散又云俄國現擬添派兵一千五百名駐守琿春已由凹提煞起程前往又云英國下議院議員有以勃而忌利亞事問諸宰臣答言此事恐有大擧故刻尙未便宣揚也又念四號來電云英國前戍埃及兵一旅刻下正資保護想須久駐此地未能調開也又云勃而忌利亞國深恐俄人侵奪故特結好於土耳其請爲保護

13

러시아의 불가리아 진출에 대한 영국의 대응책 고민(2)(滬報 기사)

英京電語

昨接西九月二十五號倫敦路透局專電致本館云今年倫敦所聚印度及英屬各國之物設爲博覽會業已畢事玆悉會中人復行集議擬於明年再擧一會又云俄國近下一哀的美頓書與勃而忌利亞約以國王及各大臣從緩議擧所獲之亂黨皆須釋放又云某外務大臣力欲塞爾維亞勃而忌利亞搖而里司及土耳奇四國聯爲一氣

14
러시아의 인도 침략 의도

露兵南侵

二月十九日日本報云據見英國新聞則魯國將欲南侵印度勢頗汲汲現已集兵於賈婁地者步兵六萬騎兵四萬又有兵四萬不日可抵矣英國亦於印度地方防禦甚密尙未開戰云若兩國兵連其勝敗未可豫料然殊屬世界之一大變局也

15

러시아의 청 및 유럽 침략 의도(申報 기사)

防俄芻言

俄國報之云有人進言於俄皇請造鐵路由俄京直達琿春以備將來調兵運餉之用蓋緣中國近來留意邊防故勸令俄皇豫爲之所云云賓紅閣主人披覽至此而不禁有感焉夫今之談時事者□以法爲不可不備其次則莫如日本從前天津之案法人幾□干戈幸得曾文正公周旋其間幾費心力始得言和至昔年安南一事法人又復大興師旅□滅我藩服蹂躪我邊疆傷夷我士卒耗費我資財後乃大創於宣光始得俯首帖耳然虎狼之國豈終能慴服其心一朝□□瀛埏能保不重修舊怨乎是宜備

16
러시아의 중앙아시아 점령(日本報 기사)

阿富汗事件

閏四月二十八日日本報云接到俄國陸軍機關新聞有俄國銳章於蠶食阿富汗印度布哥羅等地擴張中央亞細亞之版圖使英人不得履阿富土耳一步之地若使發哥及喜拉陶爲英所有則俄國該處之商務不啻頓見蕭索俄之與布哥羅及中國之路永爲間隔且影印占有喜拉陶則英國之兵商登艦必由波斯港灣渡斯俄之保護其境內港岸實與俄之裏海相接門戶之側安容敵人之止泊乎權利攸係不惟不早定取舍(*sic*)云

17

터키를 둘러싼 영·러 갈등(時報 기사)

外洋來電

英土經口歐東土之執政謂埃及之約如已允洽然則塞卜洛斯之可約否因之擧行按同治季年俄土用兵土人敗績致失黑海之濱巴統城卡斯城二鎭之地乞援于英英以勁兵駐地中海東距近小亞細亞部之塞卜洛斯島以策應之迨俄土行成土復與英立保護之約遂以此島假令徵其地租以充兵餉約載如將來該二城歸土則英亦以島見歸云云刻土人如行埃及新約則與英奧意諸國合俄國又將啓戎故敬復申明前約盖欲堅英人保護之盟也右俱係時報

18

베이징 일본 공사관에서의 회담

(明治二十三年三月淸國北京日本公使館ニ於テ)

中島 雄 稿

京城再度ノ變亂後間モナク朝鮮國王ヨリ金鏞元權東壽外四名ノモノヲ密使トシテ露國浦鹽斯德ニ差遣セシコトアリソノ密使ノ歸路ニ携ヘ來リシ露國ヨリノ回答密事ナルモノハ直チニ國王ノ手中ニ收納セラレシニ由リ當時ニ在テ朝鮮國ノ督辨交涉通商事務タル金宏集スラ最初ヨリ一向何事ヲ知ルニ至ラザルハ實ニ當惑ノ至リナリトテ同氏ヨリ京城ニ駐箚セル某國代理公使ニ直話セシコトアリ國王ヨリノ密書ニハ何事ヲ記載アリシヤ之ヲ知ル由シナケレドモ爾時世人ノ傳稱スル所ニ據レバ京城再度ノ變亂後朝鮮國ノ人心恟々トシテ今ニモ日淸ヨリ駐屯ノ兵隊ハ干戈ヲ以テ相ヒ見ントスルヲ憂惧ノ餘露國ハ隣邦ナレバソノ保護ヲ請求スベシト發議スルモノアリ彼ノモルレンドルフ氏モソノ一人ニテコノ議ハ一時廢案トナリシモ國王ハ遂ニ密書ヲ以テ浦鹽斯德ノ地方官ヲ經過シ露國ニ此事ヲ請求セシニ露國ヨリ回答セシ密書中ニハ日淸兩國ヨリ現駐ノ兵隊ヲ撤回スルニ至ルモ他日朝鮮ニ事故アルニ遇ヘバ何日ニテモ兵ヲ出スノ權ヲ有スト聞ク露國モ朝鮮ニ對シテハ日淸兩國ト一般隣國ナルノ故ニ同樣ノ權ヲ得ベキハ勿論ナリトノ事ヲ記載アル由ナルヲ以テ淸英ノ兩國ハ大イニ戒心スル所アリ此ニ其翌明治十八年 淸曆光緖十一年西洋一千八百八十五年 アフガニスタン疆界ノ案件ヨリ英露ノ和約將ニ破裂セントスルノ景況アリシ時ニ當リ英國政府ハ露國ニ先鞭ヲ着ケラレンコトヲ畏レソノ軍艦ヲシテ朝鮮國巨文島ヲ占據セシムルニ至ル是ニ於テ李鴻章ハ水師提督丁汝昌ヲシテ軍艦ニ搭坐シ先ツ朝鮮國南陽ヨリ漢城ニ入リ國王ニ謁見セシ後參判嚴世永同モルレンドルフ氏ヲ同件シ巨文島ニ廻航シテ實況ヲ查驗セシメ一面ハ總理衙門ヨリ在英淸國公使曾紀澤ニ訓令ヲ發シ英國政府ニ談判スル事ヲ命シ終ニ英艦ヲシテ巨文島ヨリ退去セシメタルモ壹ニ是レ淸國政府ト商議セシ結果ナリト思ハルソノ證據ニハ英艦ノ巨文島ヲ占據セシ當初朝鮮國督辦交涉通商事務金允植ヨリ我國ヨリ京城ニ駐箚スル代理公使ニ宛テ居間調停ヲ請ヒタル照會ニハ

爲照會事照得本年三月晦日英國水師佔住巨文島一事由我政府派送政府有司堂上嚴協辦交涉通商事務穆前往該島査看情形果見英國兵艘來泊該島々上樹有旗幟該派員不勝詑異轉往長崎見英國水師提督詰問其故並送函辯駁據該提督復函稱已電知本政府一俟回信立卽函復等因該派員回來已久杳無音信嗣於本月初七日英國總領事阿來署面談稱有英國政府信到北京英公使館由北京公館寄信前來稱巨文一島是暫住非久計也只要將煤炭在岸上寄庫更無他事等語査英國條約第八款云英國師船所用軍裝物料及一切餉需各件可在朝鮮通商各口存寄交英國委派之員看管惟煤炭係是師船物料不應在未通商口岸存寄如諸國有事則本國應守局外之分不可以地借人准其暫住此係公法所無斷不能行爲之備文照會請煩貴代理公使査照將此事由轉達貴國政府諒照爲隣誼舊好起見妥爲居間調處是所深望焉須至照會者

トアリテ同時ニ金督辦ヨリ在京城各國使臣ニ宛テタル照會モ略ボ之ト同文言ナリシニ其後英國政府ハ淸國政府ヨリノ談判ヲ辭却セザリシモノト見ヘ金督辦ヨリ再度我代理公使及ビ各國使臣ニ宛テタル照會ニハ

爲密行照會事前巨文島一事照會業經貴署收照在案嗣後再有英國總領事阿來本署有所面談該島事應由兩國政府相議庶有妥辦之道爲此請煩貴代理公使將此情由密稟貴政府亮照切冀暫勿行前送照會所請調停之事一俟日後如何辦法再行商酌奉告仍請密稟于貴政府始行調停可也爲此備文照會須至密咨者

トアルノミナラズ英艦ノ巨文島ノ退去セシニ及ビ朝鮮國王ヨリ使臣ヲ北京ニ派遣シ禮部ヲ經過シテ差出シタル謝表ナリト云フモノニハ

(前略)巨文島本朝鮮舊地橫被英人侵佔屢索不歸今蒙大皇帝執理與爭英人顧念邦交慨然讓出俾本國世守之土不致屬之他人敝國近年冦難頻仍天朝字小之心有加無已感激隆恩實無旣極(後略)

トアレバナリ而シテ前ニ朝鮮國王ヨリ密使トシテ露國浦鹽斯德ニ差遣セラレシ金鏞元權東壽外四名ノモノハ其後李鴻章ヨリ朝鮮國王ニ勸告シテ遠島ノ形ニ處セシメタリ英艦ノ巨文島ヲ佔據セシ年ノ秋間ニ於テ淸國政府ヨリ大院君ヲ開釋セシ時ノ上諭ニハ

前因朝鮮兵變幾危宗社李昰應于亂軍索餉不能禁止事後復置不問以致輿論紛々咎爲禍首朝廷軫念藩服命將出師殄厥渠魁驅除叛黨當時審察該處情勢若李昰應不離本國則亂萠尙未有艾特命安置近畿優其廩餼並准該國王歲時派員省問以慰其思慕之情所以防隱患而全私恩者無徵不至李昰應到保定後該國曾兩次咨請禮部代奏懇恩放還彼時因該國大難甫平人心未靖且李昰應甫經獲罪降旨宣示毋許瀆陳迄今時閱三年李昰應又以年老

多疾灑陳怨艾私衷具呈申懇特命李鴻章傳至天津驗視屬實玆復據禮部奏該國王遣使臣閔種默等恭賫表文籲求恩釋情詞迫切至于再三朝廷孝治爲先于藩屬彌深矜恤念省愆之日久惘逮養之情殷宜沛殊施俾伸孺慕李昰應加恩准其開釋卽著李鴻章派委妥員護送回國並著禮部傳知該國王此係朕法外施仁李昰應固應永戴洪恩愼持晩節該國王尤當痛懲前車之失去讒遠佞親仁善隣刻々以勵精圖治爲心庶幾內衅悉除外侮不作以無負朝廷覆庇矜全有加無已之至意寔於該國王有厚望焉欽此

トアリシトコロ當初閔泳翌(ママ)ハ大院君ノ歸國スルヲ欲セズ淸國政府ノ之ヲ開釋セントスルノ模様アルヲ聞キ親ツカラ天津ニ來リ百方計畫スル所アリシモ大院君ハ開釋セラレテ保定ヨリ天津ニ到達スルニ及ビ閔氏ハ大院君コソ我ガ不俱戴天ノ讎ナレト言ヒ觸ラシ之ニ面スルヲ嫌ヒ避テ芝罘ニ往シガ天津海關道周馥ヨリ李鴻章ノ內意ヲ以テ呼ビ還サレ夫ヨリ李鴻章ニ說得セラレシ末閔氏ハ大院君初メ李戴冕朴齋純等ヲ天津水師營務處ニ於テ饗應シソレヨリ大院君ト同件シテ歸國以後更ニ香港ニ渡航セシコトアリ閔氏ノ香港滯在ハ相應ニ日子ヲ消過セシヲ以テ當時世上ニテハソノ何ニカ爲メニスル所アルナリト流傳セシガ果セルカナ跡ニテ聞ケバ同氏ハ同處ヨリ轉シテ露國聖彼得堡ニ航セントセシモ英淸兩國ハ彼ノ朝鮮國王ヨリ密使ヲ浦鹽斯德ニ派遣シ露國ノ保護ヲ請求ノ一事ヨリ深ク戒心スル所アリシニヤ終ニ人ヲシテ閔氏ニ說テ國ニ歸ラシメタリト云フ是ヨリ先北京ノ言官中ニ於テ李鴻章ノ朝鮮政略ヲ非難スルモノアリ曰ク李鴻章ハ國家東顧ノ憂ヲ絶スル爲メナリトテ朝鮮ヲシテ歐米各國ト條約ヲ締結セシメシニ爾來却テ種々ノ葛藤ヲ惹キ起スニ至リタルハ是レ禍ヲ買ヒタルナリトアリシ折柄壬午[淸曆光緒八年我明治十五年]ノ夏間彗星東北ニ出現セシヨリ牽强附會ノ說ヲ立テ李鴻章ノ前言ニ驗ナキヲ咎ムルモノ多キヲ以テ皇太后モ殆ンド之ガ爲メ熒惑セラレントセシコトモアリタル由ヲ傳聞以後李鴻章ハソノ懷ヲ安ンズル能ハズ然ルニモルレンドルフ氏旣ニ用ヲ爲スニ足ラズ又淸國ヨリ總理交涉通商事宜トシテ朝鮮ニ駐箚セシムル陳樹棠ナルモノハ原來廣東ノ一富翁ニシテオ力モ氣力モナキモノナルノミナラズ巨文島及ビ露國書記官スペーヤ氏渡韓ノ事件等ニ付テモ李鴻章ニ詳細ノ報告スラ爲サヾルモノナレバ是亦用ヲ爲スニ足ラズ更ニ何人ヲ使フベキヤト正サニ思考ノ間ニ於テ袁世凱ノ大院君ヲ朝鮮ニ護送シテ歸リ來リシニ是レ用ヲ爲サシムルニ足ルモノナリト斷定セシニヤ陳樹棠ノ代員トシテ袁世凱ヲ朝鮮ニ派遣スルコトヽハナレリ袁氏ハ武人出身丈ケ氣力モアリオ氣モアリ殊ニ京城ニ再度

ノ變亂アリシ時淸兵ヲ引率シテ王闕ニ進入シ日本兵ヲ攻擊セルノ故ヲ以テ朝鮮人中ニハ好評ヲ博セシノミナラズ就任ノ當初李鴻章ヨリ朝鮮政府ニ對シ袁氏ノ人ト爲リヲ賞揚セル添書ヲ携ヘ來ルヲ以テ朝鮮人等ノ信用殊ニ重ク今ヨリ巨文島モ還ルベク金玉均モ捕フベシトテ國中ノ難題ハ細大トナク袁氏ノ考議ニ付スルニ至リシニ袁氏モ亦會釋ナク之ヲ引受ケ自ツカラ其手札ニ監國使ト刷印セシトコロ米國代理公使ニ議論セラレ之ヲ止ムルニ至リシノミナラズ其後金玉均モ捕ヘ得ズ巨文島モ袁氏ノ力ニテハ還リ來ラズ袁氏ハ却テ自ツカラ巨文島ヲ回復スルノ手段ナリトテ在京城英國領事ニ親睦ヲ謀リシ一事ノ如キハ朝鮮人ノ冷笑スル所ト爲リ爾來追々信用ヲ失ナヒシヲ以テ李鴻章ハソノ帮助ト爲スノ思考ニヤ前任米國領事デニー氏ヲ朝鮮ニ吹擧シ其行ニ臨ミ次ノ三事ヲ以テ之ニ訓令セリト云フ

第一　韓爲中國之屬邦辦事必須有益中韓大局

第二　事涉洋務必竭誠相告

第三　與中國駐韓大員尤當和衷相接

右ノ情況ナルヲ以テデニー氏モ最初ハ李鴻章ノ訓令ヲ守ラントセシモノヽ如クニ思ハル是故ニソノ朝鮮ニ赴任ノ前ニ於テ我國ニ至リ去ル貴顯ト直話セシ言語中

(前略)某ガ朝鮮政府ノ事ヲ處スルニハ一切李鴻章ニ稟議シテソノ指揮ヲ仰ガザルベカラズ是ハ某ガ李鴻章ニ對スル公然ノ職分ナリ(後略)

トアリシガ同氏ノ袁世凱ト事ヲ同フスルヲ欲セザリシハ是時ヨリ既ニソノ胸中ニ横タハリタルモノト見ヘ同上ノ言語中

(前略)聞クガ如クナレバ方今朝鮮ニテハ彼ノ袁世凱ナル者ノ勢力甚ハガ强ク殆ンド全ク同國政府ノ權ヲ握リ萬事同人ノ指揮ニ出ルガ如キ情況ナリト若シ果シテ然ランニハ某ハ迚モ彼ガ如キ不分曉漢ノ下ニ立チテ善ク同國政府ノ事ヲ處スル事ヲバ爲シ得ザルベシ(後略)

トアリシトコロ朝鮮政府ハデニー氏ヲ以テ協辦內務府事兼外衙門掌文司堂ニ任ゼントスルニ及ビ袁氏ハデニー氏ヲ以テ外衙門ニ專任シ內務府ノ事ハ外國人ヲ以テ之ニ任ゼズ若シ朝鮮人ニテ決シ難キコトアラバ自ツカラ其顧問ニ當ラント百方デニー氏ノ任官ヲ妨阻セシモ國王ノ親裁ニテデニー氏ヲ協辦內務府尹トセシヲ以テ是ヨリ袁氏トデニー氏トノ間ニ軋轢ヲ生ジ袁氏ハ世ニイフ燒ケノ氣味合ヲ以テ益々干涉主義ヲ取リ朝鮮國王ノ聽ヲ聳ヤカサセントテ差シ出シタル上書並ニ喩言四條及ビ時事急務十欵ニハ

丙戌九月日袁世凱敬上書于朝鮮大王殿下世凱于役韓邦迄今五載自壬午秋冬已見殿下有心於勵精圖治期臻富强昕夕勤勞意慮良苦至今上下解體國敝民貧變故迭生危如累卵於殿下求治之初心實有大相逕庭者如殿下自引其咎則朝野竊有未安如朝臣適當其罪則淸議亦爲非是究其所以然之故蓋上有求治之心而小人因以誤之也如欲認眞求治則前數年已行無驗之謀畫應悉改圖如依前樣而恐求治無功而變亂將起査甲申之變金玉均等侈陳自强之計密獻自主之謀蠱惑尊聽無所不至迄其稍有藉手而誅戮大臣脅迫殿下幾至一發而不可收拾試思其平日之進言與其居心行事固大不相合矣可知小人之辯亂君心希圖權利陽引外援以强國實陰藉外援以亂國其遺誤非淺鮮也設使殿下於十月十七日以前察其居心揣其行事而疑之防之當不至此倘平日奸計遂成變生不測則殿下千百年不白之寃其將何以發明耶幸而賊臣誅戮轉危爲安世凱以爲小人陰謀必不復熾前日之傾覆尙可引鑑是亦朝鮮治亂之一大轉機也迨世凱請假歸省數月家食去冬復來從事而竊窺時勢又將有不堪設想者是以日夜呶々舌敝唇焦勸戒諸臣期望殿下永固宗社以保臣民不爲力薄才踈空言無補卒有今年七月之事夫小人者無非地望疏微處心卑汚欲圖富貴而羨利權疏微則必以利口動聽而使殿下信之卑汚則不以諂諛爲恥而使殿下親之迨親信旣久復爲富强之說以誘之叔爲新奇之論以惑之一入術中不可救止殿下亦爲因時變革度可自强而不知小人特欲資以改革朝政誅戮大臣爲一已富貴利權之計而不恤忘國家敗家之禍金玉均之故可思也然而小人之甘言詭最易察覺伏願殿下將金玉均等素日所進之言使人歷書于策置之坐右以時觀覽以爲烱鑒如有小人陳說於此符合者卽以金玉均視之繼察其居心行事當不爽矣此至近至白之明證也爲殿下慮莫善於此如小人自謂可用必富國强兵之術請姑假巧以事權若不至變亂朝政誤人家國者世凱後此抉目斷舌自服瞽狂之咎以謝此人世凱從事於斯者五年匡輔者數次懷耿々豈忍坐視顚危不思拯救所望殿下時思良葯苦口之利無令世凱徒深關方涕泣之情則幸甚謹擬喩言四條時事急務十欵乞採納焉

謹擬喩言四條附呈

一曰立國如立室中國與朝鮮東西密通比隣也東隣之傾覆則西隣之庭堂亦必暴露於外世凱西隣人也見東隣之室將欹每日叫呼於東隣之門外曰爾室宜急修理不然必傾其智者聞之知其言之不謬忻然應之其愚者視之邈然反以爲東隣之室欹於西隣何千乃日聒於此不惟不應且甚惡之於是傷心者必從此閉門聽棟撓榱折而不相聞問多情者仍復不辭勞怨時々勸去惟恐隣室之傾覆況世凱已代修數次能不關心耶

二曰朝鮮如破舟木已毁腐蓬已零落必易木換蓬以求其固縱現在無力重修亦當隨時査看漏處設法彌縫不謂同舟小人希圖舟中金幣不惟不肯彌縫而且故意搖撞使舟沈陷而後可

携金幣以逃如世凱充爲舟匠已代修數次殿下及諸臣民皆舟中人也爲舟匠任其搖撞儻舟一時疎忽修之不及舟中人不知漂流何處矣世凱來此去冬至今不及十月始而穆麟德事繼而金玉均事旣以今年七月事已撞其舟將沈者三世凱充當舟匠豈不難哉

三曰治國如醫朝鮮病入膏盲善醫者必蓄良葯然良葯苦口者不知其利於病也遂惡而絶之也是有以甘美之味進者病者善其適口而食之一食而病劇再食而病革至不可救而後知進美味者遺害則已晩矣

四曰一國如一身而徒華麗其服而室如懸磬無飮無食其何能久治國者宜先修內政後務外觀譬之人日果腹充腸雖衣服簡陋亦無所損不然飢餓不堪者卽日衣文繡其何以生此必然之理也

謹擬時事急務十欵附呈

一曰任大臣大臣者皆世受國恩與共休戚者也其爵已顯其祿已榮所謀者無非安國保家社爲永遠之計國家永遠卽其祿位永遠也宗社永遠卽其勳名永遠也況諸大臣中多有閱歷多知大義縱不能建奇功亦不至僨大事信之任之民服國安然亦須用之必不疑之疑之則不用方能有濟

二曰屛細臣細急於一己之名利而不顧國家之安危一得進倖能以小忠小信固人之心小善小慧悅人之意始則甘言巧計無所不至甚者賣國求榮何所不爲其爲禍可勝道哉夫小人者非無小才之可用然祇可分隷各司效其片長而不可日親君側與聞國政設使玉均泳孝英植等初無親信之權祇奔走於各司之下豈有甲申之禍耶

三曰用庶司用一人之聰明材力斷難勝萬幾之紛紜故聖如堯舜尙有叢脞之戒苟事無鉅細必斷於上積久弊生疏虞隨之小人因以隱窃政柄外若權歸於上其實已移於下此從古之弊而萬國之所無也爲庶事紛任於庶司而殿下綜核其大綱計其得失明其賞罰則不勞而自治不擾而有成矣

四曰收民心此時民心渙散急須挽回民爲治本未有本動而枝葉能茂者然所謂收民心者非小恩小惠之謂也近年水旱疾疫民困已極如擇一二捄弊之政實力去之再由名司大官議擧賢守令與民興利去害而久任之以課其殿最民無不翻然向化如響斯應如影隨形者也

五曰釋猜疑前者上下交疑人盡謀身此事之所以日廢而不能振作也爲殿下振靡起衰破疑乾斷可疑者退之可信者進之使人々各盡其所長猜疑之間渙然永釋則臣下感奮共濟時艱政治無不烝々日上矣

六曰節財用量入以爲出古人皆然近來庫儲支絀國債積累求諸實事則所爲無一成効蓋急於不急之務小人得資富强爲名而自求利益目如典圜局製藥局機器輪船等事豈非善擧然

以朝鮮之時勢論則不宜急此宜先修內政開財之源而認其力行節財之流而事必求實國帑充裕家給人足然後次第爲之徐圖富强如不量財賦之出入而只務外觀之侈大將効無而靡費日益財用竭而貧弱愈甚失今不治不可爲矣

七曰愼所聞君人者一國之元首臣下賢愚皆賴君上之採擇每者不肖群小希圖事變幸災樂禍於中取利欺罔之弊百計叢生或揣摩上意因以利誘或甘言悅耳以夬聽聞或聳辭危語以冀恐動此俱雜類之輩可罪而不可近者也聽言者須先審其言之能否近理繼察其言之參否屬實稍有欺罔則屛棄遠方以清進言之路儻明知姑容是養癰遺患將讒說日見其多正言日見其少非國之福也引正去纔湯武所以興別纔去正桀紂所以亡殷鑒不遠可不愼諸

八曰明賞罰夫賞罰政令之本人心之所係也賞必信罰必行而後可以治國臣下或功或罪使有司論斷一秉公正嚴其黜陟不存一毫私見則賞罰明政令行人心亦治然歸服矣

九曰親所親中東相依數百年矣人心固結亦非一日朝發夕至緩急可共眞能親密相依則外人不能間訛謬亦可自息人心賴以奠安宗社賴以永保然所謂親密者非外面之具文也必推誠相與一心兩國彼此相信無世不濟況有中國之聲援外侮不作政可勵精圖治力謀富强亦何不利之有

十曰審外交在外交者萬國耳目之所係而亦爲國之要務也宜責任外署認眞周施外則盡禮內示以信方可久敦友誼各自相安如號令不一政出多門不但取笑於各國幷將見疑於外人且有不肖輩之居心叵測藉端愚弄以自逞其狡啓鯨呑之計取亂之道也如事無巨細必有諸大臣公議處之則何有陰謀何至有隱禍何至有甲申之變

以上管見迂論此下忱之所久蓄於殿下者非世凱有意祕之而諸臣故必蔽之也如前此世凱言之必有讒人議其後曰袁某將干預我內政此心叵測不可聽信世凱明知其無益故不敢仰瀆聰聽也如前此大王言之又有讒人議其後曰此人祗知保身不明大計搆誣抗陷以固奸謀此諸王明知無益而不敢出也揣諸讒人之心無非欲人盡解體聽其敗而以自取利此與金玉均等何異世凱每日不必於日本有玉均須防於朝鮮生玉均良以此也近聞殿下聰明決斷力在知非故敢有昧陳一二素性戇直於無顧忌尙乞亮察是幸

トアリ而シテデニー氏ハ彌々非干涉ノ主義ヲ取リ横流ノ極遂ニ一書ヲ著ハシ朝鮮ヲシテ獨立セシメザルバカラズトノ說ヲ立ツ世ニ謂フデニー氏ノパンフレツト便ハチ是ニテ彼ノ傳法教師ヲ以テ米國ヨリ朝鮮ニ渡航シ爾後朝鮮政府ノ雇ト爲リ在米朝鮮國公使館附ノ書記官ト爲リタルアルレン氏ノ如キモ亦デニー氏ノ說ニ左袒シ朝鮮ヲシテ獨立國ト爲サシメントト主張セシ論者ノ一人ナリキ獨立論ノコトニ付テハ因ヲ以テ玆ニ露國代理公使ウエバー氏ノ事ヲ提起スバシ前ニ露西亞ハ我國ヲ初メ西洋各國

ノ朝鮮ヲ獨立國視シテ對等ノ條約ヲ締結セシ當初ニ於テ朝鮮ヲ獨立國視スルコトニハ甚ハダ心ヲ用イザリシハ此國ヲ清國ノ屬邦トシテ置カバ假リニ中央亞細亞ニ於テ清人ガ一頭ノ露馬ヲ殺害スルモソノ償ハ朝鮮ノ土地ヨリ賠ハシムルニ足レリトノ如ク至極陰險ノ政略ナリシトコロウエバー氏露國ノ代理公使ト爲リ京城ニ駐箚セシヨリ專パラ朝鮮ヲ獨立國トスルニ心ヲ用フルハ蓋シ好意ヨリ出デタルニ非ズ朝鮮ヲシテ全ク清國トノ關繫ヲ絶セシメ而シテ後ニ爲ス所アラントスルモノナリト云フモノアリ或ヒハ然ランカ明治十九年 清曆光緖十二年西洋一千八百八十五年 朝鮮國王ハ保護ヲ露國政府ニ請求セリトノ風說再タビ朝鮮國京城ニ流傳セシ時ニ當リ袁世凱ハ清國ヨリ大兵ヲ派シ來リ罪ヲ朝鮮政府ニ問フベシトノ電報アリタリトノ旨ヲ以テ朝鮮政府ニ顚末ノ查明ヲ要求シ且ツ何故カ北洋艦隊中ノ數艘ハ之ト同時ニ仁川ニ廻航セリ

19
조선의 전략적 가치에 대한 1884년도 신문기사 모음집

RGAVMF, F.23, Op.1, D.52, L.30-34ob.

Русский Вестник в 1884 году
Сентябрь. Стр. 493, 494, 495

Прошлого года заключен и весною этого года ратифицирован торговый и мореходный трактат между Германией и Кореей, в силу коего немецким судам, приходящим в Корею и немецким купцам предоставлены обширные льготы. При обсуждении договора в парламенте, все в один голос твердили, что Германия с заключением этого договора приобрела «большие выгоды». Несколько позднее Германское Правительство внесло в палату проект закона о правительственных субсидиях пароходным компаниям, кои взялись бы содержать правильные почтовые сношения на Востоке. В числе прочих имели проектирование одного парохода, который, следуя из портов южного Китая Японским морем, должны были в определенные сроки заходить в Корею. Проект вызвал много возражений и не прошел, но и при этом никто не оспаривает важность «корейской линии», учреждение которой далеко не нравилось англичанам. В этом году в осеннюю сессию рейхстага в новом его составе, законопроект о субсидиях почтовому пароходству будет снова предложен палате, и теперь уже никто не сомневается, что в виду успехов колониальной политики правительства, законопроект будет встречен не только одобрительно, но и с полным сочувствием. Россия ближайший сосед с Кореей. Было бы даже странно, если бы Россия не воспользовалась выгодами своего положения и не вступила бы в близкие сношения с Кореей, связи с которой могут иметь значение далеко большее, нежели для Германии, или какой бы то ни было европейской державе. …установление более тесных связей с Кореей не останется без влияния на нашу промышленность, торговлю и отчасти даже мореходство в водах великого океана. Каждый торговый _______ в этих водах имеет для нас цену, поднимая значение нашего лучшего порта Владивостока, можно сказать пограничного с Кореей. Было время, когда из Владивостока мы могли продвинуться много дальше на юг и приобрести первенствующее, может быть даже исключительное влияние в Корее. Теперь время миновало и нам предстоит здесь соперничать с другими национальностями, опередившими нас. Россия может и должна стремиться приобрести силу во великом океане и особенно в морях Охотском и Японском, континентальный берег которого совершенно в нашей власти. Наши отношения с Кореей и Японией вполне дружественные, но это еще не значит, чтобы нам не оставалось ничего больше желать. Напротив и на Корею в Японии мы может иметь гораздо больше влияния, нежели теперь. И за пушкой и за обрезом ружья и за многими товарами, Япония и Корея тянутся совершенно в другую сторону. Японская военная миссия посетила __________ этим летом Россию, внимательно осмотрела наши военные учреждения, но центр своей деятельности перенесла в Германию. Могло бы быть совершенно иначе и это вполне зависит от нас. В последнее время мы обратили внимание на свой восток, стремились даже к усилению своего военного флота в домашних водах, но делаем ли мы это с полным сознанием и с важною смелостью? Не слишком ли мы осторожны и осмотрительны в ущерб своим интересам. Вклады не приобретаются без известных затрат и риска. В Корее мы почти на два года дали предупредить себя и вошли в переговоры о торговом трактате чуть ли не по примеру Германии, а у нас она под боком…. В Японском море мы у себя дома, а есть ли у нас там, хотя нечто подобное тому, что можно назвать флотом? Хорошо было заключить торговый договор с Кореей, но одного этого акта для развития торговли с этой страной далеко не достаточно. Следует подумать и о других средствах развития и поддержания зарождения отношений…

Не лучше ли было бы, чтобы эти деньги пошли на развитие наших дальних окраин, на поддержку предприимчивости в этих пределах, где эта предприимчивость теперь сопряженная с крайним риском и на первое время может быть даже совсем бездоказная, в будущем могла бы дать значительные выгоды не только окраинам, но и центру. В каком положении, например, угольная промышленность на Сахалине? Земледельческая промышленность в Южно-Уссурийском крае, находится, очевидно, в затруднительном положении? Не послужит ли торговый трактат с Кореей началом новой эры для русских прибрежий Тихого океана?

«Выгодное географическое положение Кореи с его многочисленными и трудолюбивым населением, за последнее время обращает на себя особенное внимание цивилизованных наций. Соединенные Штаты, Англия, Западная Германия и наконец непосредственная соседка Кореи, Россия, заключили с Сеульским правительством торговые трактаты, в силу которых торговыми судами этих государств открывается свободные доступ в эти или другие Корейские порты» (Новости 4 Декабря 1884 года)

«При одном взгляде на карту северной части Тихого океана нельзя не заметить выдающейся порции занимаемой в географическом отношении корейским полуостровом. Положение его можно назвать центральным, господствующим между владениями трех соседних государств, Китая, Японии и России………………» (Нов. Вр. 29 Декабря 1884 года)

«По своему положению Корея имеет огромное стратегическое значение. Она будет находиться в тылу флота оперирующего в желтом море и в заливе Пе-тжя-ли, омывающим берега столичной провинции Китая. По верному выражению английского путешественника Срифтиса, Корея является таким же важным базисом, как Канада для Северной Америки. Нет сомнений, что по справедливости Россия, так же как и Америка, должна являться первенствующей морской державой на Тихом океане……»

«Нельзя пренебрегать страной, занимающей для нас чрезвычайно важное географическое положение и обладающей почти восьми миллионами населения. Рано или поздно, нам придется считаться с китайцами, и вопрос, а чье же влияние будет преобладать в Корее — наше или китайское, имеет первостепенное значение……»

«Корея находится в непосредственном соседстве с русскими владениями в Тихом океане и для России очень важно не допускать захвата этой страны китайцами. Во всякой политическое комбинации, ___отнять Корею от китайских притязаний, русское правительство неизбежно должно будет сказать сове властное слово и поддержать его теми морскими силами, которыми располагает оно в Тихом океане……» (Н. Вр. 4 Декабря 1884 года)

«Было бы слишком несправедливо и вредно для наших национальных интересов, если бы в Корее преобладало чье-либо влияние кроме нашего. В этой стране русский национальный флаг должен быть поднять выше всех остальных……» (Н. Вр. 9 Декабря 1884 года)

«Вообще становиться все более и более очевидным, что дальний восток нельзя далее оставлять без всякого контроля со стороны европейских держав, имеющих коммерческие и другие интересы в Тихом океане. Отдаленные страны, расположенные по берегам этого водного вместилища, перестали быть недоступными для европейцев и нельзя допускать, чтобы в них беспоказанно продолжал существовать порядок вещей того времени, когда никому не было дела ни до Китая, ни до Японии……» (Н. Вр. 4 Декабря 1884 года)

Пока Корея остается, как и была долее, полу варварским, не культурным государством, до тех пор для соседей ее совершенно безразлично все то, что в ней совершается, и она могла не иметь ровно никакого влияния на судьбы и течение дней в их владениях. Но раз Корея попадет в руки цивилизованного народа, она, конечно, воспользуется ее благоприятным положением, ее удобствами для того, чтобы влиять на соседей в торговом и политическом отношении».

«Не надобно думать, что Корея уподобляется неким пустырям, которыми мы владеем по соседству с нею, нашему Южно-Уссурийскому краю. Это страна очень густо населенная, жителей в ней считается до 8 миллионов……»

«Утверждение какой-нибудь европейской державы в Корее — создало бы для наших тихоокеанских владений, соседа вовсе нежелательного. Хотя прошло уже двадцатьс лишком лет, как мы приобрели эти владения, то было бы весьма трудно утверждать, что мы их прочно укрепили за собою. Серьезное внимание на приморскую область мы обратили только с недавнего времени, когда начались правильные ____ во Владивосток.

Упрочение нашего владычества на Тихом Океане, можно сказать, теперь только начинается, а при таких то условиях, имея под боком алчного, не всегда дружелюбного и сильного соседа, вряд ли может быть покойным.

« Вот почему Корейский вопрос должен втянуть нас неминуемо в сферу этих интересов, которые с ним связанны. Если бы это было возможно, мы могли бы ограничиться противодействием захвата Кореи какою-нибудь европейскою державою, так как не имеет ни малейшего желания завоевывать Корею, как французы завоевали _____. Но ограничиваться одним противодействием захвату Кореи другою державою, в сущности, будет постепенно ничего не делать в тот пункт, где просвеченная деятельность Англии или Германии может создать базу для операций против нас, в одной из лучших частей наших азиатских владений. Не желая насильственного присоединения Кореи, мы только по необходимости должны стремиться к тому, чтобы сделать наше влияние там преобладающим……»

«Во всех вопросах колониальной политики Россия может оставаться индеферентною и как бы неподвижною до тех только пор, пока ее национальные интересы – хотя бы только интересы будущего не затронуты......»

«Германия, чувствуя себя ____ морскою державою, заняла уже тринадцать ____ станций в южной части Тихого океана и предполагает двигаться далее, к его северным прибрежьям......» (Н. Вр. 29 Декабря 1884 года)

«Почему же одной России смотреть скрестив руки на то, что происходит в ближайшем соседстве с ее уссурийскими владениями, в двух шагах от Валдивостока? Или для нас безразличн , будут ли стоять в корейских гаванях английские или китайские или японские или германские военные суда? Неужели мы можем допустить, что Корея станет операционным базисом враждебных нам военных и торговых армий. Стоит только бросить взгляд на карту, чтобы понять, почему шанхайские газеты называют Корею «ключом японского моря» и убедиться в том, что этому ключу уместнее всего быть в наших руках. Нейтральная Корея имела бы для нас такой же смысл, как и нейтральная Турция…….»

« Можно ли нам равнодушно относиться к этому вопросу, в особенности теперь, когда все великие державы Европы, успешно соперничают между собою в развитии колониальной политики……» (Моск. Вед. 29 Декабря 1884 года)

20
거문도 점령 외교사, 〈The Japan Weekly Mail〉 1887. 4. 30.

AVPRI, F.150, Op.493, D.113, L.155-156ob.

История переговоров по занятию Порта Гамильтона.

Выписка из газеты The Japan Weekly Mail, April 30, 1887.

Недавно в английский Парламент был представлен документ под заглавием: «Переписка по поводу временного занятия Порта Гамильтон Правительством Ее Величества», в котором с подробностью изложен исторический ход переговоров по сказанному вопросу.

Из этого обзора явствует, что в Апреле 1885 года английское Правительство заняло группу островов, известных под именем «Порта Гамильтон», составляющих часть корейской территории, без всякого предварительного соглашения с Кореей, Китаем и Японией и уже после такого фактического захвата, стало давать Правительствам означенных трех государств весьма шаткие объяснения, основывавшиеся на непредвиденных случайностях, (опасении захвата этого пункта другою Державою) которые якобы и побудили английское Правительство сделать этот шаг. Вместе с тем, признавая сюзеренные права Китая на Корею, великобританское Правительство изъявило готовность вступить с ним в переговоры по этому вопросу и предложило временно занять эту местность под условием известной платы Правительствам Кореи и Китая. Условия эти изложены в проекте соглашения между лордом Гранвиллем и Маркизом Цзенгом 28-го апреля 1885 года.

Китайское Правительство, однако, взглянуло на дело иначе и заявило чрез своего Представителя в Лондоне, что, в виду заявления русского Посланника в Пекине занять часть корейской территории в случае уступки Англии Гамильтона, оно не может принять подобные условия и поэтому надеется, что Правительство Ее Величества не найдет нужным занятие этих островов.

Между тем британский флаг уже был поднят над Гамильтоном и англичане, несмотря на протест Кореи, поставили минные заграждения и начали укреплять острова.

Лорд Солсбёри, ставший в это время во главе нового Министерства, продолжал делать попытки к соглашению и 7 июля предписал господину О'Конору, великобританскому Поверенному в Делах в Пекине, возобновить с китайским Правительством переговоры, в виду готовности Ямыня придти к соглашению.

Готовность эта, о которой упоминает Лорд Соолсбёри, не подтверждалась, однако, никакими документами.

Вслед за этим переговоры прекращаются на несколько месяцев (от 13 июля до 14 октября 1885 года) и возобновляются с приездом Ли-Хунг-Чжана в Пекин в октябре 1885 года. Из свидания, которое последний имел с господином О'Конором явствует, что Вице-король видел в очищении Гамильтона единственное средство к соглашению, и в виду Парламентских выборов, происходивших в это время в Англии, решился ждать ответа по истечении годового срока.

Убедившись, по-видимому, в необходимости оставить этот пункт, английское Правительство изменяет характер своих требований и в 1886 году ставит во всех своих переговорах условием sine qua non – гарантию со стороны Китая в том, что другая Держава не займет ни этих островов, ни вообще какой-нибудь части корейской территории – вопрос затрагивающий, таким образом, неприкосновенность всей Кореи.

Китайское Правительство сначала не нашло возможным дать такую гарантию, но вскоре, благодаря категорическим обещаниям данным господином Ладыженским, по поручению русского Правительства Ли-Хун-Чжану, что Россия ни в каком случае не займет корейской территории, если Англия оставит остров Гамильтон, оно решилось взять на себя таковую гарантию.

Этим и заканчиваются переговоры и 27 февраля 1887 года английский флаг был спущен с Гамильтона.

Со своей стороны газета Japan Mail дает понять, что уступчивость великобританского Правительства в данном случае обусловливалась скорее стратегическими соображениями о непригодности этого пункта, чем Китайско-корейскими требованиями.

약어표

* 한글로 표기된 것은 구한국 자료, 한자는 중국과 일본 자료, 로마자는 구미(歐美) 자료를 뜻함.
* 자료의 나열은 국가별로 분류한 후 한글과 한자는 가나다순, 로마자는 알파벳순에 따름.

〈조선〉

각국교섭 : 『各國交涉文字』 서울대학교 규장각한국학연구원 소장
거문도상황조사 : 『巨門島狀況調査』 한국학중앙연구원 장서각 소장
거문도영함 : 『巨文島英艦見聞記』 국사편찬위원회 소장
구한국 : 『舊韓國外交文書』 고려대학교 아세아문제연구소 편(서울: 고려대학교출판부, 1965-1973)
금등장록 : 『金等狀錄』 서울대학교 규장각한국학연구원 소장
대한계년사 : 『大韓季年史』(서울: 소명출판, 2003)
동래부계록 : 『東萊府啓錄』 서울대학교 규장각한국학연구원 소장
실록 : 『高宗實錄』(서울: 探究堂, 1970)
운양집 : 『雲養集』 서울대학교 규장각한국학연구원 소장
일기 : 『承政院日記』(서울: 국사편찬위원회, 1967-1968)
전라좌수영 : 『全羅左水營啓錄』 서울대학교 규장각한국학연구원 소장
통서 : 『統署日記』 서울대학교 규장각한국학연구원 소장
팔도사도삼항구일기 : 『八道四都三港口日記』 서울대학교 규장각한국학연구원 소장
한성주보 : 『漢城週報』

〈중국〉

德宗 : 『大淸德宗景皇帝實錄』(北京: 中華書局, 2008)
東華錄 : 『光緖朝東華錄』(『東華錄· 東華續錄』 朱壽朋 · 王先謙 編, 上海古籍出版社, 2008에 수록)

袁世凱 : 『袁世凱全集』 駱寶善·劉路生 主編(鄭州: 河南大學出版社, 2008)
李文 : 『李文忠公全集』 吳汝綸 編(臺北: 文海出版社, 1962)
李鴻章 : 『李鴻章全集』 顧廷龍·戴逸 主編(合肥: 安徽教育出版社, 2007)
養壽園 : 『養壽園電稿』 沈祖憲 輯(臺北: 文海出版社, 1960)
中日 : 『清光緒朝中日交涉史料』 故宮博物院文獻館 編(臺北: 文海出版社, 1970)
中日韓 : 『清季中日韓關係史料』 中央硏究院 近代史硏究所 編(臺北: 近代史硏究所, 1972)
中朝匯編 : 『清代中朝關係檔案史料滙編』 中國第一歷史檔案館 編(北京: 國際文化出版社, 1996)
清外 : 『淸季外交史料』 王彥威·王亮 輯編(臺北: 文海出版社, 1985)

〈일본〉

公文 : 『公文錄』 日本國立公文書館 所藏
別錄 : 『公文別錄』 日本國立公文書館 所藏
秘書類纂 : 『秘書類纂 朝鮮交涉資料』, 伊藤博文 編(東京: 秘書類纂刊行会, 1936)
原文 : 『原敬關係文書』, 原敬文書研究會 編(東京: 日本放送出版協會, 1985)
伊藤 : 『伊藤博文文書』(舊 秘書類纂), 伊藤博文文書研究會 編(東京: ゆまに書房, 2007)
日外 : 『日本外交文書(明治年間)』(東京: 日本 外務省, 1933-1963)
日韓資料 : 『日韓外交資料集成』, 金正明 編(東京: 巖南堂書店, 1962-1964)
井上馨文 : 『井上馨關係文書』 국사편찬위원회 소장

〈미국〉

AADM : *Anglo-American Diplomatic Materials Relating to Korea, 1866-1886*, Park Il-Keun ed. (Seoul: Shinmundang, 1982)
ADPP : *American Diplomatic and Public Papers: The United States and China, Series II, The United States, China and Imperial Rivalries, 1861-1893*. Vol. 9-11, Davids, Jules, ed. (Wilmington, DE: Scholarly Resources, 1979)
KAR I : *Korean-American Relations: Documents Pertaining to the Far Eastern Diplomacy of the United States, The Initial Period, 1883-1886*, McCune, George M. and John A.

Harrison, eds. (Berkeley, CA: University of California Press, 1963)

KAR II : *Korean-American Relations: Documents Pertaining to the Far Eastern Diplomacy of the United States, The period of growing influence 1887-1895,* Spencer J. Palmer, ed. (Berkeley, CA: University of California Press, 1963)

NARA II : National Archives and Records Administration Micro Films

RWS : Robert Wilson Shufeldt papers (Library of Congress)

〈영국〉

BDFA : *British documents on foreign affairs — reports and papers from the Foreign Office Confidential Print. Part I, From the mid-nineteenth century to the First World War. Series E, Asia, 1860-1914*, vol. 2, Ian Nish ed. (University Publications of America, 1989)

FO : Records created and inherited by the Foreign Office in UK

Parliamentary Papers : *Parliamentary papers: Corea, 1883-1898,* Great Britain. Parliament (London: [s.n.], 1883-99)

〈프랑스〉

C. P : *Correspondances politiques* (Political Correspondences, the National Archives and the Archives of the Ministry of Foreign Affairs of France, Courneuve)

M. D : *Mémoires et documents* (Memorandum Book and Documents, the National Archives and the Archives of the Ministry of Foreign Affairs of France, Courneuve)

〈러시아〉

AVPRI : Arkhiv vneshnei politiki Rossiiskoi Imperii (Archive of foreign policy of the Russian Empire)

RGAVMF : *Rossiiskii Gosudarstvennyi Arkhiv Voenno-Morskogo Flota* (Russian State Archive of the Navy, St. Petersburg)

RGIA : Rossiiskii Gosudarstvennyi istoricheskii arkhiv (Russian State Historical Archive)

문서 목록

번호	발신일/수신일* (음력)	문서제목	발신	수신	문서출처	번역문 출처	관련문서 제목	관련문서 출처
6. 거문도 사건 관련 각국의 교섭								
1	1885.4.20	榎本武揚·李鴻章 회담	榎本武揚·李鴻章		『日韓資料』 7, pp. 576-82.			
2	1885.4.21	거문도 점령의 전략적 가치 보고	Patenôtre	Ferry	MD Chine Vol. 23, f.97-102.			
3	1885.4.21	영·러 전쟁 발발 가능성에 대한 주독 청무관의 우려 보고	Patenôtre	Ferry	MD Chine Vol. 23, f.103-4.			
4	1885.4.27	청 정부에 전신 설치 승인 요청 지시	E. Granville	N. R. O'Conor	FO 405/35/14; Parliamentary Papers, No. 11, p. 3.			
5	1885.4.27/ 1885.4.27*	거문도 점령에 대한 청 정부의 입장	曾紀澤	E. Granville	FO 405/35/13; Parliamentary Papers, No. 10, p. 3; AADM, p. 492.			
6	1885.4.28	거문도 점령에 대한 영국과 청의 협정문 초안	E. Granville	曾紀澤	FO 403/35/15; Parliamentary Papers, No. 12, p. 3; BDFA, doc, No. 139, p. 244; AADM, p. 493.			
7	1885.4.28	영국의 거문도 점거에 관한 李鴻章과의 회담 보고	原敬	榎本武揚	『原文』 4, 문서번호 131.			
8	1885.5.1(光緒十一年三月十七日)	영국과의 협정문 서명에 관한 의견 요청	曾紀澤	總署	『李鴻章』 21, 電報, 1 G11-03-056, p. 522; 『李文』, 電稿 5, p. 37.			
9	1885.5.1(光緒十一年三月十七日)	영국의 제안에 대한 李鴻章의 검토 지시	光緒帝		『德宗』 205, 丙辰條, p. 911.		李鴻章의 의견 (1885.5.1)	『李鴻章』 21, 電報, 1 G11-03-063, p. 523; 『李文』, 譯署電稿 5, p. 38; 『中日』 8, 문서번호 376, p. 16.
10	1885.5.4(光緒十一年三月二十日)	영국과의 협정 조인 불가 지시	總署	曾紀澤	『李鴻章』 21, 電報, 1 G11-03-069, p. 525; 『李文』, 電稿 5, pp. 38-9.			
11	1885.5.5(光緒十一年三月二十一日)	고종의 적당한 처리 지시	光緒帝		『李鴻章』 21, 電稿 1, G11-03-071,			

					p. 525; 『德宗』 205, 庚申條, p. 913.			
12	1885.5.8/ 1885.5.9*	청 정부의 전신선 설치 승인 예정	N. R. O'Conor	E. Granville	FO 405/35/17; AADM, pp. 494-5.			
13	1885.5.9/ 1885.5.9*	러시아와 일본의 동향에 대한 청의 우려	N. R. O'Conor	E. Granville	FO 405/35/18; AADM, p. 495.			
14	1885.5.9/ 1885.7.6*	거문도 점령 기간에 대한 청 정부 견해	N. R. O'Conor	E. Granville	FO 405/35/71; AADM, p. 521; BDFA, doc, No. 176, pp. 260-2.			
15	1885.5.11	거문도 전신선 설치에 대한 청 정부와의 교섭 지침	E. Granville	N. R. O'Conor	FO 405/35/20; AADM, p. 495.			
16	1885.5.11	청 정부의 거문도 협정안 서명 거부	E. Granville	N. R. O'Conor	FO 405/35/21; AADM, pp. 494-5; BDFA, doc, No. 142, pp. 245-6.			
17	1885.5.15	영·러 전쟁 발발 가능성 저하 보고	J. Sienkiewicz	Ch. de Freycinet	CP Japon, Vol. 31, f.186-9.			
18	1885.5.15/ 1885.7.6*	거문도 전신선 설치 관련 청 정부와의 교섭 경과	N. R. O'Conor	E. Granville	FO 405/35/74.			
19	1885.5.15*(光緒十一年四月二日)	청의 입장을 각국에 통보 제안	日本代理公使	李鴻章	『李鴻章』 33, 信函 5, G11-04-001, p. 490.			
20	1885.5.16	거문도 전신선 설치 관련 추가 지침	E. Granville	N. R. O'Conor	FO 405/35/26.			
21	1885.5.18/ 1885.5.18*	청 정부와 거문도 전신선 설시 합의	N. R. O'Conor	E. Granville	FO 405/35/27; Parliamentary Papers, No. 16, p. 5.			
22	1885.5.18/ 1885.7.13*	청 정부와 거문도 전신선 설치 협상 내용	N. R. O'Conor	E. Granville	FO 405/35/93.			
23	1885.5.20	거문도 전신선 설치 관련 總理衙門에 보낸 공문	N. R. O'Conor	E. Granville	FO 405/35/94.			
24	1885.5.20	거문도 전신선 설치 위한 선박 파견	E. Granville	N. R. O'Conor	FO 405/35/30.			

25	1885.5.20	영국의 거문도 점령과 조선의 협조 요청	G. C. Foulk	Bingham	NARA II, M133, R52.			
26	1885.5.27	거문도 사건의 추이 보고	原敬	井上馨	『原文』 4, 문서번호 140.			
27	1885.5.30	거문도 조차 협상을 위해 청 정부와 사전 협의 필요성 설명	O'Conor	W. G. Aston	FO 228/793/41; FO 405/35/123, Inclosure 1.			
28	1885.6.1	청 정부를 통한 협상 타결 건의	The Secretary to the Admiralty	Currie	FO 405/35/42; Parliamentary Papers, No. 28, p. 8; AADM, p. 505.			
29	1885.6.2	영국의 거문도 점령에 대한 청 정부의 지지	N. R. O'Conor	W. G. Aston	FO 228/793/44; FO 405/35/123, Inclosure 3.			
30	1885.6.2/ 1885.7.27*	李鴻章이 조선 정부의 반대 차단 약속	N. R. O'Conor	E. Granville	FO 405/35/120; AADM, p. 566.			
31	1885.6.2/ 1885.7.27*	러시아의 반응에 대한 청 정부의 우려	N. R. O'Conor	E. Granville	FO 405/35/122; AADM, pp. 568-9; BDFA, doc, No. 210, p. 289.			
32	1885.6.4	영국의 거문도 점령에 대한 일본의 반응	Bingham	T. F. Bayard	NARA II, M133, R52.			
33	1885.6.5	러시아, 영국 사신에 대한 응대 관련 훈령	井上馨	高平小五郎	『秘書類纂』 下, pp. 127-8.			
34	1885.6.5	거문도 사건에 대한 李鴻章의 입장	原敬	井上馨	『原文』 4, 문서번호 142.			
35	1885.6.5/ 1885.7.10*	Plunkett · 井上馨 회담	F. Plunkett	E. Granville	FO 405/35/81; AADM, pp. 536-7; BDFA, doc, No. 184, pp. 271-2.			
36	1885.6.6	O'Conor · 李鴻章 회담	N. R. O'Conor	E. Granville	FO 405/35/ 132; Parliamentary Papers, No. 39, p. 12; FO 405/35/132; FO 17/981/268; AADM,			

					pp. 578-9; BDFA, doc, No. 214, p. 290; FO 405/35/132, Inclosure는 FO 228/793/47.		
37	1885.6.10/ 1885.6.27*	입안 8개조에 관해 李鴻章과의 협상 지시	井上馨	榎本武揚	『日外』 明治年間追補 第1冊, pp. 356-61.		
38	1885.6.11(光緒十一年四月二十九日)	영국의 거문도 전선 설치 및 러시아의 흑포도 점거 사실 통보	李鴻章	總署	『李鴻章』 21, 電稿 1, G11-04-076, p. 547.		
39	1885.6.12	주청 영국 공사가 조선에 거문도 점령을 통지한 사실 확인	J. Sienkiewicz	Ch. de Freycinet	CP Japon Vol. 31, f.199-205.		
40	1885.6.13	영국의 거문도 점령에 관한 대응책 훈령	井上馨	河瀨眞孝	『日外』 18, 문서번호 335.		
41	1885.6.15	거문도 전신선의 일시적 설치를 재확인	總署	N. R. O'Conor	FO 405/35/155, Inclosure.		
42	1885.6.15*(光緒十一年五月三日)	영국과의 협약 체결을 통한 중국의 권리 보전 제안	曾紀澤	總署	『中日韓』 4, 문서번호 995, pp. 1286-7.	曾紀澤이 영국 외무성에 보낸 조회	『中日韓』 4, 문서번호 995, pp. 1286-7.
43	1885.6.17/ 1885.8.11*	Plunkett에게 청 정부의 반대 가능성 통보	N. R. O'Conor	E. Granville	FO 405/35/145; AADM, pp. 592-3; BDFA, doc, No. 225, pp. 296-7.		
44	1885.6.23/ 1885.8.7*	Plunkett · 井上馨 회담	F. Plunkett	E. Granville	FO 405/35/138.		
45	1885.6.26*(光緒十一年五月十四日)	거문도의 개항 제안	徐承祖	總署	『中日韓』 4, 문서번호 1002, p. 1845.		
46	1885.6.27	거문도 점령에 대한 李鴻章의 견해	N. R. O'Conor	E. Granville	FO 405/35/56; Parliamentary Papers, No. 31, p. 8; AADM, p. 509; BDFA, doc, No. 163, p. 253.		
47	1885.6.28	李鴻章 견해 수용을 위한 總理衙門과의 교섭 진행	The Marquis of Salisbury	N. R. O'Conor	FO 405/35/58; AADM, pp. 509-10; BDFA, doc, No. 164,		

					p. 253.			
48	1885.6.29/ 1885.8.24*	청 總理衙門의 거문도 전신선 관련 입장	N. R. O'Conor	The Marquis of Salisbury	FO 405/35/155; AADM, p. 602; BDFA, doc, No. 234, pp. 302-3.			
49	1885.6.30/ 1885.8.24*	李鴻章의 제안을 Aston에게 통지	N. R. O'Conor	The Marquis of Salisbury	FO 405/35/159; AADM, pp. 604-6; BDFA, doc, No. 237, p. 304; FO 405/35/159, Inclosure 1은 FO 228/793/58; FO 405/35/159, Inclosure 2는 FO 228/793/59.			
50	1885.7.1/ 1885.8.24*	러시아를 고려한 청의 입장	N. R. O'Conor	The Marquis of Salisbury	FO 405/35/160; FO 17/982/331; AADM, p. 606. BDFA, doc, No. 238, pp. 204-5.			
51	1885.7.1(光緒十一年五月十九日)	조선 정부에 영국의 거문도 조차 제안 통보 지시	李鴻章	劉含芳	『李鴻章』 21, 電報 1, G11-05-058, p. 564; 『李文』, 電稿 6, p. 12.			
52	1885.7.2(光緒十一年五月二十日)	조선 정부에 러시아 요구 거절 권고 지시	李鴻章	劉含芳	『李鴻章』 21, 電報 1, G11-05-059, p. 564; 『李文』, 電稿 6, p. 12.			
53	1885.7.2~7.3	榎本武揚·李鴻章 회담	榎本武揚·李鴻章		『日外』 明治年間追補 第1冊, pp. 361-83.			
54	1885.7.3/ 1885.8.7*	Plunket·井上馨 회담	F. Plunkett	The Marquis of Salisbury	FO 405/35/139; AADM, pp. 583-4; BDFA, doc, No. 219, p. 293.			
55	1885.7.5/ 1885.9.7*	거문도 점령에 대한 일본의 반대	N. R. O'Conor	The Marquis of Salisbury	FO 405/35/172; FO 17/982/339; AADM,			

					p. 618.			
56	1885.7.7*(光緒十一年五月二十五日)	거문도 점령 관련 영국 정부와의 협의	曾紀澤	總署	『中日韓』 4, 문서번호 1009, p. 1856.			
57	1885.7.8/ 1885.9.7*	거문도 점령 관련 청 정부와의 협의	N. R. O'Conor	The Marquis of Salisbury	FO 405/35/175; FO 17/983/349; AADM, pp. 621-2.			
58	1885.7.8(光緒十一年五月二十六日)	거문도 개항에 대한 부정적 입장 전달	李鴻章	總署	『李鴻章』 33, 信函 5, G11-05-006, pp. 504-5.			
59	1885.7.10	조선에 대한 청의 종주권 활용 방안	The Marquis of Salisbury	N. R. O'Conor	FO 405/35/85; AADM, p. 539; BDFA, doc, No. 185, p. 272.			
60	1885.7.10	영국의 거문도 점령 관련 조선의 동향 보고	Patenôtre	Ferry	CP Chine Vol. 68, f.329.			
61	1885.7.14/ 1885.7.14*	井上馨 · Plunkett 회담(1)	F. Plunkett	The Marquis of Salisbury	FO 405/35/99; FO 46/332/182; AADM, p. 549; BDFA, doc, No. 196, p. 277.			
62	1885.7.14/ 1885.8.25*	井上馨 · Plunkett 회담(2)	F. Plunkett	The Marquis of Salisbury	FO 405/35/162.			
63	1885.7.15/ 1885.9.7*	거문도 점령 및 러시아에 대한 청의 입장	N. R. O'Conor	The Marquis of Salisbury	FO 405/35/178; FO 17/983/352; AADM, pp. 623-5; BDFA, doc, No. 247, pp. 312-4.			
64	1885.7.15/ 1885.9.7*	李鴻章 · 榎本武揚 협의 경과	N. R. O'Conor	The Marquis of Salisbury	FO 405/35/177; AADM, pp. 622-3; BDFA, doc, No. 245, pp. 311-2.			
65	1885.7.16/ 1885.9.21*	거문도 점령 및 러시아에 대한 청의 입장	N. R. O'Conor	The Marquis of Salisbury	FO 405/35/182; AADM, p. 626.		전신보고 내용	FO 405/35/103; AADM, pp. 550-1.
66	1885.7.17/ 1885.9.21*	조선 정부에 대한 청 정부의 압력 기대	N. R. O'Conor	The Marquis of	FO 405/35/184; AADM,			

				Salisbury	pp. 627-8; BDFA, doc, No. 250, pp. 314-5.			
67	1885.7.18/ 1885. 9. 21*	李鴻章에 대한 Colquhoun의 거문도 점령 반대 권고	N. R. O'Conor	The Marquis of Salisbury	FO 405/35/185; FO 17/983/357.			
68	1885.7.18	거문도 점령 철회를 위한 독· 러 협력 도모	M. de Giers	M. de Staal	CD de M. De Staal. tome I, f.127.		(1) 거문도 사건이 러· 독의 공통 위협이라는 견해(1885.7. 3) (2) 영국의 거문도 점령 철회를 위한 독·러 협력 제안(1885.7. 3) (3) 독·러 협력 불가 및 비스마르크 에게 대책 마련 촉구 (1885.7.12)	(1) CD de M. De Staal. tome I. f.127-annexe 1. Giers → Schouvalow (2) CD de M. De Staal. tome I. f.127-annexe 2. Giers → Schouvalow (3) CD de M. De Staal. tome I. f.127-annexe 3. Schouvalow → Giers
69	1885.7.19*(光緖十 一年六月八日)	조선의 교섭 상황 및 러시아 군함의 동태 보고	李鴻章	總署	『中日韓』 4, 문서번호 1017, p. 1865.			
70	1885.7.20	李鴻章에 대한 榎本武揚의 거문도 철수 요구 제안	N. R. O'Conor	The Marquis of Salisbury	FO 405/35/186; FO 17/983/359; AADM, pp. 628-9; BDFA, doc, No. 252, p. 316.			
71	1885.7.24	거문도 점령에 대한 청의 즉각적인 항의	G. S. de Bezaure	Ch. de Freycinet	CCC Tientsin, Vol. 2, f.55-6.			
72	1885.7.27/ 1885.7.30*	거문도 전신선 연결 완료 보고	The Secretary to the Admiralty	J. Pauncefote	Parliamentary Papers, No. 38, p. 12.			
73	1885.7.30	거문도와 홍콩 간의 해저 전신선 부설을 덴마크 전신회사가 담당했음을 보고	A. P. Davydov	N. K. Girs	AVPRI, F. Glavnyi arkhiv U-Az, 1885 g, D.45, L.312-4.			
74	1885.7.31	유사시 거제도 점거 건의	榎本武揚	井上馨	『井上馨文』 232-3.			
75	1885.8.15	李鴻章과의 협의 경과 보고에 대한 답신	井上馨	榎本武揚	『日外』 明治年間追 補 第1冊, pp. 383-6.			
76	1885.8.16	거문도 탐문			『普号通覽』			

		결과 보고			23.			
77	1885.8.17	거문도 점령 사건으로 인한 오스트리아-헝가리제국과 한국 간의 조약 체결 보류	A. P. Davydov	N. K. Girs	AVPRI, F. Glavnyi arkhiv U-Az, 1885 g, D.45, L.319-20.			
78	1885.8.22*(光緒十一年七月十三日)	영·러 분쟁 미결 시 각국의 움직임에 대한 풍설	李鴻章	總署	『中日韓』 4, 문서번호 1045, pp. 1919-20.			
79	1885.8.24	거문도 경비병에 대한 보고			『公文』			
80	1885.8.25/ 1885.9.12*	波多野承五郎·吳大澂 회담	波多野承五郎	井上馨	『日外』 18, 문서번호 216.			
81	1885.9.7/ 1885.9.21*	波多野承五郎·李鴻章 회담	波多野承五郎	井上馨	『日外』 18, 문서번호 217.			
82	1885.9.15	조선 문제에 대한 신중한 접근 촉구	井上馨	波多野承五郎	『日外』 18, 문서번호 218.			
83	1885.9.20	李鴻章의 거문도 점령에 대한 견해	P. S. Popov	N. K. Girs	AVPRI, F.150, Op.493, D.113, L.102-102ob.			
84	1885.9.27	조·청 간의 전신선 가설 협정 체결에 대한 보고	A. P. Davydov	A. Y. Vlangali	AVPRI, F. Glavnyi arkhiv U-Az, 1885 g, D.45, L.334-6.			
85	1885.10.2	영국의 거문도 점령에 대한 각국의 입장	J. Sienkiewicz	Ch. de Freycinet	CP Japon, vol. 31, f.264-9.			
86	1885.10.2	거문도 점령에 대한 조선의 반응 및 러시아의 계획	Mgr. Blanc		CP Japon, Vol. 31, f.270-6.			
87	1885.10.17/ 1885.11.5*	영흥만 중립에 관한 吳大澂과의 협의	波多野承五郎	井上馨	『日外』 18, 문서번호 219.			
88	1885.11.17	거문도 점령 관련 영·청 간 거래 소문	V. K. Shneur	Director of the Military-Scientific Committee of the General Staff	AVPRI, F.150, Op.493, D.113, L.104-104ob.			
89	1885.12.5/ 1886.1.26*	청 總理衙門의 전신선 작동 여부 확인	N. R. O'Conor	The Marquis of Salisbury	FO 405/36/5; Parliamentary Papers, No. 51, pp. 21-3; FO 17/986/479.			
90	1885.6.15	井上馨·徐承祖 회담	井上馨·徐承祖		『日外』 明治年間追			

					補 第1冊, pp. 352-6.			
91	1886.1.5	조선과 청국 간 전신망 연결 및 일본 정부의 부산과 나가사키 전신선 부설권 획득 보고	A. P. Davydov	N. K. Girs	AVPRI, F. Glavnyi arkhiv U-Az, 1885 g, D.45, L.386-8.			
92	1886.2.3	거문도 전신선 관련 O'Conor 지시 내용 전달	Currie	The Secretary to the Admiralty	FO 405/36/8.			
93	1886.3.12/ 1886.5.3*	李鴻章에게 Denny의 거문도 문제 개입 차단 요청	N. R. O'Conor	Earl of Rosebery	FO 405/36/28.			
94	1886.5.22(光緖十二年四月十九日)	러시아의 영흥만 측량에 따른 영·러 간 알력	袁世凱	李鴻章	『袁世凱』 1, 문서번호 1-319, p. 173; 『養壽園』 1, pp. 25-6.			
95	1886.6.26(光緖十二年五月二十五日)	거문도 문제 관련 문건 작성에 袁世凱 개입	袁世凱	李鴻章	『袁世凱』 1, 문서번호 1-374, p. 173; 『養壽園』 1, p. 53.			
96	1886.8.15	전신선의 유지 여부 문의	J. Walsham	Earl of Iddesleigh	FO 405/36/58; AADM, pp. 691-2; BDFA, doc, No. 292, p. 343.		거문도 전신선의 유지 여부 해군성 문의	FO 405/36/63.
97	1886.8.18	거문도의 조약항 지정 방안	Earl of Iddesleigh	J. Walsham	FO 405/36/64; AADM, p. 694.			
98	1886.10.14	조선의 지위 관련 Denny·李鴻章의 대담	G. C. Foulk	T. F. Bayard	KAR I, doc, No. 13, pp. 154-6.			
99	1886.12.21	거문도 전신선 처분 여부 결정 요청	Macgregor	Currie	FO 405/36/132; AADM, p. 743; BDFA, doc, No. 331, p. 371.			
100	1886.3.12/ 1886.5.3*	청 정부의 거문도 전신선 구매 거절 결정	J. Walsham	Earl of Iddesleigh	FO 405/37/2.			

7-1. 영국 내 거문도 무용론과 철군 논의

101	1885.5.25	거문도 점령의 경제적 이점	F. Plunkett	E. Granville	FO 405/35/66; AADM, pp. 517-8; BDFA, doc, No. 172, pp. 258-9.			

102	1885.7.4	무역항으로서 거문도의 가치를 다룬 Plunkett 보고서	Currie	Furrer	FO 405/35/69; AADM, p. 520.			
103	1885.9.15	해군 기지로서 거문도의 적합성 검토	The Secretary to the Admiralty	Hamilton	Parliamentary Papers, No. 44, p. 16.			
104	1886.1.20/ 1886.1.21*	거문도 주둔 해군 상황 보고	The Secretary to the Admiralty	Currie	FO 405/36/2, FO 405/36/2, Inclosure 1; Parliamentary Papers, No. 50, pp. 21-3; AADM, p. 652; BDFA, doc, No. 261, pp. 320.			
105	1886.1.25/ 1886.1.26*	거문도 매입 관련 해군성 입장	The Secretary to the Admiralty	Currie	FO 405/36/6; AADM, pp. 659-60.			
106	1886.2.4	원산항에 대한 Hetslet 각서	E. Hertslet		FO 405/36/9.			
107	1886.3.6	예상되는 청의 부정적인 견해에 대한 보고	N. R. O'Conor	Earl of Rosebery	FO 405/36/27; AADM, pp. 670-1; BDFA, doc, No. 274, p. 29, pp. 330-1.			
108	1886.3.19/ 1886.3.20*	거문도 점령 유지에 관한 해군성의 의견	The Secretary to the Admiralty	Currie	FO 405/36/19; Parliamentary Papers, No. 54, pp. 24-5; AADM, pp. 665-6; BDFA, doc, No. 270, p. 327.			
109	1886.4.30	거문도 철수의 조건	Earl of Rosebery	N. R. O'Conor	FO 405/36/26; AADM, pp. 669-70.			
110	1886.5.19/ 1886.5.20*	정부 결정에 대한 신속한 통보 요청	The Secretary to the Admiralty	Currie	FO 405/36/32; Parliamentary Papers, No. 57, pp. 24-5; AADM, p. 673.		Currie의 답신(1886.5. 22)	FO 405/36/33; Parliamentary Papers, pp. 25, No. 58; AADM, p. 673.
111	1886.7.17/ 1886.7.19*	거문도 점령에 대한 Hamilton의 부정적 견해	The Secretary to the Admiralty	Currie	FO 405/36/45; Parliamentary Papers,			

					No. 61, pp. 24-5.			
112	1886.7.10/ 1886.7.12*	O'Conor의 원산항 개방안 동의	The Secretary to the Admiralty	Currie	FO 405/36/44.			
113	1886.7.14	거문도와 원산항	E. C. Baber	J. Walsham	FO 228/830/28.			
114	1886.7.21	거문도 점령 종료 논의	The Secretary to the Admiralty	Currie	FO 405/36/46; AADM, pp. 682-7; BDFA, doc, No. 281, pp. 337-41.			
115	1886.8.18	해군성의 거문도 철수 주장	The Secretary to the Admiralty	Currie	Parliamentary Papers, pp. 24-5, No. 66.			
116	1886.11.10	거문도 방어의 어려움 통지	The Secretary to the Admiralty	Currie	Parliamentary Papers, No. 68, pp. 24-5.			
7-2. 이홍장 · 라디젠스키 회담과 각국의 철군 교섭								
117	1885.10.14/ 1885.11.30*	거문도 임대에 대한 李鴻章의 부정적인 견해	N. R. O'Conor	The Marquis of Salisbury	FO 405/35/203; FO 17/985/429; Parliamentary Papers, No. 46; AADM, pp. 645-6.			
118	1885.11.17/ 1886.1.12*	李鴻章의 거문도를 담보로 한 차관 제안	N. R. O'Conor	The Marquis of Salisbury	FO 405/36/1; AADM, pp. 651-2.			
119	1885.12.12	李鴻章에게 거문도의 타 열강 점령 방지 가능 여부 확인 지시	The Marquis of Salisbury	N. R. O'Conor	FO 405/35/208; Parliamentary Papers, No. 47; AADM, p. 648; BDFA, doc, No. 259, p. 319.		(1) 李鴻章에게 거문도의 타 열강 점령 방지 가능 여부 타진에 대한 의견 (2) 李鴻章에게 거문도의 타 열강 점령 방지 가능 여부 타진에 동의	(1) FO 405/35/206; AADM, pp. 647-8. (2) FO 405/35/207; AADM, p. 648; BDFA, doc, No. 258, p. 319.
120	1885.12.12(光緖十一年十一月十六日)	러시아의 전략에 대한 Detring의 보고 전달	李鴻章	總署	『李鴻章』 21, 電稿 1, G11-11-046, p. 628; 『李文』, 電稿 6, p. 33.			
121	1886.1.4(光緖十一年十一月三十日)	영국의 거문도 철수 여부 탐문	李鴻章	袁世凱	『李鴻章』 21, 電稿 1,			

		지시			G11-11-087, p. 638; 『李文』, 電稿 6, p. 33.			
122	1885.1.7/ 1886.3.9*	청 總理衙門에게 거문도의 타 열강 점령 방지 가능 여부 확인 지시	N. R. O'Conor	The Marquis of Salisbury	FO 405/36/16; Parliamentary Papers, No. 52, pp. 21-3.			
123	1886.3.11(光緒十二年三月六日)	Currie · Macartney 회담	Currie · Macartney		『中日韓』 1, 문서번호 1147의 부건 1, pp. 2115-6.			
124	1886.3.27/ 1886.5.17*	李鴻章 · O'Conor 회담	N. R. O'Conor	Earl of Rosebery	FO 405/36/31.			
125	1886.4.1	주청 러시아 공사의 청 정부에 대한 압력 행사	Earl of Rosebery	N. R. O'Conor	FO 405/36/22; Parliamentary Papers, No. 55, pp. 24-5; AADM, p. 667.			
126	1886.4.14	청의 조선 영토 보장 시 철수 단행 통지	Currie	Macartney	FO 405/36/23; Parliamentary Papers, No. 56, pp. 24-5; AADM, pp. 667-8; BDFA, doc, No, 272, p. 328.	[漢譯] 『中日韓』 1, 문서번호 1147의 부건 1, p. 2116.		
127	1886.4.17(光緒十二年三月十四日)	거문도 철수 관련 영국 정부의 제안	曾紀澤	總署	『淸季』 65, p. 2; 『李鴻章』 22, 電報 22, G12-03-016, p. 39.			
128	1886.4.25(光緒十二年三月二十二日)	거문도 철수 관련 영국의 추가 입장	曾紀澤	總署	『李鴻章』 22, 電報 22, G12-03-025, p. 41.			
129	1886.6.4	거문도 점령 보고 및 정부의 추가 지시 요청	The Secretary to the Admiralty	Currie	FO 405/36/36; Parliamentary Papers, No. 59, pp. 24-5; AADM, pp. 674-7; BDFA, doc, No. 277, pp. 331-4.			
130	1886.6.12	청 정부로부터의 답신 대기 중	Currie	The Secretary to the Admiralty	FO 405/36/38; Parliamentary Papers,			

					No. 60, pp. 24-5; AADM, p. 678; BDFA, doc, No. 278, p. 334.				
131	1886.6.13*(光緖十二年五月十二日)	거문도 철수 관련 영국의 공식 제안	曾紀澤	總署	『中日韓』 4, 문서번호 1147, p. 2115.				
132	1886.7.27/ 1886.7.27*	영국의 제안에 대한 청 總理衙門의 동향	J. Walsham	Earl of Rosebery	FO 405/36/51; Parliamentary Papers, No. 63, pp. 24-5; AADM, p. 689; BDFA, doc, No. 288, p. 342.				
133	1886.7.31/ 1885.7.31*	거문도·원산항의 조약항 지정 방안 제안	J. Walsham	Earl of Rosebery	FO 405/36/52; Parliamentary Papers, No. 64, pp. 24-5; AADM, p. 689.				
134	1886.8.4	러시아의 원산항 조약항 지정 요구의 군사적 의미	W. Parker	T. F. Bayard	KAR I, doc, No. 24.				
135	1886.8.12	거문도·원산항의 조약항 지정 협상 지시	Earl of Iddesleigh	J. Walsham	FO 405/36/55; Parliamentary Papers, No. 65, pp. 24-5; AADM, pp. 690-1; BDFA, doc, No. 291, p. 343.				
136	1886.8.25/ 1886.10.19*	거문도·원산항의 조약항 지정 협상 진행 상황	J. Walsham	Earl of Iddesleigh	FO 405/36/99.				
137	1886.8.30(光緖十二年八月二日)	Ladygensky·李鴻章, Brenan·李鴻章 회담	李鴻章	總署	『李鴻章』 22, 電報 22, G12-08-004, p. 98; 『淸外』 68, pp. 18-9.				
138	1886.9.7*(光緖十二年八月十日)	영국과 러시아 동향 관련 吳大徵의 보고	李鴻章	總署	『淸季』 68, pp. 24-5.				
139	1886.9.12(光緖十二年八月十五日)	Ladygensky·李鴻章 회담(1)	李鴻章· V. Ladygensky		『李鴻章』 34, 信函 6, G12-08-026, pp. 77-8.				
140	1886.9.15(光緖十二年八月十八日)	Ladygensky와의 회담 요지 보고	李鴻章	總署	『李鴻章』 34, 信函 6,				

					G12-08-032, p. 80.			
141	1886.9.24(光緒十二年八月二十八日)	Ladygensky·李鴻章 회담(2)	李鴻章·V. Ladygensky		『李鴻章』 34, 信函 6, G12-08-049, pp. 88-90.			
142	1886.9.27 (1886.11.18)	거문도·원산항의 조약항 지정에 대한 청 總理衙門의 입장	J. Walsham	Earl of Iddesleigh	FO 405/36/107.			
143	1886.9.29(光緒十二年九月二日)	Ladygensky·李鴻章 회담(3)	李鴻章·V. Ladygensky		『李鴻章』 34, 信函 6, G12-09-003, pp. 92-3; 『李文』, 譯署函稿 18, pp. 43-4.			
144	1886.9.29(光緒十二年九月二日)	Ladygensky와의 회담 요지 보고	李鴻章	總署	『李鴻章』 22, 電報 2, G12-09-005, p. 114; 『中日』 10, 문서번호 482, p. 13; 『李文』, 電稿 6, p. 201.			
145	1886.10.1(光緒十二年九月四日)	Ladygensky와의 교섭 경과 보고	李鴻章	總署	『李鴻章』 34, 信函 6, G12-09-007, p. 95.			
146	1886.10.1*(光緒十二年九月四日)	Ladygensky의 조회문 초고	V. Ladygensky	李鴻章	『李鴻章』 34, 信函 6, G12-09-008, p. 95; 『中日韓』 4, 문서번호 1177의 부건 2, p. 2142.			
147	1886.10.2(光緒十二年九月五日)	영국에 거문도 철수 촉구 지시	光緒帝		『德宗』 232, 乙未條, p. 130.			
148	1886.10.6	러시아의 對조선 방침에 대한 李鴻章의 발언	J. Walsham	Earl of Iddesleigh	FO 405/36/91; AADM, pp. 709-10. BDFA, doc, No. 305, pp. 351-2.			
149	1886.10.6	李鴻章·Brenan 회담(1)	J. Walsham	Earl of Iddesleigh	FO 405/36/111; AADM, pp. 721-8; BDFA, doc, No. 316, p. 361.			
150	1886.10.6*(光緒十二年九月九日)	Ladygensky의 수정 조회문	V. Ladygensky	李鴻章	『李鴻章』 34, 信函 6, G12-09-009, p. 96; 『中日韓』 4, 문서번호			

					1177의 부건 3, p. 2143.			
151	1886.10.7(光緖十二年九月十日)	조회문의 재수정 요구 사실 보고	李鴻章	總署	『李鴻章』 22, 電報 2, G12-09-022, p. 118; 『李文』, 電稿 7, p. 45.			
152	1886.10.8	러·청 간 교섭 경과(1)	J. Walsham	Earl of Iddesleigh	FO 405/36/112; AADM, p. 728; BDFA, doc, No. 318, pp. 363-4.			
153	1886.10.8(光緖十二年九月十一日)/ 1886.10.11*(光緖十二年九月十四日)	조회문 작성 관련 Ladygensky와의 교섭 경과	李鴻章	總署	『李鴻章』 34, 信函 6, G12-09-011, p. 97; 『李文』, 譯署函稿 18, pp. 44-5; 『淸季』 69, pp. 12-3; 『中日韓』 4, 문서번호 1177, p. 2139; 『中日』 10, 문서번호 492, pp. 15-6.			
154	1886.10.9	러·청 간 교섭 경과(2)	J. Walsham	Earl of Iddesleigh	FO 405/36/113; AADM, pp. 728-31; BDFA, doc, No. 319, pp. 364-5.			
155	1886.10.11(光緖十二年九月十四日)	조회문 재수정 지시	光緖帝		『德宗』 232, 甲辰條, p. 136; 『中日』 10, 문서번호 493, p. 17.			
156	1886.10.11(光緖十二年九月十四日)	조회문 재수정 지시 이행 상황 보고	李鴻章	總署	『李鴻章』 22, 電報 22, G12-09-030, p. 120.			
157	1886.10.13(光緖十二年九月十六日)	영국의 거문도 철수 관련 내용 보고	李鴻章	總署	『李鴻章』 22, 電報 2, G12-09-034, pp. 121-2; 『李文』, 電稿 7, p. 46.			
158	1886.10.14(光緖十二年九月十七日)	조회문 수정의 방침 지시	慈喜太后		『德宗』 232, 丁未條, pp. 137-8.			
159	1886.10.22/ 1886.12.13*	거문도·원산항의 조약항 지정 관련 중국 주둔 해군과의 협의	J. Walsham	Earl of Iddesleigh	FO 405/36/122; AADM, pp. 734-40; BDFA, doc, No. 322,			

					pp. 366-7.			
160	1886.10.22(光緖十二年九月二十五日)/1886.10.23*(光緖十二年九月二十六日)	조회문 수정 요청에 대한 Ladygensky의 반응	李鴻章	總署	『李鴻章』 34, 信函 6, G12-09-017, p. 100; 『中日韓』 4, 문서번호 1178, p. 2145; 『中朝匯編』, 문서번호 235, p. 293.			
161	1886.10.24(光緖十二年九月二十七日)	Ladygensky·李鴻章 회담(4)	李鴻章·V. Ladygensky		『李鴻章』 34, 信函 6, G12-09-018, pp. 100-1; 『李文』, 譯署函稿 18, pp. 51-2; 『中日韓』 4, 문서번호 1180의 부건 1, pp. 2168-71.			
162	1886.10.25/1886.12.13*	李鴻章·Brenan 회담(2)	J. Walsham	Earl of Iddesleigh	FO 405/36/123.			
163	1886.10.25(光緖十二年九月二十八日)	러시아 측의 조회문 수정 거절에 따른 대책 제시	李鴻章	總署	『李鴻章』 22, 電報 2, G12-09-041, p. 123; 『李文』, 電稿 7, p. 47; 『中日』 10, 문서번호 496, p. 18.			
164	1886.10.26(光緖十二年九月二十九日)/1886.10.27*(光緖十二年十月一日)	러시아 측과의 교섭 중단 사실 보고	李鴻章	總署	『李鴻章』 34, 信函 6, G12-09-019, pp. 101-2; 『李文』, 譯署函稿 18, p. 51; 『中日韓』 4, 문서번호 1180, p. 2168.			
165	1886.10.26(光緖十二年九月二十九日)/1886.10.27*(光緖十二年十月一日)	영국 측에 거문도 철수 조회 발송 요청	李鴻章	總署	『李鴻章』 34, 信函 6, G12-09-020, p. 102; 『李文』, 譯署函稿 18, pp. 54-5; 『中日韓』 4, 문서번호 1179, p. 2167.			
166	1886.10.31(光緖十二年十月五日)	청 總理衙門의 철수 요청 조회	總署	J. Walsham	『中日韓』 4, 문서번호 1180, pp. 1171-2.	[英譯] FO405/36/134; Parliamentary Papers, No. 76, pp. 24-5.	Walsham의 답신(1886. 11.10)	『中日韓』 4, 문서번호 1184, p. 2176.
167	1886.11.5/	러·청 협상 결렬	J.	Earl of	FO			

	1886.11.5*		Walsham	Iddesleigh	405/36/102; Parliamentary Papers, No. 67, pp. 24-5; ADM, p. 715; BDFA, doc, No. 310, pp. 355-6.			
168	1886.11.5/ 1886.12.27*	러·청 협상의 타결 가능성	J. Walsham	Earl of Iddesleigh	FO 405/36/135.			
169	1886.11.7	조선 문제에 대한 李鴻章과 Ladygensky의 회담 내용 보고	Ladygensky		RGAVMF, F.417, Op.1, D.312, L.7-11ob.		Li-Ladygensky 구두 협약	RGAVMF, F.417, Op.1, D.312, L.6.
170	1886.11.19	거문도 철수 이후의 협의 사항 지시	Earl of Iddesleigh	J. Walsham	FO 405/36/108; Parliamentary Papers, No. 69, pp. 24-5; ADM, p. 720; BDFA, doc, No. 314, p. 359.			
171	1886.12.10	철수 이후 청의 조선 영토 보장 문서화 지시	Earl of Iddesleigh	J. Walsham	FO 405/36/120; Parliamentary Papers, No. 73, pp. 24-5.			
172	1886.12.18/ 1886.12.18*	청에 거문도 권리 양여에 대한 일본 정부의 우려	F. Plunkett	Earl of Iddesleigh	FO 405/36/126.			
173	1887.1.20	Li-Ladygensky 협약에 대한 Girs의 견해	N. K. Girs	I. A. Shestakov	RGAVMF, F.417, Op.1, D.312, L.1-5.			
174	1887.3.6	타 열강의 거문도 점령 방지에 대한 청국 신문기사	K. I. Veber	I. A. Zinoviev	AVPRI, F.150, Op.493, D.113, L.143a-143ob.			

7-3. 철군과 사후 처리

175	1886.12.1/ 1886.12.3*	조선 정부에 거문도 철수 통보 예정	J. Walsham	Earl of Iddesleigh	FO 405/36/114; Parliamentary Papers, No. 70, pp. 24-5.			
176	1886.12.3	거문도 철수 통지	Currie	Macgregor	FO 405/36/114; Parliamentary Papers, No. 71, pp. 24-5.			
177	1886.12.7/ 1886.12.8*	중국 주둔 영국 해군에 철수 결정 통보	Macgregor	Currie	FO 405/36/118; Parliamentary Papers,			

					No. 72, pp. 24-5.			
178	1886.12.7	거문도 점령에 대한 영국, 청국, 일본의 입장과 영국의 거문도 철수에 관한 보고	P. S. Popov	N. K. Girs	AVPRI, F.150, Op.493, D.113, L.113-114ob.			
179	1886.12.11	Walsham의 보고 전까지 철수 준비 보류	Currie	Macgregor	FO 405/36/121; Parliamentary Papers, No. 74, pp. 24-5.			
180	1886.12.11/ 1886.12.13*	중국 주둔 영국 해군에 Currie의 전신 통보	Macgregor	Currie	FO 405/36/124; Parliamentary Papers, No. 74, pp. 24-5.			
181	1886.12.23(高宗二十三年十一月二十八日)	영국군 거문도 철수 결정 통보	J. Walsham	金允植	『영안』 1, pp. 215-6.	[俄譯] AVPRI, F.150, Op.493, D.113, L.134-135ob.		
182	1886.12.24*(光緒十二年十一月十九日)	영국 정부의 거문도 철수 통보	J. Walsham	總署	『中日韓』 4, 문서번호 1189, p. 2179.			
183	1886.12.25	청과 조선 정부에 거문도 철수 통보	J. Walsham	Earl of Iddesleigh	Parliamentary Papers, No. 80, pp. 24-5.			
184	1886.12.27/ 1886.12.28*	거문도 철수 결정에 따른 후속 조치 이행 계획	J. Walsham	Earl of Iddesleigh	FO 405/36/138; Parliamentary Papers, No. 77, pp. 24-5; AADM, p. 748; BDFA, doc, No. 333, p. 372.			
185	1886.12.29(光緒十二年十二月五日)	조선에 영국의 거문도 철수 사실 통고 지시	李鴻章	袁世凱	『李鴻章』 22, 電報 2, G12-12-004, p. 145; 『李文』, 電稿 7, p. 54.			
186	1887.1.3/ 1887.1.4*	거문도 주둔군에 철수 관련 지침 통보	Admiralty	Foreign Office	FO 405/37/1; Parliamentary Papers, No. 78, pp. 24-5.			
187	1887.1.3*(光緒十二年十二月十日)	영국의 거문도 철수 사실 상주	總署	光緒帝	『淸季』 69, pp. 33-4; 『中日韓』 4, 문서번호 1193, pp. 2183-4; 『日外』 18, 문서번호 335의 부기			

188	1887.1.7	조선 정부에 대한 거문도 철수 통지 일정	Admiralty	Foreign Office	FO 405/37/3; Parliamentary Papers, No. 79, pp. 24-5.			
189	1887.1.13	미국의 거문도 임대 가능성 타진	W. W. Rockhill	T. F. Bayard	KAR II, doc, No. 47, pp. 239-40; ADPP 11, doc, No. 171, pp. 222-9.			
190	1887.1.21(光緖十二年十二月二十八日)	거문도 사후 처리를 둘러싼 조선 내의 동향	李鴻章	總署	『李鴻章』 22, 電報 2, G12-12-046, p. 156; 『李文』, 電稿 7, p. 59; 『淸季』 69, p. 37.			
191	1887.1.22	영국의 거문도 철수 통보	W. W. Rockhill	T. F. Bayard	KAR II, doc, No. 50, pp. 240-1.			
192	1887.1.23	영국의 거문도 철수 및 반환에 대한 보고	K. I. Veber	N. K. Girs	AVPRI, F.150, Op.493, D.113, L.126-126ob.			
193	1887.1.24	영국의 거문도 철수에 대한 도쿄 주재 러시아 공사의 보고	A. P. Davydov	N. K. Girs	AVPRI, F.150, Op.493, D.113, L.129-129ob.			
194	1887.1.26(高宗二十四年一月三日)	거문도 철수에 대한 사은 조회의 북경 전달 요청	金允植	J. Walsham	『영안』 1, p. 218.		거문도 철수에 대한 사은 조회	『영안』 1, pp. 218-9.
195	1887.2.1	조선 정부의 거문도 점령 반대 성명서 및 영국의 거문도 철수 통첩 번역문 송부	K. I. Veber	N. K. Girs	AVPRI, F.150, Op.493, D.113, L.132-133ob.			
196	1887.2.2~2.3	영국 의회 질의, 응답			FO 405/37/10, 11.			
197	1887.2.8	거문도에 영국이 설치한 시설물 철거 관련 보고	V. Kostylev	외무부 아시아국	AVPRI, F.150, Op.493, D.113, L.130-131ob.			
198	1887.2.10(高宗二十四年一月十八日)	거문도 방어를 위한 진영 건설 제안	內務府	高宗	『일기』 高宗 24년 1월 18일; 『실록』· 『일록』 같은 날			
199	1887.2.25	거문도 철수를 조선, 청국에 통보한 내용 승인	The Marquis of Salisbury	J. Walsham	Parliamentary Papers, No. 81, pp. 24-5.			
200	1887.2.28/ 1887.3.11*	녹둔도 일대를 조선이 청국에 양여한다는 소문에 관한	杉村濬	井上馨	『日外』 20, 문서번호 146.		청국 정부가 鹿屯島를 점령했다고 하는	『日外』 20, 문서번호 146의 부기

		보고					풍설 보고 (杉村濬 ➡ 井上馨, 1886.11.15*)	
201	1887.2.28/ 1887.3.1*	2월 27일부로 거문도 철수 완료	Admiralty	Foreign Office	FO 405/37/18; Parliamentary Papers, No. 82, pp. 24-5.			
202	1887.3.1(高宗二十四年二月七日)	영국군 거문도 철수 통보	Watters	金允植	『영안』 1, pp. 223-4.			
203	1887.3.2/ 1887.3.2*	철수 통보에 대한 조선 정부의 회답	J. Walsham	The Marquis of Salisbury	FO 405/37/20; Parliamentary Papers, No. 83, pp. 24-5.			
204	1887.3.4*(光緒十三年二月十日)	조선의 거문도 사후 처리에 관한 袁世凱의 보고 전달	李鴻章	總署	『中日韓』 4, 문서번호 1199, p. 2187.			
205	1887.3.5	영국군의 거문도 철수에 관한 나가사키 주재 러시아 영사의 보고	V. Kostylev	외무부 아시아국	AVPRI, F.150, Op.493, D.113, L.142-142ob.			
206	1887.3.5(高宗二十四年二月十一日)	영국군의 거문도 철수에 대한 조선 정부의 사은 조회	金允植	Watters	『영안』 1, p. 224; 『운양집』 卷八		Watters의 답신(1887. 4.6)	『영안』 1, pp. 226-7.
207	1887.3.28	영국군의 거문도 철수에 관한 Veber의 전문	K. I. Veber	I. A. Zinoviev	AVPRI, F.150, Op.493, D.113, L.149-150ob.			
208	1887.4.10(高宗二十四年三月十七日)	거문도 유자리에 진영 설치 제안	內務府	高宗	『일기』 高宗 24년 3월 17일; 『실록』 같은 날			
209	1887.4.18(高宗二十四年三月二十五日)	長淵府使 申錫孝의 巨文島僉使 임명	高宗		『일기』 24년 3월 25일			
210	1887.5.9(高宗二十四年四月十七日)	거문도 사건 해결에 대해 청국에 사의 표시 제안	議政府	高宗	『실록』 24년 4월 17일; 『일기』· 『비변사』 같은 날		거문도 사건 해결에 대해 청 정부에 보낸 사은 자문	『실록』 24년 4월 17일
211	1887.7.9*(光緒十三年五月二十九日)	조선 국왕의 사은 상주 요청 자문 통보	禮部	總署	『中日韓』 4, 문서번호 1243, p. 2322.			
212	1887.7.13(高宗二十四年五月二十三日)	거문진 설치 문제에 대해 전라감사의 재조사 보고를 청하는 啓	內務府	高宗	『일기』 24년 5월 23일; 『실록』 같은 날			
213	1887.7.28(光緒十三年六月八日)	청 禮部의 조선 국왕 사은 대주	禮部		『德宗』 244, 甲午條, p. 280.			

214	1887.9.2(高宗二十四年七月十五日)	청산진을 혁파하고 거문진의 설치를 청하는 啓	內務府	高宗	『일기』 24년 7월 15일; 『실록』 같은 날			
215	1887.9.6(高宗二十四年七月十九日)	거문도진 水軍僉節制使를 거문도진 水軍僉節制使兼守防將으로 변경을 청하는 啓	兵曹	高宗	『일기』 24년 7월 19일			
216	1888.7.16(高宗二十五年六月八日)	거문진의 방어 강화 요청 승인	高宗	內務府	『일기』 25년 6월 8일; 『실록』 같은 날			
217	1890.4.00	거문도 실상 조사와 방비 보강에 대한 의견	李鶴圭		『거문도상황조사』(S03-07-0295)			
7-4. 철군 이후 러시아의 극동 군사정책								
218	1887.6.8	조선에서의 정치적 영향력 유지를 위한 러시아 함대의 제물포 파견 요청	N. K. Girs	Andreyev	RGAVMF, F.417, Op.1, D.312, L.13-5.			
219	1887.7.5	러시아 군함의 제물포 파견 지시에 대한 보고	I. A. Shestakov	N. K. Girs	RGAVMF, F.417, Op.1, D.312, L.17-17ob.			
220	1887.7.12	러시아 군함의 제물포 입항 보고	A. Y. Vlangali	I. A. Shestakov	RGAVMF, F.417, Op.1, D.312, L.19-19ob.		러시아 군함 '베스트닉' 호 함장의 高宗 알현 (1887.6.2)	RGAVMF, F.417, Op.1, D.312, L.20-20ob.
221	1888.4.20	'드미트리 돈스코이'호의 제물포 입항 관련 보고	Dmitry Donskoy 함장	V. P. Shmidt	RGAVMF, F.417, Op.1, D.363, L.27-9.			
222	1888.5.18	1888년 러시아 태평양 함대의 극동 해역 순항 보고서	V. P. Shmidt	N. M. Chikhachev	RGAVMF, F.417, Op.1, D.572, L.27-30.			
223	1889.1.11	영국의 거문도 재점령 가능성에 대한 정보 보고	V. P. Shmidt	N. M. Chikhachev	RGAVMF, F.417, Op.1. D.572, L.51-51ob.			
224	1889.7.10	'코레예츠'호의 블라디보스토크 하계 훈련 참가 계획	V. P. Shmidt	A. A. Peshchurov	RGAVMF, F.417, Op.1, D.572, L.122-3.			
關係資料								
1	1885.8.	거문도 사건 전말			『대한계년사』			
2	1886.1.25	영국의 거문도 점거 및 러시아의 대마도 점거 시도			『한성주보』			
3	1886.3.8	열강의 약소국			『한성주보』			

		침략 형세와 영국의 거문도 점거					
4	1887.3.4	李元會의 巨門島經略使 임명		『한성주보』			
5	1887.3.21	영국군의 거문도 철수 현황(申報 기사)		『한성주보』			
6	1887.4.4	거문도 경략사 부임 보고		『한성주보』			
7	1887.4.4	영국 하원의 거문도 관련 논의(滬報 기사)		『한성주보』			
8	1886.3.1	러시아와 영국의 군사 갈등 전망		『한성주보』			
9	1886.3.15~5.10	러시아의 싱가포르 정탐(滬報 기사)		『한성주보』			
10	1886.9.20	영국의 러시아 고립 외교(滬報 기사)		『한성주보』			
11	1886.10.4	러시아 견제를 위한 영·중 연대 제안(*Times* 기사)		『한성주보』			
12	1886.10.11	러시아의 불가리아 진출에 대한 영국의 대응책 고민(1) (滬報 기사)		『한성주보』			
13	1886.10.11	러시아의 불가리아 진출에 대한 영국의 대응책 고민(2) (滬報 기사)		『한성주보』			
14	1887.4.4	러시아의 인도 침략 의도		『한성주보』			
15	1887.6.13	러시아의 청 및 유럽 침략 의도(申報 기사)		『한성주보』			
16	1887.7.11	러시아의 중앙 아시아 점령 (日本報 기사)		『한성주보』			
17	1887.7.11	터키를 둘러싼 영·러 갈등(時報 기사)		『한성주보』			
18	1890.3	베이징 일본 공사관에서의 회담	中島 雄	『日韓資料』 2, pp. 462-73.			
19	1884.12.00	조선의 전략적 가치에 대한 1884년도 신문기사 모음집		RGAVMF, F.23, Op.1, D.52, L.30-34ob.			
20	1887.4.30	거문도 점령 외교사, <The Japan Weekly Mail> 1887.4.30.		AVPRI, F.150, Op.493, D.113, L.155-156ob.			

편찬위원회 명단

편찬위원장 : 김용구(한림대학교 한림과학원장)

편찬사업단장 : 장인성(서울대학교 정치외교학부 교수)

편찬위원 :
김형종(서울대학교 동양사학과 교수)
김흥수(공군사관학교 인문학과 교수)
우철구(영남대학교 정치외교학과 명예교수)
이근욱(서강대학교 정치외교학과 교수)
최덕규(동북아역사재단 연구위원)
최덕수(고려대학교 한국사학과 교수)

전임연구원 :

김종학(동북아역사재단 연구위원)

홍문기(서울대학교 국사학과 박사과정 수료)

연구원 :

김 경(서울대학교 동양사학과 박사과정 수료)

김정은(서울대학교 국사학과 박사과정)

김희연(고려대학교 한국사학과 박사과정)

노진국(서강대학교 정치외교학과 석사)

박한민(고려대학교 한국사학과 박사)

조병식(서울대학교 동양사학과 박사과정 수료)

한동훈(고려대학교 한국사학과 박사과정 수료)

한보람(서울대학교 국사학과 박사과정 수료)

한승훈(고려대학교 한국사연구소 연구교수)

近代韓國外交文書 제13권
거문도 사건 II

초판 1쇄 인쇄 2018년 4월 20일
초판 1쇄 발행 2018년 4월 25일

편 자 근대한국외교문서 편찬위원회
펴낸이 성낙인
펴낸곳 서울대학교출판문화원

출판등록 제15-3호

주소 08826 서울 관악구 관악로 1
대표전화 02-880-5252 팩스 02-888-4148
홍보마케팅팀(주문 상담) 02-889-4424, 02-880-7995
이메일 snubook@snu.ac.kr
홈페이지 www.snupress.com

ISBN 978-89-521-1976-6 94910
978-89-521-1356-6 (세트)